COSTA RICA
Adventures in Nature

Text and Photography by
Ree Strange Sheck

JOHN MUIR PUBLIC
SANTA FE, NEW M

John Muir Publications, P.O. Box 613, Santa Fe, New Mexico 87504

Printed in Canada.
First edition. First printing September 1998.

Library of Congress Cataloging-in-Publication Data

Sheck, Ree.
    Costa Rica: adventures in nature / Ree Strange Sheck. — 1st ed.
    p. cm.
    "Portions of this book were previously published as Costa Rica: a natural
destination"—T.p. verso.
       ISBN: 1-56261-414-2
       1. Costa Rica—Guidebooks. 2. Natural history—Costa Rica—Guidebooks.
       3. Outdoor recreation—Costa Rica—Guidebooks.
    I. Title.
    F1543.5.S53 1998
    917.286.04'5—dc21   98-10165
                                     CIP

Editors: Krista Lyons-Gould, Nancy Gillan
Graphics Editor: Heather Pool
Production: Janine Lehmann
Design: Janine Lehmann
Cover design: Janine Lehmann
Typesetting: Kathleen Sparkes, White Hart Design
Maps: Kathleen Sparkes, White Hart Design
Printer: Transcontinental Printing Inc.

All interior photographs by Ree Strange Sheck unless otherwise noted.

Title page photo: Ree Strange Sheck–Dominical Area—Looking toward Ballena
National Marine Park
Large Front Cover: Ree Strange Sheck–Chachaqua Rainforest
Small Front Cover: © Leo de Wys, Inc./Bob Krist
Large Back Cover: © Leo de Wys, Inc./Karen McCunnall
Small Back Cover: Ree Strange Sheck

Distributed to the book trade by
Publishers Group West
Berkeley, California

*While every effort has been made to provide accurate, up-to-date information, the
author and publisher accept no responsibility for loss, injury, or inconvenience sus-
tained by any person using this book.*

CONTENTS

CONTENTS

ACKNOWLEDGMENTS

I first came to Costa Rica in 1968. I came as a visitor to this country that became my home from 1990, when I finished the first edition of *Costa Rica: A Natural Destination*, to 1998. For unfailing support during the research and writing of both books, loving thoughts go to my daughter, Claren Boehler-Sheck, and to Ronald Sheck. Continuing love and gratitude go to my son, Curt, whose death in 1984 was the beginning of a new journey for me, a journey that led me back to Costa Rica and to this book.

For this edition, special thanks go to Nora Schofield, whose assistance in countless ways has been invaluable as I struggled to meet deadlines; to Omar Coto for graciously stepping in to assist with research; to Alex Segura for helping hands on dozens of occasions, and to family and friends who shared some of my travels for this edition: Ruth Hamilton (who also aided in proofing), Gayle Strange, Mildred Jasper, and Mel Jordan.

To the naturalist guides I have been privileged to travel with and to learn from, to tour operators, to the owners of private nature reserves and hotels visited, thanks for gracious attention. Travels in national parks, reserves, and refuges have given me profound respect for those who protect them, who often live and work under difficult circumstances. Thanks to each one who has taken time to talk or walk with me.

I would like to thank the Costa Rican Tourism Institute (ICT) and the staff of Expotur, an international tourism wholesalers' and retailers' fair, for their help through the years.

Thanks to the many readers of this book who have sent helpful suggestions and shared their own discoveries with me.

Finally, I express my appreciation to the people of Costa Rica for their generosity of spirit, those I know and those whose names I will never know—for smiles, for helping me get on the right bus or the right road, for walking with me to the corner to point out the street I needed, for reminding me that neighborliness transcends international boundaries. And I am forever grateful to those who have worked to preserve the extraordinary richness of Costa Rica's tropical ecosystems.

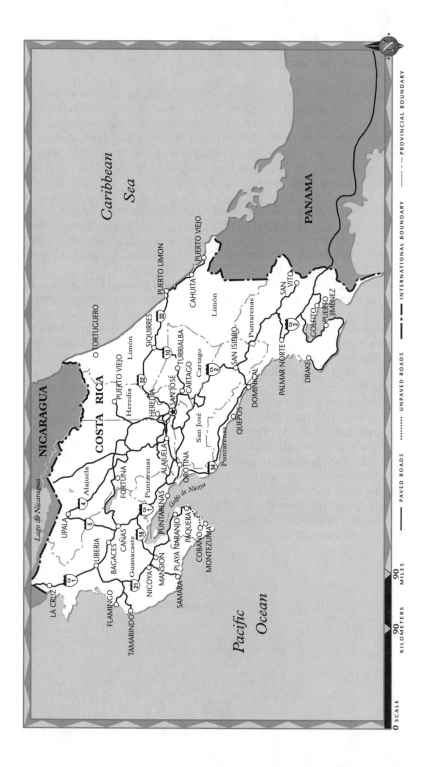

WHY COSTA RICA?

Costa Rica touches the heart and mind, not through elegant boulevards, towering cathedrals, or an imposing place in history, but through its incredible natural beauty and a gracious people disposed to peace, kindness, and a generosity of spirit. No one feels a stranger here for long.

It is one of the most biologically diverse countries in the world—a treasure-house of flora and fauna unequaled in so small an area. Casual tourist and dedicated nature traveler alike come under the spell of a natural wonderland studded with tropical forests, rushing rivers, exotic animals, uncrowded beaches, high mountains, and awesome volcanoes.

Struggling to explain why increasing numbers of people are making their way to this small Central American country, one observer finally said simply, "The greatest tourist attraction in Costa Rica is Costa Rica."

With more than 100 years of democracy under its belt in a region with a history of political strife, Costa Rica boasts "teachers, not soldiers." The country has had no army since 1948. It lays claim to one of the highest literacy rates in the world and a national health-care system that covers all its citizens. The people's inclination toward modesty, simplicity, and friendliness, along with the country's commitment to peace, create a climate of trust for travelers.

And what a place to travel! Visitors can walk among rain-forest giants, see green turtles nesting, get a ringside view of one of the most active volcanoes in the world, ogle the keel-billed toucan, and hear the howler monkey. Pristine beaches beckon on the Caribbean and Pacific. Trees alive with their own mini-forests of bromeliads, lichens, and mosses assume mysterious forms in the high cloud forests; orchids grow wild amid lush vegetation that tumbles down along road cuts.

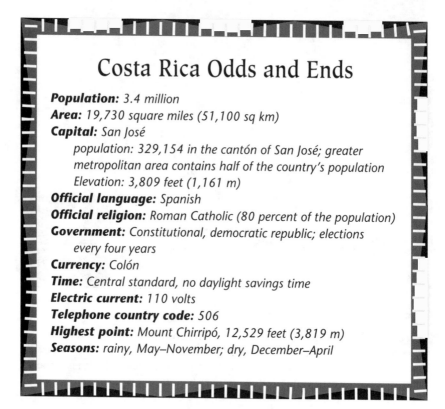

Costa Rica Odds and Ends

Population: *3.4 million*
Area: *19,730 square miles (51,100 sq km)*
Capital: *San José*
> *population: 329,154 in the cantón of San José; greater metropolitan area contains half of the country's population*
> *Elevation: 3,809 feet (1,161 m)*

Official language: *Spanish*
Official religion: *Roman Catholic (80 percent of the population)*
Government: *Constitutional, democratic republic; elections every four years*
Currency: *Colón*
Time: *Central standard, no daylight savings time*
Electric current: *110 volts*
Telephone country code: *506*
Highest point: *Mount Chirripó, 12,529 feet (3,819 m)*
Seasons: *rainy, May–November; dry, December–April*

Travelers can enjoy world-class white-water rafting, sunning on deserted beaches, bicycle touring, surfing, snorkeling, fishing, bird-watching, hiking, diving, climbing to the forest canopy, and kayaking or ballooning.

A small country, a little smaller than West Virginia or Nova Scotia, Costa Rica abounds with plant and animal species: North American, South American, and those endemic to the area. It is known around the world for its national park system, now protecting about 12 percent of the land. With the aid of other reserves, about 33 percent of its territory is protected—an enviable record for any country, remarkable for a developing one. That commitment to conservation makes it possible for resident and tourist alike to encounter the natural world in a special way. An agouti and I once surprised each other on a park trail; a paca (known locally by the marvelous name of *tepezcuintle*) amazed me by rushing from bushes to plunge into a pool at the base of a waterfall where I had been swimming. Giant blue morpho butterflies can turn any ordinary day into a mystical experience. There is the chance of coming face-to-face with a white-faced monkey or catching a glimpse of a scarlet macaw. Tropical trees towering to 150 feet (46 m) and delicate, tiny flowers blooming in a high Andean-like climate open us to not only the magnificence of the universe but also the interrelationship of all living things.

This guide is offered as a companion for your journey in Costa Rica, to help you touch and be touched by the land and people on paths that are most comfortable for you. It includes information about the national parks and privately owned nature reserves, beaches, volcanoes, and towns. It also tells what you will find at the end of the trail: a private room and bath with hot water, or a bunk in a dormitory atmosphere with a shared bath and cold water. It lets you know whether you can fly in or drive in, or whether access is by foot, boat, or horseback; what to bring along and how to call home; where and when you might see a quetzal; and which beaches turtles choose for nesting.

Find your own adventure and sense the heartbeat of this special place, from the quiet rhythm of its rural landscape to busy San José. Your experience will be your own. Just bring an open heart to contain it.

TRAVEL STRATEGIES

The first-time visitor to Costa Rica can feel overwhelmed by the banquet of choices: tropical forests to explore, steaming volcanoes to photograph, beaches to comb, mountains to climb, rivers to raft, flowers to smell along the way. Hire a guide? Take a tour? Travel independently?

If it's your first trip, you may choose to stay a day or two in San José. It has crazy traffic and crowded sidewalks, but it also has museums and parks and is the center of Costa Rican culture and government. You can stay in San José itself or choose among some wonderful small hotels and inns not far from the airport, near Alajuela, Heredia, Atenas, or Grecia. Some travelers start their experience from Liberia, landing at the country's second international airport.

Wherever you make your initial base, sign up for a trip with a naturalist guide for a good introduction to the tropical world. The guide knows where the crocodiles hang out, what time scarlet macaws fly over the trail, what tree the hummingbirds nest in, and which orchids are in bloom.

Costa Rica's essence is tied to its rural roots. Its people and its natural resources are the biggest part of what it has to offer. Privately owned reserves provide excellent opportunities for adventures in nature: for those whose bliss is tromping along muddy trails through a jungle miles from nowhere, and for those who prefer viewing plant and animal life from a shady veranda or strolling along a quiet beach. Some reserves include bilingual biologist guides; others offer local people with varying commands of English who are naturalists by life experience. Accommodations range from bunk beds to first-class hotels with hot water and fine dining. Few parks offer a place to stay, but lodges are usually nearby and offer day visits to parks and reserves.

Increased in-country flights make it easier to experience a variety of destinations. Though distances may seem short in miles, many paved roads are potholed, and unpaved roads can be slow going. A network of buses reaches into areas once remote. Major car-rental companies have offices in San José, with branches at other locations.

As for accommodations, I emphasize small and midsize lodges and hotels, many owner-operated, because I believe they give the traveler a sense of place and are more in keeping with the wonderful smallness and variety of the country itself, facilitating the connection with both people and nature.

Vacations have to do with moving you beyond the ordinary. Let your dreams come true in Costa Rica: climb a mountain, be pampered on a cruise, tramp along trails in a tropical forest, ford rivers with water that reaches to the hood of the car, stay up all night trying to photograph a volcanic eruption, or take off on horseback to explore the countryside. Sit on a beach, walk in a cloud forest, see birds and animals you know only from *National Geographic* specials, and bathe under a waterfall. Meet a warm and gracious people. Walk softly, aware of your own impact on the culture and environment.

LAY OF THE LAND

Costa Rica is a small country, but its varying geography creates a constantly changing panorama for travelers. The chain of mountains that forms a backbone down the length of Costa Rica starts in the north with the Guanacaste Cordillera (*cordillera* is the Spanish term for mountain range), continuing through the Tilarán Cordillera (location of Monteverde and Arenal), and Central Cordillera (Irazú, Poás, Braulio Carrillo). The southern Talamanca Cordillera is the highest in the country.

The Pacific coastline is almost 780 miles (1,254 km); the Caribbean, only 132 miles (212 km). Hilly peninsulas jut out from the Pacific coastline; there are two large gulfs, many small coves and bays, and two major commercial ports: Puntarenas and Puerto Caldera. On the Caribbean, a natural harbor exists only in the Moín–Limón area. The largest area of lowland plains in the country, which stretches back from the northern coastline almost to Limón, makes up about one-fifth of Costa Rica.

Costa Rica lies in the tropics between 8 and 11 degrees north of the equator, about the same latitude as the southern tip of India. Because Costa Rica is a small country without much latitude variation, you might expect the climate to be relatively uniform, but the rugged mountain chain's effect on factors such as wind, rain, and temperature creates many microclimates.

Some rules of thumb, however, can be helpful. In general, temperatures are moderate, varying more with altitude than time of year. Most people are surprised to learn that frost and ice can occur on some of the loftier peaks. Temperatures are somewhat higher on the Pacific side than on the Caribbean at the same elevation. (There are more clouds on the Caribbean watershed year-round than on the Pacific.) At sea level on either side, the annual average is always above 75°F (24°C). Some of the highest peaks in the Central Mountain Range and Talamanca Mountains average 54°F (12°C), though temperatures can fall below freezing.

Temperature variation is much greater from night to day than from

Arenal Volcano, active since 1968

season to season: difference in daily temperatures averages 14°F to 18°F (8°C to 10°C). From November to January, cold air from the north can funnel down through the mountains of North America. Though much weakened by the time they get to Costa Rica, the breezes bring a bite to the air. This is one of the few places in the world where polar air gets this close to the equator. The warmest months are March, April, and May.

Spring and fall have little meaning here; the seasons are called *verano* (summer) for dry season months, generally from December through April, and *invierno* (winter) for wet months, generally from May through November. The country's most prevalent rainfall pattern is in the range of 79 to 158 inches (2,000 to 4,000 mm). Precipitation can come in the form of a tropical downpour—a gully-washer complete with impressive lightning and thunder—or a steady rain. The downpour is called an *aguacero*; a continuous rain for several days is a *temporal*.

On the Pacific side, particularly from the central to the northern area, September and October are wettest, with the length of the wet season increasing the farther south you go. Rainfall amounts vary from less than 59 inches (1,500 mm) in the northwest and central part to more than 190 inches (4,800 mm) in the south.

On the Atlantic side, the rainy season can begin in late April and end in January, with December and January the wettest months. When it's rainy in the rest of the country in October, the southern Caribbean can be sunny. Annual rainfall averages are higher here than on the Pacific side. Heaviest rainfall is inland on the eastern (windward) face of the northern mountains: it may exceed 355 inches (9,000 mm) per year. Elsewhere in the lowlands, annual rainfall averages from 118 to about 200 inches (3,000 to 5,000 mm).

Even in the wet season, rain will not fall all day every day. It usually begins in early afternoon in the Central Valley and other highland areas and later in the afternoon in the Pacific lowlands. Rain can drum steadily at night in the Atlantic lowlands and valley bottoms.

Each season has its beauty and its particular cares. In wetter times plant life is profuse, with a vibrant greenness that seeps into the soul. In the dry season a subtler background is a perfect canvas for orchids, bougainvillea, and *reina de la noche* (queen of the night), with its large white or pink trumpet-shaped flowers, as well as for deciduous trees that flower only then.

HISTORICAL HIGHLIGHTS

Travelers often ask what has led this country on a path that sets it apart from its Central American neighbors. Different it is. Costa Rica is a country without an army in a world that counts tanks, missiles, and nuclear warheads as the measure of a nation's power. The national hero is not a general but a young, barefoot *campesino* (farmer). Schoolchildren, not soldiers, parade on Independence Day. While other countries debate the issue, Costa Rica abolished the death penalty more than 100 years ago.

Located in a region where violence has too often been the order of the day, Costa Rica lives in peace. Costa Ricans like to say they have gained through evolution what other countries try to attain through revolution. A brief look at its history, economy, and political and social systems sheds light on some of the questions most often asked.

When Christopher Columbus dropped anchor off Costa Rica in 1502, near the present-day Port of Limón, he still thought he had found a new route to the East and believed he was on the southeast coast of Asia, near Thailand. Even today, some people confuse Costa Rica with another Caribbean locale: Puerto Rico.

Stories about great wealth to be found here began at that time. The Indians offered Columbus gifts of gold, and Spanish explorers began to refer to the area as *costa rica*, or "rich coast." Later expeditions touched along the Caribbean and then the Pacific coasts, but it was not until the 1560s that the first permanent European settlement took root. Cartago in the Central Valley became the capital of what would become a province under the Captaincy General of Guatemala.

The first Spanish inhabitants of this new land found neither mineral wealth nor a large indigenous population that could be used as forced labor. The Indians they did find were not keen on servitude. Resistance ranged from warfare to retreat into the forested backcountry. Though definitive numbers on the indigenous population at the time of the conquest are not available, a range of 300,000 to 500,000 is commonly cited. By 1522, colonial authorities reported only 27,000 indigenous peoples, probably an underestimate but still

Volcanoes

Volcanoes are a hot topic. Some 112 craters, including the two on Coco Island, mark the Costa Rican landscape. They range from extinct to dormant to active, and from a mere remnant rising 328 feet (100 m) above the Tortuguero Plains to majestic peaks more than 11,000 feet (3,350 m) high that still fuss and fume along the country's spine.

If you have never heard a volcano breathe, consider a visit to 5,358-foot (1,633-m) Arenal, one of the most active volcanoes in the world. Hearing the huff of its breath one unforgettable morning made me one with primitive peoples; the mountain became a living being. When it hurled fiery blocks high in the air, not a doubt remained: Arenal was angry. It has been angry enough to kill people since beginning its current phase of activity in 1968, including a tourist who climbed its slopes. Be prudent when you visit any active volcano.

Activity at Poás and Rincón de la Vieja has caused the national parks associated with them to close occasionally since 1989. Other volcanoes with some level of activity include Irazú, Miravalles, and Turrialba. Volcanological and seismological institutions constantly monitor active sites.

indicative of greatly reduced numbers resulting from intertribal conflicts, wars with the Spanish, illness introduced from the Old World, sale as slaves to other countries, and intermarriage. By 1801, the number was 8,000.

So even though traditional Spanish colonial systems of forced Indian labor existed in Costa Rica, colonizers were effectively reduced to small landholdings that they and their families could largely work themselves. Communication was hampered by rugged terrain and lack of roads and made more difficult by seasonally heavy rains. Efforts went into survival rather than commerce, with the agrarian society based on subsistence farming and ranching.

Throughout the colonial period, Costa Rica was a poor, neglected outpost of the Spanish empire. The poverty and isolation gave rise to a simple life, strong individualism, hospitality, and a certain spirit of equality that cut across existing social class lines, contributing to the beginnings of rural democracy.

Even the name Costa Ricans call themselves, *ticos*, is said by some to come from a colonial saying: "We are all *hermaniticos* (little brothers)." (Diminutive endings of *-ito* and *-ico* are used in everyday speech. For example, you may hear *pequeñito* for "small" rather than *pequeño*.)

The Latin American wars for independence from Spain were far removed from this solitary enclave. When victory finally came in 1821, Costa Rica received word about a month later. A popular story is that a messenger on a mule delivered the official victory letter. Costa Rica joined the Central American Federation for a time but declared itself an independent republic in 1848.

A war that did have an impact on the country came in 1856, when William Walker, a U.S. adventurer who had gained control of the armed forces of Nicaragua and dreamed of controlling all of Central America, invaded Costa Rica. The strong national identity forged during the colonial period of isolation brought volunteers from around the country to defend the nation. In a battle that lasted only a few minutes, the well-armed invading force was routed at Hacienda Santa Rosa in Guanacaste. The site of the confrontation is now protected in Santa Rosa National Park. When you visit there, remember how remote it was at the time; the ragtag citizen army of 9,000 marched 12 days from San José to get there. The army pursued Walker's forces into Nicaragua, where a second battle occurred.

In the fighting at Rivas, a brave young campesino from Alajuela named Juan Santamaría volunteered to set fire to the Walker stronghold, losing his life in the act. He became the national hero for his part in this crucial battle. Walker's dream ended in 1860 before a firing squad in Honduras.

The first true popular elections came in 1889, which is why Costa Rica claims more than 100 years of democracy. The president at the time tried to cancel the promised vote in order to name his successor, but the elections were held when the peasants invaded San José and demanded their say.

By this time, the exportation of coffee was ending Costa Rica's isolation. Soon, bananas thrust the country further into international commerce. The population grew, frontiers expanded, and transportation routes carried produce out and the world in.

Costa Rica's own brief "revolution" came in 1948, when Congress annulled the presidential election to keep the opposition candidate from

Monument in Alajuela honoring Costa Rica's national hero, Juan Santamaría

Haga Fila: Get in Line

Waiting your turn is a surviving piece of the "everyone is equal" mentality born in colonial times. No one is exempt. In fact, the more important a person is, the more essential it is that this tenet be respected. I observed this for myself one lunchtime when I noticed the Costa Rican president entering a downtown McDonald's. It was almost as if a ritual—understood by all the players—was being performed as he took his place in line to order and looked for an empty table. That president was Oscar Arias, winner of the 1987 Nobel Peace Prize.

The same decorum is expected when waiting at a bus stop, store counter, grocery store, or public telephone.

taking over. It was a short but savage civil war in which more than 2,000 people died. The leader of the revolt was José "Pepe" Figueres, who took control of an interim government for 18 months before the elected opposition candidate assumed office. Figueres abolished the army; military facilities were converted into schools, a prison, and the National Museum. The Constitution of 1949 set up a government of checks and balances.

Succeeding governments have spent money on roads, schools, hospitals, electricity, and running water instead of arms. Compromise and negotiation are the key words in resolution of conflict. Citizens do, however, take to the streets to protest or pressure the government for action.

Today, large landholdings exist alongside small farms; wealth exists alongside poverty. But there is still a genuine faith in peace as a force, in democracy, and in fundamental human dignity. Social, economic, and political mobility are possible. The national character is still tied to the land. Even in urban centers, Costa Ricans tell you their strength is in the hard-working, loyal campesino and the land. It will be interesting to see how this idealization of the past holds up as more and more campesinos become *peónes* (day laborers) and the pressures on the land increase. You can be sure of one thing: it will be a Costa Rican solution.

POLITICAL SYSTEM

Governmental power is divided among executive, legislative, and judicial branches, with a Supreme Election Tribunal in charge of elections. The decentralized form of government reflects Costa Ricans' aversion to a concentration of power.

A president is elected every four years by secret ballot and cannot be reelected. Two vice-presidents are elected at the same time. Numerous checks and balances were written into the 1949 constitution, under which the country is governed, to prevent abuse of power, especially by a strong president. The unicameral Legislative Assembly is considered to have more power than the president. Its 57 deputies are also elected every four years and may not serve consecutive terms. Seats are allocated according to population in each of the country's seven provinces.

Magistrates of the Supreme Court of Justice are named by the legislature for staggered eight-year terms. These magistrates name justices at the provincial level.

Municipal elections take place at the same time as national elections. These are the two important levels of government.

To safeguard against electoral fraud, a kind of fourth branch of government is set up as an autonomous body. This Supreme Election Tribunal oversees everything from voter registration to counting of votes. It also oversees registration of political parties and keeps an eye on political campaigns for misconduct. As a further check, six months before the election, command of the Civil and Rural Guard, essentially police forces, passes from the president to the tribunal.

Campaigning can be dirty, but election day itself is a party. Even children turn out to help get people to the polls, wave party flags, and shout slogans. Do not, however, mistake fanfare for frivolity. *Ticos* take their voting seriously. Women have the vote, as do 18-year-olds. Even those who cannot read and write are entitled to cast a ballot. Women have been elected to high office, both in the legislature and as vice-president.

Political parties come and go; the two principal ones today are the National Liberation party and the Social Christian Unity party. Factions split off and coalitions form. The Communist party is recognized but does not carry much weight at the polls.

Costa Rica has a large bureaucracy. The government produces electricity, runs the telephone service and a national banking system, builds houses, and distills liquor, along with doing all the other things one expects a government to do. About 15 percent of the country's workers on fixed salaries are employed in the public sector.

SOCIAL WELFARE AND EDUCATION

The Social Security system, referred to by *ticos* as the *Caja* and identified by the initials CCSS, was instituted in 1941 by the same president who helped enact a labor code that set minimum wages and guaranteed workers the right to organize. Though complaints about inefficiency and the level of care are common, no one denies the vital role Social Security has played in improving health care. Infant mortality rates are among the lowest in Latin America.

Life expectancy at birth in the early part of the century was 40 years; today it is 75 years. When the system started, coverage was limited, but now practically all citizens have access to care.

Rural health-care programs geared to both prevention and treatment touch the lives of the poor even in remote corners of the country. Scenarios may include a medical center staffed by paramedics and visited regularly by doctors and nurses. I was once visiting a rural highland school when the doctor came for his scheduled community visit. He used one room of the two-room school for consultations. In a coastal Caribbean village, a young mother told me the doctor came by boat once a month. Poor urban neighborhoods are also targeted.

As you travel around the country, you'll see clinics in small towns and a growing number of regional hospitals. The Red Cross (*Cruz Roja* in Spanish) is a strong, highly respected organization in Costa Rica, working closely with health-care agencies and providing ambulance service.

Housing, another focus of social programs, has been particularly emphasized in recent years. Both urban and rural public projects have been implemented in an attempt to meet a serious housing shortage.

Costa Rica and schools are practically synonymous. The country was among the first in the world to mandate free, compulsory, tax-supported education; children must attend school through the ninth grade. More than 22 percent of the national budget goes to education. The literacy rate is an impressive 93 percent.

In rural areas the schoolhouse may be one room, with six grades divided between morning and afternoon classes. Continuing on to secondary school can mean real commitment for students, for while primary schools are abundant, secondary schools are centered in areas with larger populations. Two young people on a mountain road explained to me that they were on their way to the nearest bus stop for a 30-minute ride to school in Turrialba. The daily walk to and from the bus stop was 90 minutes each way, with the return trip after dark.

Most visitors ask about the rationale behind school uniforms for primary and secondary students. This, too, harks back to egalitarian roots. The idea is to minimize differences between social classes. Private schools also have uniforms. Many private primary and secondary schools do exist, an option for those who complain about inferior levels of instruction at public schools.

Costa Rica has four state universities in the Central Valley, with branches in outlying areas. University education is not free, but tuition is generally low (although increasing) and scholarships are available. Technical and vocational schools outside the San José metropolitan area also put higher education within reach of more students as well as promote other regions in the hope of stemming the flow of people into the heavily populated Central Valley. The number of private universities has mushroomed.

Debates on quality of education, and even what constitutes an education, rage here as elsewhere. Resources are stretched thin. Urban areas have an

Traditions tied to the land

advantage because of backup facilities (such as libraries) and easier access to educational support; it is often difficult to retain teachers in small, isolated areas. The overall picture, however, has some positive hues. For the most part, schools remain the nucleus around which a sense of community forms. Dedicated teachers do exist, often working with few of the materials that teachers in the United States or Canada take for granted. Innovative projects include radio programs aimed at primary schoolchildren in rural areas, a growing program to provide computers to classrooms, and initiation of English-language training in primary schools. Bilingual materials in the surviving Indian languages (Maleku, Cabecar, Guaymí, and Bribrí) have been incorporated into the curriculum on Indian reserves, including history and legends that have passed down through oral tradition.

While some historians question aspects of the rural democracy thesis (such as whether the colonial social structure was egalitarian, whether there was universal poverty, or whether landholdings were uniformly small), no one seems to debate the importance of early emphasis on public education to the democratic process—a major difference from its neighbors. Until universal suffrage came with the 1949 constitution, literacy was a requisite for voting. Enlightened education policies enfranchised the populace and gave them power at the polls.

ECONOMY

Starting from a base of subsistence agriculture in colonial times, Costa Rica moved into the world economy only in the latter half of the 19th century with exportation of coffee to Europe, followed soon by banana exports. A Costa Rican journalist, lamenting his country's dependence on agricultural exports, once said to me, "What makes it worse is that the country produces *postres* [desserts]—coffee, bananas, sugar, and chocolate. When importing countries are in an economic bind, demand for these things drops first."

Some of Costa Rica's current economic problems have roots in the crisis of 1979 to 1982, when the country went through one of the worst economic crunches in its history. World prices for its traditional crops collapsed at the same time that petroleum costs soared. Since Costa Rica imports all its oil, the dynamics were devastating. The country had borrowed heavily from eager banks, with the money used largely, as one Costa Rican put it, "to maintain our accustomed standard of living." It has been difficult to cut the social programs citizens take as their due. National spending still outstrips income earned from exports and taxation, while juggling foreign-debt payments demands enormous energy.

However, there is light on the horizon. Investment in nontraditional products for export and to cut dependence on the *postres* is paying off. In 1988, for the first time, nontraditional exports edged past traditional ones in dollar value. Textiles, fresh flowers, ornamental plants, pineapples, frozen fish, pharmaceutical products, and tires are among the items filling out the menu. Check the label of the next shirt or pair of pants you buy—it could very well say, "Assembled in Costa Rica." The country has become one of the largest brassiere manufacturers in the world. A good percentage of the hair dryers imported by the United States come from Costa Rica, and the manufacture of microprocessors is taking off in a big way. You will probably not be aware of the fact that the person who answers your software questions via a U.S. 800 number may be sitting in Costa Rica.

The nation's stability, a large and educated middle class that provides a stable workforce, competitive labor costs, and national and international incentives have drawn foreign firms and spawned joint ventures with Costa Rican companies. Average annual per-capita income is $2,738 (in U.S., $25,000).

The U.S. Caribbean Basin Initiative, which provides preferential customs treatment to many products from the region, has been a stimulus; the United States is the country's biggest business partner, but multinational companies from Europe and the Far East have set up shop. Tourism has edged out coffee and bananas to become the country's number-one foreign exchange earner. This is a result of both increasing numbers of visitors and decreasing income from those traditional crops because of falling prices, competition, and restrictive trade agreements.

Debate continues regarding the privatization of state-owned companies that dominate sectors of energy, telecommunications, banks, petroleum, and insurance.

POPULATION PATTERNS

The Central Valley, home to many of the country's 3.4 million people, has been the center of population since colonial times. As was the pattern in other Central American countries, settlement centered in the highlands. Early Spanish colonists in Costa Rica shunned the hotter, rainier coastlands in favor of this mountain valley and its rich volcanic soil. This New World enclave continued in relative isolation until the 19th century. As late as 1700, Cartago, with a population of 2,535, was the country's only permanent urban center. In 1821, when Costa Rica and its 60,000 residents gained independence from Spain, 90 percent lived in the Central Valley. About 5 percent had ventured out toward Esparza (not far from Puntarenas) and Bagaces (16 miles [26 km] south of present-day Liberia) to raise cattle, and another 5 percent were indigenous peoples living in dispersed settlements on their traditional lands in the north and south.

A small bean introduced into Costa Rica around the beginning of the 19th century ended up transforming the life of this agrarian society, pushing the frontier farther and farther away from the Central Valley. Coffee was its name. The export of coffee led to the opening of a road to Puntarenas, since the first loads went to Panama, then Chile, and finally to Europe via the Strait of Magellan. To transport the beans to the port of Limón for more direct European market access, a railroad was built, indirectly bringing about the beginning of large banana plantations on the Caribbean.

Blacks brought to work on the railroad and plantations, mainly from Jamaica, added another ethnic group and an English-speaking component.

Population

Costa Rica	**3,432,665**
Province	
San José	1,242,302
Alajuela	614,187
Cartago	385,065
Heredia	275,522
Guanacaste	270,643
Puntarenas	382,788
Limón	262,158

Source: Dirección General de Estádistica y Censos, January 1, 1997, census figures

The African American population today is about 3 percent. The estimated Indian population is about 1 percent; East Asian, mainly Chinese, is 3 percent. As Central Valley land values rose, small farmers sought new territory. Satellite towns took shape around colonial centers, but Costa Rica still had an abundance of unoccupied land at the beginning of the 20th century.

In 1938, banana activity moved to the southern Pacific coastal region from the Atlantic; roads followed, and so did settlement. With the opening of the Pan American Highway south of the Central Valley to San Isidro de El General in 1946, the trickle of pioneers who had braved the high, chilly climate of Cerro de la Muerte on foot or horseback became a flood of immigrants looking for new land, following the transportation route as it made its way to Panama in the 1960s. (The Pan American Highway is called the Inter-American Highway in Costa Rica, as it is throughout Central America.)

Immigrants added to Costa Rica's population. Italians, for example, developed San Vito, and Quakers from the United States settled Monteverde. New transportation routes helped drain some of the population pressure in the central region. In 1956, Costa Rica had 1 million inhabitants; by 1976, 2 million. The limits of settlement extended to the Plains of San Carlos and Sarapiquí, to Guanacaste and Tilarán, to the Nicoya Peninsula, and to the San Isidro de El General and Coto Brus regions.

Today Costa Rica is facing the pressures of a growing population with little remaining public land. Most of what exists is in Indian reserves, forest reserves, national parks, and wildlife refuges. Since one of the frontier legacies is a belief that every campesino has a right to a piece of land to work, pressure on this protected land is going to be enormous.

As you travel on the road to San Isidro de El General, remember that most settlement along here dates from the middle of this century. As you drive over the new road to Limón through Guapiles, look at what has developed in this decade. If you sense a frontier spirit as you get to know outlying areas, you will understand why.

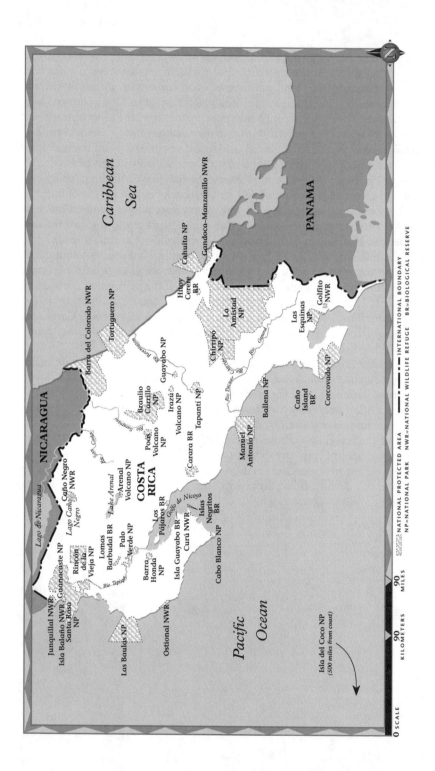

2

CONSERVATION AND RESPONSIBLE TOURISM

In pre-Columbian times, the area now known as Costa Rica was inhabited by small, dispersed indigenous groups who caused little human impact on the land. Spanish colonial settlement was also limited in both size and location, being focused in San José, Cartago, Alajuela, and Heredia. Even then, however, there are records of governmental action to control the burning of fields and forests. After Costa Rica gained independence from Spain, the frontier began a retreat pushed by roads and the development fanning out from them. Environmental controls reflected the concerns of an agrarian society: laws maintained forested watersheds and forests along main riverbanks. Population growth and expansion of towns and agricultural activities in the 20th century made it clear that forest and the incredible life in it, left unprotected, would not long survive.

Today, the combination of public and private initiatives that keeps Costa Rica on the cutting edge of conservation strategies has earned international acclaim for this small country. The national park system is perhaps the best-known of these strategies, but the stage is crowded with other players, including large and small private reserves, biological corridors, carbon credits and carbon sinks, "eco" labels, ecotourism, biological prospecting, reforestation incentives, and private nonprofit conservation organizations. Dedicated individuals, both Costa Rican and foreign, working in both the public and private sectors, have made the difference.

At stake are richly diverse ecosystems estimated to contain half a million plant and animal species: about 5 percent of the species that exist on the planet are in Costa Rica. There are more butterflies in this tiny country than in the United States, nearly as many bird species as in all of North America, and almost half its number of plant species. Here and around the world, species are being lost before they have even been identified, much less studied for their importance to humanity. Plants are gone before their medicinal value is known. Disappearance of a species of fauna can cut a link in a food chain that directly affects other species. Preservation of this biological diversity holds importance far beyond national boundaries.

Successes so far have not come without struggle, and much remains to be done. The following pages list some of the challenges and achievements. A common theme runs throughout: conservation of nature cannot be separate from the satisfaction of human needs. Sustainable development is the watchword.

PARKS, RESERVES, AND WILDLIFE REFUGES

Today, protected wildlife areas cover about 33 percent of Costa Rica. Most are categorized as national parks, biological reserves, and wildlife refuges. The remaining areas are in forest reserves, protected zones, and wetlands. All are part of 11 conservation areas that form part of the National Conservation Areas System, referred to by its Spanish acronym SINAC. The conservation areas (listed in Appendix B) were created to facilitate the regional protection of ecosystems and cultural resources.

The cornerstone of the wildlife areas is the national parks. Although "paper parks" had been created earlier, the national park system did not come into existence until the late 1960s. The park system grew from three in 1970 (Cabo Blanco, Poás, Santa Rosa) to 17 in 1978, and today numbers 24.

While preservation was the necessary initial step, the goal and challenge

No longer standing tall—deforestation near San Miguel

of parks and protected areas in general today is not only conservation of bio-diversity but also putting people into the conservation equation. Population pressures are increasing at a time when public land available for new settlement is practically gone. Neighbors who receive some benefit from those protected lands will be more inclined to preserve them.

This is where SINAC comes into play. The conservation areas encompass not only the wildlife areas but surrounding private lands. Each has offices to coordinate conservation efforts within its area and to work with communities in the buffer zones around the protected areas. Participation by private entities is fundamental. The Arenal Conservation Area, for example, has assisted local communities in organic vegetable farming development, ecotourism trails and lodges, medicinal plant nurseries, tree nurseries, handicrafts for sale, and reforestation projects.

In some conservation areas, private lands are being promoted for scientific research: community members have been trained to work as parataxonomists or naturalist guides or to start a butterfly farm or raise pacas. They work as caretakers and environmental education teachers in protected areas. These activities tie livelihoods directly to conservation.

One challenge facing not only parks but all public and private reserves is poaching, which involves hunting, nest-robbing, and trapping of tropical birds for pets to sell to national or international buyers. In the short term, preventing poaching requires constant surveillance, both costly and difficult. In the long term, education and developing alternative sustainable economic activities are the best solution.

Squatters sometimes pose a dilemma, especially for private reserves, but national parks have also been a target. The best-known examples are the gold miners who invaded Corcovado National Park, at its worst in the 1980s. I saw for myself in 1985 the destruction of mountainsides and streams caused by mining inside the park. In interviews with miners, it was clear that preservation of the forest came in a poor second to earning a living the way they knew how. They saw no direct economic benefit from keeping Corcovado pristine.

Budgets continue to be tight, with personnel stretched thin. Most parks lack sufficient staff to patrol protected areas adequately, much less meet needs of visitors. While infrastructure for tourists at most parks is still limited, a few visitor centers are now in place. The most-visited parks have management plans that incorporate guidelines on tourist capacity to prevent the places from being loved to death. Substantial improvement has been made in printed information available for visitors, usually in a bilingual format. Some information is free (especially trail maps). Attendants at entrance booths are not always good salespeople, so be sure to ask for a booklet or brochure.

Another challenge facing parks is lack of funds to purchase inholdings, which amount to perhaps 15 percent of total park land. Some private owners, who have waited for years to be paid, demand resolution—either pay or give back the land.

For wildlife refuges, incorporation of private reserves into the national system is a new wrinkle. Landowners who comply with requirements receive several benefits: exemption from the territorial tax, assistance in case of problems with squatters, free technical help on wildlife management, and the prestige that comes with being a government-recognized wildlife refuge—the latter a marketing edge for private reserves involved in tourism.

Want to Be a Park Volunteer?

If you are open to a different kind of vacation, are 18 years of age or older, and speak at least basic Spanish, the National Parks Service may have a deal for you. As a volunteer in the parks, you can work alongside rangers or in the San José office—minimum 30 to 45 days.

Depending on skills and interests, you could be a lifeguard at park beaches during high tourist season, work on an archaeological dig, help fight forest fires, protect nesting sea turtles, cook, or maintain trails. Extra hands and minds are always needed in environmental education and to assist visitors.

The work can be hard, hours long, and living conditions rustic. You pay for your food (about $10 a day) and transportation, handwash your own clothes, and bring your own sheets. Some stations have no electricity, with outside contact only by radiophone. Both men and women are welcome, and there is no upper age limit.

What does a volunteer get out of all this? A rare opportunity to experience Costa Rica's parks in a way no tour or day visit can offer, to learn, and to contribute to conservation efforts. Parks are understaffed and for the most part work within severe budget constraints.

If you're interested, write for an application to ASVO, Servicio de Parques Nacionales, Apartado 11384-1000, San José, Costa Rica. State when you can come—writing in Spanish may speed up the answer. Allow at least three months for the exchange of letters to arrange your stint. The office is at Calle 25, Avenida 8/10, San José, (506) 233-4533, fax (506) 233-4989; open weekdays 9 a.m. to 4 p.m.

The refuge status does not preclude development but regulates it, gaining wildlife habitat without displacing landowners or removing land from productive private use. The owner can still raise livestock, live there, build a hotel, restaurant, or shop, or permit scientific research. This seems a useful approach to protecting habitats not found within the parks, reserves, and government refuges at little cost to the government.

PRIVATE RESERVES

Some private nature reserves belong to nongovernmental organizations who use them for research, education, or tourism, with large areas simply for preservation. Well-known examples are the Monteverde Cloud Forest Preserve operated by the Tropical Science Center, La Selva and Las Cruces Biological Stations that belong to the Organization for Tropical Studies, and Bosque Eterno de los Niños that belongs to the Monteverde Conservation League.

Other private reserves are oriented principally to ecotourism, though they may also incorporate research and education. Perhaps 150 such reserves now function in the country, initiatives by both individuals and communities who see tourism as a way to bring in income and maintain their forests.

Some reserves belong to individuals who inherited forested land or bought it simply to protect it from destruction, expecting virtually no economic benefit. In reality, farmers who maintain forest on their farms have private reserves. Many reserves function as important buffer zones around public conservation areas.

Whatever the category, these reserves face threats from hunters and squatters just as public protected areas do; management and protection costs come out of their own pockets. The Costa Rican Network of Natural Reserves is an organization that began in 1995–96 as a mechanism to share information among private reserves as well as to represent their common interests and seek solutions to problems in the community. The government of Costa Rica favors this initiative: these landowners are protecting important habitats and species without the necessity of incorporating them into the nationally protected wildlife areas.

The value of the forest and other biological resources is one issue the network addresses. Value goes far beyond cost per hectare. What about roles in protection of biodiversity and watershed, in carbon fixation, in gene banks, in production of water and energy, in preservation of scenic beauty?

This issue, confronted by this small group of farmers, biologists, and lodge owners, is one that faces politicians, businesspeople, and all of us who share the planet. What are the costs of conservation? Who is paying them now? Who should pay them? What are the benefits? Who is receiving them?

I recommend that your travels in Costa Rica include at least one private reserve. You will experience firsthand their contributions to conservation and quality of life.

Bosque Eterno de los Niños: A Children's Rain Forest

Once upon a time, there was a teacher from the United States who came to Monteverde, Costa Rica, to do biological research. Her enthusiasm for the rain forest and her concern about its destruction found its way into a small primary school far away in rural Sweden. There, a class of 9-year-olds wondered if there were something they could do to save the trees, the waterfalls, and the many animals who lived in the tropical forest. With their teacher, they decided there was. They wrote a play and presented it for their parents; they drew cards and sold them; they gave from their allowances. That money was sent to the Monteverde Conservation League, a group working hard to protect the threatened rain forest. It was enough to buy 15 acres (6 ha).

The idea of a rain forest saved by children for children spread to schools in Sweden, England, and Germany, and to Maine, where the biology teacher lived. Today, children in other European countries, Japan, and Africa—more than 44 countries in all—have lent a hand. These children ask for donations instead of birthday presents, collect materials for recycling, and sponsor "green days." The result is Bosque Eterno de los Niños (Children's Eternal Forest), the first international children's rain forest.

Since it began in 1989, BEN, as the children's reserve is often

NATIONAL BIODIVERSITY INSTITUTE

Individuals from science, government, and industry are beating a path to the door of INBio, the National Biodiversity Institute, in Santo Domingo de Heredia near San José. Here, work is underway to systematically inventory the estimated half-million species in the country, to look for and promote sustainable uses of these resources, and to transfer the accumulated knowledge in ways that increase biological literacy at all levels and sectors of society.

INBio was set up as a private nonprofit organization so it could be apart from political whims and more flexible than a governmental entity. Its activities require.a close integration with many public and private institutions, both national and international.

called, has grown to protect thousands of acres of trees and wildlife—
about 46,000 (18,652 ha). Living in this lush vegetation are quetzals,
monkeys, bare-necked umbrella birds, ocelots, jaguars, and tapirs.
Long vines trail to the forest floor.

As children learn about this Costa Rican forest, they begin to think
in a new way about their own environments. Often, their parents join
in the campaign. An educational center at BEN will bring together children from around the world to learn more about natural history and
each other. Research stations, where people learn about the tropical
forest, are open already. Maybe you would like to visit one.

You can help BEN. Long-term protection of the rain forest means
more than buying land. It means patrols by forest guards, environmental programs in neighboring schools and communities, planting
trees, and continuing research. Donations of any size help. Send contributions to the Monteverde Conservation League, Apartado 10581-
1000, San José, Costa Rica. For information on tax-deductible gifts,
contact the league: (506) 645-5003, fax (506) 645-5014; e-mail
acmmcl@sol.racsa.co.cr; Web site www.monteverde.or.cr. (See Chapters 7 and 8 for more BEN information.)

Species Inventories

Years of research in Costa Rica by national and international investigators
have been incorporated into INBio's program; scientists willingly collaborate
in this mutually beneficial project.

INBio also uses its own unconventional brand of field researcher in an
enormously popular and productive program. Men and women are chosen
for intensive training to be collectors and initial catalogers of species. These
parataxonomists, in turn, serve as vital links with the community, sharing the
information being revealed about that environment. Many are neighbors to
protected areas. As you visit parks and reserves, you may be lucky enough to
come across one of these young people. The ones I have met are dedicated

Cataloging Costa Rica's species at the National Biodiversity Institute

and enthusiastic, and obviously love their work. Though they hold no Ph.D.s, they are becoming respected specialists. In 1996 they discovered 400 to 500 new species: insects, mollusks, and microorganisms.

Counting species is one thing. Knowing enough about them to protect them and manage their use for the public good is another challenge. What does a species eat? What does it produce? Where is it found? How does it reproduce? How tolerant is it to changes? Where else can it grow? What is it good for? Answers to these and other questions require studies over time and collaboration with researchers from other countries where this species exists. INBio says such information exists for only a small fraction of Costa Rica's species.

Chemical Prospecting

Regarding sustainable use of the biodiversity, the idea was that a tropical country could conserve its species in the wild to the extent that they generate enough benefits to cover the costs of conserving them. How? Pharmaceutical and agrochemical industries are interested in prospecting rights in Costa Rica's conservation areas. Companies sign contracts with INBio, with money up front as well as a promise of a percentage of the royalties from any product developed as a result of what is found here. At least 10 percent of the contract payments go to the Ministry of Environment and Energy (MINAE) to help cover conservation costs. If a product is developed, INBio will give 50 percent to MINAE for use by SINAC, the system of conservation areas.

Research into new products takes years, especially in medical research. The average drug takes about 14 years to get from the plant or microorganism sample to the pharmacy shelf. Though perhaps one in 10,000 samples collected is significant, arrival of an important new drug on the shelf could be a golden egg for INBio and the conservation areas.

Information and Technology Transfer

Part of INBio's plan is to facilitate training so that professionals in Costa Rica can carry out more and more of the detailed chemical analyses on organisms: the chemical analysis along with the botanical classification is much more valuable. Foreign universities currently carrying out this work help train Costa Ricans to do the job. A portion of proceeds from prospecting will support scientific and technological infrastructure here.

INBio shares information about natural history and taxonomy with schools and universities, assists lawmakers, takes part in natural resource-management events, trains conservation-area personnel, and publishes field guides and other types of literature about biodiversity. One powerful means of communication you can check for yourself is at www.inbio.ac.cr, e-mail askinbio@quercus .inbio.ac.cr; (506) 244-0690, fax (506) 244-2816.

FOREST PROTECTION

Forest was the natural cover of this tropical land for about 2 million years, and until this century the forests continued to dominate. However, commercial logging and the clearing of land for agriculture and settlement has taken a heavy toll. Costa Rica lost 26 percent of its forest cover between 1963 and 1989. Though trees are still being cut today, private and government efforts and national and international attention are focused on integrating conservation and

How Many Species?

Mammals	209
Birds	850
Reptiles	220
Amphibians	163
Freshwater fish	130
Arthropods (insects, spiders, and crabs with segmented bodies and jointed limbs)	366,000
Plants	13,021
Trees	1,500
Orchids	1,400

Look Who's Interested in Biodiversity

Pharmaceutical companies sign contracts with INBio to look for sources of new drugs: Merck & Co. has been working with INBio since 1991, searching for veterinary and human drugs, including a cure for Alzheimer's disease. Cosmetic companies are interested: a Swiss perfume company receives biological data on plants with interesting scents, using the data to create similar scents in their laboratories. Forest scents can also be used in household products. Agriculture is interested: a natural nematocide can be derived from the seeds of a dry-forest tree, with enormous implications for the environment.

sustainable development to preserve what remains. A 1997 satellite survey suggests a turnaround in the past 10 years, with reforestation outpacing deforestation. The reported 40 percent forest cover includes, however, not only natural forest and regenerating forest but tree plantations.

One issue is how to move beyond the familiar "frontier" mentality in which forests were seen as something to be conquered in order to carve out farms and ranches. Not much value was given to a tree, except what it could bring from cutting it. In fact, not so many years ago thousands of hectares of forest here were burned simply to clear the land; the trees were not even logged.

Legal Considerations

In Costa Rica, statutes have been around for a while forbidding tree-cutting in erosion-prone areas such as steep slopes, hilltops, and riverbanks. While they came too late to save some of the almost-perpendicular denuded slopes you will see on your travels, they do protect what's left.

The forestry law passed in 1996 embodies the government's intention to remove elements of the previous law that unwittingly stimulated deforestation. The 1996 law encourages people to see forests as valuable resources from which they can receive economic benefit, rather than as obstacles to development. Under the previous law, those who developed tree plantations were granted subsidies and tax concessions. In ten years, $120 million was spent on subsidies and 346,000 acres (140,000 hectares) planted. Sounds good, but what actually happened is that in too many cases, natural forests were felled to make room for plantations. In effect, the government paid people to deforest.

These subsidies have stopped. A new approach offers incentives to keep natural forests standing. Forest Conservation Certificates pay landowners for the environmental services provided by the forest they are conserving, such as protection of biodiversity, watershed, and soil, and carbon sequestering. Currently, money to compensate landowners comes principally from an environmental fuel tax introduced in 1996, but Costa Rica has big hopes for major funding via Joint Implementation projects with highly industrialized countries (see Carbon Credits, below).

Critics of the New Forestry Law have pointed to loopholes that could favor deforestation; some enforcement regulations have already been changed as a result. Environmentalists are watching to see how the law works out in reality. Proper enforcement in line with the intent of the law is the key.

A Success Story

The Central Volcanic Range Conservation Area can be considered a showcase for agreements on forest preservation and sustainable use. The target is

The Fig and the Wasp

There are 65 species of fig trees in Costa Rica, adapted to a variety of habitats. Each is pollinated by a different species of wasp. After the female wasp pollinates the fig, she lays her eggs inside the fruit. The wasp depends on the fig, and the fig depends on the wasp. Remove either and the cycle of survival is broken. Complex relationships between flora and fauna are not fully understood, but what is understood points dramatically to nature's intricacies. Maintaining a rich animal mix is crucial to preservation of diverse plant species. Animals are more important to seed dispersal in tropical forests than in temperate ones, where wind is the primary agent.

Reforestation counts, but preservation of natural forests is crucial. Replacing a primary forest of mixed species with one or two types of trees will not maintain the diversity: the fig wasp is not going to make it in a teak plantation. While reforestation projects on already cleared lands are essential—erosion control and watershed protection alone merit the effort—they are not going to replace what has been lost.

247,000 acres (100,000 hectares) of forest in private hands here. Under the impetus of a nongovernmental organization known as FUNDECOR (Central Range Development Foundation), agreements exist with more than 370 landowners, about 80 percent of whom receive payment for environmental services; the rest benefit economically through sustainable lumber extraction under forest management plans handled by FUNDECOR. Funds have come from the environmental tax on fuels and through contracts with private power-generation companies. These companies pay a set amount yearly per hectare of forest existing in watersheds of their hydroelectric projects. Properties are inspected by FUNDECOR twice a year; infringements cause loss of the agreement and legal charges.

Along with programs to maintain natural forest and foster sustainable logging practices, FUNDECOR encourages reforestation. When the organization began to address deforestation in 1991, almost 17,300 acres (7,000 ha) of area forest were lost every year. Satellite images indicate that more land is now forested in the Central Volcanic Range than in 1991.

Reforestation Strategies

The government estimates between 988,400 and 3.7 million acres (400,000 to 1.5 million ha) of deforested land could be recovered. Diverse strategies to reestablish forest cover are in use. Tree plantations do have a place, especially where established on already cleared or degraded land. Natural regeneration moves cleared land from scrub vegetation to secondary forest and over time can result in a primary forest.

Some exciting work in reforestation focuses on planting native species of trees to connect existing forests, large and small. These biological corridors allow seasonal migrations of species as well as genetic maintenance of populations such as the jaguar, puma, and tapir. They help ensure survival of the biodiversity that is jeopardized in isolated units.

Research in Monteverde has shown the importance of small forest fragments in survival of the region's biodiversity: remnants contain species absent in the large private reserves there, and they are feeding sites for altitudinal migrants such as the quetzal and three-wattled bellbird. More than 42 species of Neotropical migrant birds were tallied in these fragments. As a result of this research, the Monteverde Conservation League has worked with local farmers to help them reforest, connecting forest patches to each other and to the larger protected areas.

Biological corridors are also a component of a far-reaching effort spearheaded by MINAE to guarantee conservation of as much as 90 percent of the country's biodiversity. A ministry study coordinated by a group called GRUAS identified 54 vegetation types in Costa Rica, of which only 38 percent are protected in national parks and biological reserves. Recommendations specify new areas that should be included in the national park system as well as areas in private hands that should remain in forest. The plan proposes corridors to unite parks, biological reserves, and refuges. On an even grander

Illegal Timber Goes to School

Under a new governmental program, the Ministry of Natural Resources fabricates illegally cut, confiscated wood into chairs, tables, and desks that are donated to schools around the country. Previously, much confiscated wood—often mahogany—was left to rot. So this wood that should never have been cut goes to benefit students who will one day assume responsibility for protecting forests.

scale, international initiatives call for corridor connections throughout Central America, even continent-wide.

CARBON CREDITS

Costa Rica was in the forefront a few years ago in debt-for-nature swaps that reduced foreign debt while providing money for in-country conservation projects. Now this tiny, progressive country is at the front of the line to try to cash in on carbon credits, a novel concept proposed as a way to help industrialized countries reduce their emissions of carbon dioxide gas.

The carbon-credit idea grew out of the 1992 Río de Janeiro Earth Summit, where goals were set for industrialized countries to reduce greenhouse gas emissions to 1990 levels. Then in 1995, at the United Nations Climate Change Convention, a Joint Implementation program was proposed under which industrialized countries would be allowed to mitigate their emissions by channeling money into conservation, reforestation, and alternative energy generation projects in developing countries. Under a joint implementation agreement, a country such as Costa Rica could receive compensation from an industrialized country for extracting greenhouse carbon emissions from the atmosphere.

How would Costa Rica do that? One way is to protect existing forests, reforest cleared land, or develop commercial forest plantations: trees absorb carbon dioxide, which is one of the gases that contribute to global warming, and they store carbon and release oxygen. Another is to promote wind farms or hydroelectric plants, "clean" ways to generate energy.

While the rest of the world still debates whether this should or will be a way for countries to meet emission requirements, Costa Rica has already issued its first carbon bonds and has mechanisms in place to administer the money raised from the sale. The first buyer was Norway, which has purchased 200,000 tons worth of carbon bonds for $2 million. The tons of carbon it bought will be sequestered for 25 years through reforestation and forest conservation programs in an area where hydroelectric projects with Norwegian interests are being built. Part of the money came from the private sector.

Why would a country or company get involved before credits are even approved by international bodies? First, they might speculate that the investment will result in approved credits. For governments in the more than 100 countries who have pledged to reduce emissions, joint implementation for carbon credits may be one way toward compliance. Another reason stems from the public relations benefits a country or gas-emitting corporation reaps from helping protect forested land or aiding energy efficiency abroad. Also, these pioneers could get a seat at the table where details on how the plan will work are to be hammered out. Costa Rica has a seat already.

Trading of carbon bonds on the stock market? Not so far-fetched, really. Nitrogen oxide and sulfur oxide are already traded in Chicago right alongside pork bellies as a result of the Clean Air Act of 1990. Watch out for the carbon bonds, already known in financial circles as CTOs (Certifiable Tradable Offsets).

GREEN SEALS

Eco-labeling is another conservation strategy bearing fruit in Costa Rica. Green seals of approval are the result of negotiated environmental standards among industry, environmental advocates, and government. Rather than mechanisms such as boycotts, which harden the line between conservationists and industry, this approach favors working together toward environmentally sound solutions.

Plastic bags placed around bananas—pollutants or resource for recycling?

A company that meets standards is certified and may mark its products with a seal, a marketing advantage to increasingly environmentally aware consumers in Europe and the United States.

An ECO-O.K. Banana Project begun here in 1992 has been credited with virtually stopping deforestation to plant bananas. For certification, plantations must protect rivers, the watershed, and worker health and safety. Requirements promote greenways along rivers and roads and preserve forest patches. Reforestation on cleared land is encouraged.

So far, plantations enrolled in the program have planted thousands of trees (some trees produced in community nurseries and sold to the producers), modified packing plants to provide primary treatment of waste waters which formerly contaminated rivers, and reduced worker exposure to fungicides. Some have stopped—and others reduced—use of herbicides. The plastic bag placed around each bunch of bananas as it grew often ended up in a river and made its way to the ocean, where it killed wildlife and harmed habitat. All plastic waste is now collected and most is recycled.

Environmental education with schools in banana zones is a component of the ECO-O.K. program, and environmental workshops for plantation managers and workers are offered. ECO-O.K.-sponsored research looks at plantations' effects on wildlands and watersheds to help identify conservation priorities. Past research has already shown that patches of remaining forest within plantations are critical habitat for migratory birds. ECO-O.K. was begun by two conservation groups, U.S.-based Rainforest Alliance and Costa Rica's Fundación Ambio, telephone/fax (506)222-3182; e-mail ecook@expreso.com.

Other important eco-labeling programs in Costa Rica involve the Smart Wood program, which in Costa Rica encompasses both plantation reforestation and natural forest restoration, and coffee, which promotes a return to coffee grown traditionally, in shade, in order to limit erosion and provide wildlife habitat. Certification requires reforesting plantations with native trees and reducing the amount of pesticides used.

RESPONSIBLE TOURISM

Tourism has come to play an important role in the economic life of Costa Rica: since 1993 it has edged out both coffee and bananas as the number-one foreign income earner. Enormous change has come quickly with the tourism boom that began at the end of the 1980s: in number of visitors, size and number of hotels, growth of tourism-related businesses, and types of tourists and what they expect.

The lifeblood of the tourism industry until now has been the traveler focused on the natural world—the ecotourist. By definition, the ecotourism industry seeks to make a low impact on the environment and local culture while simultaneously helping to create jobs and to conserve wildlife and vegetation. Its ends are responsible tourism that is ecologically and culturally sensitive. While other types of tourism are developing in the country today, the measuring stick by which they are evaluated is that set by ecotourism. The tourism industry, the many conservation groups located around the country, government agencies, community groups, and travelers themselves play important roles in determining the impact tourism has on resources and culture.

Big or Little?

In less than 10 years, large chain-operated hotels have moved in to join the traditionally small hotels and lodges, often owner-operated, that had dominated the industry. Though the prospect of thousands of additional hotel rooms in a single development causes concern, the issue is not simply small hotels versus big but more one of overall impact and appropriateness to landscape and culture. Are ten 30-room hotels on the beach inherently better than one 300-room hotel? My bias for smaller has already been stated, but the answer is not simple. As this kind of question is debated in the country, issues such as environmental impact studies, water resources, infrastructure, carrying capacity related to natural resources, and impact on communities and their way of life enter in.

Sustainable Tourism

A green seal for tourism-related companies is being developed through the Costa Rican Tourism Institute (ICT), in cooperation with other government agencies, nonprofit organizations, and international entities. Although several private rating systems have attempted to evaluate hotels and lodges in the past, this is the first large-scale government effort. While the program has been designed for all tourism-related companies, the first stage encompasses only lodges and hotels. Participation in the program is entirely voluntary to businesses and is offered at no cost other than providing necessary information. At this writing the ratings have not been completed; they should be by your arrival. For a list of certified businesses, contact ICT: e-mail info@tourism-costarica.com, Web site www.tourism-costarica.com.

The Sustainable Tourism Certification Program encompasses proper stewardship of natural and cultural resources, improvement in quality of life of local communities, and economic success that can contribute to national development. Businesses are rated on a scale of 1 to 5, with 5 considered outstanding in terms of sustainability.

The following are some of the aspects considered: degree of harmony with the physical setting (including how it affects the local environment), policies regarding consumption of water and electricity, disposal of wastes, use of biodegradable products, relationship between hotel guests and staff, and social integration in the host community—benefits the community receives, contribution to local infrastructure, promotion of local culture (via information to guests and social contact), and safety.

Since studies indicate that the majority of tourists to Costa Rica are environmentally concerned, ICT believes the rating system will influence travelers' choices about where to stay. Tourism operators will respond by upgrading their operations to climb the green ladder.

I encourage travelers to support those businesses that participate in this program. By mentioning the importance you place on the green seal in choosing where to spend your time and money, you help determine the success of this countrywide initiative toward responsible tourism.

In conjunction with other government entities, ICT also administers a Blue Flag (Bandera Azul) program for beaches, taking into account factors such as water quality (both ocean and drinking water), public bathrooms, and amount of trash on the beach. Heavily visited beaches are checked monthly, others bimonthly.

Other Ways to Travel Responsibly

Perhaps you are already among the growing number of tourists who want to vacation in a place that reflects at least some sensitivity to physical and social surroundings, travelers who want to contribute rather than deplete.

It is all too easy for those who travel to Costa Rica this year, Kenya next year, and Bali last year to ignore long-term impact of their travels, their tours, and their actions. Some have a philosophy that having paid to come to a country, they have the inalienable right to see and do exactly what they wish.

All tourism has an impact—be aware of your own. Stay on the trails, don't feed the animals, keep your garbage-generation level down, avoid public nudity, don't molest an animal to get a good picture, and don't litter. We all know these guidelines. Take it a bit further. If a tour guide bothers a monkey or feeds the crocodiles so you can get a good picture, let the guide know you prefer that animals not be molested, and tell his or her company.

Responsible tourism is not just some list of rules to follow; it's more a way of thinking. I trust that your experience with Costa Rica's biodiversity will help put you in touch with the interconnectedness of all living things, and give you a better understanding of the individual responsibility each of us has to protect our natural resources.

Show your appreciation for all of the human and financial resources that have gone into protecting the natural beauty you enjoy in Costa Rica by supporting a local conservation group, donating to the National Parks Foundation, or volunteering your time. Assist the growing number of lodges and tour groups who support public and/or private conservation efforts and local community schools or clinics.

Most of all, keep your travels simple. Make time to hear the message of a place, to learn what it has to teach. Be aware of others as fellow travelers in this time and place.

Three-toed sloth

3

FLORA
AND FAUNA

Rising between the Atlantic and Pacific as part of the land bridge from North to South America, Costa Rica lies in a region unique in the world, between two continents and two oceans. This species-rich land is home to plants and animals from both North and South America as well as to species indigenous and exclusive to Costa Rica. They exist in a variety of habitats: tropical dry and seasonally deciduous forests, rain forests, cloud forests, mangrove swamps, oceans, coral reefs, rivers, and *páramos* (high, cold, humid landscapes). Costa Rica is the northern limit for Andean *páramo* vegetation.

This small country, which covers less than three ten-thousandths of the Earth's surface, is home to 5 percent of all the plant and animal species known to exist. As a matter of fact, species are still being discovered in the country's rich mix of tropical habitats. The National Biodiversity Institute (INBio) has begun a multiyear project to discover and catalog all plant and animal species found in the country (see Chapter 2).

Some scientists believe that as many as a half-million species exist in Costa Rica, among them a number of endemic species, those species not found anywhere else in the world: five species of mammals, six of birds, 41 amphibians, 24 reptiles, and 16 species of freshwater fish.

With such a wealth of flora and fauna, it is difficult to highlight only a few. This chapter includes some of the most common species, ones you might expect to encounter as you explore. The English name for each is followed by the scientific name in parenthesis and the name in Spanish. See "Recommended Reading" in Appendix B for books on plants and animals found in Costa Rica.

FAUNA

MONKEY BUSINESS

Four species of monkeys live in Costa Rica: squirrel, white-faced capuchin, howler, and spider monkeys. Reports of the night or owl monkey in southern Atlantic coastal forests so far have not been accepted as proof that it exists here. All are arboreal; they don't generally spend much time on the ground except to cross an open space—or, in the case of the white-faced monkey, sometimes to forage for insects. Monkeys migrated from South to Central America via the land bridge. I describe squirrel and howler monkeys here.

Squirrel monkey *(Saimiri oerstedii)*, *mono tití*, *mono ardilla*

This colorful, active creature has a captivating white face with black encircling its mouth and nose, a black cap, and orange-gold fur on back and limbs. Shoulders, hips, and tail (except for the black tip) are a yellowish green. The smallest monkey in Costa Rica, it's found only in the southern Pacific lowlands, south of the Tarcoles River. Scientists classify it as the Central American squirrel monkey, and many believe it was introduced here by humans because of its small range far from South America's squirrel monkeys. Don't confuse the squirrel monkey, with the white-faced capuchin. If you can't distinguish coloring, look at the tail. Capuchins coil theirs, while squirrel monkeys keep their tails straight.

A research project by Grace Wong, of the National University of Heredia's wildlife management program, focused on the titís in Manuel Antonio National Park, which are endemic to Costa Rica. Another subspecies farther south, such as those you might see on the Osa Peninsula, is endemic to

White-faced capuchin monkey

Costa Rica and Panama, though few remain in Panama.

Wong's study identified 14 troops, totaling 681 individuals; six of the troops, varying from 15 to 65 individuals, ranged mainly inside the park. She found that from May to October, when fruit is abundant, the titís have more time to rest and play, but by November they spend most of the day looking for food. Up at 5 a.m., they retire for the night around 6 p.m. Young are born from the end of February to the end of March, one birth per pregnancy. Females bear young every two years. Babies are carried for their first three months, with other adults taking turns helping the mother.

When food is scarce, there is often

competition between capuchins and titís. When they clash, the smaller tití leaves; Wong has seen a capuchin grab a tití and throw it to the ground. When food is plentiful, they eat together. In the park, natural enemies of the tití are mainly boa constrictors and tayras.

The increase in tourists and tourism infrastructure has reduced the habitat of monkeys and other animals living outside the park, in some cases isolating troops through destruction of forested corridors. Another impact of tourism is that monkeys near a trail or road where people stop to observe them spend more energy on guard and less time foraging. Natural events also influence habitat. Tropical Storm Gert in 1993 affected about 60 percent of the forest canopy (upper layer), reducing sites where monkeys look for insects and fruits. Although short-term effects are negative, Wong explained that long term results can be beneficial because of the mosaic of different types of forest that regenerates.

Howler monkeys *(Allouatta palliata), mono congo*

Howlers are all black except for a saddle-like mantle of long, brown or golden hairs on sides and backs; males have a white scrotum. Some field guides list them as mantled howler monkeys. The loud bass vocalizations of adult males reverberate over the tropical landscape from lowland dry forest to mountainous cloud forest. The roars carry about a mile (more than a kilometer). It is thought that these roars or barks not only allow members of the same troop to communicate with each other but also are territorial, advertising location to another troop to prevent feeding conflicts.

Since the average troop size is 10 to 20, keeping everybody together requires a system. Once in Monteverde I heard a big ruckus in the forest near the house. I stepped outside: howler calls told the story. The dominant male bellowed, and from a distance I heard what sounded like the distressed answer from one separated from the group. The calls moved closer to each other as I watched the progress from movement in the trees. Once the stray was back in the fold, the forest again fell silent.

If you get the chance, watch the dominant male through binoculars: see the threatening stance, mouth wide open as he roars. Daybreak and sunset are vocal times, but howlers also respond to thunder, loud noises, airplanes, other howlers, and even guides who imitate their call. But don't stand directly under the monkeys—they have been known to defecate on people below.

Since howlers do not need large areas of forest, you may see them in the forest ribbons along streams, river, or roads. Strictly vegetarians, they feed on fruit, leaves, flowers, and leaf stems. They are the only monkey species in Costa Rica to eat significant amounts of leaves: specialized bacteria in their digestive tracts help break down cellulose, and they produce enzymes to counteract toxins in leaves, which many plants have developed to ward off herbivores. Research has shown that when presented with a variety of leaves, howlers choose those with highest nutrients and lowest toxicity.

Because of their low-energy diet, howlers are more sedentary than other monkey species. They spend long hours in the same tree resting, scratching, grooming, the adults draped over a tree branch while babies play. Adult males weigh up to 15 pounds.

Predators for adult monkeys are harpy and crested eagles and cats. Tayras, ocelots, and boas prey on the young.

CENTRAL AMERICAN AGOUTI *(DASYPROCTA PUNCTATA)*, *GUATUSA, CHERENGA*

Though the agouti is a member of the rodent family, its body is shaped more like that of a miniature deer. It has no tail, but does have telltale rodent-like whiskers. Its generally reddish-brown coat can be more yellow on the belly and throat, and the lower legs are a darker brown. Inside the ears is a distinctive pink.

The agouti moves through the forest looking for seeds and fruits that have fallen on the ground: it eats seedlings, flowers, insects, and fungi. It's most active in late afternoon and early morning, though you may see it at any hour of the day. If you come upon an agouti at night, you know it must be extremely hungry.

In times of plenty, the agouti buries single large, hard-husked nuts so that when pickings get slim, it can return for them. It chooses nuts that will survive in damp soil. Because it doesn't dig up all the buried seeds, which then may sprout, the agouti is considered an important disseminator of some species of trees. The agouti sits on its haunches while eating, with the nut in the front paws, gnawing on one spot until it gets the nut open.

Usually solitary during the day, agoutis form monogamous pairs that sometimes travel together. Young are born in nighttime dens, which can be in hollow logs, under fallen brush, or in burrows. But the next day the mother leads the single offspring (occasionally twins) to a burrow where it lives for about eight weeks. The burrow's entrance is small to discourage predators, too small even for the mother to enter. She calls her offspring out every morning and evening to nurse and care for it. As a further precaution against predators, before nursing, the mother stimulates the offspring to urinate and defecate by licking its perineum; she then eats the wastes. Researchers say this probably also strengthens the odor bond between offspring and mother. The mother may give birth two or three times a year, but more than half of the offspring don't survive beyond the first few months of life. Adults can live three to five years.

A frightened agouti stamps its feet and sounds repeated high-pitched barks as it flees. A swift runner, it also has another defense—longer hair on the rump that can be raised so predators end up with a mouthful of hair instead of flesh. Predators include cats, large snakes (the boa and fer-de-lance), coyotes, coatis, tayras, owls, and eagles, some preying only on the young. Humans, of course, have been major predators—hunting agoutis for meat and also destroying their habitat.

Wary where hunted, agoutis can be easy to see in some protected reserves, even where there are many people. Visitors to La Selva Biological Station, where researchers have worked for years, see agoutis foraging in open areas. In Monteverde they are seen crossing the road through town, and in Manuel Antonio and Cabo Blanco, they rustle leaves alongside trails.

THREE-TOED SLOTH *(BRADYPUS VARIEGATUS)*, *PEREZOSO DE TRES DEDOS, PERICO LIGERO*

Yes, sloths usually move slowly, but no, they do not spend their lives in a single tree. Yes, they are often seen in cecropia trees, but no, they don't feed exclusively in these trees. Some studies indicate they feed on more than 96 species of trees. Sloths are seen more often in cecropias because of the tree's open growth and because cecropias grow along roads, trails, and clearings. Arboreal animals that feed, live, and reproduce high above the forest floor, the Costa Rican brown-throated three-toed sloth has pale brown shaggy fur; a small, round head; long limbs; and three long, curved, hook-like claws on each foot. The face is light-colored, with dark stripes slanting down over the eyes and what looks like a perpetual slight smile. Males have a patch of shorter yellow hair on their backs with a black stripe down the center. Their fur may take on a greenish cast from algae that live in it.

Since the diet of leaves and fruit is relatively energy-poor, sloths have an energy-conserving lifestyle: they move slowly, have heavy fur that provides insulation, and use body postures that conserve heat. They often hang upside down by their claws or sit in tree forks with heads tucked between front legs. To get their body temperatures up, they bask in the sunlight, preferring tree crowns exposed to early morning sun.

A solitary creature, the sloth has the surprising habit of descending to the ground about once a week to defecate at the base of a tree it feeds in. It digs a slight depression in the ground with its short, stubby tail, defecates there, and goes back up the tree; the whole procedure over in 30 minutes. Though no one knows for sure why it does this, one theory is that it is the sloth's way of returning nutrients to a tree it feeds from. Since sloths tend to return time and again to favorite trees, it's a kind of investment in the tree's health.

This ritual is important in the life cycle of arthropods (mainly moths, mites, and beetles) that live on sloths as adults. For example, moths apparently leave the sloth to deposit eggs on the feces. The larvae feed on dung and form pupae among the pellets. When the adult moth emerges, it flies to the canopy in search of a sloth to live on. It is similar for the more than 900 beetles that may make their home in the fur of a single sloth.

Fairly helpless on the ground, a sloth pulls itself slowly along with its forearms on the rare occasions when it leaves the trees. Sloths can swim—I once saw one in the waters of the Tortuguero Canals.

An adult female produces about one offspring a year. She nurses it for six weeks but begins giving the baby leaves by the time it is two weeks old. The mother carries the baby for about six months, showing it the trees and lianas she feeds on. Abruptly, mother leaves the baby on its own to live in a home range where it has learned which species it may eat. If the young sloth can survive the separation stage (mortality of young sloths is high), it can live to be 20 to 30 years old. Predators include large forest eagles and jaguars; habitat destruction and hunting also affect them.

The three-toed sloth is found in moist and wet forests up to 5,900 feet (1,800 m). Look for it on the Perezoso Trail in Manuel Antonio, from Guapiles to Limón and along the Caribbean coast, and at Caño Negro.

The other sloth in Costa Rica is Hoffman's two-toed sloth (*Choleopus hoffmani*). Though larger, it is harder to see because it is nocturnal, sleeping during the day. It has two toes instead of three and lacks the three-toed male's golden back patch. Its face is different, with a longer snout and brown eye rings. It can live up to 5,900 feet (1,800 m). You might see it in Monteverde.

RESPLENDENT QUETZAL
(*PHAROMACHRUS MOCINNO*), QUETZAL

The name is exotic. The bird is exotic. A member of the trogon family, the resplendent quetzal was a symbol of freedom and independence to some indigenous Central American peoples. It thrives in Costa Rica.

Travelers are more likely to see it here than in Guatemala, where the quetzal is the national bird, because of the protected forests at its home elevations: 5,000 to 10,000 feet (1,524 to 3,048 m) in the Central and Talamanca ranges; above 4,000 feet (1,219 m) in the Tilarán Cordillera.

Monteverde is a famous locale for this fantastic iridescent bird with its shimmering green head, neck, and body, and its crimson belly. The male has graceful tail streamers more than 2 feet (.6 m) long. While the female's barred black-and-white tail and duller crimson belly cannot match the male's magnificence, she is regal. Depending on light, quetzal feathers can shine in shades of blue. Braulio Carrillo, Poás, and Chirripó National Parks and areas around them are also home to the quetzal: some birders say the easiest place to see quetzals is near San Gerardo de Dota off the Inter-American Highway before Cerro de la Muerte, where they live year-round. Quetzals are usually solitary or in pairs, though several can gather in a fruiting area.

The birds depend heavily on fruit from wild relatives of the avocado, in the laurel family. At Monteverde, quetzals move seasonally, apparently following fruiting patterns; they become altitudinal migrants facing peril as they move away from protected lands. As reserves become isolated by deforested land, survival of migrating species such as this one is jeopardized.

As quetzals depend on laurels, laurel trees depend on quetzals to distribute their seeds. The birds swallow the fruit whole and cough up the seed after digesting the nutritious pulp—quetzals' intestines are too small to allow the large seeds to pass. The seed falls to the ground below the bird's perch, with a chance to take root.

Breeding period is March to June, peaking in April and May. This is the easiest time to see quetzals because they come down lower in the trees to nest, making do with a hole already hollowed out by a woodpecker or excavating space in rotting limbs or dead tree trunks with their short bills. The female generally lays two blue eggs, which hatch about 18 days later. As soon as the first babies fly away, she lays eggs again. Both male and female take part in building the nest, incubating eggs (parts of the male's longer tail streamers sometimes protrude from the hole when it is his turn on the nest), and feeding young. Though adults are primarily fruit-eaters, at first they feed offspring insects and small lizards to supply the proteins needed for rapid growth. After August the male sheds his by-now-tattered streamers and grows new ones.

The main predators of eggs and chicks are short-tailed weasels, toucanets, tayras, and perhaps snakes, but the quetzal also faces great threat from loss of trees for feeding and nesting.

If you expect such a colorful bird to be easy to spot, think again. Like other members of the trogon family, quetzals tend to sit still for long periods. Its greens blend in with surrounding leaves, the male's long streamers can look like fern fronds, and red bellies could be distant flowers. Go with a guide who knows how to spot a resplendant quetzal; once you see one, it's easier to find others.

SCARLET MACAW *(ARA MACAO), LAPA ROJA*

Flock after flock of spectacular red, blue, and gold scarlet macaws squawk overhead on their return from forested feeding places to communal roosting sites in mangroves along the Pacific coast. The silhouettes of these largest of the Neotropical parrots are unforgettable, with their long, pointed tails stretched out behind and their rhythmic wing movements. I have observed them many times near the Tarcoles River and Carara Biological Reserve. You can, too—it's a daily occurrence in early morning and late afternoon.

The Osa Peninsula also offers good opportunities to see large numbers of these lowland forest birds, while only a few still exist in dry forest around Palo Verde. Once they were plentiful along both coasts, but destruction of lowland forest and capture for the pet trade have put them on the CITES (Convention on International Trade in Endangered Species) endangered species list.

Noisy while flying, macaws are fairly silent when feeding in the canopy. With large, powerful bills they extract nuts and seeds from unripe fruit, their main food, though they also eat leaves and fruit pulp. They are actually seed

Scarlet macaw

predators, not seed dispersers since they digest plant embryos. You might hear the sound of the discarded pieces of seeds or fruit falling from the canopy to the ground as you walk on trails in Carara or on the Osa.

Macaws reach sexual maturity at five years of age, and a macaw pair may maintain a monogamous partnership for years. Nesting is from December to July, with the female laying one or two eggs high in cavities in tall trees. They tend to reuse the same trees year after year.

Several approaches to protecting the species are underway in Costa Rica, one being placement of boxes that serve as artificial nesting sites. Lack of suitable nesting trees is a problem in some areas; the boxes are put where they can be watched to reduce poaching of chicks. Unfortunately, selling macaws is extremely lucrative for someone living in an economically depressed rural area.

In a pilot project developed by the Pro Iguana Verde Foundation and approved by the Ministry of Environment and Energy, scarlet macaws are being raised in captivity and released into the wild, rescuing a limited number of eggs from nests that are regularly poached. So far the birds released into the wild have come from the rescued eggs, from chicks confiscated by park rangers at Carara, and from chicks born in captivity to macaws that cannot be set free because of injuries. Until freed birds learn to fend for themselves by contact with wild macaws, park rangers continue to provide food at feeding stations. (In the wild, a chick stays with its mother during its first year.) The controversial program has critics who express concerns about the possible introduction of domestic diseases into wild populations and removal of eggs from nests.

The only other macaw in Costa Rica, except in captivity, is the endangered great green macaw, currently the focus of an effort to protect *almendro* (tonka bean) trees, whose fruits it favors. Some estimates put the number of breeding pairs of green macaws in Costa Rica at 30 to 35 pairs. One of the focal areas is the Sarapiquí region in north central Costa Rica.

HUMMINGBIRDS (*TROCHILIDAE* FAMILY), *COLIBRI*

Among the names early Spanish explorers gave to hummingbirds was *joyas voladores* (flying jewels). And indeed they are. The iridescent colors of these small New World birds delight and mystify observers. Since the colors of hummingbird plumage are structural rather than pigmented, the play of light on them creates different hues. Tiny air- and melanin-filled feather structures called platelets are the key. Almost all of the bird's feathers are iridescent but some parts display more brilliant color. Hummers at flowers or feeders may appear dark and without color, while at other times they glitter with dazzling flashes of red, green, purple, blue, or turquoise.

Costa Rica has at least 57 of the 330 species of hummers known to exist from Alaska to Tierra del Fuego (there are only 21 in all of the United States and Canada). No doubt you will see several species during your travels.

Observe the lengths and shapes of their bills as clues to which flowers provide their nectar. Hummingbirds are important pollinators of tropical plants, and these plants' flowers have developed features that allow access to hummers while excluding other species. Many flowers are tubular and trumpet-shaped, and many bloom at branch tips, which facilitates feeding from a hovering position. Perhaps you will get a glimpse of the bird's tongue as it feeds, a tongue that can measure twice as long as the bill itself. Hummers are attracted by color, not scent. As the hummingbird probes the blossom for nectar, some of the pollen brushes off on its feathers, which is then deposited on the next blossom of the same kind the bird visits, allowing fertilization.

High-energy creatures (up to 80 wing beats per second), hummingbirds need protein as well as nectar, which they get from flying insects, spiders, and tiny insects in some of the flower tubes. To maintain their high rate of metabolism, they must feed about every 10 minutes during the day. At night they slow their metabolism to conserve energy, going into a torpor state in which the heartbeat slows from as many as 1,260 beats per minute to 50 per minute.

From studies so far, it appears that after mating, the female assumes total responsibility for building the nest, sitting on the eggs (usually two), and feeding the young, who remain in the nest about three weeks.

SEA TURTLES

Six of the world's eight species of sea turtles nest on Costa Rica's coasts—English, scientific, and Spanish names are

- green turtle (*Chelonia mydas*), *tortuga verde*
- leatherback turtle (*Dermochelys coriacea*) *baula* or *canal*
- hawksbill turtle (*Eretmochelys imbricata*), *carey*
- olive ridley turtle (*Lepidochelys olivacea*), *lora* or *carpintera*
- Pacific green turtle (*Chelonia agazzisii*), *negra*
- loggerhead turtle (*Caretta caretta*), *cabezona*

The Pacific green, hawksbill, and leatherback are found on both coasts, while the ridleys are only on the Pacific. The loggerhead is mainly in the Caribbean. Hawksbills, loggerheads, and leatherbacks are usually solitary nesters; the greens come ashore to lay eggs in concentrated colonies; and the ridleys come singly, in small colonies, or in massive *arribadas* (large numbers of turtles). Though it's possible to see a turtle laying eggs on a beach almost any night of the year, there are times when turtles arrive in *arribadas* at particular sites. The most important nesting beaches are listed here.

• Tortuguero: Green turtles nest from June to September; hawksbills are also easiest to see here at this time, though they nest year-round on both coasts. Leatherbacks nest from March to May, as do loggerheads.

• Playa Grande in Las Baulas National Marine Park: Peak nesting for leatherbacks, the largest sea turtles, is from October to March.

• Ostional Wildlife Refuge: July to December are peak months for olive ridley turtles, though there are nesting turtles or hatchlings almost all year.

• Santa Rosa National Park: July to December brings *arribadas* of olive ridley turtles, especially on Nancite Beach. Leatherbacks and Pacific greens also nest at Nancite and Playa Naranjo.

• Barra de Matina Beach, north of Limón: Leatherbacks come ashore from F*e*bruary to July, with peaks in April and May; green turtle nesting peaks from July to September; hawksbills also come ashore.

Green turtles are prized for their meat, especially in the Caribbean area. Hawksbills are hunted for their shells (source of tortoiseshell jewelry) along both coasts. While eating turtle meat is not a tradition on the Pacific, the eggs are prized as aphrodisiacs. Turtle protection and conservation programs range from beach patrols and public education to egg hatcheries, controlled harvesting of eggs, and setting of legal catches of turtles to sell for meat.

Practice proper turtle-watching etiquette. Stay still when a turtle comes onto the beach—movement may scare it back into the water. Light disturbs the turtles, so restrict use of flashlights; no flash cameras. Wear dark clothing. Wait until turtles are laying their eggs before drawing near. Be quiet!

AMERICAN CROCODILE
(*CROCODYLUS ACUTUS*), *COCODRILO*

To set the record straight: there are no alligators in Costa Rica! None. Caimans and American crocodiles are here.

Although not much research has been done on the American crocodile in Costa Rica, there is general information based on a study of the species elsewhere. Found from southernmost Florida to the northern coast of South America, American crocodiles prefer mangroves, estuaries, and deep, rapid rivers.

American crocodile

Crocodile or Caiman?

Color is one distinguishing factor between these two species. The American crocodile is olive to grayish, while the caiman is dark brown. Length is not much help, except for the largest specimens: Costa Rica's caimans rarely measure more than 6½ feet (2 m), so if it's longer than that, it's a crocodile. If you get close enough to observe the head, two clues help. The crocodile's snout has a definite indention behind the nostrils, while the caiman's snout is uniform. Observe the lower jaw through binoculars. If a lower tooth (fourth one from the front) protrudes outside the upper jaw when the mouth is closed, it's a crocodile; in caimans, this tooth is hidden under the lip.

The crocodile continues to grow throughout its life span, with some rules of thumb to help estimate age related to length. A crocodile about 2 feet (.6 m) long is probably about two years old, while a four-year-old will measure about 3½ feet (1 m). If you spot one along the banks of the Tarcoles or Tempisque Rivers that measures 7 feet (2 m), you're looking at a crocodile that's probably about eight years old. The rate of growth slows with the years: at 20, a male crocodile could be 12 feet (3.7 m) long. There used to be a granddaddy on one of the small islands in the Tarcoles. See if you can spot it from near the bridge with your binoculars.

Females don't begin to breed until their ninth year. Nesting sites are on sandy beaches. The crocodile digs a hole and deposits 25 to 30 eggs, covers them, and packs the sand down much like the sea turtle. She does this during the dry season to protect nests from flooding. About 90 days later hatchlings appear, usually May to July. The female often tends the nest and may help the young emerge.

Crocodiles eat fish, birds, turtle eggs, snakes, and even small mammals. When young, they eat insects and crustaceans. Humans and habitat destruction are the biggest threats to adult crocodiles, but the young fall prey to herons, hawks, and other predators, with highest predation in the first year of life.

POISON-DART FROG *(DENDROBATES PUMILIO)*, *RANITA ROJA*
This tiny frog with the bright red body and dark blue hind legs is famed for the toxins it secretes from its skin glands. Toxins from some dendrobatid

species were used by Colombian Indians to poison the tips of blowgun darts—hence the name. Although there is no documentation to suggest that toxins from this particular genus were used that way, the whole family was tagged with the name. The skin toxins of the blue and red poison-dart frog are actually much less potent than that from some of its relatives.

Lest you underestimate the potency, however, I pass along a research note reporting that the pumiliotoxin secreted by the frogs caused convulsions and death to rats when injected subcutaneously. You wouldn't want these secretions to get into a cut or wound.

Species with conspicuous colors usually have strong toxins: their colors warn predators. These frogs, active in daytime, feed mostly on ants and termites, so their search for food exposes them for long periods. Coloration varies somewhat: frogs can be completely red or sport black spots on the back; limbs can be red or partly or entirely blue or black. Because of the blue or black legs, naturalist guides sometimes refer to them as the blue-jeans frog.

Found at elevations from sea level to 3,150 feet (960 m) throughout the Caribbean lowlands, they are fairly easy to see in the area around Puerto Viejo de Sarapiquí and Tortuguero. Look for them in leaf litter along trails or on tree trunks or exposed tree roots. Listen for their calls to each other, which resemble some insect sounds.

As the life history of these tiny creatures is being discovered, we learn about a fascinating breeding strategy. Females come to calling males and follow them to appropriate sites to lay the eggs. The male deposits sperm in curled leaves or a dry leaf beneath other fallen leaves on the ground. The female lays from three to five eggs on top of the sperm. About a week later when the tadpoles hatch, the female (possibly the male also) carries them off one or two at a time to a site where they can develop, perhaps to a reservoir of water in a bromeliad high in a tree.

Some studies indicate that the female continues to visit her young (only one per pool). The tadpole rapidly vibrates its tail to show her it's still there, and then she lays an unfertilized egg in the water as food. The tadpole bites a hole in the egg and sucks out the nourishment. At intervals of one to nine days, the female provides a tadpole with from seven to 11 eggs. When tadpoles become frogs, they descend to the forest floor. First documented in captive frogs, this extraordinary parental care has now been observed in the wild. Other studies are needed to see how common the use of eggs in rearing tadpoles is, as well as to research courtship behaviors.

FLORA

CECROPIA *(CECROPIA)*, *GUARUMO*

A member of the mulberry family, the cecropia tree grows throughout the country at elevations up to approximately 6,500 feet (2,000 m). It is called a pioneer species because it is among the first to return to cleared land or to grow when forest is opened up by the fall of a big tree. Cecropia grows rapidly and requires a lot of light; you'll notice it along road cuts. Look for a tree with a ringed trunk that resembles bamboo; leaves are large and lobed, resembling hands.

Because it is a relatively short-lived tree, maybe 20 years, the cecropia has not developed the chemical protection, such as toxic leaves, that longer-lived trees tend to have. However, its hollow stems are usually home to aggressive Azteca ants, which tend to live in large colonies and swarm out over the tree at the slightest disturbance, attacking unsuspecting caterpillars, other ants, and even a hand lightly placed on the tree. Aztecas do not seem to bite birds, who eat the fruits and scatter the tree's seeds, but they zero in on epiphytes and vines, chewing off any vine that starts up the trunk. In return, the tree provides glycogen-rich food at the base of leaf stalks for ants to feed on and hollow stems for them to live in.

Ant patrols are not effective against all predators. Sloths are among the animals that like cecropia leaves and fruit. Apparently their heavy fur gives them some protection from the ants. Howler monkeys also eat in cecropia trees.

Countless symbiotic relationships exist in the natural world. Some we know about; others remain to be discovered. Even in the tree–ant relationship, all the answers are not in on why the tree has developed lodging and food to attract these ants or the degree of protection ants actually give. Lower-elevation species of the Cecropia family almost always contain ant colonies while a higher-elevation species does not.

EAR FRUIT *(ENTEROLOBIUM CYCLOCARPUM)*, GUANACASTE

The word *guanacaste* came from the Aztec words *guautil* (tree) and *nacaztli* (ear)—tree with ears or the tree that hears. The strange name comes from the shape of the fruit, which looks like a flattened ear. A legume, it grows on the Costa Rican Pacific coastal plain. The tall, stately tree with its large crown can attain a height of 130 feet (40 m) and have a 3-foot (1-m) diameter. The trunk is reddish-brown, and it has rather inconspicuous white flowers in March and April. For one to two months during the dry season the tree loses its mimosa-like leaves.

When flowers come, the mature brown fruit from flowers of the previous year falls to the ground. The fruits are eaten by cattle or horses, but if none of these are around, there do not seem to be many other takers—tapirs occasionally eat them. Conjecture is that the large mammals who roamed Central American forests more than 10,000 years ago ate these fruits.

However, the seeds inside the fruit are another matter, usually 10 to 16 per fruit. Parrots and peccaries like them, and a small terrestrial rodent harvests the seeds big-time. Seedlings that come up in pastures are apparently trampled, destroyed by fire, crowded out by grasses, or maybe eaten by horses or cattle. The dry season also takes its toll. Whatever the reason, seeds from pasture trees are not producing more trees. There may come a day when the national tree will be conspicuously absent, except in parks and reserves.

Guanacaste trees are found up to about 3,300 feet (1,100 m) in drier parts of the country, but they are not limited to dry forest. Though rare, they are found occasionally on the Osa Peninsula and appear to be native from Mexico to Brazil. The hard wood is used for fenceposts, cabinet-making, and crafts.

This is the national tree of Costa Rica, declared in 1959 as the result of a newspaper campaign to honor the people of Guanacaste (formerly a part of Nicaragua) who voted to become a part of Costa Rica by annexation.

ORCHIDS (*ORCHIDACEAE* FAMILY), *ORQUIDEAS*

More than 1,400 orchid species are found in Costa Rica. This is the largest family of flowering plants (*Orchidaceae*). From tall terrestrials that wave in the breeze to tiny miniatures whose flowers you can really appreciate only with a magnifying glass, orchids add amazing richness to the biological landscape. They grow as vines (up to 98 feet [30 m] long) and as the plants more commonly recognized as orchids.

While you see orchids growing on branches and trunks of trees, they are not parasites; that is, they do not take their nourishment from the tree. They are epiphytes, using the tree only as a mean of support. Eighty-eight percent of all orchids are epiphytic, while 12 percent are terrestrial.

Miniatures can be so tiny that it is difficult to pick out the three sepals, two petals, and a modified petal (labellum) that are characteristic of orchids. They can measure not more than 1 inch (3 cm), including roots, foliage, and flower. At the other extreme, some orchids have a stem up to 16 feet (5 m) long.

Orchid pollination has some bizarre twists. They are usually pollinated by bees, flies, moths, butterflies, wasps, birds, and beetles. Some orchids have developed flowers that look like certain species of bees or wasps. A male bee or wasp attempts to copulate with the flower and in the process goes away carrying pollen, ideally to another orchid flower. Some orchids produce oils that are collected by certain kinds of bees to be used as food for larvae; in the process of collecting, the bees move pollen from one flower to the next. To ensure cross-pollination, flowers in the same

Hanging orchid

species in one area produce their fragrances at different times of day so bees will fly from one to the other. Some flowers last only a day; others last several weeks if they are not pollinated.

The national flower is the *guaria morada* orchid (*Cattleya skinneri*), a showy species chosen in 1939 because it grows easily around the country and was a part of the national folklore. It is said that Guatuso Indians adorned their hair with *guarias* because they thought the blossoms had magical qualities.

You can see orchids in the forest, along roadsides, in landscaped hotel gardens, and in botanical gardens. The largest collection is at the Lankester Botanical Garden near Cartago; a smaller, fine one is in Monteverde.

Aerial Tram

NATURE/ ADVENTURE COMPANIES AND ACTIVITIES

4

Nature/adventure travel tours in Costa Rica run the gamut from one person with a guide to a microbus of travelers; from hiking, bicycling, sailing, rafting, ballooning, or kayaking to overland jaunts by horseback, car, or bus. Some remote destinations are best reached by short flights in small planes—don't be surprised by landings on grass runways. Just as Costa Rica is small and friendly, so are the nature tours I have taken. Chances are that by the time even a one-day tour is over, the guide will call you by name and you will have made a friend.

Here are some of the activities available and the people who can help you enjoy them, companies that specialize in nature and adventure travel. First are Costa Rican tour operators, followed by U.S. companies. Though prices vary from season to season, these 1998 rates offer an idea of what to expect. Listings of each company's offerings are intended to give you a glimpse of possibilities; they are not all-inclusive.

HIKING, BIRD-WATCHING, GENERAL NATURE TRAVEL OUTFITTERS

Camino Travel, downtown location, Calle 1, Avenidas 1/Central, San José, (506) 257-0107, fax (506) 257-0243, sales office (506) 225-0263, (506) 234-2530, fax (506) 225-6143; e-mail caminotr@sol.racsa.co.cr. The downtown office, open weekdays, offers travelers a "one-stop travel shop" to fit individual budgets and preferences. Services include hotel reservations, tour reservations, and purchase of bus tickets and domestic airline tickets, which can be delivered to any hotel in San José's metropolitan area. Rent a car, with a driver or a private guide if you wish. You pay the same as if you book directly. What's more, if you go in with this book, you receive free an updated list of buses with station addresses and hours of service. Trip planning is a specialty, so travelers can contact Camino before arrival as well.

Camino offers its own three-day tour to Chirripó National Park. The first day gets you from San José to base camp in a park refuge at 11,155 feet (3,400 m), requiring an eight- or nine-hour hike of 10 miles (16 km). Day Two is the trek to the peak, San Juan Lagoon, and Los Crestones. The return to San Gerardo de Rivas on the last day takes only four hours, which gives you an idea of the terrain. Cost is $385 for transportation, meals, guide, cook, park fees, and a donation to the park. Bring backpack and sleeping bag. Minimum three persons.

A seven-day, six-night Costa Rica Verde trip goes to Poás and Arenal Volcanoes, Tabacón Hot Springs, Caño Negro wildlife refuge, Valle Escondido Lodge for its private forest reserve and ornamental plant farm, La Ensenada Lodge on the Gulf of Nicoya for horseback riding and a boat trip to the mangroves, and Monteverde. Cost includes trained English-speaking guide, lodging, specified meals, entrance fees, and in-country transportation: $843 double occupancy November through mid-April, $798 in other months.

Costa Rica Expeditions, Avenida 3, Calles Central/2, San José, (506) 222-0333, (506) 257-0766, fax (506) 257-1665; e-mail costaric@expeditions .co.cr; Web site www.expeditions.co.cr. This company pioneered natural history travel in Costa Rica and has a team of excellent naturalist guides. It offers one-day Tropical Forest Adventure tours to Poás Volcano, Tapantí National Park, or Cerro de la Muerte for $99 including transportation, guide, lunch, and park fees (minimum four people). Another one-day option is a visit to internationally known La Selva Biological Station; $119 each, minimum: four. Travelers who want their own guide can take advantage of the private naturalist guide service: $119 per day for the guide, transportation cost depends on the destination.

Costa Rica Expeditions also has fixed-departure multiday packages that combine several destinations: for example, the eight-day Costa Rica Odyssey travels to Poás, Monteverde, and Corcovado; $1,498 per person. The 10-day Costa Rica Explorer takes in Tortuguero, Arenal, the Reventazón River (for white-water rafting), Poás, and Monteverde; $1,698. Prices for both of these are based on double occupancy from December to March (less in other months); they include in-country travel, lodging, guides, park fees, taxes, and some meals.

The company also offers white-water tours and owns three lodges: Tortuga Lodge at Tortuguero, Corcovado Lodge Tent Camp, and Monteverde Lodge; packages available.

Costa Rica Sun Tours, Avenida 4, Calle 36, San José, (506) 255-3418, fax (506) 255-4410; e-mail suntours@sol.racsa.co.cr. Sun Tours offers several day trips from San José. The 12-hour Arenal Volcano Night Tour includes stops at

Zarcero for the topiary and at Tabacón for a swim in the hot springs, as well as volcano-viewing time. Others include Barva Volcano, Carara Biological Reserve, Guayabo National Monument, Cerro de la Muerte, Irazú/Lankester Botanical Garden/Orosi, and Poás Volcano/Sarchí. The company also operates horseback riding, rafting, boat trips, turtle nesting tours, kayaking, cruises in the Gulf of Nicoya, and park tours in day trips from the Arenal area, Guanacaste, Jacó Beach, Manuel Antonio, and Monteverde.

Eight- and nine-day nature and adventure programs cover the country. The New Southern Rainforest Odyssey includes Cerro de la Muerte and the chance of seeing the resplendent quetzal, lovely Wilson Botanical Gardens at the Las Cruces Biological Station, Tiskita Rainforest Reserve, and Corcovado; $1,320 including transport, lodging, specified meals, and taxes. Ask about Best of Costa Rica (Corcovado, Tiskita, Arenal, Monteverde, Carara) and Coast to Coast (Tortuguero, southern Pacific rain forests, and Corcovado).

Sun Tours has a number of multiday tours to the two private nature reserves it operates: Arenal Observatory Lodge and Tiskita Jungle Lodge. It also offers a four-day hike from Monteverde to Arenal with a Sunday departure date; $495 per person, double occupancy.

Horizontes Nature Adventures, Calle 28, Avenidas 1/3 (just north of Pizza Hut on Paseo Colón), San José, (506) 222-2022, fax (506) 255-4513; e-mail horizont@sol.racsa.co.cr; Web site www.horizontes.com. With a well-deserved reputation for quality nature-based tourism, Horizontes offers personalized service to individuals and small groups interested in travel for nature observation, conservation, education, soft adventure, and connections with local people. The staff designs custom trips, taking into account physical abilities, budget, length of visit, and time of year; they want to make sure clients don't take off on a trip that's too long or too tough. High-quality bilingual guides are chosen according to each client's specific interests and needs.

Horizontes has a wide array of packaged programs from which individual travelers may choose, including both single- and multiday tours. Horizontes has received international recognition for its leadership in ecotourism, the latest from *Condé Nast Traveler* magazine.

Jungle Trails, Calle 38, Avenidas 5/7 near Centro Colón, San José, (506) 255-3486, fax (506) 255-2782; e-mail jungletr@sol.racsa.co.cr. Staff custom-plan one-day trips or multiday expeditions throughout the country taking into account travelers' interests and budgets. Jungle Trails creates an itinerary suited to travel independently or with a guide. Its team of guides includes biologists, many of whom have taught or are teaching at Costa Rica's universities, with specialists in botany, ornithology, ecology, and other branches of biology. The small company is committed to personalized attention and has experience with all modes of travel, from hiking to flying. Jungle Trails continues with its program to plant a tree in San José for every tour sold. The native species of trees are purchased from Arbofilia (the Association for the Protection of Trees), a grassroots ecological organization.

Tikal Tour Operators, Avenida 2, Calles 7/9, San José, (506) 223-2811, fax (506) 223-1916; e-mail advtikal@sol.racsa.co.cr. This full-service travel agency also specializes in nature travel. One-day tours include a city tour ($22), Carara ($70), and the aerial tram ($70). Several eight-day Ecosafari series are $1,067 each, double occupancy, all-inclusive. The Rainforest Ecosafari visits Cerro de la Muerte, San Gerardo de Dota for quetzals, San Isidro and the Alexander Skutch farm at Los Cusingos, Dominical, Drake Bay, Caño Island, and Corcovado. The Ecoadventure tour goes to Las Baulas (including mountain biking), Culebra Bay (snorkeling), Coter Lake near Arenal, the Corobicí (a river float), and a Pacific dry forest (horseback riding).

AIR TOURS
Skytours, (506) 383-3673, telephone/fax (506) 228-9912; e-mail skytours @sol.racsa.co.cr; Web site www.greenarrow.com/travel/skytours.htm. Operated by Pitts Aviation, Skytours offers travelers a bird's-eye view of some of the country's greatest attractions. It's all set to music that complements the symphony of nature played below. Each passenger has use of a pair of quality binoculars and a stereo headset along with a description of the route and tips on what to look for along the way.

Dance on the Volcanoes flies over Poás, Barva, Irazú, and Turrialba Volcanoes as well as the forested expanse of Braulio Carrillo National Park

Small planes get to remote places

($99 per person). The Pirate Treasure route includes Quepos and Manuel Antonio, south over Punta Uvita, Corcovado, Caño Island, Golfito, Sierpe River, and up to the heights of the Talamanca Mountains and the country's highest peak, Chirripó ($165). The Ocean Connection is a full day, with 3½ hours of flight time: Tortuguero, then over Arenal Volcano to Puerto Carrillo on the Pacific where passengers deplane for a gourmet lunch, swim in the pool of a small resort, or walk on the beach before returning to San José, enjoying the sunset over the coast of the Nicoya Peninsula ($359).

A four-day trip, with seven hours of flight time, covers volcanoes, the Talamanca Mountains, the Caribbean coast, the Pacific coast, the Gulf of Nicoya Islands, Manuel Antonio, Corcovado, and Caño Island. Lodging is in Tortuguero, the Osa, and Guanacaste. In-country and international charter flights offered.

BALLOONING

Costa Rica Serendipity Adventures, (506) 556-2592, fax (506) 556-2593, e-mail serendip@sol.racsa.co.cr, Web site www.serendipityadventures .com, U.S. number (800) 635-2325, fax (313) 426-5026. Experience the country by hot-air balloon. The Naranjo option goes over coffee fields and mountain villages and includes breakfast at the central market in a farming community; $235 per person includes ballooning, transportation to and from launch site, and breakfast; flight only is $195 per person. A two-day Arenal option includes views of Arenal Volcano at night, soaking in hot springs, and a sunrise balloon flight; $495, minimum four. Another trip features the Turrialba Valley, with a visit to Lankester Botanical Garden and a sunrise balloon flight; $545 per person, minimum four. Flight-only rates for these two are $225 per person. All pilots are U.S. FAA-licensed commercial pilots. Office in Turrialba.

Serendipity also offers rafting, kayaking, mountain biking, climbing, and rappelling (horseback ride to a giant strangler fig tree to climb it from the inside, emerging in the canopy), camping, and horseback riding (one- to four-day treks into the Talamanca Mountains, following Indian trails and river banks to hot springs, ruins, and villages). The staff works with travelers who lack physical ability to allow them to experience the adventure to its fullest, while challenging those with high-level skills.

CRUISE OUTFITTERS

Several companies offer day trips by yacht through the Gulf of Nicoya to Tortuga Island or other destinations. Passengers are wined and dined during the day-long outing, with time for swimming, snorkeling, or just relaxing.

Bay Island Cruise, (506) 258-3536, fax (506) 258-1189; e-mail bayislan@ sol.racsa.co.cr. The trip to Tortuga Island includes an air-conditioned bus ride from San José to Puntarenas, the cruise on the *Bay Princess*, snacks, cocktails, and lunch; $70.

Calypso Tours, (506) 256-2727, fax (506) 256-6767; e-mail calypso@
sol.racsa.co.cr; Web site www.calypsotours.com; U.S. number (800) 948-
3770. Sail to Tortuga Island on the catamaran *Manta Raya,* with two
Jacuzzi pools on deck and an underwater viewing window; $99 includes
air-conditioned bus, continental breakfast, and lunch (with wine). Other
$99 cruises include one on the yacht *Calypso* to Punta Coral Private Re-
serve on the Nicoya Peninsula in front of Negritos Island Biological Reserve. You can walk nature trails to see monkeys and parrots, or you can
kayak, snorkel, or swim. Chilled white wine accompanies lunch to live
marimba music. A late tropical sky cruise is led by a bilingual astronomer.
Stargaze on the way to Punta Coral, where you have a torchlight gourmet
dinner (baked fudge with whipped cream for dessert), and a look through a
star-finder telescope. Return to San José about 1 a.m.

Sea Ventures of Costa Rica, (506) 257-2904, fax (506) 257-3139; e-mail
seavent@sol.racsa.co.cr. Cruises include a day trip to Tortuga Island. Guests
enjoy an air-conditioned salon featuring Neptune's Bar. Sit on the lower
deck, or relax on the upper deck while listening to the tropical band. Swim,
snorkel, and hike before a full buffet lunch; $70, including transport from
San José, guide, drinks, and food.

Temptress Adventure Cruises, (506) 220-1679, fax (506) 220-2130;
e-mail TemptressA@worldnet.att.net; Web site www.temptresscruises
.com/; U.S. number (800) 336-8423. Cruise on the *Temptress Explorer,* a
99-passenger, 185-foot boat, all outside cabins, private baths, and air conditioning. Voyages include morning natural history walks with naturalist

Cruising the Pacific coast on the Temptress

guides and afternoons of snorkeling, scuba diving, sea kayaking, waterskiing, or swimming. The three-night Curú Voyage embarks from Puntarenas, with time at Curú wildlife refuge, Tortuga Island, Drake Bay, Corcovado National Park, and Golfito, flying back to San José. The three-night Caño Voyage begins with a flight from San José to Golfito, visiting Corcovado, Caño Island, and Manuel Antonio. Each of these is $895 per person, double occupancy. A six-night Pacific voyage combines the two previous itineraries; $1,695, double occupancy. These rates are November to May; June to September rates are lower. Naturalist guides are excellent and food is superb.

SCUBA DIVING AND SNORKELING

Costa Rica has coral reefs off both coasts for snorkeling and scuba, along with world-class diving around Coco Island and Caño Island. Caribbean reefs are better-developed and more diverse than Pacific reefs, and the southern Caribbean still has some of the best coastal diving, though sedimentation from deforestation and agriculture is damaging the reefs. There is less coral on the Pacific, but the abundance of big fish makes it popular with divers. See Chapter 8 for dive centers in the Ocotal, Playa Hermosa, Flamingo, and Montezuma areas.

Diving Outfitters For Coco Island

Cocos Travel, telephone/fax (506) 290-6737; e-mail info@divecocos.com; Web site www.divecocos.com. On diving trips to Coco Island see schools of 200 or more hammerheads during rainy season, orcas, dolphins, green sea

Protecting Rivers and Peoples

Fundación Ríos Tropicales is a private nonprofit foundation whose mission is to preserve, protect, and restore watersheds of the Pacuare and Reventazón Rivers and the well-being of the surrounding communities. Government hydroelectric projects on these rivers is the concern, some proposed and some already being built. The foundation was established in 1991 by Ríos Tropicales. For information about contributions or volunteer work, telephone Ríos Tropicales or contact the foundation directly via e-mail: frt@riostro.com. Send tax-free donations through Friends of the River/Fundación Ríos Tropicales, 128 J Street, 2nd floor, Sacramento, CA 95814-2203.

turtles, white-tip reef sharks, marble stingrays, sailfish, mantas, and silk sharks. The 115-foot *Sea Hunter* has eight cabins for 18 passengers, private baths. *Underseas Hunter,* a research vessel, holds 14 passengers. A sample itinerary is a 12-day trip that includes diving on seven days (three to four dives per day), transport between San José and Puntarenas, and lodging and meals during the cruise; from $2,970 per person. Park fees are additional.

Okeanos Aggressor, (506) 256-6428, fax (504) 384-0817; e-mail okeano@sol.racsa.co.cr; Web site www.aggressor.com/; U.S. number (504) 385-2628. This 120-foot, 22-passenger vessel features diving trips (for experienced divers) to Coco Island. Passengers have four dives per day in waters where hundreds of hammerheads and white tip sharks are at home, along with dolphins, manta rays, tuna, reef fish, stingrays, and spiny lobster. Water visibility is 80 to 100 feet, temperature 74°F to 82°F (27°C to 30° C). The 11-day cruise offers seven full days of diving for $2,795; the 10-day offers six full diving days, $2,495.

RAFTING/KAYAKING OUTFITTERS

Costa Rica's wealth of sea and river resources make it an ideal destination for both rafting and kayaking. The Pacuare River is among the five wildest and most scenic rivers in the world, with class III–V rapids and virgin forests. The Reventazón River is rated as the third-best river for world-class kayaking. The Caribbean and Pacific coasts, as well as the Pacific gulfs, offer terrific sea-kayaking opportunities.

All of the following specialists in rafting and kayaking have trained, bilingual guides and good equipment. If you have never rafted or kayaked before, this is a wonderful way to experience the natural world. There are trips for beginners, and each company offers instruction. Standards are one-day trips year-round on the Reventazón near Turrialba, which offers rapids and calm stretches passing through spectacular landscapes, from $70 to $90. Another popular one-day is a float trip on the Corobicí River near Cañas (class I–II) for wildlife viewing, especially birds and monkeys, $70 to $85. The one-day rafting trip on the Pacuare River is about $90. Check the Mountain Biking section for tours that also include rafting and/or kayaking.

Aguas Bravas, in San José (506) 292-2072, fax (506) 229-4837; in La Fortuna (506) 479-9025; Web site www.hway.com/arenas/abravas/. Offers whitewater rafting from San José, La Fortuna, and Sarapiquí, with trips on the Sarapiquí, Sucio, Pacuare, and Peñas Blancas Rivers. The Peñas Blancas, just 30 minutes from Arenal Volcano and relatively new to the white-water scene, class II–III rapids, $37 for the half-day trip. The class IV–V upper Sarapiquí is $80 ($50 from Sarapiquí), but there are beginners' trips on the Sarapiquí, some especially for bird-watching. The company's White-Water Center is in the Sarapiquí area between La Vírgen and Puerto Viejo. Its Adventure Center is in La Fortuna.

Aventuras Naturales, (506) 225-3939, fax (506) 253-6934; e-mail avenat @sol.racsa.co.cr; Web site www.toenjoynature.com, U.S. number (800) 514-0411. Its two-day Pacuare River rafting trip (class III–IV) is great for seeing wildlife and enjoying the thrill of white-water rafting. Overnight is in the company's rustic, two-story Pacuare Jungle Lodge. Each of five screened bungalows has beds with orthopedic mattresses and private bath, no electricity—dinner by candlelight; $249 per person. Hiking in Aventuras Naturales' forest reserve is added on the three-day Pacuare trip, with waterfalls and trails into the mountains to the land of the Cabecar Indians; $324. A one-day Sarapiquí trip (class III) is $75. Multiday trips include rafting, hiking, and biking. One 10-day adventure package offers hiking in Monteverde, a visit to Arenal and thermal springs, a canopy experience, biking, kayaking, white-water rafting, overnight at Pacuare Jungle Lodge, and Tortuguero canals; $1,365 per person. The company operates the Fleur de Lys Hotel in San José. Custom packages available.

Costa Rica White Water (part of Costa Rica Expeditions), Avenida 3, Calles Central/2, San José, (506) 222-0333, (506) 257-0766, fax (506) 257-1665; e-mail costaric@expeditions.co.cr; Web site www.expeditions.co.cr. Its rafts are custom-made by Demaree Inflatable Boats. Two one-day Reventazón tours for experienced rafters run daily with a minimum of four: the Pascua run (class III–IV) and the more dangerous Guayabo Run (class IV–V); $85 for either. First-time rafters run the Tucurrique section of the Reventazón, which the company describes as "exciting but forgiving rapids in a tropical setting";

Photo courtesy of Riós Tropicales

White-water excitement

$69. A two-day trip on the Pacuare includes beautiful side hikes and overnight camping on the riverbank. Ask about fixed departure dates.

Ríos Tropicales, Calle 38, Paseo Colón/ Avenida 2, San José, (506) 233-6455, fax (506) 255-4354; e-mail info@riostro.com; Web site www.riostro.com. This company is recognized internationally for its efforts in conservation, reforestation, and environmental education; owners are authors of *The Rivers of Costa Rica*. A three-day Pacuare trip offers rafting (class III–IV), and hiking, with overnights in the Cabecar-style bungalows of Ríos Tropicales Camp on the river's banks—electricity from hydropower. On Day Two, trail guides lead a five-hour hike into Garcia's Indian Village; Day Three is back on the river for more waterfalls, rapids, and wildlife. Two one-day Sarapiquí tours, one for beginners and one a scenic float trip with class I–III rapids, are each $85. The four-day Río General trip (class III–IV) is $440.

Ríos Tropicales has a number of multiday kayak trips. A four-day Curú trip includes hiking at the wildlife refuge, beach camping, and an estuary trip; $600. The nine-day Golfo Dulce tour starts and ends at Golfito, and includes the Esquinas River area, Caña Blanca, Puerto Jiménez, camping where dolphins play, and an Osa Peninsula beach where squirrel monkeys, scarlet macaws, toucans, and other wildlife are regular visitors. Kayaking continues to Pavones (with one of the longest left-breaking waves in world) and Punta Zancudo; $1,370. No experience necessary. Ask about the four-day Rafting and Hiking in the Rain Forest tour. Ríos Tropicales has a small outdoor store, with equipment for camping, hiking, climbing, and water sports: Calle 22 Bis, Avenida 3, (506) 255-0618.

MOUNTAIN BIKING

Costa Rica's terrain offers terrific mountain-biking opportunities. Several agencies provide logistical support and equipment on adventurous tours. Some of the popular one-day tours are in the Orosi Valley and Tapantí National Park, to the pre-Columbian ruins at Guayabo near Turrialba, or between Irazú and Turrialba Volcanoes.

Aguas Bravas, in San José (506) 292-2072, fax (506) 229-4837; in La Fortuna (506) 479-9025; Web site www.hway.com/arenas/abravas/. Half-day and full-day mountain bike routes for each level are arranged at its Adventure Center in La Fortuna. Tours include transport, bikes, and bilingual guide; half-day, $45; full day, $65 including lunch.

Bi.Costa Rica Bike Tours, (506) 258-0303, (506) 258-0404 (leave message), cellular (506) 380-3844, fax (506) 258-0606; e-mail kitcom @yellowweb.co.cr; Web site www.yellowweb.co.cr/bicostarica.html. In small groups (maximum six riders) explore the country's diverse ecosystems with expert guides. Lodging is in small, luxurious country inns, most with swimming pools for relaxation after the daily ride. Luggage is shuttled daily in the support vehicle, which also has cold tropical fruits and drinks. Riders average 30 miles (48 km) a day, and tours include other adventures: hiking, swimming in the pool at the base of a waterfall, sunset cruise, sea kayaking, white-water rafting, caving, and fishing.

One-day tours visit such sites as Tapantí National Park and the Orosi Valley; $85 including breakfast, lunch, park fee, and a hot-springs entrance fee. The one-day to Poás Volcano, Grecia, and Sarchí is also $85. Two-day trips are in the Arenal area or to Carara and Jacó. A three-day trip cycles on the Osa Peninsula with a visit to Corcovado. The nine-day Rain Forest, Volcanoes, and Beaches tour is $1,550, starting in San José. Another nine-day tour is Bike the Beaches, taking off from Liberia and including Ocotal, a monkey trail, Bahía Potrero, Playa Conchal, Playa Langosta, Tamarindo, Bahía Garza, Ostional, and Sámara; $1,795. Tours also custom designed.

Costa Rica Sun Tours, (506) 255-3418, fax (506) 255-4410, e-mail suntours@sol.racsa.co.cr. The one-day Irazú trip is $90; a two-day trip adds rafting on the Reventazón, $250. The three-day trip includes biking in the Irazú area and rafting on the Pacuare, $420. These tours can also be booked through Costa Rica Connections in the U.S., (800) 345-7422, (805) 543-8823, fax (805) 543-3626, e-mail crconnec@crconnect.com, Web site www.crconnect.com.

Rock River Lodge, at Lake Arenal northwest of Tilarán, telephone/fax (506) 695-5644, e-mail rokriver@sol.racsa.co.cr, Web site www.rockriver .mastermind.net. Explore unusual mountain-biking routes: the three-day Volcano Trail for intermediate bikers goes all the way to Orosi Volcano near Nicaragua, $100 per day. A Quipilapa trail goes to Miravalles, and two- to five-hour day tours go to Cañas for a swim in the Corobicí and to a waterfall for swimming in the Tenorio River.

Costa Rica Serendipity Adventures, (506) 556-2592, fax (506) 556-2593; e-mail serendip@sol.racsa.co.cr; U.S. number (800) 635-2325, fax (313) 426-5026. Bike trips range from rugged single-track to gentle downhills. The Espíritu Sanctu is six hours of off-road and gravel adventure in mountain coffee country; trip includes an introductory rappel, $135 per person. Misty Waterfalls starts at 6,300 feet (1,920 m), descending through dairy farms to forest and a 45-minute hike to the first waterfall and lunch; then single-track through forest to a hanging bridge, and finally through coffee fields and villages; $155 per person. Ask about the three-day Beach Glory expedition in Guanacaste that includes camping, hiking, and rappelling.

MOTORCYCLING
Rent-a Harley Davidson, (506) 289-5552, fax (506) 289-5551, e-mail matour@sol.racsa.co.cr. See the country on a Harley Davidson. On Ride by Your Own tours, travelers rent a Harley and follow one of the company's

suggested tours, from one to multiple days, or ask for a custom itinerary that includes hotel reservations, airport transfers, the works. Rates : XL 883 Sportster, daily $80, weekly $480; XL 1200 Sportster, daily $100, weekly $600; FXD Dyna Super Glide, daily $140, weekly $840. Free mileage, no charge for second passenger. Rates include helmets, rain gear, lock, motorcycle cover, and insurance. Minimum age for rental is 25, and the driver must have a valid motorcycle license.

WINDSURFING

At its northern end, Lake Arenal is one of the world's best windsurfing sites. Daily wind average in dry season is 33 mph, best for experts, but rainy-season winds are calmer, good even for beginners. See Chapter 7 for hotels and lodges offering windsurfing tours or packages.

U.S. COMPANIES WITH NATURE TOURS TO COSTA RICA

Many tour companies offer trips to Costa Rica. Here are a few of those that specialize in nature and adventure travel.

Costa Rica Connection, (800) 345-7422, fax (805) 543-3626; e-mail tours@crconnect.com; Web site www.crconnect.com. A nine-day, eight-night national parks tour begins at $1,479 from Los Angeles or $1,255 from Miami, with visits to Tortuguero and Manuel Antonio parks. Specialty tours focus on beaches, adventure, language and culture, and family tours. The eight-day, seven-night Costa Rica Odyssey tour combines the Monteverde Cloud Forest Preserve, Sarchí, Manuel Antonio, a Pacific island cruise, and sightseeing in San José. Ask about a fly–drive package or a sea-turtle conservation expedition at Ostional. The weekly fixed departures are ideal for single travelers. Tropical Adventure program includes hiking, rafting, and mountain biking. Also available are sport-fishing, diving, surfing, and student programs. Call or write for a Costa Rica Trip Planner.

Earthwatch (800) 776-0188, (617) 926-8200, e-mail info@earthwatch.org, Web site www.earthwatch.org). This nonprofit organization teams up interested volunteers from age 16 to 85 with university scientists and cultural experts worldwide to work on field research expeditions around the world. No special skills are required, though they are welcomed. Contact Earthwatch for information about projects in Costa Rica.

Geo Expeditions, (800) 351-5041, (209) 532-0152, fax (209) 532-1979; e-mail drisard@geoexpeditions.com. A 12-day fixed-departure tour travels through Tortuguero canals by boat, to Arenal for volcano-viewing and relaxing in nearby thermal waters, to Monteverde to learn about the tropical forest at the Monteverde Cloud Forest Preserve, to the Osa Peninsula to hike in Corcovado, and to Caño Island to snorkel and see Indian artifacts; from $2,295, excluding international airfare.

A 10-day natural history tour, led by first-class naturalist guides, focuses on Poás and Tortuguero parks, Monteverde, Arenal Volcano, and rafting on the Reventazón. December through March fixed departures are $1,698. Custom-designed tours available.

Geostar Travel, (800) 624-6633, (707) 579-2420, fax (707) 579-0604. Specialties are bird-watching, botanical, and natural history tours. Naturalists lead multiday trips to sites such as the Monteverde Cloud Forest Preserve, Arenal Volcano, Tortuguero, and Corcovado National Park. Activities include hiking in tropical forests; white-water rafting; wildlife river trips; bathing in thermal waters; bird-, butterfly-, and turtle-watching; and volcano-viewing. High-season prices, double occupancy, for these eight- to 10-day trips are $1,498 to $1,698, excluding airfare.

Green Tortoise Adventure Travel, in Costa Rica (506) 761-1035; e-mail info@greentortoise.com; Web site www.greentortoise.com; U.S. and Canada numbers (800) 867-8647, (415) 956-7500, fax (415)-956-4900. Finds tours for budget-minded travelers. It operates a bed and breakfast on 17 acres (7 ha) of rain forest near La Vírgen de Sarapiquí, specializing in rafting, kayaking, and mountain biking. Accommodations are rustic, yet comfortable. Lodging in Green Tortoise bed-and-breakfast is $15 per person double, camping $5, rafting $40 per person, kayaking $50, mountain bikes $20 per day. Bed-and-breakfast package also includes sack lunch and rafting or kayaking, $55.

Holbrook Travel, (800) 451-7111, fax (352) 371-3710; e-mail travel@ holbrooktravel.com; Web site www.holbrooktravel.com. Choose from an array of all-inclusive natural history tours, some fixed departures. Birding, photography, biodiversity, and national parks tours are available, generally led by individuals noted in their fields, as well as naturalist tours. Ask about the 11-day Birds of Costa Rica; $1,297, excluding international airfare. The eight-day Costa Rica's Natural Riches—From the Caribbean to the Cordillera is led by an expert naturalist guide; $1,097 per person, double occupancy. Holbrook also has Turtle Tagging in Costa Rica in association with the Caribbean Conservation Corporation, nine or 16 days from March to May and July to September. Staff create custom tours.

International Expeditions, (800) 633-4734, (205) 428-1700, fax (205) 428-1714; e-mail intlexp@aol.com; Web site www.ietravel.com/intexp. High-quality, educational natural history expeditions stress environmental awareness and resource conservation. Its 10-day Wildlife Sanctuary of the Americas features Monteverde, Poás, Tortuguero, Santa Rosa National Park, and Lomas Barbudal; $2,398 per person. An eight-day Volcanos, Rivers, and Rainforests tour visits Palo Verde National Park on a river trip, Monteverde, Tortuguero, and Arenal. Classic Costa Rica, 15 days, includes

Monteverde, a float trip on the Bebedero to Palo Verde, Tortuguero, Arenal, the Savegre Valley in search of the quetzal, Hacienda Baru, and Manuel Antonio and Carara. Ask about educator workshops. Itineraries designed for independent travelers.

Mariah Wilderness Expeditions, (800) 462-7424, (510) 233-2303, fax (510) 233-0956; e-mail rafting@mariahwe.com; Web site www.mariahwe.com. Emphasizing natural history and adventure travel, it offers several eight- to 10-day itineraries. The nine-day Best of Costa Rica includes Tiskita Rain Forest Reserve, Arenal Volcano, Tabacón Hot Springs, Monteverde cloud forest, and Carara Biological Reserve. With the Adventures a la Carte program, travelers put together their own adventure, guided by the 16-page Costa Rica Trip Planner, which includes one-day and multiday options. Expedition staff researches and designs custom trips based on special interests and budgets. Ask for a full-color Costa Rica brochure and the trip planner.

Overseas Adventure Travels's (OAT), (800) 955-1925. Excellent naturalist guides lead small groups on 11-day trips to explore a variety of habitats, from cloud forest to beaches: hikes, rafting, wildlife boat trip, volcano watching, hot spring experience, thermal mud bath, river trip for crocodile observation, cruise on a yacht, and guided walks at private nature reserves. Eat with a local family and visit a rural school and local cantina. Trips are designed to have no negative impact on the physical or cultural environment while providing a glimpse of the natural riches and contact with Costa Ricans. Real Affordable Costa Rica is from $1,990, including airfare from Miami; three-day extension to Tortuguero National Park available. Cost includes donation to support research and community projects in Costa Rica. The company is also a member of Grand Circle Foundation, a nonprofit organization that has contributed to a number of cultural and environmental projects in the country.

Preferred Adventures Ltd., (800) 840-8687, (612) 222-8131, fax (612) 222-4221; e-mail paltours@aol.com. Customized individual adventure and natural history travel featured as well as special-interest tours for birders, horticulturists, and student groups. A Tropical Birding and Discovery Journey to the Rainforests of Costa Rica is led by Noble Proctor, author of *A Manual of Ornithology*. The 11-day trip goes to top birding destinations; $2,595 per person, double occupancy. New are Rain Forest Ecology Workshops in collaboration with the Organization for Tropical Studies: one at Las Cruces Biological Station and Corcovado, the other at La Selva and Tortuguero.

Remarkable Journeys, (800) 856-1993, (713) 721-2517, fax (713) 728-8334; e-mail cooltrips@remjourneys.com; Web site www.remjourneys.com. A diverse array of packaged tours and personalized itineraries available. The nine-day Costa Rica: An Active Adventure explores Venado Caves, bikes from Irazú to Turrialba Volcanoes, visits Guayabo National Monument, travels by horseback from Arenal to Monteverde, and hikes in a rain forest; $1,355 starting in San José, $1,605 from Houston, Texas. A Costa Rica Adventure for Women offers 10 days of white-water rafting, rain-forest hiking, biking, horseback riding, canoeing, and kayaking; $1,355 from San José, $1,615 from Houston, Texas. Nine-day Costa Rica Naturally explores Corcovado, including a tent-camp experience, Bosque del Cabo, and the Golfo Dulce.

Wildland Adventures, (800) 345-4453, (206) 365-0686, fax (206) 363-6615; e-mail info@wildland.com; Web site www.wildland.com. Tours and individual trip planners allow travelers flexibility. Trips support the company's nonprofit Travelers Conservation Trust. The company aims to provide opportunities for individuals, groups, families, honeymooners, and teacher and student groups, to experience natural habitats and discover local cultures in ways that enrich not only the traveler but also local people. The eight-day Tropical Trails Odyssey travels to Monteverde and the Osa Peninsula. A 10-day Family Adventure takes in Sarapiquí and Selva Verde Lodge, Arenal Volcano, and Tamarindo beach. Choose a nature adventure–wellness vacation at Nosara Retreat Center: yoga, turtle-watching, hiking, mountain biking, horseback riding, sailing, and wellness activities; minimum two days.

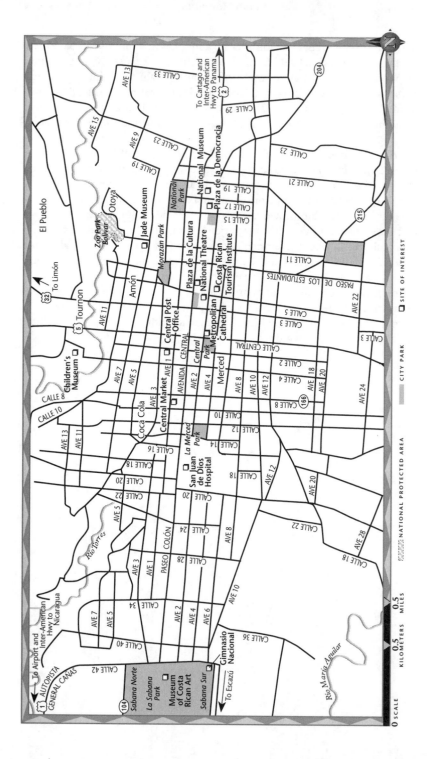

5

SAN JOSE
AND ENVIRONS

San José, founded in 1737, is the center of government, theater, and art, as well as air pollution and congestion. This capital city has beautiful parks and museums, along with a few beggars on the streets. It is big and often noisy, but even from its crowded downtown streets, you can manage a view of surrounding mountains, green against the sky. I find it a friendly, interesting city. Increased theft, however, is a reality—be alert.

With all the traffic, it's hard to realize that the era of the automobile began here only in the 1950s. It is not uncommon to see carts scattered among the cars even now, though they are generally pulled by people rather than oxen as in the countryside. Walk along Avenida 1 to the area around the Central Market, Calles 6/8, or Borbón Market, Avenida 3, Calles 8/10, in the early morning to see carts being loaded and unloaded.

In recent years San José has paid attention to its parks, and it shows. Morazán and España parks start at Calle 5 near Avenida 3, a place to join *ticos* eating their sack lunches and watching schoolchildren play. Do a little bird-watching even here: blue-gray tanagers, a few parrots, and a woodpecker or two. The elaborate bandstand in Morazán reverberates with music on special occasions. The metallic school building you see nearby was built in the 1890s; the plates were designed by Alexandre Gustave Eiffel of Eiffel Tower fame and shipped from Belgium by boat to be assembled here. The National Park, farther down Avenida 3 at Calle 15, is another good place to escape crowds; and the park in front of the Metropolitan Cathedral, Avenida 2/Calle 2, has had a facelift. San José's moderate temperature makes sitting outside and seeing the sights pleasant: average high is 77°F (24.9°C); low, 61°F (16.3°C).

Morazán Park in downtown San José

Because of the country's small size and San José's central location, a traveler can use it as a base to touch many parts of Costa Rica in one-day excursions. National parklands with easy access are Irazú and Poás Volcanoes, Tapantí, and Braulio Carrillo. Package tours by air bring Tortuguero and Barra de Colorado National Parks into the picture. Guayabo National Monument, the only archaeological park, is also a good road trip. A cruise in the Gulf of Nicoya or a tour to Carara Biological Reserve takes you to the Pacific. Exploring the historical and biological treasures of the Central Valley is possible with tours to the Orosi Valley, Lankester Botanical Garden (for orchids), the colonial capital of Cartago with its religious shrine, and the handcraft city of Sarchí. One-day tours take you rafting or kayaking on the country's waterways and hiking on Barva Volcano.

GETTING YOUR BEARINGS

Avenida? Calle? These are words to add to your vocabulary. *Avenida* (pronounced ah-vay-NEE-dah) means "avenue." Avenidas run east and west. *Calle* (CAHL-yay) means "street," and calles—you got it—run north and south. It helps to get your bearings early, because when you stop to ask for directions, answers generally are in terms of so many meters to the north, east, south, or west. A city block is about a hundred meters long, so when a helpful person tells you to go *"200 metros al norte,"* it means two blocks north. *Metros* is pronounced "MAY-tros."

Street numbers on calles originate from Calle Central, with odd-numbered streets running parallel on its east, even-numbered streets west. Avenida numbers originate from Avenida Central; odd numbers are north of it and even numbers south. Thus, if you go north from Avenida Central, you cross in succession Avenida 1, Avenida 3, and Avenida 5. Walking west from Calle Central, you encounter Calle 2, Calle 4, and Calle 6. Few buildings have numbers. A typical address is Calle 1, Avenidas 2/4, which means the place is on Calle 1 in the block between Avenida 2 and Avenida 4. Calle and Avenida numbers are posted on buildings, at intersections, or on street corners. Keep looking; you'll find one eventually. The Costa Rica Tourism Institute (ICT) map of the country has a large city map on the back.

Things to See and Do in San José

Clodomiro Picado Institute (Dulce Nombre de Coronado), (506) 229-3135. This snake "farm," about 30 minutes from San José, is where the snakes are "milked" for the production of serum used to treat snakebite victims. Low fatality rate from snakebites in Costa Rica is attributed to widespread availability of antivenins, which the lab also exports. Visitors view snakes in enclosures weekdays from 8 a.m. to 4 p.m. On Friday at 2 p.m. see a slide show and demonstration of venom extraction. Admission free.

Pedestrian Safety

One of the most dangerous things facing a traveler in downtown San José is crossing the street. The pedestrian's job is to keep out of a driver's way—whatever the driver may decide to do. The tico's gentle nature seems to give way to rampant individualism behind the wheel. Cars turning right do not yield to pedestrians, even though the traffic law requires it. Expect no mercy if the light change finds you in the middle of the street. To meet the challenge, I follow a Costa Rican woman who is hanging onto at least two small children. When she goes, I go. If I don't see the light turn green at a wide street like Avenida 2, I wait a full cycle, ready to sprint across when it next turns green. I suggest you do the same.

One other word of caution: back up on corners where buses make turns on narrow streets; you could actually be hit by the bus while standing on the sidewalk. The downtown pedestrian walkway on Avenida Central keeps getting longer. It's great.

The small **Insect Museum,** University of Costa Rica campus in San Pedro, (506) 207-5318, in the basement of the Music Arts Building (Facultad de Artes Musicales). It has a dazzling display of butterflies, bees, exotic-looking beetles and walking sticks, poisonous spiders, the large bala ant found in the Atlantic zone, and a 162-pound wasps' nest from near San Isidro de El General. If the entrance at the bottom of the stairs is locked, ring the bell. Open weekdays 1 to 5 p.m. Admission $2.

Jade Museum, Avenida 7, Calle 9, 11th floor of Instituto Nacional de Seguros (the National Insurance Institute), (506) 287-6034. Here is a marvelous collection of jade objects, pre-Columbian ceramic and stone works, and archaeological and ethnographic displays. Clean public rest rooms. Open weekdays 8:30 a.m. to 4:30 p.m. Admission $2.

Museos, Calle 5 between Avenidas Central and 2, (506) 223-0528. A three-level museum under the Plaza de la Cultura was established by the Central Bank of Costa Rica. The **Pre-Columbian Gold Museum** contains a spectacular collection of gold objects dating from A.D. 500. The **Numismatic Museum** displays collections of coins and bills dating back to the 16th century. Changing expositions of pre-Columbian pottery and contemporary art fill out the menu. The museum shop sells original art pieces and gold reproductions of collection pieces as well as books. Open 10 a.m. to 4:30 p.m., closed Monday. Admission $4.

Museo del Niño (Children's Museum) (506) 223-7003. Follow Calle 4 past Avenida 9 to the castle and you're there. It may be for children, but this museum, housed in a former prison, delights all ages with its hands-on exhibits (biology, astronomy, electricity, natural history), television and radio studio, art galleries, and mechanical talking figures (including astronaut Franklin Chang of Costa Rica). In an arboretum, look at Costa Rican tree species and learn about their uses. Open 8:30 a.m. to 4 p.m. Tuesday through Friday; 10 a.m. to 5 p.m. Saturday and Sunday; closed Monday. Admission $2 adults, $1.25 children.

Museum of Costa Rican Art, Calle 42, where Paseo Colón comes to La Sabana Park, (506) 222-7155. Until 1955, La Sabana Park was the international airport (Charles Lindbergh landed here); the museum is in the old terminal. Open 10 a.m. to 4 p.m., except Monday. Admission $3. The Sabana–Cementerio bus will get you there from downtown. A delightful restaurant in the museum building, Café Ruiseñor, (506)256-3168, looks out on Sabana Park. Open Monday–Saturday 10 a.m. to 6 p.m.

Museum of Natural Sciences (Colegio La Salle), across from the southwest corner of La Sabana Park, (506) 232-1306. Take Sabana–Estadio bus from downtown and ask to be let off at Colegio La Salle for the Museo de Ciencias

Naturales. Though some specimens appear a bit moth-eaten, exhibits show many of the mammals and birds to be found in Costa Rica, along with insects, reptiles, and crustaceans. It may be your only chance to see the harpy eagle, an endangered species, even if it is stuffed. There are also mineralogy, anthropology, and paleontology sections. Open Monday through Saturday 8 a.m. to 4 p.m., Sunday 9 a.m. to 8 p.m. Admission $1.25 adults, $1 children.

National Museum, Avenida Central/2, Calles 15/17, (506) 257-1433. An exhibit on modern history joins pre-Columbian art, natural history, and religious art in this 19th-century building that was converted from a military fortress after the army was abolished. Open 8:30 a.m. to 4:30 p.m., closed Monday. Admission $5. The adjoining Plaza de la Democracia, dedicated in 1989, commemorates 100 years of democracy in Costa Rica.

National Theater, beside Plaza de la Cultura. Start-up funds for the building came from coffee-growers through a voluntary tax on every bag of coffee exported. Later a tax on all imports was levied to complete construction. The reason? A famous European opera star appearing in Guatemala had refused to perform in Costa Rica for lack of an adequate performing space, one of a number of snubs from touring music and theater groups. National honor resulted in this neoclassical treasure, inaugurated in 1897. Attend a performance, or take a tour between 9 a.m. and 5 p.m. daily. Admission $2.50.

Zoológico Nacional Simón Bolívar, Avenida 13, Calles 7/11, (506) 233-6701, fax (506) 223-1817; e-mail fundazoo@sol.racsa.co.cr. The zoo tends to be jammed with local folks on weekends. Most of the wildlife is from Costa Rica, but an African lion, Bengal tiger, and assorted other foreign species round out the picture. Bolívar once again has a tapir, and a herpetological aquarium displays all five of Costa Rica's colorful poison-dart frogs. The zoo is open year-round, 9 a.m. to 4:30 p.m. daily. Admission $1. Bolívar Zoo can use financial help. Ask about donations through Fundación Pro-Zoológico.

Plaza de la Cultura, Avenida Central, Calles 3/5. This is a good place to people-watch. A mime, juggler, marimba band, Andean music group, or magician may be there, drawing clusters of onlookers. Artisans display wares.

Pueblo Antiguo in Parque de Diversiones, 1 mile (2 km) west of Hospital Mexico, (506) 296-2212. The site recreates the ambiance of an earlier Costa Rica, from 1880 to 1930, portraying life of city, country, and coasts: reconstructed rural houses, milking barn, train station, traditional trapiche (for extraction of cane juice), pulpería, Indian ranchitos, and a mini-plantation of banana and coffee. Open weekdays 9 a.m. to 5 p.m., weekends 9 a.m. to 9 p.m. Admission $2. Ask about weekend programs in English.

Serpentarium, Avenida 1, Calles 9/11, second floor, (506) 255-4210. You may not encounter a single snake during your forays into the natural world, so here is a chance to see some: the boa constrictor, coral snake, brightly colored tree viper, and fer-de-lance. More than 45 species of reptiles and amphibians (including tiny poison-dart frogs) are here, along with a photographic exhibit of Costa Rican wildlife. Learn how to distinguish between venomous and nonvenomous snakes. A bilingual biologist is on hand; most signs are in English and Spanish. Open year-round, weekdays 9 a.m. to 6 p.m., weekends and holidays 10 a.m. to 5 p.m. Admission $4.

Spirogyra, 1 block east and 1½ blocks south of El Pueblo Shopping Center, (506) 222-2937. This small urban butterfly garden showcases hundreds of butterflies of some 30 species. Visitors learn about butterflies from egg to metamorphosis to feeding habits and defense systems. A video is followed by a self-guided tour in what surely is one of the last small forests in town, close enough to the zoo to hear the lion roar. Spirogyra also exports butterfly pupae, including those raised by eight rural groups (mainly women) who breed butterflies to augment family incomes, people for whom the $20 or so per week they can make is a big difference. Spirogyra staff train representatives from each group, who go back and train others. Open daily 8 a.m. to 3 p.m. Admission $5 adults, $2.50 children.

Gift Shops
Find a wide variety of quality products in San José: jewelry, wooden items, furniture, T-shirts, leather goods, and artwork. Many shops also sell natural history posters, postcards, and slides; most accept credit cards.

Arte Plaza San Pedro, 150 meters north of Hispanidad Fountain near San Pedro Mall. More than 20 shops feature arts and crafts from Costa Rica and

Driver's Alert

Parking can be a problem in San José. Parking lots are called parqueos. *A few streets have token-operated parking meters. There is usually a self-appointed car watcher who has tokens for sale and keeps an eye on your vehicle. Independent guards will often offer to watch your car. Accept. Pay 100 to 200* colones *when you return.*

other Latin American countries, along with a restaurant and mini-rain forest complete with butterflies and small, colorful frogs. Open daily. Guided tour $3.

Artisan Street Fairs. In downtown San José, find arts and crafts stands at various locations. Try the fair for independent artisans near Plaza de la Democracia in front of the National Museum, Calle 15 between Avenidas Central and 2, active Monday through Saturday.

Atmósfera, Calle 5, Avenidas 1/3, (506) 222-4322. Art and handcrafts are displayed on three floors in a lovely old building, itself worth the visit. Open 9 a.m. to 6 p.m., closed Sunday.

Flower market in front of the Central Post Office

Boutique Annemarie, Hotel Don Carlos, Calle 9, Avenidas 7/9, (506) 221-6707. More than 400 paintings on display, along with one of the most complete selections of handcrafts around: gifts in wood and leather, pottery, jewelry, T-shirts, cards. Open daily 9 a.m. to 7 p.m. year-round, even holidays.

Central Market, Avenidas Central/1, Calles 6/8. Handcrafts are sold here along with rubber boots, fish, flour, herbal remedies, shirts, flowers, and pots and pans. Be ready for crowds and watch your belongings. Open daily early until late.

La Casona, Calle Central, Avenidas Central/1, (506) 221-8303. Two floors of shops, open 9:30 a.m. to 6 p.m., closed Sunday.

Mercado Nacional de Artesanía, Calle 11, Avenidas 4/6, (506) 221-7009. Open weekdays 9 a.m. to 6 p.m., Saturday 9 a.m. to 5 p.m.

Suraska Gallery, Avenida 3, Calle 5, (506) 223-2110; and **La Galería**, Calle 1, Avenidas Central/1, (506) 221-3426. Both show off handcrafts and elegant jewelry like the works of art they are. Don't miss upstairs sections. Open weekdays 9 a.m. to 6 p.m.; Suraska also open weekends 9 a.m. to 4 p.m.

General Shopping
Head west from the Plaza de la Cultura on Avenida Central to find **Librería Lehmann**, Calles 1/3, for books and magazines; **Librería Universal**, Calles

Central/1, for books, posters, maps, film, photo developing, and department-store items; and **La Gloria** department store, Calles 4/6.

Next to the Avenida 1 "back door" of Librería Universal is a photo shop (look for the "Fuji" sign), where you can get film and same-day print developing. An IFSA photo shop is at Avenida Central, Calle 5.

Chispas bookstore at Calle 7 between Avenida 1 and Avenida Central, (506) 256-8251, has a marvelous selection of natural history books along with interesting history, science, cultural studies, and fiction volumes, magazines, newspapers, and new and used books. Open 9 a.m. to 6 p.m. daily.

If disaster strikes with your camera, don't despair. Try **Equipos Fotográficos Canon**, Avenida 3, Calles 3/5, (506) 223-1146. They also have camera equipment. Open weekdays 8 a.m. to noon and 1 to 5:30 p.m., Saturday 9 a.m. to 1 p.m.

Farmacias (*pharmacies*) abound, but one downtown is Fischel, Avenida 2/Calle. A very complete drugstore/pharmacy is 7 blocks from the Plaza de la Cultura on Calle Central, Avenidas 8/10: Botica Mario Jiménez.

Taking the Bus

Thousands of people ride buses in San José every day. You can, too. Fares are inexpensive. Hotel staff or the ICT office can tell you where stops are. Wait your turn in line and pay as you enter. Though correct change is not necessary, don't pay with a large bill. Fare should be posted on the front window.

If there is no vacant seat, hang on. Men and women passengers relinquish their seats to pregnant women; parents with a small child or two in tow; the handicapped; and frail, elderly persons. Men sometimes surrender seats to females. Microbuses cost more but are quicker, and a seat is guaranteed.

Buses are great for people-watching, eavesdropping, and catching glimpses of local people's everyday lives. When it's time to get off, push a button, pull a cord, or yell "Parada," and the driver will stop at the next scheduled place. Again, watch your money and passports.

International Bookstore in San Pedro, near the San Pedro mall, (506) 253-9553, has a good selection of books in English, Spanish, German, and French. Open Monday through Saturday 9:30 a.m. to 7 p.m.

Supermarkets. Closest to the Plaza de la Cultura is La Gran Via, just west of the plaza; other large supermarkets downtown are Mas x Menos, Avenida Central, Calle 13, and Automercado, Avenida 3, Calle 3.

Where to Eat in San José

San José has many restaurants serving typical fare as well as French, Italian, Thai, Chinese, German, Spanish, Peruvian, Mexican, and Japanese cuisine. Check the English-language newspapers, *Tico Times* and *Costa Rica Today*.

American food chains have downtown locations: Burger King, Hardee's, Kentucky Fried Chicken, McDonald's, Mister Pizza, Pizza Hut. San José has good ice-cream shops. Helados Pops has two near the plaza: Avenida Central, Calles 1/3; and Avenida Central, Calle 11. Helados Monpik has a downtown site at Avenida 4, Calle Central.

A 13 percent sales tax is included in your restaurant bill, usually along with a 10 percent service charge (tip). Some restaurants close Sunday or Monday.

Restaurants in or near Downtown

Try any of the **Café Ruiseñor**s for light meals: quiches, sandwiches, memorable pastries, or cappuccino. One is in the National Theater next to the Plaza de la Cultura, and one at the Museum of Costa Rican Art.

Churrería Manolo, Avenida Central, Calles 9/11, has superb typical Costa Rican breakfasts. *Churros* are long, thin, addictive, doughnut-like pastries for sale at the front. Another Manolo's is at Avenida 1, Calles Central/2.

City Cafe, Hotel del Rey, Avenida 1, Calle 9, has great pastrami sandwich, hamburgers, full meals.

El Balcón de Europa, Calle 9, Avenidas Central/1, offers excellent Italian food. Photos of yesteryear line the walls.

El Pueblo, Calle 3 past Avenida 13, left at La República, is a Spanish-style complex with gift shops, galleries, nightclubs, and restaurants. Here are some: **La Cocina de Leña**: traditional food far beyond rice and beans—plantain ceviche, black bean soup, *olla de carne*—served in quaint surroundings. **El Fogón de Leña**: regional specialties from Guanacaste, Limón, and Central Valley. **La Estancia**: for steak lovers. **Rías Bajas**: seafood specialties, attentive waiters.

Gran Hotel Costa Rica, Avenida 2, Calle 3, offers the ambiance of an outdoor terrace next to the National Theater, live marimba music, breakfast and lunch menu plus á la carte; for late-nighters, open until 2 a.m.

Hotel Grano de Oro, Calle 30, Avenidas 2/4, has unusual fare inside or on peaceful patio, a merging of Costa Rican tropical with European cuisine.

Le Chandelier, 100 m west and 100 m south of ICE, San Pedro, is an exquisite French restaurant—dishes are also a feast for the eyes; expect superb attention.

Restaurante El Chicote, north side of Sabana Park, 400 m west of ICE, has excellent baby beef and seafood (fresh lobster, New Zealand mussels); traditionally a favorite with Costa Ricans for good dining.

Restaurante Italiano Il Ponte Vecchio, San Pedro near Hispanidad Fountain, serves gourmet Italian in a picturesque setting.

Restaurante La Masía, Sabana Norte, has paella and things Spanish as well as international food; nice atmosphere.

Restaurante Terra Mar, Calle 41, 250 m north of Avenida Central, serves beef, fish, and chicken with a flair; marvelous pastry tray; excellent attention; dine indoors or on the covered patio by a lovely tropical garden.

Restaurante Tin-Jo, Calle 11, Avenidas 6/8, offers Chinese and Thai food. Try a dish served in a nest of taro.

Restaurant La Galeria, 125 m west of ICE in San Pedro, has German food and classical music. A second location has opened in Escazú.

Restaurants a Bit Farther Out

Barbecue Los Anonos,600 m west of Los Anonos bridge in San Rafael de Escazú, has charming rustic decor. Known for good beef, it also serves chicken and fish. Closed Monday.

Hotel Bougainvillea, Santo Domingo de Heredia—take the shuttle service. Dishes have European flair and country elegance, well worth the trip.

Hotel Chalet Tirol, above San Rafael de Heredia, serves superb French food with attention in a charming Tyrolean-style restaurant in a mountain setting.

Le Monastere Restaurant, San Rafael de Escazú. Enjoy French food in a 1940s monastery—spectacular views from the hillside setting, great Belgian beer and wine cellar. Follow the green crosses on signs.

Las Orquídeas, 12 km north on Limón highway. This is a getaway place with nice atmosphere, good food, good service, and Costa Rican cuisine.

Where to Stay in San José

Not a comprehensive list of hotels, this represents a range of prices with emphasis on smaller places and interesting options.

The **Costa Rican Network of Youth Hostels**, Avenida Central, Calles 29/31, telephone/fax (506)224-4085, offers lodging at Toruma (its own facility) and Don Paco Inn in San José, plus reduced rates at other sites: Cabinas Rossi in La Fortuna, Estero Azul in Tortuguero, Hotel Finca Valverde in Monteverde, Hotel Marparaiso in Jacó, Hotel Yaré at Cocles Beach, Rara Avis near Horquetas, Rincón de la Vieja Mountain Lodge, San Isidro Hotel and Club in Puntarenas, and Santa Clara Lodge in Guanacaste.

The following hotels are in the greater San José metropolitan area. Look also at Chapter 6 for others with easy access to San José, close to the airport.

Larger Hotels

San José has a growing number of hotels affiliated with international hotel chains. Since the emphasis of this book is on smaller and owner-operated hotels, I do not include detailed information about the chains. If your tastes run to larger hotels, here are a few that you can check on through their respective companies: **Aurola Holiday Inn, Best Western Irazú, Costa Rica Marriott Hotel and Resort, Hotel Camino Real, Hotel Radisson Europa, Meliá Cariari Conference Center & Golf Resort, Meliá Confort Corobicí, San José Palacio, Sheraton Herradura Hotel & Spa**.

Rates and Reservations

All rates, listed in U.S. dollars, were valid at the time of publication. They do not include the 13 percent tax unless specified. These are high-season rates, which usually last from December to April; green-season rates are often less. Some hotels have higher rates for Christmas and Easter weeks.

Reservations are recommended. When calling from outside Costa Rica, use the country area code, 506, before the number. Inside the country, do NOT use the 506 code. Because mail service can be slow and unreliable, it's better to phone, fax, or e-mail.

Smaller Hotels

The hotels and inns that follow are arranged according to price, beginning with higher rates. Many are in what were once lovely old homes in residential areas whose use changed as the city grew.

Britannia Hotel is in a 1910 mansion I have long admired, Avenida 11, Calle 3, (506) 223-6667, fax (506) 223-6411; e-mail britania@sol.racsa .co.cr. Great care has been taken in its restoration and conversion into a 24-room hotel. The entrance is grand. Large rooms have hardwood or carpeted floors, air conditioning, tiled baths with tubs and showers, cable TV, writing desks, pretty comforters with matching window treatment, and wallpaper wainscoting. Restaurant has atmosphere. Standard single $77, double $89. Single deluxe $93, double $105.

Hotel Rosa de Paseo is in a restored century-old residence on Paseo Colón, (506) 257-3213, fax (506) 223-2776; e-mail rosa@yellowweb.co.cr; Web site www.yellowweb.co.cr/rosa.html. The 19-room hotel has beautiful antique pieces—chests, benches, wardrobes; painted, stenciled friezes at ceiling level in some rooms; charming alcoves and bay windows on the front; some of the original painted-tile floors; and stained glass. Rooms have high ceilings (when did you last stay in a room with a transom?), matching drapes and bedspreads, a wardrobe, desk, and large baths with tubs. A two-story addition in keeping with the older house shares a pretty garden. Sitting areas have attractive wicker furniture. The restaurant serves light meals. Single or double with fans $72, air-conditioned junior suites $77, and master suites with Jacuzzi $100; tropical breakfast included.

Hotel Grano de Oro, Calle 30, Avenidas 2/4, 150 m south of Paseo Colón, (506) 255-3322, fax (506) 221-2782, e-mail granoro@sol .racsa.co.cr, is a personal favorite. Inner patios bright with tropical plants and intimate courtyards, peaceful with the music of the fountains, weave the gracious turn-of-the-century mansion and attractive rooms into a harmonious whole. By day, see volcanoes from the rooftop garden terrace where there are Jacuzzis and a bar; at night, city lights sparkle. Each of 32 rooms has a writing desk, direct-dial phones, satellite TV, and wardrobe closet; all rooms are nonsmoking. I am partial to bathtubs; these are spotless, with charming brass and porcelain fixtures. Try the creative fare at award-winning Restaurante Grano de Oro: great bocas, an array of tropical cocktails, delicacies such as stuffed palm heart pie, tempting desserts. The hotel is a member of Small Distinctive Hotels of Costa Rica. Standard double $72, superior $88, deluxe $98. Suites, one with Jacuzzi tub and private garden, begin at $125.

La Casa Verde is a lovely Barrio Amón mansion at Avenida 9, Calle 7, telephone/fax (506) 223-0969; e-mail casaverde@sol.racsa.co.cr; Web site www.zurqui.com/crinfocus/verde/cverde.html. Renovated as an exclusive small hotel, the green Victorian house has five rooms and two suites, with soaring ceilings, king- or queen-size beds, cable TV, ceiling fans, and private baths—some claw-foot tubs and canopy beds. Suites are enormous. The upstairs Victorian lounge, with its 110-year-old German-made baby grand piano, wicker furniture, and polished wooden floors, is stunning. Original art for sale on the walls gives the hotel the air of a gallery. Guests enjoy a complimentary breakfast buffet in a downstairs garden room open to the patio, and an enclosed terrace looking out over the city or a sun deck at the back. The loving restoration, supervised by owner Carl Stanley, earned the building a National Historic Site designation and the Best Restoration Award-Costa Rica in 1994. Deluxe rooms $72 to $86, suites $86 to $126, family rooms $86 to $106, double occupancy.

Hotel Le Bergerac, half a block south of Avenida Central on Calle 35, in pretty Los Yoses, (506) 234-7850, fax (506) 225-9103; e-mail bergerac @sol.racsa.co.cr, offers roses on the table, balconies and gardens, a sun terrace, fountains, spacious rooms, Monet prints on the walls, and personalized service. French Canadian owners pay attention to detail. The two-story establishment, with the flavor of a fine French inn, has 18 airy rooms (in three buildings connected by gardens and archways) with framed, padded headboards, ceiling fans, cable TV, direct-dial telephones, hardwood floors, and baths with dark forest-green fixtures. The gourmet

Quiet breakfast at Hotel Grano de Oro

restaurant opens onto a central garden and its musical fountain, now home to the well-known French restaurant Ile de France, open to the public from 6 to 10 p.m. Standard single $58, double $68; superior (garden or balcony) single $68, double $78. Continental breakfast included.

Fleur de Lys Hotel, Calle 13, Avenidas 2/6, (506) 222-4391, fax (506) 257-3637; e-mail avenat@sol.racsa.co.cr; Web site www.crica.com/tours/ aventura.html, is in a renovated three-story Victorian built more than 60 years ago. Its 19 unique rooms, named for flowers, are all tastefully furnished, with private baths, cable TV, and telephones. Some original tile and hardwood floors remain; rooms are carpeted. Fresh flowers brighten comfortable sitting alcoves; skylights bring the sunshine in. An intimate restaurant specializes in nouvelle Costa Rican cuisine. The hotel's tour agency is affiliated with Aventuras Naturales, which specializes in rafting, mountain biking, and nature tourism. Single $60, double $70; suites from $80, breakfast included.

Gran Hotel Costa Rica, in the very heart of San José next to the Plaza de la Cultura at Avenida 2, Calle 3, (506) 221-0796, fax (506) 221-3501, has been a meeting place since it opened in 1930. Diners at the popular terrace café are often treated to marimba music. The 108 pleasant, carpeted rooms have satellite TV and writing desks. Single $54, double $71; suites $81 to $127 for two.

Hotel del Rey, Avenida 1, Calle 9, (506) 257-7800, (506) 255-3232, fax (506) 221-0096; e-mail delrey@ticonet.co.cr, is a comfortable 104-room hotel. A large, gracious lobby has tropical plants and cushioned wicker furniture. The six-floor neoclassical structure has a skylight-covered central atrium that washes the building with light. Carpeted rooms have quilted bedspreads, cable TV, direct-dial telephones, and private baths with tubs. Handcarved wooden doors to each room depict quetzals, butterflies, iguanas, a coffee-picker, and other Costa Rican motifs—works of art. The hotel has a travel agency, streetside bar, casino, car rental, parking, and restaurants. Standard single $55, double $68; deluxe single or double $75; master suites from $125 for two.

Hotel Santo Tomás, Avenida 7, Calles 3/5, (506) 255-0448, fax (506) 222-3950; e-mail Hotelst@sol.racsa.co.cr; Web site www.hotels.co.cr/santomas. html, is in a renovated circa-1910 mansion where a coffee plantation once flourished. Each of 20 rooms is different but all feature high ceilings, reproduction Louis XV furniture, orthopedic queen-size beds, ceiling fans, telephones, and cable TV. Persian rugs decorate gleaming hardwood floors. Corridors have the original tile floors, and the comfortable parlor area sets a nice tone. A former courtyard is now an appealing place to start the day, (complimentary tropical breakfast of fruits and pastries served on glass-topped tables) or to wind down after a day of sightseeing for a drink at the bar. Staff arranges tailored tours. Parking is nearby at a discount. Standard single $50, double $60; superior from $70 to $90, double occupancy; deluxe doubles have two queen beds, $80 up to two.

Casa Morazán, Calle 7, Avenida 9, in Barrio Amón, (506) 257-4187, fax (506) 257-4175; e-mail anakeith@sol.racsa.co.cr; Web site www.grafic .com/casamorazan/, home of a former president, is a stylish 11-room hotel. Rooms have restful green and rose carpeting, air conditioning, high ceilings, cable TV, and telephones, some with tubs and king-size beds. The dining room opens onto a patio. The Costa Rican owner-operators arrange tours and airport transfers. Single $55, double $65, suites $70; continental breakfast included.

El Sesteo, 2 blocks from Sabana Sur park is less than 10 minutes from downtown, (506) 296-1805, fax (506) 296-1865; e-mail SESTEO@sol .racsa.co.cr. The two-story apartotel has 16 hotel rooms and 20 apartments with equipped kitchens, dining and living area, and one or two bedrooms. All have ceiling fans, cable TV, and direct telephone. Units are around a garden with Jacuzzi and pool. Single or double $50; one-bedroom apartment $60; two-bedroom $80.

Hotel Europa Centro, Calle Central, Avenida 5, (506) 222-1222, fax (506) 221-3976; e-mail europa@sol.racsa.co.cr, has 70 carpeted rooms and a pretty outdoor swimming pool surrounded by plants. Good-sized rooms have cable TV, air conditioning, large closets, direct telephones, and a writing desk, some with balconies. There is a restaurant and cozy downstairs bar. Single or double $50.

Hotel Petit Victoria, Calle 28, Avenida 2a, (506) 233-1813, telephone/fax (506) 233-1812, is a two-story Victorian house more than 70 years old. It has elaborate tile floors in the reception area and wood floors in some of the high-ceilinged rooms. Pretty, quilted bedspreads brighten rooms, some with king-size beds and cable TV. Seven rooms with shared baths are $40 for two persons. Single from $35, double $45 to $55 in 15 rooms with private baths. Taxes and continental breakfast included.

Hotel Don Carlos, Calle 9, Avenidas 7/9, in Barrio Amón, (506) 221-6707, fax (506) 255-0828; e-mail hoteldc@sol.racsa.co.cr; Web site www.doncarlos .co.cr, has character. Find patios with fountains, a sun deck, sculpture, lots of tropical plants, walls covered with original art, most rooms with a small balcony, terrace, or view of an interior courtyard garden. The 36 rooms have private baths and cable TV; including access to a computer to send and receive e-mail messages. The Pre-Columbian–style lounge and restaurant offers typical Costa Rican fare with live guitar and piano music at lunchtime and happy hour. The gift shop, Boutique Annemarie, is one of the best. The main lobby's remarkable mural of San José at the turn of the last century, made of 272 hand-painted tiles, has drawn visitors for years. (Along Avenida 9 are more tile artworks, created around phrases of one of Costa Rica's beloved poets. Take a look.) Don Carlos Tours offers natural history trips (volcanoes, turtles, quetzal search) with a bilingual naturalist guide, rafting, and city tours; reservations for domestic airlines and car rental. Single $40 to $50; double $50 to $60, including continental breakfast.

Hotel Hemingway, Avenida 9, Calle 9, in Barrio Amón, (506) 257-8630, telephone/fax (506) 221-1804, is in a Spanish-style house built in 1930. The 17 rooms are named for 20th-century authors: you could be in the Steinbeck, Faulkner, or T. Williams room. Shoulder-high wooden wainscoting, hardwood floors, and high ceilings predominate; plants and Costa Rican and South American wall hangings add to the decor. Rooms have cable TV, and the interior courtyard features a Jacuzzi. Single $30, double $40, including breakfast.

Hotel La Amistad Inn, Avenida 11, Calle 15, (506) 221-1597, fax (506) 221-1409; e-mail wolfgang@sol.racsa.co.cr; Web site www.centralamerica. com/cr/hotel/amistad.htm, is a German-owned and -operated bed-and-breakfast a 10-minute walk from Plaza de la Cultura. The 22 rooms have cable TV, telephones, ceiling fans, and orthopedic mattresses. Single $25, double $35, suites $50; all include German-style breakfast and taxes.

Hotel Kekoldi, Avenida 9, Calle 3b, in Barrio Amón, (506) 223-3244, fax (506) 257-5476; e-mail Kekoldi@sol.racsa.co.cr, is colorful, from bed coverings to a multicolored balustrade and murals that bring sea views right into San José. The 14 large rooms have telephones, king-size beds, and wicker furniture. The house, more than 80 years old, has a young spirit. Breakfast is served. First-floor room single $27, double $32; second-floor single $39, double $45.

Hotel Aranjuez, Calle 19, Avenidas 11/13, (506) 256-1825, fax (506) 223-3528, in one of San José's oldest districts, has 23 rooms with the flavor of a Costa Rican home. Rooms have typical Costa Rican bedspreads and bamboo chairs with bright cushions. Single with private bath and cable TV $25, double $35; with shared bath single $20, double $23. Rates include breakfast buffet, local calls, and parking.

Toruma Youth Hostel, Avenida Central, Calles 29/31, (506) 234-8186, fax (506) 224-4085, has 19 rooms (105 beds). In shared rooms, nonmembers pay $14 per person, members $11. Private rooms are $30 for nonmembers, $28 for members, double occupancy with a shared bath. Toruma stores luggage and has safety deposit boxes.

Where to Stay near Escazú

Tara Resort Hotel Spa and Conference Center, (506) 228-6992, fax (506) 228-9651; e-mail Taraspa@sol.racsa.co.cr; Web site www.crnn.com /tara is centered around an antebellum three-story mansion in San Antonio de Escazú. There are Scarlett and Twelve Oaks suites, Rhett's Boca Bar, and the Atlanta Dining Gallery. The restaurant is excellent; meal plans available. Scarlett's Fountain of Youth Spa offers a full range of treatments, from body cocoons, massages, facials, reflexology, aromatherapy, and private specialty baths to nutritional consultation and fitness classes. Tours include overnight to Arenal, white-water rafting, horseback riding, and hikes to Pico Blanco. Single $90, suites $125 to $190; bungalow $200. A two-night, three-day package is $369 each, double occupancy, including some meals, lodging, use of spa facilities, some spa treatments, and other specialties.

Posada El Quijote Inn, in the hills of Bello Horizonte de Escazú, (506) 289-8401, fax (506) 289-8729; e-mail quijote@sol.racsa.co.cr; Web site www.pmtl.com/peq/peq.html, offers a fine collection of modern art, personalized service, and an unimpeded view of the Central Valley. Owners Gordon and Lucy Finwall cater to guests' needs and whims, making travel and tour arrangements, even arranging theater and concert tickets. Eight spacious rooms, some with private terraces, have cable TV, telephones, and king or queen beds. Single $60 to $70, double $70 to $80, including full breakfast.

Pico Blanco Inn, (506) 289-6197, fax (506) 289-5189, is on 12 acres (5 ha) above San Antonio de Escazú, about 20 minutes from San José at an elevation of 5,000 feet (1,524 m). The 22 pleasant rooms have private balconies with breathtaking views of the Central Valley. A fireplace in the restaurant is welcome on chilly nights. Hike nearby trails, rent horses, choose from a range of tours, or swim in the pool. A terrace bar on this edge-of-the-mountain place is spectacular. Owners John and Flor are gracious hosts and proud caretakers of free-flying macaws, both scarlet and great green. Single $35, double $45 to $55, two-room suites $55 to $65.

Costa Verde Inn in San Rafael de Escazú, 20 minutes from downtown San José or airport, (506) 228-4080, fax (506) 289-8591, is a country home with 15 charming rooms surrounded by quiet gardens. Swimming pool, Jacuzzi, lighted tennis court, sun deck, king-size beds, and a fireplace in the lounge area are only a few of the extras. The inn is associated with Costa Verde Hotel at Manuel Antonio. Single $45, double $55, one-bedroom apartment with balcony $70; breakfast included (typical Costa Rican address: 100 m west and 300 m south of Escazú cemetery).

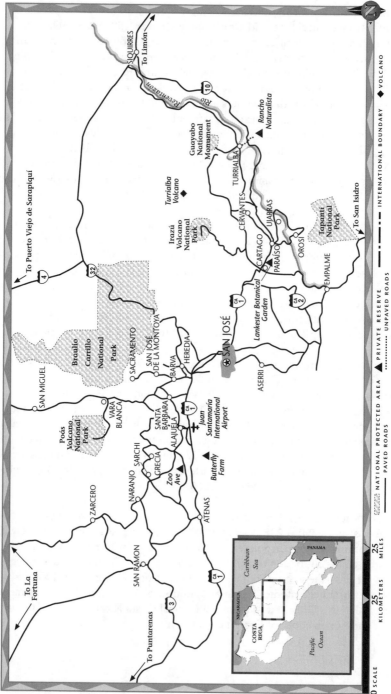

To Limón

To Puerto Viejo de Sarapiquí

SIQUIRRES

Río Reventazón

10

Guayabo National Monument

Rancho Naturalista

Turrialba Volcano

Irazú Volcano National Park

TURRIALBA

CERVANTES

UJARRAS

CARTAGO

PARAISO

OROSI

Tapantí National Park

To San Isidro

EMPALME

CA 2

Lankester Botanical Garden

CA 3

SAN JOSÉ

HEREDIA

ASERRI

SACRAMENTO

SAN JOSÉ DE LA MONTOYA

BARVA

Braulio Carrillo National Park

SAN MIGUEL

32

4

VARA BLANCA

Poás Volcano National Park

ZARCERO

NARANJO

SARCHI

GRECIA

Zoo Ave

SANTA BARBARA

ALAJUELA

CA 1

Juan Santamaria International Airport

Butterfly Farm

ATENAS

SAN RAMON

3

CA 1

To La Fortuna

To Puntarenas

NICARAGUA

Caribbean Sea

PANAMA

COSTA RICA

Pacific Ocean

0 SCALE

25 KILOMETERS

25 MILES

NATIONAL PROTECTED AREA   PRIVATE RESERVE   INTERNATIONAL BOUNDARY   VOLCANO

PAVED ROADS   UNPAVED ROADS

6

CENTRAL COSTA RICA

Since colonial times, the Meseta Central (Central Valley) has been Costa Rica's population center. In addition to the valley where San José, Heredia, Alajuela, Grecia, Naranjo, Atenas, and San Ramón are located, it encompasses the higher, eastern valley that contains Cartago, Paraíso, and Turrialba.

The four colonial cities of Costa Rica were San José, Cartago, Alajuela, and Heredia, each with its own character and strong sense of identity. That is still true today. As you travel to or through these places, remember that this land was once covered with forest. Imagine what travel must have been like on foot or horseback up and down these mountains and across rivers now spanned by bridges. Life here was hard; it helped forge the national character.

Beauty, not hardship, is the sensation travelers experience today. Protected forests remain, but the landscape is also painted with coffee fields, sugarcane, small farms, picturesque villages, and pastures for dairy cows. Rural houses have flowers, a porch to sit on when work is done, a few banana and coffee plants, fruit trees, and perhaps beans, squash, and corn—a link back to agrarian self-sufficiency.

Natural history/adventure destinations include the archaeological site at Guayabo as well as Irazú Volcano, the Barva sector of Braulio Carrillo National Park, and Tapantí park. Heredia, Alajuela, and Grecia are gateways to Póas Volcano National Park. Visitors can learn about birds, snakes, orchids, and butterflies from those who work with and study them. Some of the best rafting is here, out of Turrialba. In colorful Sarchí, watch artisans at work. The country's patron saint is honored in Cartago.

Lodging in the valley of San José, close to Juan Santamaría International Airport, is an alternative to staying in San José on arrival or departure.

ALAJUELA AREA

Alajuela

Capital of the province of Alajuela, this pleasant town (population 50,586) is a stone's throw from Juan Santamaría airport and 10.5 miles (17 km) northwest of San Jose. It was the home of Juan Santamaría, the country's national hero. A statue honors him as a symbol of the Costa Ricans' desire for peace and freedom. **Juan Santamaría Cultural and Historical Museum** documents the campaign against William Walker and his filibusters in which the young farmer lost his life; open 10 a.m. to 6 p.m., closed Monday; free admission; (506) 441-4775.

Stop by Central Park, a veritable orchard of mango trees. Blue-gray tanagers are among the birds that flock to eat ripe fruit. The July Festival of Mangoes brings nine days of music, parades, farmers' markets, and an arts and crafts fair.

Take advantage of the meals provided by the following Alajuela area accommodations. If your hotel offers breakfast only, ask about other area restaurants.

Getting There

By bus: 30 minutes from San José, five minutes from the airport.
By car: Off the Inter-American Highway near the international airport.

Where to Stay and Eat in Alajuela Area

Hotel Buena Vista, 3 miles (5 km) north of Alajuela, is in the tiny village of Pilas de San Isidro, 15 minutes from airport, (506) 442-8595, (506) 442-8605, fax (506) 442-8701, e-mail bvista@sol.racsa.co.cr; Web site www.arweb.com/buenavista; U.S. number (800) 506-2304. This gracious, 25-room, Spanish-style mountain hotel with a hilltop view of coffee, banana, and citrus farms; the Central Valley; and forested slopes of three volcanoes: Poás, Barva, and Irazú. Spacious, carpeted rooms have two queen-size beds, cable TV, and writing desks. Landscaped grounds include a pool and pleasant patios. The restaurant features dishes from around the world, open to the public by reservation: breakfast $6, lunch $8, dinner $12. Hosts Connie and Ed Pratt offer tours in a 12-passenger van to nearby Poás volcano, Sarchí, Zoo Ave, Butterfly Farm, and other area sites. Single $65, double $80, breakfast included; deluxe second-floor with balcony, $5 more.

Orquídeas Inn, 10 minutes north of Alajuela on the road to Poás, (506) 433-9346, fax (506) 433-9740; e-mail orchid@sol.racsa.co.cr; Web site www.yellowweb.co.cr/orquideas.html, is a charming hotel in a garden setting. The 18 rooms feature arched windows that let in lots of light, with colorful bedspreads, fresh flowers (orchids, of course), and glass-topped tables with antique Singer sewing-machine bases. Owners Fred and Darlys McCloud serve Buffalo-style chicken wings in the Marilyn Monroe Bar as complimentary bocas. Guitarist/composer/singer Rolando and daughter Leidy give a great evening performance most weekends. Relax by a pretty swimming pool and walk along paths bordered by eye-catching tropical plants on this 5-acre (2-ha) estate; keep your eyes open for sloths. Staff arrange van and driver for custom tours apart from a long list of day trips that include Poás, nearby Sarchí, Los Chorros Waterfall, Zoo Ave, Zarcero, Arenal Volcano and Tabacón Hot Springs, San José city tour, horseback riding, or ballooning. Single $55, double $65 with fans, air conditioning available; rooms away from the road are quieter. Two mini-suites, each with two double beds, are $120. A geodesic dome suite has a living room with kitchenette, downstairs bedroom, and sleeping loft, $130 for up to four. Breakfast is included; dine in company of free-flying toucans that have made Orquídeas Inn home—watch your toes. No children under 13.

Tuetal Lodge, north of Alajuela, 10 miles (6 km) from the airport, telephone/fax (506) 442-1804; e-mail tuetal@sol.racsa.co.cr; Web site www.islandnet.com/~tuetal/, is a chance to try something different. Owners Arnold and Carolyn Wiens offer 30 campsites, six cabins, and two treehouses. Yes, treehouses. Sleep in a bamboo structure built among the branches, sharing bath facilities with campers—washrooms, solar-heated showers. The lodge is on 7 acres (2.8 ha), with a pool in the tropical gardens. Campsites are $10 for two (tents for rent); treehouses, $14 for two; cabins with kitchenette, $45 for two, without $40. Breakfast and dinner are served in a pleasant restaurant (Canadian and American cuisine). No credit cards.

Xandari Plantation, 3 miles (5 km) from Alajuela, (506) 443-2020, fax (506) 442-4847; in e-mail paradise@xandari.com, Web site www.xandari.com,U.S. number (800) 686-7879, is a classy tropical paradise designed by owners architect/designer Sherrill and artist Charlene Broudy. White villas against the backdrop of forested mountains and coffee plantations are stunning. Spacious high-ceilinged rooms with touches of stained glass, dramatic art, custom-designed furniture, sculpture, refrigerator, bar sink, fresh flowers, and tropical plants open onto large private outdoor terraces with spectacular daytime views and romantic sunsets. Health-conscious meals include fruits and vegetables from the plantation's organic gardens.

Guests hike on 2 miles (3 km) of scenic trails, experience the magic of bathing in a secluded river pool, bird-watch, meditate, have a picnic by any of five waterfalls, or ride horses along country roads to small villages. The hotel has two 60-foot-long lap pools, a library, open-air exercise rancho, Jacuzzi, palm-roofed studio for painting, and therapeutic massage. Villas are $135; with kitchenettes $195; breakfast and airport transfer included (15 minutes from airport).

Convenient to airport and Alajuela is the **Hampton Inn**, affiliated with the international chain of Hampton hotels.

Things to See and Do in Alajuela Area

ZOO AVE, WILDLIFE CONSERVATION PARK, PRIVATE RESERVE

Location: La Garita de Alajuela.
Hours: Daily 9 a.m. to 5 p.m.
Cost: $8 for adults, children $1.
Information: (506) 433-8989, fax (506) 433-9140; e-mail
ZooAve@sol.racsa.co.cr.

Walkways wind through beautifully landscaped grounds which are home to more than 800 birds representing 100 species, four monkey species, a crocodile that measures about 10 feet (3 m), boa constrictors, green iguanas, and turtles, along with a few non-native species. Educational signs in English and Spanish and large, well-done enclosures make visiting Zoo Ave a treat. Birds include scarlet, great green, and blue and gold macaws; chestnut-mandibled and keel-billed toucans; the resplendant quetzal; ornate-hawk eagle; long-tailed manakin; scarlet-thighed dacnis; six parrot and five parakeet species; and many more birds often so elusive in the rain forest. Get close-up photos of macaws, who preen and squawk right beside the path, and of nimble spider monkeys as they move from tree to tree.

The zoological park occupies 10 acres (4 ha). The remaining 25 acres (10 ha) are being reforested with native trees that provide food and nesting sites for wild birds. Zoo Ave is operated by the nonprofit Nature Restoration Foundation, created by Dennis and Susan Janik, who started Zoo Ave in 1990.

Rehabilitation and Rescue

Behind the scenes is an animal hospital, where injured and orphaned animals are cared for until they can be returned to the wild. According to Suzanne Chacón, scientific officer, those whose injuries prevent release become part of the breeding program. Former pets also find a home here. Since 1990, nine species of rehabilitated birds have been successfully released back into the wild, as well as foxes, anteaters, sloths, porcupines, raccoons, iguanas, caimans, and turtles.

Captive Breeding and Reintroduction

Seventy native species are currently in breeding programs. Not all are in immediate danger of extinction but, according to Suzanne, all are species whose wild populations are at historically low levels. Some face a loss of genetic diversity in parts of the country: the goal is to release animals into these genetically isolated populations.

All of the park's adult monkeys were once pets; while they cannot survive in the wild, the goal is to release their offspring. Sixty-five native monkeys are bred and maintained in large enclosures.

The endangered scarlet macaw and great green macaw are bred here.

Having produced 47 scarlet macaws in the first five years of the program, Zoo Ave is working toward releasing birds into protected areas where they have vanished due to poaching and habitat destruction. I felt privileged to see a pair of two-month-old great green macaws in the bird nursery. As few as 30 to 35 pairs are breeding in the wild in Costa Rica.

To minimize human contact with animals to be released in to the wild, hospital and nursery areas are closed to the public. However, a stroll through the grounds reveals animals released on the property that choose to stay: chachalacas, toucans, owls, crested guan, white-fronted parrots, a collared aracari (which has paired with a wild bird), and curassows.

The ultimate success of release programs depends on enforcement of wildlife protection laws, habitat restoration and/or protection, and educational programs. Almost 16,000 schoolchildren learn during class visits to Zoo Ave. For travelers who want to help, look for a donation box near the exit or contact the foundation.

Getting There
By bus: From Alajuela, take a Dulce Nombre or La Garita bus; they pass in front of Zoo Ave—a 20-minute ride from Alajuela.
By car: From the Inter-American, take the Atenas/Punta Leona exit (watch for a large Zoo Ave sign), turn right, continue 1.2 miles (2 km) to Zoo Ave.
Other: Taxi from Alajuela, fare less than $6.

BUTTERFLY FARM, PRIVATE RESERVE
Location: La Guácima, Alajuela.
Hours: Daily 9 a.m. to 3 p.m. (when last tour begins).
Cost: Adults $14, children 5 to 12 years $7, under 5 free.
Information: (506) 438-0400, fax (506) 438-0300; e-mail cres@butterflyfarm .co.cr; Web site www.butterflyfarm.co.cr.

Owners Joris Brinkerhoff and María Sabido have created a beautiful opportunity to observe, learn about, and photograph butterflies and tropical flowers. An introductory video focuses on butterfly stages of life, habits, and habitats, while live specimens waft through the room and dozens of eye-catching species vie for your attention through a glass wall. An enclosed garden of native plants is home to about 1,000 breeding butterflies, some 70 species.

A two-hour guided tour touches on butterfly defense mechanisms, predators, host plants, and reproduction and visits breeding facilities. It's a hands-on experience for those who choose to touch pupae, feel caterpillars, and spot butterfly eggs. See the cracker butterfly: listen for the noise that explains its name. Observe morphos, clearwings, sweethearts, swallowtails, tigers, zebras, and the large owl eyes of the caligo.

The gift shop and snack bar, which has a view of Poás, Barva, and Irazú Volcanoes, weather permitting, has loads of butterfly handcrafts and literature, along with other natural history offerings. Look for an amazing poster of the alphabet created by the patterns on butterfly wings. Make a day of it by combining the Butterfly Farm with the Café Britt Coffeetour, $50 including lunch, guide, and transportation.

Breeding Butterflies

Joris and María began the farm to export butterflies as a way of promoting sustainable development and protecting natural resources. From one client in England in 1984, business has expanded to clients in France, Germany, Italy, the United States, Canada, and Singapore, shipping about 12,000 pupae per month, up to 50 species. The Butterfly Farm produces only a small percent of what it exports; most pupae come from small producers—about 100 families are involved. All take part in training programs, with conservation as the key philosophy. On export days, see sorting and packing.

While survival rate of eggs in the wild is 2 percent, here it is 90 percent. Eggs develop into larvae that feed for an average of one month before forming pupae, the stage for export. Butterflies emerge from pupae in seven to 10 days and, since transport to clients takes three days, timing is of the essence.

Butterflies are released to replace ones originally taken from the wild. Flora that butterflies need have been planted on the farm to create a natural butterfly refuge.

Getting There

By bus: From San José, take La Guácima bus. Check with Butterfly Farm for times. Get off at the last stop and follow signs for about 300 m. From

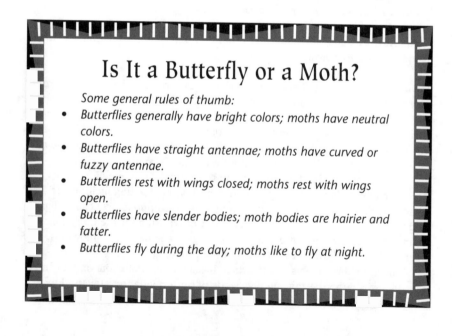

Is It a Butterfly or a Moth?

Some general rules of thumb:
- *Butterflies generally have bright colors; moths have neutral colors.*
- *Butterflies have straight antennae; moths have curved or fuzzy antennae.*
- *Butterflies rest with wings closed; moths rest with wings open.*
- *Butterflies have slender bodies; moth bodies are hairier and fatter.*
- *Butterflies fly during the day; moths like to fly at night.*

Alajuela, take La Guácima Abajo bus and ask to be let off at La Finca de Mariposas, a 40-minute ride.

By car: From San José, take the Inter-American toward Alajuela; get off at the San Antonio de Belén exit, go left across the bridge, and continue 6.2 miles (10 km) through San Rafael and La Guácima.

Other: Tour and round-trip transfer from San José $20 for adults, $14 for children.

SARCHÍ, GRECIA, AND ATENAS AREAS

SARCHÍ

Sarchí (population 10,237) is an artisan center 35 miles northwest of San José where even trash cans and bus stops are decorated with bright, colorful paintings. The most famous product is the painted oxcart. Sarchí was a stopping place for caravans that carried coffee to Puntarenas for shipping; this spurred an industry in cart repair, and eventually cart production took hold. Even into the 1940s, caravans of 700 carts were still making the trek—but when motorized vehicles took over, cart-makers began to produce them as decoration.

Several stores have workshops where you can watch local artisans paint delicate freehand designs. In addition to carts—from miniatures to full size—you can select from an array of salad bowls, wooden fruit, lamps, jewelry, and more. Sarchí-style chairs are famous, created in wood or wood and leather. Factories and shops are around every turn along the 2-mile (3-km) road from South Sarchí to North Sarchí. Two large ones are Fábrica de Carretas Joaquín Chaverri and COOPEARSA, a cooperative. Plaza de la Artesanía has dozens of stores exhibiting arts and crafts. Restaurants abound. Try the one next to the Chaverri store or one at the plaza.

Getting There

By bus: From Alajuela, Grecia, or Naranjo, transfer to a Sarchí bus, most frequent from Alajuela.

By car: From the Inter-American, turn off at Grecia or Naranjo intersections.

Where to Stay and Eat in Sarchí

Villa Sarchí Lodge, telephone/fax (506) 454-4006, has eight triple rooms, a small pool, shaded patio, and quaint open-air bar that shows off painted handcrafts of the region; on weekends hear marimba music. Meals allow guests to sample Sarchí specialties along with typical Costa Rican fare. Owner Ramón Rodríguez has been known to escort guests for shopping to ensure they get the best value. He offers tours to impressive waterfalls in the Bajos del Toro area, cloud forests of Bosque de Paz, and Poás Volcano—areas he has known most of his life. Double $40, including breakfast.

GRECIA

Just 13 miles (21 km) northwest of Alajuela, off the Inter-American Highway and 4 miles (6 km) southeast of Sarchí is the small community of Grecia. Visit the metal church imported from Belgium and sit in the park in front to feel the friendly rhythm of this place.

Things to See and Do near Grecia

Jewels of the Rain Forest, housed in the Grecia Cultural Center, in front of the Banco Nacional (506) 494-5620, is a marvelous display of butterflies and beetles (spectacular scarabs) along with spiders, centipedes, and crustaceans. Margaret and Richard Whitten share this collection of the world's arthropods—more than 1,000 exhibits—along with information focused on the importance of saving these creatures' habitats. Open daily 9 a.m. to 5 p.m. Admission $5.

World of Snakes is a wonderful snake exhibition, as well as breeding and research center, in the hills of Grecia, telephone/fax (506) 494-3700; e-mail snakes@so.racsa.co.cr. More than 50 species are housed in large outdoor enclosures, about 5 feet high (1.5 m) with solid walls on the bottom half and reinforced glass and mesh screens on the upper half to allow spectacular, safe observation even for the squeamish. See the endangered ringed tree boa, colorful eyelash vipers, false corals, tropical rattlesnakes, even a Burmese albino python. Most species are natives, but visitors also find beautiful and interesting snakes from Vietnam, Australia, New Guinea, Brazil, Mexico, and Africa.

Begun by two young Austrians, Nikolaus Schwabe and Robert Meindinger, the project focuses on protecting Costa Rica's snakes as well as endangered species from other countries. The exhibition area is a key player on the educational front. A two-hour tour explains these animals' role in the ecosystem, their habits and behavior. It teaches how to distinguish venomous from nonvenomous snakes and how to behave in an encounter with a snake. Prevention of both habitat destruction and indiscriminate killing of snakes is a goal. Already, educational efforts at the local level are paying off. Some snakes that would have been killed are brought to the snake farm: venomous ones are kept and nonvenomous ones are sometimes released on farms whose owners welcome them: snakes are natural predators to rodents.

Another threat to snakes in the wild is a growing international market for them—the terrarium trade and the need for research specimens. World of Snakes has a breeding program that will allow sale of snakes in compliance with CITES regulations. So instead of dealing with poachers and contributing to an illegal animal trade, buyers can obtain captivity-bred snakes. The tour tells why buyers prefer captive-bred specimens for reasons above and beyond environmental ones. Snakes for this project were captured according to wildlife regulations; all foreign species came with CITES documents.

The project's research phase aims to expand basic knowledge about snakes—mainly species description, range, habitats, and ecological importance—to lesser-known topics such as behavior and reproduction patterns.

World of Snakes is open daily 8 a.m. to 4 p.m. Admission $11 adults, $6 children (under 6 free). To get there, go to Grecia's metal church and continue east 1 mile (2 km) on the road toward Tacares and Alajuela.

ATENAS

Founded in the 16th century, Atenas is a lovely, small (population 6,261) town in an area known for the quality of its fruits, 26 miles (41 km) northwest of San José. *Ticos* travel to Atenas and Garita on weekends just to buy fresh produce. If you decide to stay in Atenas, check out the local produce, and explore nearby attractions on day trips from local lodges. This area is easily accessible from the airport and on a road that leads to Pacific beaches, such as Punta Leona, Jacó, and Quepos, and to Carara National Biological Reserve.

Where to Stay near Atenas

El Cafetal Inn, (506) 446-5785, fax 506-446-7028; e-mail cafetal @yellowweb.co.cr; Web site www.yellowweb.co.cr/cafetal.html, is delightful. The spectacular two-story house with rounded glass corner alcoves overlooks the Colorado River Valley and fields of coffee and sugarcane, with views of Alajuela, part of Heredia, and Poás, Barva, and Irazú Volcanoes. Lee and Romy Rodríguez greet you at the door and treat you as an honored guest throughout your stay. It's a classy place—shiny marble floors, soothing waterfall in the two-story atrium, light and airy rooms, deep cushions on wicker furniture, and lots of floor-to-ceiling windows. Each of 10 doubles has a private bath. Meals are a treat. Romy dons the chef's hat and cooks with a flair. Down a garden path through coffee plants is a large pool and rancho: try the cappuccino and coffee raised on the farm. Tours go to Poás Volcano; orchid, butterfly, iguana, and coffee farms; Las Musas Waterfall, Sarchí, Jacó, Tortuga Island, and Carara; to San José for a city tour and Alajuela for a night mariachi tour. Standard double $60, with balcony $65; corner tower rooms $70.

El Cafetal is 20 minutes from the airport. In Atenas, turn right toward Santa Eulalia de Atenas and follow signs. From the Inter-American, watch for the sign after the Grecia-Sarchí intersection; turn left before the bridge.

El Cafetal near Atenas

Vista del Valle, (506) 450-0800, telephone/fax (506) 451-1165; e-mail mibrejo@sol.racsa.co.cr; Web site www.vistadelvalle.com, formerly Posada Las Palomas, is an upscale country inn on a lush plantation at the edge of the Río Grande chasm. Palms embellish tropical gardens around the swimming pool, Jacuzzi, main house, and two cottages. Beautiful hardwoods, glass, and stone complement the high ceilings and open floor plan of the two-story house. Each of two guest rooms has a private bath and balcony with views to garden, mountains, and coffee and citrus plantations; single $85, double $95. Enjoy breakfast on a glass-ceilinged veranda, pretty with earthen pots, fresh flowers, and tropical plants. The larger cottage has two doubles, each with a separate entrance and veranda, plus a shared kitchen. A smaller cottage has a double bed, wraparound veranda, and kitchenette; $85 to $120. A full breakfast is included. With prior notice, dinner with owners Johanna and Mike Bresnan is available.

Guests are invited to explore paths that wind through the plantation or hike to the waterfall. Take a walk to the nearby village of Rosario. The inn furnishes a van and bilingual driver to guests, $28 per day, and offers tours to Sarchí, Poás and Barva Volcanoes, Butterfly Farm, Zoo Ave, Tabacón and Arenal, Orosi Valley, and Los Angeles Cloud Forest. Half-day trips are $50 to $60; full-day excursions $95 to $110. Rafting trips arranged.

The inn is located 20 minutes from the airport. From the Inter-American, turn left about 1 mile (2 km) west of the Río Colorado bridge and follow signs.

HEREDIA AREA

HEREDIA

Founded in 1706, Heredia (population 29,935) is capital of the province by that name. Known as the city of flowers, it's also home to the National University. Visit the 1796 church and the nearby tower of an old fort that remains in pretty gardens. On Sunday morning or Thursday evening, listen to a band play *paso dobles*, *boleros*, tangos, mazurkas, and waltzes in Central Park, a 150-year tradition. Heredia (7.5 miles [12 km] north of San José and east of the airport) is the gateway to the Barva sector of Braulio Carrillo National Park. Adjacent mountains are settings for secluded hotels and lodges.

Visit nearby **Butterfly Paradise,** (506) 265-6694, in San Joaquín de Flores, 7 miles (14 km) from San José. It features hundreds of butterflies, 30 species, in a tropical garden with some 50 species of host plants. Admission $5 adults, $1.25 children, including a guided walk through the laboratory (breeding and export of pupae), gardens, and a small museum—handicapped accessible. Open daily 9 a.m. to 4 p.m.

Getting There
By bus: Frequent buses from San José to Heredia.

By car: Routes from the Inter-American, from La Uruca intersection in San José, and from Alajuela.

BARVA SECTOR, BRAULIO CARRILLO NATIONAL PARK

Location: *19 miles (30 km) N of San José through Heredia and Sacramento.*
Hours: *8 a.m. to 4 p.m., closed Monday.*
Cost: *$6, camping $2.*
Information: *Telephone hotline 192 (see Appendix A: Parks and Reserves Information), (506) 290-1927, fax (506) 232-5324.*

Braulio Carrillo National Park protects a large area north and east of San José. The highest part of the park is accessible at the Barva entrance. Barva volcano is also one of the highest summits in the Central Volcanic Mountain Range; its three peaks are known as Las Tres Marías.

To walk in this lofty sector is to experience the mystical silence of the cloud forest. See quetzals more between January and March when they are nesting, though park rangers report some stay year-round. They are among 125 bird species, including the three-wattled bellbird and volcano hummingbird. Mammals are not seen as often as in lower sections of the park, though tracks of jaguar and tapir are found. Agoutis, mountain lions, tayras, porcupines, coyotes, and two-toed sloths live here. Keep an eye out for smaller things, like scarabs; some 21 species of beetles are registered.

Trails are lined with large-leafed poor-man's umbrella and tiny blossoms of trees and shrubs; there is a veritable banquet of bromeliads. Exquisite rain-fed lakes shimmer in volcanic craters. The trail from the ranger station to Barva Lagoon, 1.8 miles (3 km) of breathtaking beauty, climbs gently in spots and is almost level in others. Air is a bit thin—it's about 9,500 feet (2,900 m) elevation. Flock after flock of mixed species of birds feed along the path; tiny flowers and colored leaves found at this elevation demand attention. The view from the *mirador* (view point) above the crater lake is worth the short climb, sparkling in sunshine and magically shrouded in mists. Linger a bit on the chance of seeing a magnificent hummingbird feed in nearby flowers. From Barva Lagoon, it's 1½ miles (2½ km) to Copey, a shallow lake that becomes isolated ponds in dry season. A third lake, Danta, is the largest and least accessible.

Barva lies at the upper end of an important migration corridor that joins Braulio Carrillo with lowland forest protected by the Organization for Tropical Studies' La Selva Biological Station near Puerto Viejo de Sarapiquí, extremely important for migrating species of birds, butterflies, moths, and perhaps bats. Research has shown that this ecosystem is home to 17 species of threatened birds; 81 species of North American migratory birds depend on this habitat during migration or for wintering.

Camping is allowed at the station and bunks can be rented when not in use by parks. Bathrooms and a covered picnic area are at the entrance, and

Gigantic sombrilla del pobre *leaves in the Barva sector of Braulio Carrillo Park*

more covered shelters are in the forest off the trail. In addition to rain gear, bring a jacket. Temperatures range from 37°F to 68°F (3°C to 20° C).

Getting There
By bus: From Heredia, take Paso Llano bus from Central Market; continue by foot 4 miles (6 km) to park or take Heredia bus to Sacramento.
By car: From Heredia, continue to Sacramento; in rainy season the 2½ miles (4 km) on to the ranger station require four-wheel-drive—one terrible road.
Other: Area hotels and agencies in San José offer one-day tours.

Where to Stay and Eat in and near Heredia (and Barva Volcano)
Bougainvillea Santo Domingo Hotel, (506) 244-1414, fax (506) 244-1313; e-mail bougainvillea@centralamerica.com; Web site www.centralamerica .com/hotel/bougain.htm; in Santo Domingo de Heredia, is located on 10 acres (4 ha) of gardens. The 83 nicely furnished, carpeted rooms are spacious, with a separate sitting area, cable TV, twin double beds, and direct-dial phones; each room opens onto a balcony with great views. Single $55, double $75. Sculpture and paintings by Costa Rican artists are displayed throughout the hotel. Facilities include tennis courts, solar-heated swimming pool, sauna, and jogging trail. Food, served in a stylish country inn setting, is superb. Plan to dine here even if you stay elsewhere. Free shuttle service to San José, about 15 minutes away.

Finca Rosa Blanca Country Inn, (506) 269-9392, fax (506) 269-9555; e-mail rblanca@sol.racsa.co.cr; Web site www.finca-rblanca.co.cr, outside

Santa Barbara de Heredia, is 30 minutes from San José and 15 minutes from the airport. The white two-story building with its domed tower room soars above surrounding coffee plantations. Enormous windows open to dramatic views of the Central Valley, Irazú Volcano, picturesque towns, and landscaped grounds. Inside, rich-colored tropical hardwoods gleam in floors, ceilings, and doors. A curved, cushioned *banco* (long seat) in the atrium-like, two-story living area faces a unique freestanding fireplace.

Each of six bedrooms is unique. La Ventana is famous for its mural: the actual landscape visible from the room continues from the large window onto the wall in a painting done by artists from nearby Barva. The Black-and-White Room, with its checkered floor, has a private garden. Down a spiral staircase from the glass-walled tower bedroom of Rosa Blanca Suite is an unforgettable rain-forest bathroom where a waterfall drops over stones into a two-person pool for bathing. Each of two separate villas has two bedrooms, sitting area with distinctive arched windows, and kitchen. A huge deck affords panoramic valley views. Murals and hand-painted Talavera tiles add accents. Double $140 to $225, including breakfast.

To allow parents to enjoy romantic four- or five-course evening dinners. Rosa Blanca has an earlier children's dinner, with video entertainment afterward. Dishes include produce from an organic garden. Dinner $25, a light lunch $10. The swimming pool is spring fed, no chemicals. Guests can explore the grounds (where more than 200 fruit trees attract birds), walk a trail where butterflies await, visit the river, or ride horses—perhaps to the Barva entrance of Braulio Carrillo. Owner Glenn Jampol and staff arrange special tours and have a van and English-speaking driver available. Glenn initiated a profit-sharing system with the local employees, and the hotel is helping create a library for the small primary school in nearby Barrio Jesus. Guests are welcome to assist with book purchases.

Hotel Chalet Tirol, (506) 267-7371, fax (506) 267-7050; e-mail tirolcr@sol.racsa.co.cr; Web site www.arweb.com/tirol, looks like an Alpine village in its 5,900-foot (1,800-m) mountain setting: 10 picturesque wooden chalets with red roofs and window boxes. Across the "village square," with requisite fountain, is church-like Salzburg Theater, site of musical performances that include International Music Festival artists. A sloped-roof restaurant and a building housing 14 suites round out the scene.

The rustic chalets, my personal favorite, face each other across a garden of tropical flowers. Double doors open onto back porches and forest, some to a small stream. Downstairs living areas have carved wooden chairs, cloth-covered tables, and knickknacks that add a homey touch. Up narrow wooden stairs is a cozy bedroom under the rafters. Spacious suites have wood-burning fireplaces, each room with a different decor. Chalets and suites have private baths, telephones, and TV. Chalets and junior suites are $66 for two; honeymoon suite $100.

Chalet Tirol's award-winning French restaurant offers gracious service and a charming atmosphere—good music, fires in the fireplaces. For more casual dining, try Bugatti pizza parlor, with its wood-fired oven.

Here in this cloud-forest setting, guests ride horses, play tennis, and explore paths in the 38-acre (15-ha) private forest to see ferns, bromeliads, orchids, mosses, toucanets, motmots, hummingbirds, and trogons. Or they venture to Braulio Carrillo park with a guide. Tirol's Quetzal Route involves a three- to four-hour hike with a bilingual naturalist guide in Tirol and Braulio Carrillo forests, and perhaps views of quetzals, sooty robins, redstarts, violet-sabrewing hummingbirds, white-faced monkeys, or peccaries. Then it's back by car to a gourmet meal. This tour is also offered as a day trip from San José. Another exclusive is a Giant Trees tour to San José de la Montaña to see fig and Spanish cedar trees with diameters up to 14 feet (4 m), a crystalline spring, and a 19th-century farmhouse with its medicinal plant garden.

The hotel is 45 minutes from San José; head north out of Heredia through San Rafael and Los Angeles, following signs. The Batalla family, owners, also operates Dundee Ranch Hotel near Orotina.

Las Ardillas Resort Health Spa, 15 minutes from Heredia in San José de la Montaña, telephone/fax (506) 260-2172, has 15 rustic cabins with kitchenettes, a restaurant serving food cooked over a wood fire, a Jacuzzi, sauna, massage rooms, and a trail along the river out back. At 4,762 feet (2,000 m) elevation, air can be chilly; each cabin has a fireplace, as does the Jacuzzi room. Owner Milea Zeledón's spa program includes hydrotherapy, herbal treatments, and volcanic-mud baths, along with Swedish massage. The restaurant features Costa Rican and international dishes, served to sounds of live marimba music in the evenings. A cabin for two with Jacuzzi and spa privileges is $60; $100 with meals included. It is 19 miles (30 km) from San José

For those who choose to stay in Heredia, here are two good choices. **Valladolid Hotel,** (506) 260-2905, fax (506) 260-2912, not far from the National University, has 11 air-conditioned rooms, with telephone, cable TV, and kitchenette. Sauna and Jacuzzi are in fifth-floor solarium. Single $58, double $62, breakfast included. Downtown **Hotel America,** (506) 260-9292, fax (506) 260-9293, has 36 rooms and four junior suites, solar hot water, telephones, and TV (local channels). Tours arranged to volcanoes, rivers, and parks. Single $35, double $45, suite $60 for double.

CARTAGO AREA

Across the Continental Divide from San José lie mountains, rivers, lakes, and valleys along what once was the main road between the Central Valley and the Caribbean port of Limón. When the faster highway opened through Braulio Carrillo National Park, pass-through traffic lessened, though travelers to Cerro de la Muerte and points south still start through Cartago. The area has superb adventure and natural history destinations.

CARTAGO

Once the colonial capital, Cartago (population 32,218) now is capital of Cartago province. Founded in 1563, the city still has remnants of its colonial heritage. Tranquility and a genuine friendliness create a pleasant atmosphere. If you like public markets, stop by the one here (Avenida 4, downtown).

The Cartago area makes a great day trip from San José, or stay in one of the lodges in the Orosi Valley or near Tapantí National Park. Cartago is 14 miles (23 km) southeast of San José.

Things to See and Do in and near Cartago

On Avenida 2, Calle 2, are reminders of the city's colonial roots. Ruins of a stone church (**Ruinas de la Parroquia**) surround a peaceful garden. This first parish church in Cartago was founded in 1575. During the colonial period it was reconstructed several times, having been almost destroyed by an 1841 earthquake. But it was a 1910 quake that brought rebuilding efforts to a halt. In front of the ruins is a remnant of a colonial cobblestone street.

Basílica de Nuestra Señora de los Angeles is the most famous church in the country; it honors La Negrita, Costa Rica's patron saint. The church was built over the rock where the tiny stone image of a black Virgin first appeared to Juana Pereira, a young woodgatherer, in 1635. (See the rock downstairs to the left of the altar. The image is above the altar.) Cases along walls in the anteroom contain countless tokens celebrating miracles attributed to her.

Basílica de Nuestra Señora de los Angeles in Cartago

Outside, behind the basilica, the faithful and the hopeful come to holy water that flows from a spring. On August 2 all roads lead to Cartago, as half a million pilgrims gather at the shrine for the Day of Our Lady of the Angels, many having come on foot over long distances.

Getting There

By bus: Frequent buses from San José.
By car: From San José, take Bernardo Soto highway.

LANKESTER BOTANICAL GARDEN

Location: *2½ miles (4 km) E of Cartago toward Paraíso.*
Size: *26 acres (10.7 ha).*
Hours: *Daily 8:30 a.m. to 3:30 p.m.*
Cost: *Adults $4, children 65 cents.*
Information: *(506) 552-3247, fax (506) 552-3151; e-mail lankeste@cariari*
.ucr.ac.cr.

Established in the 1950s by English naturalist Charles Lankester to preserve local epiphytes, beautiful Lankester garden was bought in 1973 by the North American Society of Orchideology and Stanley Smith Foundation of England and donated to the University of Costa Rica. Thousands have walked these paths to see the orchids—more than 800 species of local and foreign orchids, from tiny miniatures to flowers with stalks more than 15 feet (5 m) high. Though peak months for orchids to bloom are February through May, there are enough in flower to dazzle visitors at any time of year.

Well-maintained trails lead over brooks, under arbors, and to greenhouses, through a breathtaking display of flowers and trees that attract more than 100 species of birds. You may be surprised to find a cactus and succulent garden here. Though most Costa Rican cacti grow in tropical dry forest, some live as epiphytes in the rain forest. Palms, bromeliads, bamboo (40 varieties), heliconias (35 varieties), gingers, aroids, and ferns abound. The secondary forest is in the premontane life zone. Research and education go hand in hand with plant production. Though there are currently no guided walks, some descriptive signs are in place and a written guide for the self-guided tour may be available by your arrival. Allow one to two hours to enjoy the garden and gift shop, where you'll find T-shirts, books, and a video about the garden. Bring insect repellent in rainy season.

Getting There

By bus: From Cartago, catch Paraíso bus; ask to be let off at the entrance to Jardín Botánico Lankester. Walk a half-mile (1 km) to the reception area.
By car: From Cartago, look for the entrance on the right just past Casa Vieja Restaurant, next to Campo Ayala.
Other: Taxi from Cartago $5.

IRAZU VOLCANO NATIONAL PARK

Location: *20 miles (32 km) NE of Cartago.*
Size: *5,706 acres (2,309 ha).*
Hours: *Daily 8 a.m. to 3:30 p.m.*
Cost: *$6.*
Information: *Telephone hotline 192, (see Appendix A: Parks and Reserves Information), (506) 290-1927, fax (506) 232-5324.*

Indians who lived on the mountain's slopes named it Iztarú: "mountain of trembling and thunder." Indeed Irazú Volcano has a history of showing off. Its awesome power is evident long before you reach the impressive craters. Near Cartago, notice the devastation from the most recent major eruptions, 1963 to 1965. Whole areas were buried in mud, floods were significant, and volcanic rock still peppers the countryside. But as you travel the paved road to the park, credit the volcano for the rich soils that now produce cabbages, potatoes, onions, and dairy cows' grasslands.

Highest peak in the Central Volcanic Range, Irazú reaches 11,260 feet (3,432 m). It has been known to send ash as far away as the Nicoya Peninsula; steam clouds have billowed 1,640 feet (500 m) high, and debris has shot up 984 feet (300 m). The rumbling giant tossed boulders weighing several tons from its innards in 1963, and its tremors rattled buildings miles away.

Today, with Irazú in a sometimes-restless resting phase, visitors can go to the top of a lunar landscape that muffles its fiery nature. But thin streams of steam or gas and occasional tremors remind us that Irazú is not dead; it only sleeps. Walk along the rim of the main crater, which has a 3,445-foot (1,050-m) diameter; peer down to a bright green lake almost 1,000 feet (300 m) below. Volcanic grays and blacks are highlighted by swatches of reds and oranges in the steep sides. The other principal crater, linked by a trail, is Diego de la Haya, 1,968 feet (600 m) across.

Tenacious plants dot largely empty areas around the craters; some bravely sport bright flowers. On slopes where the green of secondary growth testifies to nature's powers of recovery, old, barren branches rise like ghostly fingers above the new forest. Animal life is scarce at the park because of both human and volcanic activity. Where cougar and jaguar once thrived, today you can see rabbits, coyotes, armadillos, and squirrels. Hummingbirds are numerous; you might spot a volcano junco, mountain robin, ruddy woodcreeper, or ant-eating woodpecker.

For clearest views and a chance to see both oceans, go early. The park closes earlier now, but I remember seeing Irazú at sunset. Buffeted by a cold wind, I stood on a narrow path between two craters and watched as the setting sun lit swirling clouds of mist with rich tones of orange and gold.

Whatever time of day you visit, take a jacket. Average temperature is 52°F (11°C)—lowest recorded temperature, 26°F (−3°C). Frost is possible December through February. Annual rainfall is 85 inches (2,158 mm).

Irazú park, one of the country's most visited, is the birthplace of rivers that flow into major waterways: Chirripó, Reventazón, Sarapiquí, and Río Grande de Tárcoles Rivers. Within the park is a small information hut with posters and park information, rest rooms, and a picnic area.

Getting There

By bus: Bus from San José to the park only on weekends.
By car: From Cartago, head for San Rafael de Oreamuno and Cot, follow park signs.
Other: San José tour companies offer day trips, some in conjunction with a visit to Lankester garden, Cartago, or Orosi Valley.

OROSI VALLEY AND ENVIRONS

Here are big rivers, fantastic scenery, forests, small towns, and small lodges that offer genuine Costa Rican hospitality. Travelers can head for Tapantí National Park, see the dam for the large hydroelectric project, or, if driving, make a loop from Ujarrás around the lake.

From Paraíso, roads go east and south for magnificent views of both Orosi and Ujarrás Valleys and the lake formed by Cachí Dam. The east road leads to ruins of the 17th-century church of **Ujarrás**. The colonial town that once surrounded it lies over pre-Columbian roads. Stop at the view point (*mirador* in Spanish) overlooking Ujarrás. South of Paraíso is the town of **Orosi** and its 18th-century church, the oldest house of worship still in use in the country. Beside it is a small museum of religious art, open daily, housed in what was a Franciscan monastery.

TAPANTI NATIONAL PARK

Location: 31 miles (50 km) SE of San José, 17 miles (28 km) SE of Cartago.
Size: 15,024 acres (6,080 ha).
Hours: Daily 7 a.m. to 5 p.m.
Cost: $6.
Information: Telephone hotline 192 (see Appendix A: Parks and Reserves Information), (506) 771-3297, telephone/fax (506) 771-3155.

"Dripping forest" is not a scientific term, but for me, it describes this park in the Talamanca Mountain Range. Inside the forest, raining or not, the air is moist, plants seem wet, the earth smells fresh. Sounds of water are pervasive: 150 rivers and rivulets run here, important sources for hydroelectric projects. Average rainfall is 256 inches (6,500 mm), though it has on occasion reached 315 inches (8,000 mm). Even in the drier months of January through April, wise travelers bring rain gear. Average temperature is 68°F (20°C), and elevation is from 4,000 to 8,400 feet (1,220 to 2,560 m).

Tree crowns form a leaky umbrella under which grow delicate ferns (including 18 species of tree ferns), orchids, bromeliads, lianas that tempt one to take a swing, mosses, and multicolored lichens. Along the road and on forest slopes grows a plant with immense leaves and a tall reddish flower that Costa Ricans call "poor man's umbrella." I have, in fact, seen its leaves used in the countryside by people caught in the rain.

Tapantí is a favorite with bird-watchers. Among more than 260 species identified here are ones everybody wants to see: quetzals, hummingbirds, toucans, parakeets, parrots, great tinamous, and squirrel cuckoos. Endangered mammals among the 45 resident mammal species are jaguar, ocelot, and tapir; you're more likely to see squirrels, monkeys, raccoons, opossums, coyotes, agoutis, and red brocket deer. There are porcupines, silky anteaters, otters, and, among the 28 amphibian species, lots of toads. Reptile species also number 28, so be on the lookout for lizards and snakes, including the venomous eyelash viper, also commonly known as palm viper, which you might spot on leaves or branches along the road or trails. Butterflies are everywhere: watch for the blue morpho.

The new visitor center is a good starting place to orient yourself via exhibits and conversation with a friendly ranger; buy a park brochure that includes a trail map, and visit the gift shop. Backpackers can leave packs at the center for day visits. Four trails lead through the extravagance of rainforest vegetation. Oropendola Trail, an easy loop, begins about a half-mile (1 km) from the visitor center. For a longer hike, continue on Sendero Pantanoso, which dips down near the Río Grande de Orosi, whose swift, cold waters rush over and around impressive boulders. Bring a picnic and enjoy the covered shelters while you soak up the scenery. The map indicates the best swimming area in the river: brace yourself for cold water. Sendero Natural Arboles Caídos (Fallen Trees Trail) is more rugged; Sendero La Pava (Guan Trail) also leads to the river. At the parking and picnic area near the end of the public road, climb a short trail to the covered shelter at the *mirador* to look across at a gorgeous waterfall and down the river valley—glorious interplays of light and clouds along the forested mountains.

The main road is good because of a Costa Rican Electric Institute (ICE) dam about 9 miles (15 km) from the park entrance. Waters from the Río Grande de Orosi produce hydroelectric energy and help quench San José's thirst. A wildlife refuge by 1982, Tapantí became a national park in 1992 and is within the Amistad Pacific Conservation Area.

Getting There

By bus: From Cartago, catch the Orosi bus—leaves every hour from the south side of the church ruins. From Orosi, take a taxi for the last 7½ miles (12 km). Park personnel can radio for a taxi for return trip. Or take a taxi from Cartago or Paraíso.

By car: From Cartago, continue through Paraíso, Orosi, Río Macho, and Purisil. Watch for "Tapantí" signs. Road passable year-round.

Other: Tours from San José may combine Tapantí with other area attractions; local lodges offer tours and/or transfers.

Where to Stay and Eat near Tapantí

Kirí Lodge, half a mile (1 km) from the Tapantí entrance, Tapantí (506) 284-2024 or beeper phone (506) 225-2500(Kirí Lodge); San Jose (506) 257-8064, fax (506) 257-8065, is a charming mountain hideaway, a natural reserve in its own right where you're likely to see troops of white-faced monkeys along with coatis, deer, armadillos, and other fauna found in the park. Blue morpho butterflies are abundant, as are a variety of hummingbirds.

Kirí's six cabins, terraced up the hillside, have memorable vistas. Rooms are simple but comfortable, with good mattresses and river rocks in the decor. Owners Alvaro and Dagoberto Torres and family offer Costa Rican hospitality. Among the restaurant's tasty dishes are trout fresh from the farm's own ponds and organically grown vegetables and fruits. Stop by for a meal if nothing else, but be advised: you will wish you were staying. Double $30, breakfast and taxes included.

More than 7 miles (12 km) of trails lead into misty mountains to rivers and waterfalls on some of the farm's 124 acres (50 ha). Besides transport to Tapantí, the lodge offers tours to Irazú Volcano, Guayabo National Monument, Lankester garden, and the Orosi Valley.

Monte Sky, (506) 232-0884, cellular (506) 382-7502, fax (506) 231-3536; e-mail montesky@intnet.co.cr; Web site www.intnet.co.cr/montesky, is a rustic mountain retreat that is as much a philosophy as a place. Owner Rafael (Billy) Montero seems to have a sacred agreement with his mountain to keep impact low, to let the forest reveal its truths to visitors, and to share the history of the place. That history starts in the 1920 lodge with old photographs and memorabilia. Rooms are basic (shared baths), with a nearby cabin for up to six people; $28 per person, including meals, lodging, and guide. Camping is permitted.

One- to four-hour guided walks reveal a spectacular waterfall, 400-year-old oaks, and 260 species of birds. From the mountaintop setting on a clear day, four volcanoes are visible, with an inspirational mountains-and-sky panorama even on cloudy days. Day trips from San José, only 90 minutes away, start at $60, minimum five people, and usually include the opportunity to plant native trees. Without transport, rates are $8 for entrance fee, $13 with lunch, and $15 with a guide.

The turnoff to Monte Sky is 3 miles (5 km) from Orosi toward Tapantí, continuing almost 2 miles (3 km) on an exciting dirt/mud road to the parking area. The lodge is up a well-marked trail; allow 30 minutes for the climb to enjoy vistas and read inspirational signs. Because of its remote location, overnight and day visits are by reservation only.

Sanchirí Mirador and Lodge (1½ miles [2½ km] from Paraíso toward

Kirí Lodge next to Tapantí National Park

Orosi), telephone/fax (506) 533-3210, has an out-of-this-world vista of beautiful Orosi Valley from the restaurant and six cabins. Expect personalized service from nine brothers and sisters of the Mata family, who have lived and worked this land for five generations. Each wooden hillside cabin is simply furnished, with telephone and attractive local-stone bathroom walls and floors. Double $60, including taxes and breakfast.

Across from the cabins is forest where quetzals reside year-round; the Matas continue to plant native trees that provide food for these resplendant birds and other wildlife. Optional tours go to Tapantí (25 minutes away), Guayabo, and Irazú (one hour away); local tours, via jeep or horseback include a look at the hydroelectric plant and a coffee stop at a rustic campesino house. Rafting trips on the Reventazón or Pacuare are arranged; airport pickup and other transfers available. Restaurant open to the public.

TURRIALBA AREA

The road from Cartago to Turrialba is spectacular as it winds up and over the mountains. Ahead are the only archaeological monuments in the coutry and fantastic river rafting, birding, and hiking.

In the town of Cervantes, watch for **La Posada de la Luna** restaurant. I cannot pass this place without stopping for a freshly made *tortilla de* *queso* (cheese tortilla) and a glass of hot *agua dulce con leche* (a hot drink made with boiling water, brown sugar, and, in this case, milk). Some people swear that the best *gallo pinto* (beans and rice) in the country is served here. Showcases hold bits of history, from Indian artifacts to old telephones, radios, and flatirons. Open 8 a.m. to 8:30 p.m., closed Monday.

The agricultural lands around Juan Viñas are among the most beautiful in Costa Rica. Fields of sugarcane wave across this top-of-the-world setting. Then comes the winding descent into the Turrialba Valley.

A back door to Turrialba snakes through San Isidro de Coronado and Rancho Redondo, dairy country, and oak forests often shrouded in mist. The last time I was on this road was Corpus Christi Sunday. Flowers strewn in the road marked the path of religious processions in village after village. In one, a milk cow stood in the middle of the road eating the flower petals while worshippers sang in a nearby church. Past Llano Grande is the turnoff for Irazú Volcano. Continue on to Cot and Pacayas for Santa Cruz, watching for waterfalls on the skirts of Turrialba Volcano. At Santa Cruz, turn to Turrialba. This road is passable even in the rainy season. From Santa Cruz, a jolting road goes on to Guayabo and the national monument.

TURRIALBA

This town (population 32,273), center of a rich agricultural region, is increasingly a destination for nature and adventure travelers. No need for an alarm clock here—at 6 a.m., three strong blasts of the town's
fire alarm do the trick. Once you're up, there's plenty to do. Kayakers and white-water rafters use the town as a base for forays on the Reventazón and Pacuare Rivers. Its location is ideal for those interested in archaeology, agriculture, and nature. Turrialba is 40 miles (64 km) from San Jose.

Things to See and Do in and around Turrialba

CATIE (east of Turrialba on the main highway), (506) 556-6431, fax (506) 556-6431; e-mail info@catie.ac.cr; Web site www.catie.ac.cr, is an agricultural education, extension, and research center. Studies focus on agroforestry, dairy and beef livestock, cacao, coffee, plantains, spices, fruit trees, and *pejibaye* (peach palm). Students from more than 34 nations hold master's degrees from its programs in agriculture and natural resources. On a day tour, look at plant collections, seed bank, and agroforestry projects: three hours is $6 to $15 per person depending on number; advance reservations required. CATIE is the Spanish acronym for Tropical Agronomic Research and Education Center.

Viborana is a small serpentarium 7 miles (12 km) east of Turrialba, 1,312 feet (400 m) past the turnoff for Pochotel, that also has a natural butterfly garden. Admission $4 adults, $2 children, including an educational demonstration with the snakes.

Getting There

By bus: San José to Turrialba by express bus.
By car: Through Cartago, Paraíso, and Juan Viñas.

Where to Stay and Eat in and near Turrialba

Casa Turire (turnoff is 3 miles [5 km] east of Turrialba), (506) 531-1111, fax (506) 531-1075; e-mail turire@centralamerica.com; Web site www. centralamerica.com, is a splendid country house on the Atirro Hacienda. Set in a curve of the Reventazón River, Casa Turire reigns over nearby forest as well as fields of sugarcane, coffee, and macadamia nuts. The hacienda belongs to the Rojas family, who extended their enterprises to include tourism in 1991. The 12-room, four-suite grand "plantation house" sits amid formal gardens, whose tropical plants, flowers, and trees attract colorful birds. The attractive swimming pool and Jacuzzi are spring fed.

Rooms are elegant, furnished in soft tones, with two full beds. Each has satellite TV, shower and tub, ceiling fan, hair dryer, direct-dial telephone, and a stunning view of mountains from a private balcony. Floor-to-ceiling windows welcome light that shines on polished hardwood floors. Single $95, double $110, suites from $130. No children under 12; the building is not equipped for the handicapped.

Guests choose from mountain biking, rain-forest tours, horseback riding, kayaking and white-water rafting on the Reventazón, and tours to Irazú Volcano, Guayabo, and Lankester Botanical Garden. On the hacienda, guests visit processing plants for cane, coffee, and macadamia nuts; relax in the Jacuzzi; play tennis, or enjoy a putting green and driving range.

The gourmet, family-style restaurant is open to the public for lunch and dinner; reservations required. Service is excellent, staff friendly. Transfers from San José and the airport are available, and there's a nearby airstrip for charter flights. The hotel is a member of the Small Distinctive Hotels of Costa Rica.

Hotel Wagelia, (506) 556-1566, fax (506) 556-1596, annex telephone (506) 556-1142, has two locations. The 18-room downtown hotel offers parking and a restaurant with good food and a pleasant atmosphere. Simple, comfortable rooms with ceiling fans open onto terraces around a courtyard; some have air conditioning, refrigerator, and TV. The 17-room annex, on a quiet street backed by coffee fields at the edge of town, has a swimming pool. Tours arranged through local agencies to Guayabo, Turrialba Volcano, and CATIE, as well as rafting trips. At either, single $30, double $45; $50 for doubles with air conditioning, refrigerator, and TV.

Pochotel, (506) 284-7292, (506) 556-0111, fax (506) 556-6222, is 7 miles (11 km) from Turrialba. From its *mirador* on a clear day, see not only the Reventazón Valley but also Cerro de la Muerte, Chirripó, the Caribbean coast, and Irazú and Turrialba Volcanoes. Eight rooms are simply furnished;

ones in more secluded bungalows along the edge of the forest have rustic charm. There is a pool, and the restaurant has a *cocina de leña* (wood-burning stove) in the dining room so guests can be a part of this traditional cooking method. Owner Oscar Garcia arranges rafting tours, horseback riding in the forest, helicopter rides, and visits to Lagunas de San Joaquín for fishing and hiking. Double $40, $10 per person extra, taxes included.

Turrialtico, (506) 556-1575, telephone/fax (506) 556-1111, is 4 miles (7 km) from Turrialba. Twelve rooms with private baths are above the lodge's locally popular restaurant, which has a dynamite view of the valley. Pleasant rooms, brightened by Guatemalan bedspreads, open onto a common space with two appealing sitting areas. Owners Hector Lezama and Lucrecia Garcia offer trips to a serpentarium and to Guayabo and Turrialba Volcano (four-person minimum); other options are rafting, horseback riding, and hiking. Camping permitted. Single $25, double $30.

Volcán Turrialba Lodge, telephone/fax (506)273-433; e-mail voturri@sol.racsa.co.cr, between Irazú and Turrialba Volcanoes, is at 9,186 feet (2,800 m). Owner Tony Lachner converted an old milking house into a comfortable, rustic, nine-room lodge that offers hiking, horseback riding, and biking—magnificent ways to see Turrialba's crater, old lava beds, and Irazú's hot springs. The crater is less than 4 miles (6 km) from the lodge. Another flora and fauna tour visits a 208-acre (84-ha) primary forest on the farm where ocelots, river otters, quetzals, porcupines, coyotes, and kinkajous live.

Single $48, double $95, including lodging, meals, and taxes. The lodge is accessible only by four-wheel-drive vehicles, but transportation is provided from San José; cost depends on number of passengers. Lodge activities are open to day visitors. A one-day tour from San José is $60. Packages available include a $195 two-night, three-day trip that includes transportation, lodging, meals, taxes, and tours to lava beds, Turrialba Volcano, hot springs, and fumaroles.

GUAYABO NATIONAL MONUMENT

Location: 12 miles (19 km) NE of Turrialba; from San José, 40 miles (65 km).
Size: 538 acres (218 ha).
Hours: 8 a.m. to 3:30 p.m., closed Monday.
Cost: $6
Information: Telephone hotline 192 (See Appendix A: Parks and Reserves Information), (506) 290-1927, fax (506) 232-5324.

Guayabo National Monument is the blue morpho butterfly, the yellow flash of a Montezuma oropendola flying through tall trees, flowing water, patches of profuse pink impatiens, and ancient carved stones. It is the quiet of centuries-old ruins hidden in the rain forest.

Costa Rica's only archaeological park, Guayabo protects the remains of a city that flourished and disappeared before the Spaniards arrived. People

may have occupied the area as early as 1000 B.C.; at its peak Guayabo is estimated to have had 300 to 500 residents, though perhaps as many as 10,000
lived in surrounding villages, supplying labor and revenue to this religious
and political center. There was little new building after A.D. 800, and the site
was abandoned by 1400. Some theorize that wars and disease contributed to
the abandonment.

Visitors today see *calzadas* (cobbled roads), stone-lined water-storage
tanks, open and covered aqueducts that carried water through the site (many
still in use), and *montículos* (mounds) with stone-covered bases. Park information signs depict conical houses believed to have been built on the
mounds out of wood and palm leaves. Trails lead past open tombs, plundered before the park was established. Stylized forms of a jaguar and caiman
decorate a striking monolith; 63 petroglyphs picture birds and animals as
well as art whose meaning is still unknown. Many mysteries of people and
place remain.

A conservation and excavation project, begun in August 1989, increased
the excavated area to half of the almost-50-acre (20-ha) archaeological site.
Among items found are golden bells, carved stone tables, roasted corn ker-
nels, beautiful pottery, a copper-and-gold frog, and a sacrificial stone. Some
pieces are exhibited at the National Museum in San José.

Guayabo protects the only remaining primary forest in the province of
Cartago, accounting for 22 percent of the park; other forest is rich, naturally
regenerating secondary forest. More than 80 varieties of orchids and other epiphytes adorn trees; toucans are present, as are hummingbirds, woodcreepers,
chachalacas, woodpeckers, and brown jays (*ticos* call them *piapias* and say they
are the scouts of the forest, their warning cries signaling that an intruder is
near). Notice long, hanging nests built by oropendolas. Mammals include
sloths, kinkajous, coatis, rabbits, squirrels, and armadillos.

Local guides accompany visitors on Sendero de los Montículos, the
interpretive trail that leads through the archaeological site to a *mirador*
with a fantastic view of the ruins below, mountain peaks, and Turrialba's
valley. Another view point overlooks the excavation of a road that ran from
Guayabo to an outlying area. Visitors can explore Los Cantarillos nature
trail, which offers either a short or longer loop down to the Lajitas River. It
can be muddy in the wet season. Rainfall averages 138 inches (3,500 mm),
with driest months February and March. Average temperature is 68°F
(20°C), and elevation is 3,150 to 4,265 feet (960 to 1,300 m).

A small visitor center is opposite the park entrance. A nearby camping
area has tent sites, bathrooms, and potable water.

Getting There
By bus: From Turrialba, take the bus to Guayabo.
By car: Paved from Turrialba; signs point the way. A more adventurous
route is described in the Turrialba section.
Other: Taxi from Turrialba.

Where to Stay near Guayabo Park
Any of the lodges and hotels in this section have easy access to Guayabo.
Day trips are available from San José.

RANCHO NATURALISTA PRIVATE RESERVE
Location: *1.7 miles (2.8 km) SE of Turrialba up a dirt road from Tuis.*
Rates: *$125 day per person, $750 a week per person, double occupancy, including*
meals, lodging, guides, horseback riding, and tours in the reserve, Río Tuis Valley,
Chirripó reserve.
Information/Reservations: *Telephone/fax (506) 267-7138.*

Fields of cane and coffee spread out below this mountain retreat, while Irazú
and Turrialba Volcanoes dominate the skyline across a vast valley. Tropical
forest is steps away from the lodge. Tranquility is the key word.
    The ranch, belonging to the Erb family, caters strictly to nature travelers.

Coffee, Anyone?

Coffee, which originated in Ethiopia and Arabia, was Costa
Rica's number-one export until this decade. Though today it's
the third-largest foreign exchange earner, after bananas and
tourism, a drop in the price of coffee still sends a shudder
through the country. Most is sold to Germany, the United
States, and Great Britain.

Grown in nurseries for about one year, coffee plants are
transplanted to the field, where they begin to bear commercially
after two years. Some growers harvest from coffee trees for 15
to 20 years and then prune them way back for 20 more years
of production.

Planting is in May and June. Harvest time depends on
elevation: October to January in the San José Valley, June to November in Turrialba and Coto Brus. Pickers are paid by the ca-
juela (basket). All ages take to the fields for the harvest; Costa
Ricans are joined by thousands of temporary workers from
Nicaragua. Each berry, which turns from green to red when
ripe, contains two seeds: the coffee beans. The pulp of the fruit
must be removed and beans dried before they can be roasted
and exported.

Enthusiastic, knowledgeable guides lead visitors on the trails and farm roads to look for the birds, butterflies, and moths that abound here. More than 345 bird species have been seen within 2 miles of the lodge. All guides are biologists/ornithologists or expert birders. With their encouragement, even neophytes experience the thrill of spotting species after species. You may spot a blue-crowned motmot (notice the telltale tick-tock motion it makes with its racket-tipped tail), a scarlet-thighed dacnis, or a green honeycreeper; and you're likely to see toucans, manakins, trogons, tanagers, and a world of hummingbirds.

If you have yet to see the gorgeous morpho butterfly, this is your chance. Several of the six Central American species of this butterfly live near the lodge. The blue flash of one of these beauties against the forest's green is a treasure that glows ever after in the mind's eye.

The Erbs don't claim to have all 12,000 of Costa Rica's species of moths, but they believe they have enough to keep you occupied. Just ask, and they'll put up a sheet and plug in a lamp outside at night to attract them. The variety is awesome. Guided night walks are available.

A neighbor down the road has a trapiche, an old-style sugarcane press, that guests can visit. Horses are available at no extra charge. Explore roads in the 125-acre (50-ha) farm, outside the farm on neighboring roads, or along the Tuis River.

With a one-week stay, the Erbs give a complimentary all-day field trip to a different elevation to see other flora and fauna. Popular choices are Tapantí National Park or Irazú Volcano. Optional tours can be arranged to volcanoes, beaches, or national parks, as well as white-water rafting.

The main house has six comfortable bedrooms, one a suite and three with private baths. There is great birding from the upstairs balcony and long porch off the downstairs living room. Nearby are a one-bedroom cottage and newer cabins, each with two queen beds, private baths, and forest views. Laundry service is part of the package. Meals are family style; food is plentiful and delicious, from filet mignon to Mexican and Costa Rican cuisine. The Erbs are gracious hosts who have lived in Costa Rica for many years.

Rancho Naturalista is at 2,953 feet (900 m), in the transition zone between premontane wet forest and premontane rain forest. Daytime temperatures are in the 70s (21°C to 26°C), nights in the 60s (15°C to 20°C). Afternoon rain is common, especially May through November; rubber boots recommended. Four main trails on the ranch are well-maintained, not difficult; shelters and benches along the way are ideal spots to sit and wait for nature to reveal its treasures.

A stay of a week or more can be split between Rancho Naturalista and the Erbs' other property on the Pacific, Tarcol Lodge near Carara Biological Reserve—same rates (see Chapter 9).

Getting There
Transfer from San José free with three-night stay; pickup at airport or elsewhere arranged.

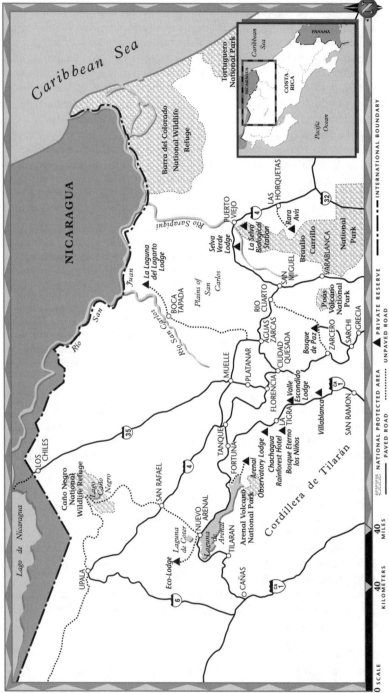

7

NORTH CENTRAL COSTA RICA

Mountains, plains, volcanoes, lakes, rivers, forests, fruit farms, and cattle ranches form a colorful and diverse mosaic in this region. Some of the major natural history attractions include Arenal Volcano National Park and Lake Arenal, Caño Negro National Wildlife Refuge, Braulio Carrillo National Park, and well-known private nature reserves such as Rara Avis and La Selva. Visitors bathe in thermal waters, windsurf, fish, bird-watch, raft, hike, and take river wildlife tours.

Several highway routes facilitate moving within the north central region and simplify combining destinations here with Caribbean or Northwest region attractions. Direct buses go from San José to Ciudad Quesada, Puerto Viejo de Sarapiquí, Braulio Carrillo National Park, and Tilarán, with connections to other destinations, such as Arenal and Boca Tapada. So far there are no scheduled airline flights to the region, but SANSA has plans for service to La Fortuna—check it out.

SAN RAMON-LA FORTUNA ROUTE

The area between San Ramón and La Fortuna is rich in magnificent scenery of forested mountains, pleasant villages, ornamental plant farms, and colorful flower gardens in front of houses from humble to elegant along the paved road. Whether you start or end the route in **San Ramón**, watch for killer speed-bumps near San Ramón. Signs warn, "*Reductor de velocidad*" ("Reduce speed"). A good route to Arenal, Caño Negro, and other north central destinations, this area is a worthy destination in itself with interesting private reserves to explore, some of which also welcome day visitors.

VILLABLANCA AND LOS ANGELES CLOUD FOREST, PRIVATE RESERVE

Location: 12 miles (19 km) N of San Ramón, 50 miles (80 km) NW of San José.
Rates: Single $68, double $89. Breakfast $5, lunch or dinner $11.
Information/Reservations: (506) 228-4603, fax (506) 228-4004.

Villablanca was built to resemble a small village: an 1800s colonial settlement centered on the *casa grande* (big house), the dwelling for the family that owned the land. The landowners in this case are former Costa Rican president Rodrigo Carazo and his wife, Estrella, who bought the site in 1989.

Individual *casitas* (little houses) where the workers would have lived serve as charming guest cottages. They have the look and feel of adobe, with rough white plaster and blue trim. Some are suites with separate sitting rooms. All have corner fireplaces with *bancos* extending out on each side, rocking chairs in front of the hearth, and writing desks. Colorful comforters on the beds and bright rugs lend a cozy look. Nights can be cool here, so the comforters and fireplaces are not merely decorative. The big house contains a dining room, bar, small library, and sitting areas. Upstairs are five rooms. There's also a dormitory-style building (shared baths) for student groups. Meals are buffet-style.

The 48 *casitas* and four family villas have small gardens in front and a 2,000-acre (800-ha) forest out back. The Los Angeles Cloud Forest is wet, exuberant, and green. There are two easy 1-mile (2-km) trails, with walkways of wooden planks covered with wire to prevent slipping. The forest is home to about 280 bird species, including bare-necked umbrella birds, tawny-capped euphonias, black guans, great curassows, chachalacas, and hummingbirds, along with three species of monkeys, sloths, raccoons, squirrels, *tepezcuintles*, ocelots, and snakes. Tree ferns are magnificent. A guided walk on these trails is $22. A more difficult 3.7-mile (6-km) trail is for those who like to walk alone in the forest. The cloud-forest elevation is about 3,600 feet (1,100 m). Driest months are March to May; go prepared for rain.

A Canopy Fair allows visitors to travel through tree crowns, viewing the forest from seven platforms in five trees. After a guided walk to the site, visitors climb to the first platform, at 33 feet (10 m), moving to other platforms via cable. The highest platform is 72 feet (22 m); the longest distance between platforms is 345 feet (105 m). Cost is $35. From a *mirador* about a mile from the main house you can see Arenal Volcano, Lake Nicaragua, and the Plains of San Carlos on a clear day.

Guests can also visit the farm's cultivated land (coffee, sugarcane, vegetable crops) and the dairy operation that provides the dining room's milk and cheese. Rent a horse to explore the farm or a two-hour forest trail. Villablanca can arrange car and driver to destinations such as Tabacón, Poás, Arenal, and Sarchí.

Day visitors are welcome. A one-day tour from San José includes guided forest walk or horseback ride, transfers, and continental breakfast and lunch; $77. A one-day package with the Canopy Fair is $80. The guided forest walk ($22) and Canopy Fair ($35) are also available by reservation to those who come on their own.

Getting There
By car: From San Ramón, turn off just past km 8 at the guard station.
Other: Transfers from San José, $35 per person; from San Ramón, $15.

VALLE ESCONDIDO LODGE, PRIVATE RESERVE
Location: 56 miles (90 km) NW of San José, 21 miles (33 km) N of San Ramón.
Rates: Single $56, double $67. Multiday packages.
Information/Reservations: (506) 231-0906, fax (506) 232-9591; e-mail valle@ns.coldnet.co.cr; Web site www.cmnet.co.cr/valle/.

At Valle Escondido Lodge, combine fantastic forest treks with walks through acres of ornamental plants grown for export, while you enjoy very nice quarters. The lodge has 25 rooms, each opening onto a covered terrace with a magical view of a valley and green, green mountains that appear and disappear in the mists. Large frogs convene on the porch in the evenings. Rooms are spacious and bright, with beautiful polished hardwood furniture, including an ample writing desk. Bathrooms have big lighted mirrors and bidets.

The restaurant, a short walk downhill from the rooms, offers an international menu with Italian specialties—food that's a feast for the eyes as well as the palate. Remember to take binoculars to the dining room to enjoy birds in the back garden while you eat. The restaurant is open to the public, a five-minute drive from the highway turnoff. A swimming pool and Jacuzzi have a fantastic mountain view.

Owner Marco Hidalgo grows and exports more than 20 species of ornamental plants to Italy, the Netherlands, and Belgium. Guests can visit greenhouses and packing sheds.

The farm includes 150 acres (60 ha) of forest and an abundance of mountain streams. The tall forest's understory is a natural tropical greenhouse with heliconias and fascinating tree roots. I watched one masked tityra feed another. An aracari, a member of the toucan family, frustrated my attempts to photograph him but allowed wonderful glimpses. Near one trail is a huge tree with enormous buttresses where bats live.

Wide forest trails begin and end at the plantation. The lodge offers a tour—on foot, horseback, or mountain bike—to the San Lorenzo River for a swim in a natural pool or a hike to a three-tiered waterfall. A guided tour of the ornamental plant farm combined with a forest hike is $12; a trail hike without guide is $5 (free to hotel guests). Horses are $10 per hour; mountain bikes, $5. Boots for rent.

Elevation is about 2,000 feet (600 m); temperature ranges from 68°F to 86°F (20°C to 30°C). Day visitors are welcome.

Getting There
By bus: From San Ramón, take La Tigra/La Fortuna bus to sign at turnoff, short hike in.
By car: From San Ramón, turn north for La Tigra and watch for "Valle Escondido" sign.
Other: Transfers provided; or take a taxi from San Ramón.

BOSQUE ETERNO DE LOS NIÑOS, POCO SOL SECTOR, PRIVATE RESERVE
Location: Office at La Tigra, 31 miles (50 km) N of San Ramón. Poco Sol Field Station is 7.4 miles (12 km) by unpaved road into the mountains to the west.
Rates: Lodging and meals $27.
Information/Reservations: (506) 645-5003, (506) 645-5200, fax (506) 645-5104; e-mail acmmcl@sol.racsa.co.cr; Web site www.monteverde.or.cr.

Bosque Eterno de los Niños, the Children's Eternal Rain Forest, is a 46,100-acre (18,652-ha) reserve created by and protected with gifts from children and adults around the world. The Monteverde Conservation League, a private nonprofit organization, owns and manages this valuable resource, which reaches over the Tilarán Mountains to Monteverde on the Pacific slope.

Here on the Atlantic slope is Poco Sol Field Station, where natural history visitors can be a part of the special magic spun by nature, children's love, and the dedication of countless individuals. The rustic, two-level main building has a kitchen and dining area (buffet-style meals) and two dormitory-style bedrooms, each with eight beds (bunks) and shared bathrooms; no hot water. The upper level has another room and bath.

Vistas lift the soul: forest across undulating hills; Poco Sol Lagoon, mysterious in the mists, shimmering in the sun; the San Carlos Valley below in the distance. From the covered porch off the dining room, watch toucans, hummingbirds, oropendolas, and other of the 330-plus species of birds that have been identified around the station.

More than 6 miles (10 km) of well-maintained trails lead through a variety of habitats (regenerating pasture and primary and secondary forest) to the lake, small hot springs, and a waterfall that speaks of eternity. Vegetation is incredible: epiphytes, lianas, philodendrons; on the way to the waterfall, your first glimpse of a giant fig will stop you in your tracks.

You may see a white-fronted nunbird, white hawk, bare-necked umbrellabird, scarlet-rumped cacique, red-legged honeycreeper, rufous-tiled jacamar, ornate hawk-eagle, ocellated antbird, or some of the more than 20 species of tanagers here. Butterflies, including the morpho, waft by. More than one visitor has mistaken the large hawkmoth for a hummingbird. Keep your eyes open for snakes. A beautiful but venomous fer-de-lance, camouflaged beside the trail, was inches from my rubber boots—fortunately, he slept. Hear and see howler monkeys, along with white-faced monkeys, coatis, kinkajous, sloths, and agoutis.

Altitude ranges from 1,640 to 3,280 feet (500 to 1,000 m). Bring rain gear. Have your camera ready for the one-lane suspension bridge over the Peñas Blancas River on the way to Poco Sol.

An educational center for children and visitors, 2 miles (3 km) from La Tigra, should be finished by the time you arrive. See more about the children's forest in Chapter 8 and the box in Chapter 2. Because of the shelter's small size and isolation, prior reservations are necessary for visits to Poco Sol.

Getting There

By bus: Bus from San Ramón to La Fortuna goes by the office, leaving an uphill trek.

By car: From San Ramón or La Fortuna, head to La Tigra. Turnoff to Poco Sol is 1,640 feet (500 m) north of the La Tigra office.

Other: La Fortuna tour agencies offer day trips to Poco Sol.

BOSQUES DE CHACHAGUA, PRIVATE RESERVE

Location: 8 miles (12 km) S of La Fortuna.

Rates: Single or double $80, triple $90. Breakfast $7, lunch or dinner $11. Multi-day packages.

Information/Reservations: (506) 239-1164, fax (506) 239-1311; e-mail chachagua@novanet.co.cr; Web site www.novanet.co.cr/chachagua/. Contact with hotel by radio.

Where else can you awaken to a morning greeting from two collared aracaris pecking at the window? Bosques de Chachagua in the Tilarán Mountains offers an unforgettable experience in a tropical paradise.

In the 10-minute dirt-road drive up from the paved highway, you move from the workaday world to a rain-forest hideaway which, in some wondrous way, helps put that other world in better perspective. The 23 attractive individual bungalows of the Chachagua Rain Forest Hotel offer creature comforts: broad wooden-plank walls and polished hardwood floors harmonize with the soft colors of comforters and matching drapes; a ceiling fan, big dresser and mirror, two queen beds, reading lamps, artwork, and flower arrangements of heliconia, anthurium, and varicolored tropical leaves complete the picture. Wood and glass doors open onto a generous terrace with benches and chairs. The pièce de résistance, however, has to be the bathrooms, as large as some hotel rooms. Bilevel, each one has two small garden areas, mirrored windows providing privacy and a view of the outdoors at the same time, and an open, chest-high shower.

Wood and cement walkways lead from bungalows across a stream to the reception area, a natural swimming pool, outdoor rancho/bar, and the open-air dining room, a tablecloth place with excellent service by friendly staff.

Meals are delicious. You may find owner Carlos Salazar in the kitchen adding his special touches, especially at breakfast. Some of the food served is grown here: pineapple, papaya, yuca, squash, and black beans. Beef, poultry (despite an ocelot's interest in the chicken population), eggs, milk, and cheese are also produced on the ranch. Dining was embellished one morning with a flight overhead of at least 60 red-lored parrots. An anteater appears more often than not at 8 a.m. The resident scarlet macaw, who hangs out at the dining room, may deign to speak to you.

Chachagua is an almost-250-acre (100-ha) ranch with a glorious rain forest. The magic of the contiguous International Children's Rain Forest spills over into this rich reserve. Trails go to small waterfalls, along rivers, and through forest inhabited by sloths, white-faced and howler monkeys, keel-billed toucans, blue morpho butterflies, and poison-dart frogs. Have the guide show you the Blood of Christ plant and monkey ladders, and watch for the large, beautiful golden spider that lives here. Boots and walking sticks provided.

The reserve can be a base for trips to nearby Arenal, Tabacón Hot Springs, and Caño Negro wildlife refuge. Packages include some tours. Half-day horseback tours are available.

Groups and individuals who visit Chachagua are invited to donate to the nearby community's school for books, supplies, and building improvements. A new classroom and bathrooms have already been added, the building painted, and students now have books and school supplies.

A three-day package includes lodging; meals; visits to Sarchí, Tabacón, and Arenal; and a guided walk and natural history slide presentation: single $370, double $274 each. A four-day package adds a visit to Caño Negro: single $616, double $430 each. Chachagua offers packages with Palma Real in San José and El Ocotal Beach Resort on the Pacific.

Getting There

By car: From San Ramón, head north through La Tigra and San Isidro; watch for hotel sign before the town of Chachagua. From La Fortuna, go south past Chachagua.
Other: Transfer provided with fixed-departure packages.

NARANJO–CIUDAD QUESADA ROUTE

The route through Naranjo, which turns off the Inter-American after km 44, heads north on a narrow mountain road through coffee plantations and small communities. As it ascends, dairy cattle paint the landscape. Views as the road climbs are stupendous, but wait until the El Mirador restaurant to pull off for photos; narrow road, curves, and no shoulders make roadside stops dangerous.

This was the traditional route to La Fortuna, Arenal, and Caño Negro until the route from San Ramón was paved, and it's still popular, especially for those who want to visit Sarchí and Zarcero en route. A private reserve, Bosque de Paz, is just off this route in the beautiful area known as Los Bajos del Toro Amarillo.

The friendly, picturesque mountain town of 3,692 people, **Zarcero** is famous for its animals—that is, animals sculpted from plants: topiary art. The fantastic gardens in front of the church hold an evergreen elephant, bull, and rabbit, plus dozens of other forms. Tours to Arenal often include a stop here. Zarcero is 15 miles (24 km) north of the Naranjo turnoff and 43 miles (69 km) northwest of San José.

If you want to stay in Zacero, there's **Hotel Don Beto,** telephone/fax (506)463-3137, across from the church and gardens. Flory Salazar and son Luis offer guests the comfort of their two-story home. Eight shining-clean rooms, some with beautiful parquet floors, are tucked off sitting rooms and balconies and down halls. Doña Flory can tell you about the natural beauty around Zarcero: waterfalls, *miradores*, parks, and India Dormida (Sleeping Indian Maiden) mountain. She or Luis accompany guests on area excursions or pick them up at Juan Santamaría airport. Double with shared bath $20; with private bath $25. Breakfast is served with advance notice.

BOSQUE DE PAZ, PRIVATE RESERVE

Location: E of Zarcero between Poás Volcano and Juan Castro Blanco National Park; 1½ hours NW of San José.
Rates: Day tours from $65, including transport from San José, guide, trail walks, and lunch; without transport, $35. A two-day, one-night visit is $100 per person, double occupancy, including lodging, meals, trail walks, and local guide.
Information/Reservations: (506) 234-6676, telephone/fax (506) 255-0203; e-mail bosque@sol.racsa.co.cr, Web site www.expreso.co.cr/bosque.

Bosque de Paz, Forest of Peace, has centuries-old trees, waterfalls, orchids, valleys, mountains, and rivers. Birdlife is abundant: frequently seen are the quetzal, red-headed barbet, emerald toucanet, black guan, collared trogon, green violet-ear hummingbird, and golden-browed chlorophonia. More than 17 miles (28 km) of well-built trails take visitors into the forest to see forest-dwelling species such as the black-faced solitaire, ruddy-capped nightingale-thrush, red-faced spinetail, and eight of the country's 12 breeding species of warblers, including the endemic flame-throated warbler. Monkeys are here, too: the spider, howler, and white-faced capuchin. The 988-acre (400-ha) private biological reserve serves as a corridor between two national parks: Poás and Juan Castro Blanco.

Visitors may choose among various trails. The short, easy Natural Garden Trail is between two rivers whose pools offer crystal-clear water for bathing. Forest Canopy Trail, 1.8 miles (3 km), allows observation of the crowns of ancient trees. The Waterfall and Poás Volcano Lookout is for those in good physical condition. Benches along some trails allow perfect places to absorb the peace, for which this place is named. The Pinto family,

The lodge at Bosque de Paz

owners of Bosque de Paz, believe that intimate contact with nature transmits peace, and they offer it as a sanctuary. The hospitality they provide in this rain and cloud forest is unsurpassed.

While most visitors come to Bosque de Paz for a one-day tour, the farmhouse has two charming rooms, each with private bath and double and single beds for overnight guests. Four new rooms are in the works. Reservations necessary.

Getting There
By car: From Zarcero, east through Palmira and follow signs, 20 minutes; from Sarchí, follow road NE to Toro Amarillo.
Other: Tours from San José include transport.

CIUDAD QUESADA

Ciudad Quesada (population 32,747) is a center of this rich agricultural area. Located 60 miles (95 km) northwest of San José, it lies on the edge of the Plains of San Carlos. It is often referred to as San Carlos. Watch on the left as you come into town for the CATUZON office, (506) 460-1672, tourism chamber for the northern zone. Open weekdays 8:30 to 11:30 a.m. and 1:30 to 5 p.m.; Saturdays 8 a.m. to 3 p.m. Staff is helpful. Pick up brochures, pamphlets, and map.

Things to See and Do around Ciudad Quesada

Remember that distances are short and main roads paved in this area, so access to Caño Negro, Arenal, Venado Caves, and La Fortuna is good from here. **Juan Castro Blanco National Park**, east of Ciudad Quesada, was created in 1992 but so far has no developed facilities for visitors. Its more than 35,000 acres (14,258 ha) protect primary forest and important watershed for the northern zone.

La Marina Zoo, (506) 460-0946, is just west of Aguas Zarcas. Something amazing is going on here: tapirs are reproducing like crazy. The three that owner Alba María Alfaro had taken in, named Clarisa, Chepa, and Toñio, have been joined by three offspring—and the females are expecting again. Most of the animals in this small, private zoo were brought to La Marina because they were sick, wounded, or had been abandoned either by former owners or in the wild. At last count, Doña Alba María has 65 species of birds and about 30 of mammals and reptiles, including toucans, a crested eagle, a king vulture, an ocelot, four jaguars, white-tailed deer, and both collared and white-lipped peccaries (including one albino). Open daily 8 a.m. to 4 p.m. Admission $2 adults and $1 children, but dig deeper and leave a donation: the jaguars need a bigger enclosure and there are always more mouths to feed. A gift shop has handcrafts, T-shirts, ice cream, and cold drinks.

Where to Stay and Eat in and near Ciudad Quesada

If you choose a small-city setting or are caught between buses and need to stay in Ciudad Quesada, here are two hotels. **Hotel Conquistador,** (506) 460-0546, fax (506) 460-6311, a few blocks from downtown near the CATUZON office, is a 47-room, two-story hotel, simply furnished and clean. Single $25, double $40, taxes included. **Hotel & Casino Central,** (506) 460-0301, fax (506) 460-0391, on the west side of the park downtown, is a 48-room, three-story hotel. Pleasant rooms offer comforters, reading lamps, TV, and fans; $15 to $25. Guided tours available to Arenal Volcano and Caño Negro.

El Tucano Resort and Thermal Spa is 5 miles (8 km) northeast of Ciudad Quesada on the road to Aguas Zarcas, (506) 233-8936, (506) 460-3152, fax (506) 221-9095, (506) 460-1692; e-mail meliatuc@sol.racsa.co.cr; Web site centralamerica.com/cr/hotel/tucano.htm. The country inn set amid 500 wooded acres (182 ha), complete with a fine Italian restaurant, tennis courts, swimming pools, miniature golf, health clinic, paths through a primary forest, a natural sauna whose steam comes from hot springs, and two Jacuzzis fed by thermal water. Fresh flowers grace the desks in the 90 spacious, carpeted, tastefully furnished rooms. Guests can bathe at the base of a small waterfall in the cold river water and choose the temperature they like best by their distance from the hot springs. The small resort offers ample opportunity to enjoy nature by bird-watching, hiking, horseback riding, or simply contemplating the forest from river or pools. One mile (1.5 km) of trails wind through the hotel's forest, and more are being added. Double $85; suites from $105.

An outdoor fitness area in the forest promotes exercise in harmony with nature. The spa has dry and humid saunas, Jacuzzis, and a gym, with separate areas for men and women. These thermal waters were long believed to be effective for treatment of arthritis, skin and kidney disorders, rheumatism, and sinus problems. Based on tests of the water, a clinic has been established here to offer treatments for healing, beauty, body care, and rejuvenation. Therapies include the thermal water, mud baths, massage, aromatherapy, and electrotherapy. Customized programs based on a patient's diagnosis are supervised by experts from Romania. Packages available.

Trips are arranged to local attractions such as Arenal Volcano, Caño Negro, and Venado Caves. Transfers from San José arranged.

Hotel La Garza (15 minutes north of Ciudad Quesada between Florencia and Muelle), (506) 475-5222, telephone/fax (506) 475-5015; Web site www.magi.com/crica/hotels/lagza.html, is built along the Platanar River within sight of Arenal Volcano. Twelve spacious rooms are in bungalows with river and volcano views. French doors open onto private terraces. Each high-ceilinged room has pretty hardwood floors, large windows, two double beds, telephone, and ceiling fans. Single $64, double $74.

The restaurant, a cloth-tablecloth place, and bar are in what was the gracious main house of the Hacienda Platanar. Polished wooden floors inside continue onto the wide veranda for outdoor dining. The place exudes tranquility. Access to the restaurant and a swimming pool/Jacuzzi area is across a photogenic hanging footbridge over the river.

Hotel La Garza, along the Platanar River

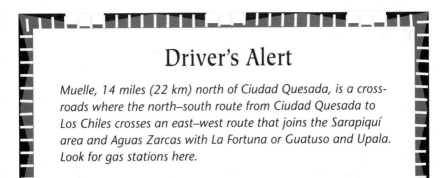

Driver's Alert

Muelle, 14 miles (22 km) north of Ciudad Quesada, is a cross-roads where the north–south route from Ciudad Quesada to Los Chiles crosses an east–west route that joins the Sarapiquí area and Aguas Zarcas with La Fortuna or Guatuso and Upala. Look for gas stations here.

Garza means egret or heron, and the hotel's name hints of abundant birdlife here. Some 740 acres (300 ha) of rain forest have trails for guests to hike or horseback ride. La Garza is a working dairy and cattle ranch, so mount up and join the cowboys if you wish. Guided bird tours can be arranged, as can trips to Arenal Volcano (30 minutes away), Tabacón Hot Springs, Caño Negro, Venado Caves, La Fortuna waterfall, and La Marina Zoo. Hot-air balloon rides are an option.

Tilajari Resort Hotel, (506) 469-9091, fax (506) 469-9095; e-mail tilajarians.goldnet.co.cr; Web site www.200.9.63.176/Tilajari/, has 60 rooms situated near the banks of the San Carlos River in sight of Arenal Volcano. Facilities include pools, four outdoor lighted tennis courts, two indoor courts, racquetball courts, sauna, Jacuzzi, restaurant, and bar. Newest addition is a butterfly garden (so far, about 200 butterflies representing 20 species) with a pretty fountain and flowering plants; a rancho alongside has educational displays. The 30 acres (74 ha) of hotel gardens contain more than 150 species of fruit trees and tropical plants, including 50 orchid species. A butterfly, medicinal plant, and garden tour is free to overnight guests.

Gracious lodging quarters are quiet, located away from the sports areas, restaurant, and pools. Surrounded by manicured lawns and gardens, spacious rooms have air conditioning, ceiling fans, satellite TV, and telephones; singles from $72; doubles, $82; junior suites, $110. All open onto private covered terraces.

Watch for crocodiles along the riverbank. Keel-billed and chestnut-mandibled toucans raised here have chosen to stay—their wings are not clipped—and seem to enjoy posing for photos. Owners Jaime Hamilton and Ricardo Araya hope that a great green macaw added to the menagerie will do the same. I saw a young sloth curled up in one of the many fruit trees that supply produce for the restaurant, which is open to the public. Meals are excellent: breakfast $8, lunch or dinner $13.50. Bring your camera to breakfast or lunch: bird-feeding stations are nearby. You're sure to see scarlet-rumped tanagers.

Tours of the 750-acre (300-ha) Tilajari rain forest are either by horse or tractor-drawn cart to the forest's edge for a hike on foot ($10). Other tours include visits to the Caño Negro refuge (full day, with a drive to Los Chiles and a boat trip on the Río Frío, $48); Venado Caves; La Fortuna waterfall ($45 each for two persons); and Arenal Volcano (a late afternoon/night tour that stops at Tabacón Hot Springs). Tilajari offers a safari float on the Peñas Blancas River in two-man rubber duckies (easy paddling) and white-water rafting on the Sarapiquí ($60). Guides for Tilajari trips are trained, bilingual, excellent at spotting species, and knowledgeable about local history and geography.

Packages include round-trip transfer from San José. The Tilajari is just west of the Muelle intersection, 73 miles (117 km) from San José, about 2½ hours; 40 minutes from Arenal Volcano.

CAÑO NEGRO NATIONAL WILDLIFE REFUGE

Location: 22 miles (36 km) E of Upala, 14 miles (23 km) SW of Los Chiles.
Size: 24,633 acres (9,969 ha).
Hours: 8 a.m. to 4 p.m.
Cost: $1; camping $2 per person per day.
Information/Reservations: Telephone hotline 192 (see Appendix A: Parks and Reserves Information), (506) 460-1412, fax (506) 460-0644.

The centerpiece of this refuge for about 400 species of resident and migrant birds is Caño Negro Lake, which covers some 2,225 acres (900 ha) with up to 10 feet (3 m) of water in the rainy season. As the dry season progresses, it diminishes to a few pools, streams, and an arm of the river that feeds it. In drier months, January to April, visitors who wait patiently and discreetly in sight of the remaining water holes can watch a variety of animals come to drink.

The country's largest colony of Neotropical olivaceous cormorants is found here, and it's a good place to see roseate spoonbills, wood storks, species of ducks you never imagined existed, snowy egrets, five species of kingfisher, and green-backed herons. Jabiru storks sometimes visit. Other animals live at Caño Negro as well: three species of monkeys, sloths, river otters, peccaries, white-tailed deer, silky anteaters, bats, and tayras. Endangered mammal and reptile species include the tapir, jaguar, ocelot, cougar, and crocodile.

During a few magical hours on a boat, I saw some of these birds plus jacanas, two groups of spider monkeys, three of howlers, a red-lored parrot, a black-bellied whistling duck, anhingas with their wings spread to dry, caimans, iguanas, a great egret, and, for the thrill of the day, a common potoo looking for all the world like a part of the branch on which it was perched. How the boatman spotted it is a mystery.

From January to April, less than 4 inches (100 mm) of rain falls; the total averages 138 inches (3,500 mm). South and west of the lake, where the land rises abruptly from the plain to the Guanacaste Mountain Range, rainfall can reach 158 inches (4,000 mm) a year. Elevation of the lake is about 100 feet (30 m).

One aim of this refuge is to help improve the economic well-being of its neighbors by promoting sustainable ways to exploit natural resources. A tree nursery established with area families provides trees to reforest parts of the refuge and the basin of the Río Frío, with some sold for profit. Freshwater turtles are raised; 30 percent are released and the rest sold. Families are allowed to fish in the lagoons when they are drying up, and the refuge helps find a market for the catch. About 50 species of fish are found at Caño Negro, including an unusual gar. Under an agreement with the local development association, the wildlife department allows cattle to graze here in dry season when the lake recedes, a controversial issue with some who point to the erosion cattle cause along riverbanks and damage to wildlife, such as destruction of caiman eggs.

Protection of these wetlands and remaining forest has received a shot in the arm with creation of a Friends of the Earth biological research center at Caño Negro, near refuge headquarters. Laboratories and accommodations for tropical wetland researchers facilitate study of the fragile ecosystem. Equally important is the focus on sustainable development projects with the 200 families who live within the refuge, to provide economic alternatives and discourage poaching.

Camping is allowed. Limited overnight space in a house at the ranger station in Caño Negro is $5 per person. In dry season, visitors can explore on foot or rent horses; in rainy months, community members take visitors out in their boats for $11 an hour.

Getting There

There are two main entrances to the refuge: the town of Caño Negro, site of the headquarters, and on the Río Frío from Los Chiles. Many river tours do not go all the way to headquarters.

By bus: From Upala to Caño Negro; from Ciudad Quesada to Los Chiles.
By car: Town of Caño Negro accessible by road from Upala, San Rafael de Guatuso, and Los Chiles (latter not recommended). For Los Chiles entrance, take a tour from your lodge that includes guide, land transport, and boat trip, or hire a local guide and boat at Los Chiles. During the rainy season four-wheel-drive may be needed for the final part of route from Upala. Other: Hotels and agencies in the north central section offer day tours.

Where to Stay near Caño Negro

Small, inexpensive, very rustic cabins are near Caño Negro's western entrance. In Upala, try **Cabinas Maleku** near the bus station, (506) 470-0142; in Caño Negro, **Cabinas El Querque**, (506) 460-4164 (leave a message). Lodging is sometimes available at refuge headquarters. Most travelers enter through the more-visited eastern entrance near Los Chiles, staying in hotels listed in this section and the La Fortuna-Arenal-Tilarán section.

LA LAGUNA DEL LAGARTO LODGE, PRIVATE RESERVE

Location: 93 miles (150 km) N of San José, 23 miles (37 km) N of Pital, 4 miles (7 km) from Boca Tapada.

Rates: Single $72, double $54 each, including meals and taxes plus trail walks and canoe rides. No credit cards. Four-day, three-night package with lodging, meals, taxes, and transportation, $198 per person.

Information/Reservations: (506) 289-8163, telephone/fax (506) 289-5295; e-mail lagarto@sol.racsa.co.cr; Web site www.worldheadquarters.com.

Spider monkeys moved through tall treetops, sometimes with spectacular leaps. I would swear I saw one slide down a long liana. Sitting on a bench across a small pond from them, I watched as they hung by their tails to feed on tall-forest fruits. Flock after flock of noisy parrots and parakeets flew in, stayed a bit, and moved on. Jesus Christ lizards skittered across the water. On the short walk to the pond from the lodge, I had stopped to watch white-fronted parrots, a Montezuma oropendola, and squirrels eating *pejibayes*. This was all before breakfast.

La Laguna del Lagarto is a watery world—lagoons, rivers, swamps—but also a place of striking forest. Owner Vinzenz Schmack has almost 250 acres (100 ha), and a neighboring forest of 1,000 acres (400 ha) extends the habitat for such species as white-faced, howler, and spider monkeys, *tepezcuintle*, great curassow, aracaris, chestnut-mandibled and keel-billed toucans, and great green macaws. Some 350 bird species have been identified so far. A butterfly garden focuses on species found in the area, especially the remarkable morpho.

A Tayra? Never Heard of It.

So, what's a tayra? A member of the weasel family, it has a glossy chocolate-brown to black coat and a long, bushy tail, its long back slightly humped at the hindquarters. Although in some of its range the tayra's head and neck are tan, gray, or yellowish, in Costa Rica the entire animal is dark-colored. Its den is in a tree hollow or a hole in the ground, and it searches during the day for food both on the ground and in trees—it's an agile climber. Tayras (Eira barbara) include bird eggs and nestlings in their diets, along with small mammals, lizards, insects, and fruit.

Ten miles (16 km) of marked trails open the forest for exploration. Tiny red frogs with blue legs, known as poison-dart frogs, are easily seen on the forest floor. Small green frogs with black spots are more elusive. Look for tapir tracks.

A different habitat can be explored by canoe in two swamp lagoons. Moving silently, with only the sound of the oar dipping into the water, brings you close to the spirit of the place. On my quiet trip, the green-backed heron made several appearances, kingfishers flashed by, and a lineated woodpecker perched on a lifeless trunk in the water. Vinzenz pointed to another trunk where small sleeping bats made a dark line down the tree. Orchids and bromeliads were everywhere.

A nighttime walk with a good flashlight reveals bright eyes of caimans along the edge of the lagoons. Caimans, or *lagartos*, are also visible during the day, and gave the place its name. Lodge guests can ride horseback along the edge of the forest ($15) or take a boat down the San Carlos River to the San Juan ($25), which forms Costa Rica's border with Nicaragua. I longed for more time just to sit on the veranda and bird-watch. Local guides are available, and a trained naturalist guide can be arranged with prior notice.

Twenty rooms are distributed in several buildings; some baths have hot water. Furnishings are simple; tropical wooden walls shine. Each room has ceiling fans. Windows are screened, with reason—bring repellent. In the open-air dining room, food is an appetizing mix of Costa Rican and European. Pineapple, papaya, oranges, yuca, *tiquisque*, and *pejibaye* are grown near the lodge. The *pejibaye* also supply heart of palm—watch it being cut fresh for your meal. Black pepper is another crop.

The lodge is about 330 feet (100 m) above sea level, and temperatures range from 68°F to 95°F (20°C to 35°C). February to mid-May are the driest months, but for rainy times, boots and ponchos are available.

Getting There

By bus: From San José and Ciudad Quesada, go to Pital, and take connecting bus to Boca Tapada; with advance notice, lodge personnel will pick you up there.

By car: Road paved to Pital, then 22 miles (35 km) of gravel road through Boca Tapada to the lodge.

Other: Round-trip transfers from San José, $150 for up to four people.

LA FORTUNA–ARENAL–TILARAN ROUTE

LA FORTUNA

Located 93 miles (150 km) northwest of San José, La Fortuna is the eastern gateway to the Lake Arenal region. Arenal Volcano, a presence in this small place, dominates the horizon. The town (population 6,977) is a convenient base for trips to the volcano, Lake Arenal, Caño Negro National Wildlife

Refuge, hot springs at Tabacón, the 230-foot (70-meter) La Fortuna waterfall just south of town (very steep trail), and Venado Caves, a nearly 2-mile (3-km) subterranean adventure not for the claustrophobic. A bank and gasoline stations are the last you will see for a while if you're heading west, and sodas (small cafes), restaurants, and gift shops are strung along the main street.

The 10 miles (16 km) to the turnoff to Arenal Volcano National Park skirt the volcano; forested slopes give way to ash and fumaroles as you approach its western face. Lava flows are usually visible only on the western side, though the sound and eruptions are impressive from La Fortuna and environs.

Tour Companies in La Fortuna

Aguas Bravas, (506) 292-2072, (506) 479-9025; fax (506) 229-4837; Web site www.hway.com/arenas/abravas/, has an Adventure Center in La Fortuna that offers rafting on the Peñas Blancas River, class II–III, for $37; and two rafting trips on the Sarapiquí, for beginners or experienced rafters, $60. Half-day and full-day mountain-bike trips range from $45 to $65, with guides and bicycles provided. The horseback ride to Monteverde takes 6 hours, $65. The Adventure Center is directly across from the plaza.

Aventuras Arenal, (506) 479-9133, fax (506) 479-9259; e-mail avarenal@sol.racsa.co.cr; Web site www.cmnet.co.cr/adarenal, offers a four-hour mountain-bike tour that takes in Lake Arenal and Arenal Volcano plus a forest trail ($45); horseback riding to La Fortuna waterfall is $20 per person (bilingual guide arranged for an added fee). Venado Caves is $35 and Caño Negro $45. Transfers are available from La Fortuna and area hotels to anywhere in the country; for example, to Sugar Beach ($145 per person), Manuel Antonio ($160), or Montezuma ($180). Ask about three- and four-night packages from San José that include Arenal Volcano, Tabacón Resort, and Caño Negro. The office is on the main road, 1 block east of the gas station; international telephone and fax service.

AveRica Bird Tours, telephone/fax (506) 479-9456; e-mail averica @yellowweb.co.cr, specializes in small groups (usually four persons max), personal service, and unique tours. Owners Aaron Sekerak and Elissa Conger design bird tours and offer a number of single- or multiday tours, with the welcome out for novices as well as life-list birders. An early-bird or afternoon walk in the Fortuna area might show birders parrots, toucans, oropendolas, tanagers, and parakeets. The more experienced might see royal flycatchers, white-fronted nunbirds, or cinnamon woodpeckers. Rates are $25 in the morning, $15 in the afternoon. A full day is $40, including lunch, birding, and a look at some farming practices. One two-day Caño Negro special includes opportunities to see land, forest, and water birds; another visits Juan Castro Blanco National Park for resplendent quetzals, toucanets, collared redstarts, and spangled-cheeked tanagers. Aaron and Elissa, authors of *Travel and Site Guide to the Birds of Costa Rica*, lead most of the tours.

La Fortuna

Sunset Tours, (506) 479-9415, fax (506) 479-9099; e-mail sunset@ns
.goldnet.co.cr; Web site www.goldnet.co.cr/sunset/home.html, has a full
menu of area tours: hiking at Arenal Volcano National Park ($25), Caño
Negro ($45), Venado Caves ($25), and the children's rain forest, Bosque
Eterno de los Niños ($45). Pickup service is available from other area sites
for a fee and transfers elsewhere in the country. A car-and-boat journey takes
visitors from La Fortuna to Monteverde in three hours ($45). Ask about
one- and two-night packages from San José; Mainor Castro will do his best
to fit your needs. The office, located one block north of the plaza, offers fax
and international telephone services, sells stamps, and has a gift shop.

Getting There
By bus: Buses run from San José, Ciudad Quesada, and Tilarán.
By car: From Ciudad Quesada or via San Ramón; from the northern Pacific
region, via Cañas and Tilarán.
By air: No air service yet, but SANSA has plans. Check.

Where to Stay and Eat in and Just East of La Fortuna
Friendly **Hotel Las Colinas,** (telephone/fax (506) 479-9107; e-mail
hcolinas@sol.racsa.co.cr, is one block south of main street. Its 17 spacious
rooms are plain but very clean. Rates range from $12 to $34. Front rooms
have a view of Arenal Volcano.

Hotel Rancho Corcovado (506) 479-9300, telephone/fax (506) 479-9090,
is 4 miles (6 km) east of La Fortuna; Arenal Volcano looms in the distance.

The 23 rooms face a pretty swimming pool; each is spacious, with telephone and private bath. The restaurant and bar are in a large open-sided structure overlooking a small lake, where you may spot a caiman or two. Birds abound, including violaceous trogons, kingfishers, and four types of toucans. Egrets sleep here at night. Notice the gourd tree near the restaurant. Tours arranged to Caño Negro ($45), Arenal and Tabacón ($37), and La Fortuna waterfall ($15). Single $37, double $50, taxes included.

Hotel San Bosco, (506) 479-9050, fax (506) 479-9109; e-mail sanbosco @ns.goldnet.co.cr, is a pleasant place to stay, created by owners Celso, Flor, and family. Not all 29 rooms have volcano views, but not to worry. A covered open-air volcano-viewing room on the third floor has chairs and tables where you can watch to your heart's content. Porches, verandas, orthopedic mattresses, architectural accents of river stone, and reading lamps are among the amenities; the swimming pool is new. Tour arrangements are through Sunset Tours across the street. Rancho La Cascada Restaurant is handy for meals. Guarded parking. The hotel is 150 m north of the plaza on the main road through La Fortuna. Eighteen air-conditioned rooms in the two-story portion are single $40, double $46; the 11 with fans in the refurbished original structure are single $30, double $35, taxes included.

Las Cabañitas Resort, (506) 479-9343, fax (506) 479-9408, half a mile (1 km) east of La Fortuna, looks like a tiny village with its cluster of 30 individual cabañas, swimming pool, restaurant, gift shop, and snack bar. Delightful rooms have vaulted wooden ceilings, polished wood floors, ceiling fans, and some king-size beds. Guests enjoy individual porches. Handicapped accessible. The tour office offers a late afternoon/evening trip to Arenal ($25), Caño Negro ($45), or Venado Caves, or horseback ride to La Fortuna waterfall. Transfers available. Single $65, double $73.

ARENAL VOLCANO NATIONAL PARK
Location: 10 miles (16 km) W of La Fortuna, 85 miles (137 km) NW of San José.
Size: 29,692 acres (12,016 ha).
Hours: Daily 8 a.m. to 10 p.m.
Cost: $6.
Information: Telephone hotline 192 (see Appendix A: Parks and Reserves Information), (506) 460-1412, fax (506) 460-0644.

Arenal is one of the world's most active volcanoes, thundering and blowing since 1968. Signs along the dirt road caution visitors to view the fiery colossus from a safe distance. Climbing to the crater would be hazardous to your health; in fact, it could be fatal. Respect the warning signs.

The volcano, located in the Tilarán Mountains, dominates the landscape of this park and of the region. After a 400-year dormancy, Arenal devastated more than 4 square miles (10 sq km) in the last three days of July 1968. It has been continuously active ever since. The flow comes from a horseshoe-shaped crater open to the northwest, west, and southwest. Eruptions send clouds of ash and fiery materials into the sky. Lava flows, visible with binoculars in daytime, are spectacular at night. Actually, the volcano has four craters, three new ones created on the west flank when it blew on July 29, 1968, at 7:30 a.m. Eighty-seven people from the villages of Tabacón and Pueblo Nuevo died; two days later, eight rescue workers died from a cloud of hot gases.

Las Coladas Trail, which begins at the first park station from the highway, goes to a lava bed from a 1993 flow. Allow about 90 minutes for the 1.7-mile (2.8-km), mostly level trail. Los Tucanes Trail, named for the five species of toucans here, crosses the lava flow and continues into forest from this same entrance (allow about three hours) though you can enter it farther down the road. Howler and white-face monkeys also roam these parts. Heliconias Trail, which can be walked in 30 minutes, shows visitors some of the vegetation that has returned since the big eruption. It crosses Las Coladas Trail, for those who wish to continue to the lava flow.

Though Arenal Volcano is the most popular attraction, the park also includes habitat along Lake Arenal's shores and protects important watershed for Lake Arenal, whose waters feed the country's largest hydroelectric project and an irrigation project that encompasses some 172,970 acres (70,000 ha) in Guanacaste. Take Sendero Los Miradores Trail near the park's main entrance; less than a mile long (1.2 km), it leads to a lookout point for the lake, volcano, and dam.

Temperatures here are between 55°F and 64°F (12.6°C and 17.5°C); average annual rainfall, 138 to 197 inches (3,500 to 5,000 mm). Maximum elevation in the park is 5,538 feet (1,633 m).

Though Arenal became a national park only in 1994, it had previously been in a protected zone. It is part of the Arenal Conservation Area. The park station has rest rooms, a parking area, and water. By the time you arrive, a visitor center should be open with a cafeteria, gift shop, small auditorium, and exhibits on the area's volcanology, biodiversity, history, energy potential, and cultural archaeology.

Getting There

By bus: San Carlos/Arenal/Turrialba bus passes about 1 mile (2 km) from the main park entrance. Get off at the road at the east end of the dam.
By car: From Pacific beach areas, take the Inter-American to Cañas, go northeast to Tilarán and Nuevo Arenal. From San José, come either via San Ramón or Ciudad Quesada to La Fortuna and head west toward Tilarán. Road to entrance is at the east end of the dam.
Other: Area hotels and tour agencies offer trips to the park, many with the option for nighttime viewing. Day trips from San José.

Where to Stay and Eat from La Fortuna
to Arenal Volcano National Park

(*In order of location going west from La Fortuna*) **Albergue Ecoturistico La Catarata,** (506) 479-9522, fax (506) 479-9178, is 1 mile (2 km) west. Owned and operated by a community association, it has eight rustic cabins with private baths and a typical restaurant. Single $21, double $31, including breakfast.

A sustainable development project started with help from World Wildlife Fund Canada, the Canadian International Development Agency, and the Arenal Conservation area, this ecolodge brings increased income to members of this farming and dairying village while helping protect the region's biological diversity. Community members do all the cooking, cleaning, and guiding, in addition to working on the farms. They have organic, butterfly, and orchid gardens; and are developing a *tepezcuintle* breeding area. (*Tepezcuintles*, large, nocturnal rodents, have been hunted heavily in Costa Rica for their excellent meat.)

Members lead trips to Cerro Chato Volcano, La Fortuna waterfall, hot springs, or Lake Arenal fishing or boating. The restaurant is open to the public, so stop by, meet the members, and see community and conservation at work. This is one of three such ecolodge projects: the others are Las Heliconias in Bijagua near Upala, and in Monte Los Olivos near Monteverde.

Jungla y Senderos Los Lagos, telephone/fax (506) 479-9126, is a marvelous spot for viewing the volcano from several perspectives. About 3.7 miles (6 km) from La Fortuna on the main road to Arenal, Los Lagos is owned and operated by the Cedeño Villegas family. It offers bungalows near the entrance and rustic cabins in a secluded lakeside setting. Near the road is an eye-catching multilevel swimming pool with a water slide; at the top, water flows out of a cone-shaped replica of the volcano, which rises like a giant behind it. A large Jacuzzi is fed by hot water from the river. The rancho-style restaurant is open to the public.

Nineteen rooms in four bungalows have small refrigerators, big showers, porches with tables and chairs, and fans. Construction is a nice mix of river stone and wood. Standard double $60, deluxe double $70; single $35 and $45, taxes included.

A 10-minute drive, with dramatic volcano views, goes to a placid lake with reflections of forest around it, the quiet sound of the chestnut-mandibled toucan, and a sky dominated by Arenal Volcano. It is a special, silent place. Picnic areas are spaced along one side of the lake, along with rustic cabins of river rock, wood, and bamboo. Each has a private bath, cold-water shower, tile floor, and electricity, $25 for two. Covered ranchos offer outdoor areas for relaxing and cooking.

In this other-world atmosphere under the volcano, where no music and no motorcycles are allowed, you can walk forest trails, paddle the lake, or ride horseback. An 2,624-foot (800-m) trail leads to lava beds. The family plans to keep this secluded area nature-oriented.

An admission fee of $5 for adults and $3 for children entitles day visitors to swim in pools, visit the lake, and hike trails. A guided horseback tour ($13) takes guests through primary forest, over an old lava flow, to a *mirador* with impressive views of Arenal, Tenorio, and Miravalles Volcanoes. A tractor-driven cart gets visitors without transport to the lakes.

Cabañas Arenal Paraíso is 4.3 miles (7 km) west of La Fortuna (cellular phone 506-383-5658, telephone/fax 506-479-9006); 20 individual cabins with the volcano practically in the front yard. Rooms of beautiful tropical woods have ceiling fans, small refrigerators, good mattresses, and floral comforters. Each cabin has a front porch and windows that face the volcano—deluxe units have glassed-in porches for protected volcano-viewing in windy weather. Guests enjoy the Jacuzzi and pool, natural mineral waters, and forest trails to a hot spring, small river, and the Arenal River. Standard double $47; deluxe, $52.

This working 148-acre (60-ha) farm has 49 acres (20 ha) of primary forest. Wake up to the sounds of howler monkeys, toucans, parrots, and oropendolas; watch hummingbirds in the pretty gardens, and the cows being moved on the highway to the milking barn—with Arenal as a backdrop. The pool and restaurant are open to the public, as is the gift shop, which offers T-shirts hand-painted by members of a local cooperative. Owners Oscar and Roxana and family are gracious hosts who offer tours to Los Lagos and La Fortuna waterfall and arrange transfers.

Linda Vista del Norte Lodge, (506) 380-0847, fax (506) 479-9443, is beyond the Arenal Volcano National Park visitor center, across some rivers and up a mountain, about 16 miles (25 km) from La Fortuna. Owned by the Badilla Picado family, the modest 11-room lodge has simple furnishings and gorgeous views of forested mountains, Lake Arenal, and the volcano from its hilltop setting. The glassed-in dining room and its outdoor terrace have the best vantage point for volcano-viewing. Rooms on the front face the lake. Single $47, double $65, breakfast and taxes included.

A horseback ride to the volcano is $20, and a tour of the 593-acre (240-ha) farm, which has cattle, forest, and a waterfall, is $12. Horseback trips to San Gerardo Abajo near Monteverde can be arranged. Guests can hike trails on the farm—more than 200 species of birds are in the area. Ask about packages.

To reach Linda Vista del Norte, turn at the road to the park visitor center and follow signs along the gravel road for 5 miles (8.5 km).

Arenal Vista Lodge, (506) 220-1712, fax (506) 232-3321; e-mail explore @sol.racsa.co.cr; Web site www.com/arenal.htm, is across an unbridged river, but not to worry—fording it simply adds to the adventure. Each of the 25 spacious rooms, terraced up a hillside with views of lake and volcano, has its own balcony, reading lights, pitched ceiling, and large walk-in closet. Single $60, double $70. Meals are served buffet-style in the large dining room: $6 breakfast, $8 lunch, $10 dinner, plus taxes. Lectures and videos are presented in a theater area. An open-air *mirador* with tables and chairs allows guests to view the volcano in community.

The forest comes right up to the buildings, with three marked, self-guided trails available. You'll hear howler monkeys in the morning and owls at night and see some of the 200 resident bird species (or perhaps Neotropical migrants) found in this area. Watch for toucans at the papaya trees. Enjoy horseback tours of the forest ($10) and boat trips on the lake for fishing or birdwatching ($20 per person). Boat transfers across the lake are $15 per person.

From the Arenal park entrance, follow Arenal Vista Lodge signs.

TABACON HOT SPRINGS

Location: 7.5 miles (12 km) from La Fortuna, toward Arenal.
Hours: Daily 10 a.m. to 10 p.m.
Cost: Adults $14, children 4 to 9 $7.
Information/Reservations: (506) 222-1072, telephone/fax (506) 479-9033, fax (506) 221-3075.

In the shadow of Arenal Volcano, Tabacón is a wonderland of gardens, paths, ponds, streams, and pools: five thermal and one with cool water, plus a whirlpool. The rush of river water blends with the sound of the small waterfalls where bathers sit beneath naturally heated waters. Rising steam lends mystery to this fairyland with a phenomenal view of the volcano. Tabacón also has a gift shop, bar, lounging areas, a restaurant overlooking the gardens, packages including one or two meals. Mud facials and massages are available.

Guests may hike a half-mile (1 km) trail along the forest to a small volcanic lake. Don't forget binoculars—birding is good here. After-dark visits are also popular for a chance to relax after a day of sightseeing or to experience the glow of Arenal's fireworks.

Across the road Tabacón offers another attractive, less-expensive option: bathe in the hot springs for $5. With a more natural ambience, set in the forest along the river, it lacks the volcano view but offers such amenities as changing rooms, restrooms, and landscaped grounds.

Getting There

By bus: La Fortuna/Tilarán bus passes directly in front.
By car: Watch for signs on the road between La Fortuna and Arenal. Guarded parking.
Other: Tour agencies and hotels in Central Valley and the La Fortuna–Arenal area offer day and night tours, often as part of a volcano tour.

Where to Stay and Eat near Tabacón Hot Springs

Tabacón Lodge, (506) 233-0780, (506) 256-0036; fax (506) 221-3075; e-mail tabacon@sol.racsa.co.cr, is 200 m before the hot springs on the road from La Fortuna. In the finishing stages when I saw it, this first-class lodge has 42 lovely rooms (one super-deluxe suite) featuring handcrafted Costa Rican furniture, individual terraces and balconies, volcano views, air conditioning, in-room telephones, and hot mineral-water showers. Many rooms are handicapped accessible and all have front-row seats for volcano-watching. Single $85, double $100, including breakfast and entry to Tabacón Hot Springs.

Five acres (2 ha) of grounds include gardens (more than 300 plant species), forest, trails, artificial lake, swimming pool (half hot and half cold), and a natural Jacuzzi. Bird-watching decks look at canopy level into the Tabacón River Canyon, and spider and howler monkeys move through this habitat.

A snack bar and a rancho serve food; guests may also eat at the restaurant at the hot springs, run by the same company. Massages, manicures, and pedicures are available. Tabacón Lodge offers daily transport from San José and La Fortuna.

ARENAL OBSERVATORY LODGE, PRIVATE RESERVE

Location: *15.5 miles (25 km) W of La Fortuna; 44 miles (71 km) NE of Tilarán; 5.6 miles (9 km) from the turnoff to Arenal Volcano National Park.*
Rates: *Observatory standard rooms, single $52, double $64; superior single $82, superior double $94. Smithsonian superior rooms, single $72, double $84; Casona farmhouse single $35, double $42. Breakfast buffet $8, lunch $12, dinner $13, box lunches $8, plus taxes. Rates including breakfast and dinner available. Packages include a three-day, two-night tour: $345 (double occupancy), including round-trip from San José, lodging, most meals, guided waterfall, lava flow, and Cerro Chato hikes.*
Information/Reservations: *(506) 257-9489, fax (506) 257-4220, lodge telephone (506) 695-5033; e-mail suntours@sol.racsa.co.cr.*

At 4:30 a.m. a thunderous explosion brought us from our beds to the door in one swift leap. Outside, Arenal Volcano's cone, about 1.2 miles (2 km) away, was sharp against the dark blue of the night sky; stars were brilliant. From the crater, red rocks and thin streams of lava began to make their way down the slopes.

Arenal Observatory Lodge is front-row center for viewing eruptions of one of the world's most active volcanoes. Built in 1987 as a laboratory and base for scientists doing long-term geological and biological research, the facility is now a top destination for nature travelers, Smithsonian scientists, and Earthwatch groups.

I was in a small group that jumped up twice during dinner to pay homage to the spectacle of steady, hot rain. Later, two of us sat patiently on the elevated, covered observatory platform trying to elicit a command

A volcano in your backyard at Arenal Observatory Lodge

performance, but Arenal seemed unconcerned with our schedules—the real show began after everyone was in bed. In all, I sprang up for four explosions and saluted two rumbles from beneath the covers.

That was in the old days before volcano-view rooms were added, rooms from which, theoretically, you can lie in bed and watch what some call "cosmic fireworks." I, for one, cannot do it: each explosion brings me to my feet—the power and the beauty somehow demand it.

Two of the nine standard observatory rooms have direct views of the volcano, while four superior rooms have excellent volcano views. The beautiful Smithsonian block of 10 rooms, across a long suspension bridge from observatory rooms and the dining room, has plate-glass windows that bring the energy of the fiery colossus into each room. These larger rooms have Tiffany-style lamps, ceiling fans, and pretty comforters, some king-size beds. A volcano-viewing room upstairs offers yet another perspective. In the original farmhouse a short distance from the lodge are five rooms that share two hot-water baths, a sitting area with a fireplace, and views of lake and volcano from the porch.

Guests have access to almost 300 acres (120 ha) of primary and secondary forest and a 432-acre (175-ha) reforestation project of pine, eucalyptus, and macadamia (watch macadamia nuts being harvested and husked). Trails through lush forest lead to a lovely waterfall or to Cerro Chato (an extinct crater near Arenal) and its green lagoon. Incredibly beautiful forest entices you step after step up the steep crater trail, even when it's bathed in cloud or washed by rain. Once there, you can canoe on the lake. Guided Cerro Chato walk is $5. Walking is easy around the farm and along roads.

Free to overnight guests are guided waterfall and lava-flow walks, a night lava tour, horseback riding, and mountain biking. Other options include a night tour to Tabacón Hot Springs, day trips to Caño Negro ($65), rafting on the Sarapiquí River ($70), and fishing or boat tours on Lake Arenal.

Elevation at the observatory is 2,428 feet (740 m); annual rainfall is 197 inches (5,000 mm). Drier months are December through May, but rain can occur anytime. In the dining room, guests sample fruits from the area and such typical meals as *olla de carne* (a meat-and-vegetable soup) or *arroz con pollo* (chicken and rice), buffet-style.

Getting There

By bus: Not easy—the Ciudad Quesada/La Fortuna/Tilarán bus leaves a 5.6-mile (9-km) trek to the lodge.

By car: From the turnoff to Arenal park, follow the signs. The road to the observatory is quite tame now—bridges over the rivers and everything. No more standing at the rushing water's edge in rainy season with a thumping heart, wondering if you and the jeep will make it through.

Other: Taxi from La Fortuna. Packages from San José include transportation.

LAKE ARENAL

Archaeological studies show that Indians had small settlements around Lake Arenal, near the volcano, as long ago as 2000 B.C. Today the lake has been greatly enlarged by a dam, completed in 1979 to provide hydroelectric energy. The 24-mile (39-km)-long reservoir is a favorite for fishing, sailing, boating, and kayaking. Windsurfing, however, might be considered king. With its steady strong winds from December to March (60 mph), Lake Arenal is one of the world's best windsurfing destinations. Even in the other months, 15-to-25 mph winds prevail.

The lake covers about 87 square kilometers at 1,791 feet (546 m) elevation. Dam construction began in 1974 and required the relocation of two towns: Arenal and Tronadora. The Arenal-Corobicí Hydroelectric Complex is the country's largest. Waters that feed the turbines flow into an irrigation project in the drier Guanacaste lowlands. Magnificent forests on slopes above the lake, preserved by the park and private reserves such as the Bosque Eterno de los Niños, protect this all-important watershed.

Going west on the road around the northeast side leads to the dam, Nuevo Arenal, and Tilarán. Be alert for one-lane bridges that seem to be mostly on curves. The road can be more potholes than pavement in some places and pavement ends altogether at Nuevo Arenal for about a 6-mile (9-km) stretch going east. While the road is much improved, the perennial paving plans are still just plans. But the scenery is magnificent; you may spot howler monkeys in trees along the road or see the colorful scarlet-rumped tanager flash by. Volcano views framed in forest are memorable; tree ferns, glorious.

Nuevo Arenal was built by the Costa Rican Electrical Institute to replace,

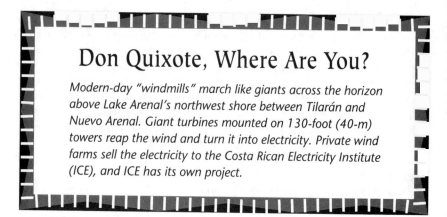

Don Quixote, Where Are You?

Modern-day "windmills" march like giants across the horizon above Lake Arenal's northwest shore between Tilarán and Nuevo Arenal. Giant turbines mounted on 130-foot (40-m) towers reap the wind and turn it into electricity. Private wind farms sell the electricity to the Costa Rican Electricity Institute (ICE), and ICE has its own project.

house by house, the existing town of Arenal flooded by the dam for the hydro-electric project. A quiet little place (population 2,434) with friendly folks, it offers a gas station, inexpensive *cabinas*, and several places to eat. A must is **Pizzaría e Ristorante Tramonti**. Gianni and Adriana make 16 types of pizza and homemade pasta—lasagna, fettuccine, and spaghetti—with Italian cheese and oil. Italian wine available too. Open 11:30 a.m. to 3 p.m. and 5 to 10 p.m., closed Monday in low season. Telephone (506) 694-4282.

Nuevo Arenal is 25 miles (41 km) northwest of La Fortuna, 20 miles (32 km) northeast of Tilarán.

As you continue around the lake, watch for wind energy projects and, on clear days, for views of Arenal Volcano and, to the north, three others: Rincón de la Vieja, Miravalles, and Tenorio.

Getting There
By bus: The Ciudad Quesada/Fortuna/Tilarán bus serves this area.
By car: Take the main road between La Fortuna and Tilarán.

Where to Stay and Eat between Lake Arenal and Nuevo Arenal Town
Arenal Lodge, (506) 228-3189, fax (506) 289-6798; e-mail ArenaLodge @centralamerica.com, is just past the dam and up a paving-stone road through a macadamia farm. Front rooms at the main lodge have impressive volcano views, while those in back are around a brick courtyard graced with orchids. The 12 view rooms are junior suites, with upholstered bamboo couch and chairs, private balconies, and both shower and tub. Single $81, double $87. Six standard rooms, showers only, are single $50, double $55, breakfast included. Ten spacious rooms with kitchenettes, balconies, and good volcano views are in five chalets up from the lodge, doubles $107. The lounge area has a fireplace. There is a Jacuzzi, billiard table, and small library.

Guests often see howler monkeys in the forest at the edge of the gardens and may even spot a tayra or anteater. Hummingbird feeders and platforms for fruit bring a variety of birds to the grounds. The lodge offers lake fishing and tours to Caño Negro, Venado Caves, the hot springs, the base of the volcano, and La Fortuna waterfall. Owner Woodson Brown wrote a handy driving guide covering routes to San José, available for guests.

Los Héroes, (506) 284-6315, fax (506) 441-4193, has 11 rooms in an imposing chalet-style structure on the main road around the north side of Lake Arenal, 18.6 miles (30 km) northwest of La Fortuna and 10.5 (17 km) from Arenal volcano. The pool and Jacuzzi have lake and volcano views. The restaurant, with decor straight from the Swiss Alps—big cowbells, red-and-white-checkered curtains—is open to the public. Choose from a menu that includes meat or cheese fondue, *rösti* (a great potato dish), spaghetti, and sausages. Double $55 to $65, suite $75, including breakfast and taxes. Two apartments for up to six people are $115 each. No credit cards.

Marina Club Hotel is 22 miles (35 km) northwest of La Fortuna, telephone/fax (506) 284-6573. Twelve split-level rooms in bungalows face Lake Arenal. Two couches and cushioned wicker chairs next to a writing table are on the lower level, with beds and a pretty wardrobe on the upper. Water flows from a big clay pot (*tinaja* in Spanish) into a small swimming pool in a garden of colorful shrubs and flowering plants. The restaurant is open to the public. Options include a day trip to Venado Caves, horseback rides around the lake, and free use of canoes. Rooms are $75 including breakfast. (VISA only accepted.)

La Ceiba Tree Lodge is about one hour from La Fortuna and 4 miles (6 km) before Nuevo Arenal, telephone/fax (506) 385-1540, (506) 694-4297; e-mail fingrspm@sol.racsa.co.cr. The bed-and-breakfast has four bright, airy rooms that open off a tiled terrace with a panoramic view of Lake Arenal and spectacular sunsets. Single $30, double $42, including breakfast. Owner Malte von Schlippenbach can provide evening meals on request, from simple dishes to exclusive dinners. In front of the lodge is its namesake: the 197-foot (60-m) ceiba tree, thought to be more than 500 years old. Ceibas (kapok trees in English) were revered by indigenous peoples; let its energy speak to you. On paths in the forest on three sides of the lodge, guests may see three kinds of toucans, howler monkeys, or sloths and enjoy two brooks with small cascades. Rent boats for sailing, rowing, and fishing; take sailing lessons; tour the lake on a Hobie Cat; rent a mountain bike; or go horseback riding. Malte suggests day tours to the hot springs or volcano, rafting, or jungle hikes.

Villa Decary is about 1 mile (2 km) west of Arenal Botanical Gardens and 1 mile east of Nuevo Arenal, (506) 383-3012, fax (506) 94-4330; Web site www.hotels.co.cr/decary.html. Here guests are more than just a name on the register. Owners Jeff Crandall and Bill Hemmer are innkeepers in the finest tradition. They tell guests about local fairs—even go with them—and advise on local restaurants and sightseeing. Take time to enjoy the orchids in the garden and the path around some of this 7-acre (2.8-ha) former fruit-and-coffee farm. Howler monkeys cross the yard to eat in the papaya trees. Jeff is a birder and Bill's specialty is palms. The pretty dining room opens onto a deck through two sets of double doors. With notice, lunch or dinner can be served.

Each of the main building's five tastefully decorated rooms has a queen and full bed with orthopedic mattresses, reading lamp, ceiling fan, desk, private balcony set up for bird-watching, and great lake views. Beautiful tropical woods, woven Guatemalan bedspreads, hand-carved doors, and other decorator touches make this a real jewel. Single $49, double $59, including full breakfast. A separate *casita* for up to four persons, including equipped kitchen, is available for longer stays, $69. No credit cards.

ARENAL BOTANICAL GARDENS
Location: 2.5 miles (4 km) E of the town of Nuevo Arenal.
Hours: 9 a.m. to 5 p.m. daily.
Admission: $4.
Information: (506) 694-4273, fax (506) 694-4086; e-mail exoticseeds @hotmail.com; Web site www.allgoods.com/botanical.

Heliconias, begonias, orchids, tree ferns, gingers, anthuriums, euphorbias: 2,500 varieties of plants from around the world thrive here, including many native to Costa Rica. In 1991 owner Michael LeMay, who has collected plants for 19 years, began to convert degraded pastureland into a breathtaking garden; he opened it to the public in 1993. Easy trails weave through dazzling displays laid out to resemble natural forest but with groupings that permit the visitor to stand in one area and see varieties in the same genus or family. There are 200 kinds of bromeliads, 200 orchid varieties, and more than 300 types of palms and ferns. See cycads, dracaena, euphorbia, gingers, heliconias, passiflora, schefflera, spathifphyllum, and many more. Booklets are available in English, Spanish, and German for self-guided walks. There's also a trail through natural forest that can take up to an hour. Flowers attract butterflies and birds, including six species of hummingbirds.

Michael, who can tell you where he got each plant, set up the garden to preserve native species of plants, create a habitat for birds, insects, and other wildlife, and provide a living classroom for the study of plants.

ECO-LODGE, LAGO COTER, PRIVATE RESERVE
Location: 17 miles (28 km) NE of Tilarán, above Lake Arenal.
Rates: Bungalow single $48, double $66; lodge single $41, double $49. Breakfast $5, lunch or dinner $10. Two-night, three-day package includes lodging, meals, hiking, horseback riding, canoeing, one water sport, and visits to Arenal Volcano, hot springs, and Caño Negro, plus transfers: $420 each double occupancy in the lodge, $454 in bungalows, taxes included.

Villa Decary—an inn above Lake Arenal

Information/Reservations: *(506) 257-5075, fax (506) 257-7065; telephone at lodge for non-office hours (506) 382-3043; e-mail ecolodge@sol.racsa.co.cr.*

Marvelous nature trails traverse the biologically rich forest here. Learn about such things as flying sticks and why some tropical trees shed their bark (to keep epiphytes from taking hold). See a huge mound built by busy leaf-cutter ants and marvel at the free-form sculpture of a vine called "monkey ladder."

On 13 marked trails, well-trained bilingual naturalists help guests appreciate that tropical forests are more than monkeys jumping from branch to branch, than coatis darting across a trail, than the turquoise flash of a scarlet-thighed dacnis against the varied greens of trees and plants. Tropical forests are all of these things, but they're also the tiny flower almost hidden among fallen leaves, an insect disguised as a dried leaf, an animal track in the mud, an elegant tree fern, and thousands of plant and animal species intertwined in a web of life.

A half-day canopy tour ($35) permits visitors to view this web in the upper levels of the forest, where so much of the life is found. The tour begins with a hike to the first platform, reached by climbing a ladder. Treetop travelers move between four platforms along cables and finally rappel back to the forest floor. Platforms range from 92 to 115 feet (28 to 35 m) high.

Guests are invited to record the wildlife seen here; more than 350 birds have been sighted. Leafing through the book, you find monkeys, brocket deer, keel-billed toucans, bare-necked umbrella birds, squirrel cuckoos, and coatis, among others.

Eco-Lodge is a comfortable home base for horseback riding, fishing, windsurfing, canoeing, or sailing on Lake Arenal or Coter Lake; for trips to the volcano and hot springs ($59), Bebedero River and Palo Verde National Park ($73), Rincón de la Vieja volcano ($69), and Caño Negro ($69); or for rafting on the Corobicí ($55). Rubber boots, flashlights, and rain ponchos provided.

The main building feels like a mountain lodge, with its spacious living/recreation area, welcoming fire in the fireplace, conversation areas, TV and VCR with a supply of videos, billiard table, bar, and dining room. Ample, tasty meals are served buffet-style. Interesting photographs, many of an earlier Costa Rica, adorn the walls of the lodge; one of the most intriguing shows a flying saucer near Arenal volcano and mysterious, heart-shaped Coter Lake.

The 23 cozy, carpeted lodge rooms are of rock and wood, each with pretty comforters. Fourteen attractively furnished rooms in seven bungalows are within a five-minute walk of the lodge. Rooms have high ceilings and a glass wall that faces the porch and volcano, Arenal and Coter Lakes, and Nuevo Arenal's nighttime lights.

In the distance, Arenal Volcano rumbles. Twenty-three miles (37 km) away, from some vantage points on the property it seems to rise out of Lake Arenal. It's not visible from the lodge, but is from a covered observatory and bungalows.

Dry season is not as pronounced here: rainfall amounts to about 152 inches (3,857 mm) a year. Elevation is 2,297 to 3,609 feet (700 to 1,100 m), with the lodge at 2,329 feet (710 m). Forested slopes have both rain-forest and cloud-forest characteristics.

Getting There
By bus: Tilarán/Ciudad Quesada (San Carlos) buses pass by on the highway 2 miles (3 km) below.
By car: Turnoff near kilometer 46 marker between Nuevo Arenal and Tilarán.
Other: Transfers from San José or Tilarán, minimum four.

Where to Stay and Eat between Nuevo Arenal and Tilarán
Hotel Joya Sureña, (506) 694-4057, fax (506) 694-4059; e-mail joysur@sol.racsa.co.cr; Web site www.allgoods.com/joyasurena, is an attractive 28-room hotel on 8 acres (3 ha) of grounds with views of Lake Arenal, the Tilarán Mountains, coffee fields, and lovely tropical gardens. On clear days you'll get a glimpse of Arenal and Tenorio Volcanoes. Surprising amenities for a small hotel in a rural area include a swimming pool, sheltered sunning terrace, sauna, exercise room, heated Jacuzzi, massage therapy, and room service. The hotel, owned by Canadian James William Swan, offers short nature trails, mountain bikes, boats, kayaks, volleyball, croquet, windsurfing, and horses. Staff custom-design tours or arrange package tours to Venado Caves, hot springs, and Arenal Volcano plus lake

fishing. The restaurant and bar looking out on landscaped gardens, are open to the public.

Rooms with lovely arched windows have telephones, TV, ceiling fans, and desks. Larger deluxe rooms have sitting areas and small refrigerators, some with balconies. Standard single $55, double $65; deluxe single $65, double $75; special discounts for children sharing room with two adults. Watch for Joya Sureña sign at main highway intersection in Nuevo Arenal.

Rock River Lodge, telephone/fax (506) 695-5644; e-mail rokriver@sol. racsa.co.cr; Web site www.rockriver.mastermind.net/, is delightfully casual. Most nights find a fire in the big fireplace near the main building's open-air lounge. There are views of the volcano and the lake, pretty at night with the lights on the far shore. Tropical woods warm the cozy bar—good music. The restaurant and bar are open to the public. Owner Norman List's breakfasts are famous and he may serve you himself; no lunches, but the $10 dinner with a variety of main dishes is excellent.

Rooms are terraced on the hillside behind. Standard rooms are wood-paneled and inviting; each has a lighted mirror in the private bath and windows onto a terrace facing the lake. Single or double, $45. Eight newer bungalows ($65) have a definite Southwestern United States flair, with built-in *bancos*, a rounded wall on one corner giving the feel of adobe, and inside walls with a hand-plastered look. Norman engineered the unusual bathtubs. Sitting on the private terrace could be habit forming.

Guests windsurf or bicycle (Rock River's two specialties), as well as raft the Corobicí River ($35), ride horseback, take a Canopy Tour near Rincón de la Vieja, fish, or bird-watch. Check out the mountain biking: the three-day Volcano Trail for intermediate bikers goes to Orosi Volcano near Nicaragua, $100/day. A Quipilapa trail goes to Miravalles, and two- to five-hour day tours visit Cañas for a swim in the Corobicí, a waterfall for a swim in the Tenorio River, or other of the unusual bike tours Norman has created. The lodge is at kilometer 40, 11 miles (18 km) northeast of Tilarán, about 31 miles (50 km) from La Fortuna.

Mystica Resort, cellular phone (506) 382-1499, fax (506) 695-5387, offers mist, hills, lake, volcano—it's a mystical place, hence its name. One rainy night it was a haven for this traveler. I was welcomed by the warm fire in the fireplace, calmed by the soft music, and tempted by the smells of pizza and pasta from the Italian kitchen. Owners Barbara Moglia and Francesco Carullo serve 12 kinds of pizza and nine kinds of pasta, most from $4 to $7. Pizzas are cooked in a big brick oven. I recommend the pasta with Gorgonzola sauce—terrific.

Each of six large, comfortable rooms, up a garden path from the restaurant, sleeps four in a double and bunk beds. Patchwork-quilt coverlets and wooden chairs and desk give a Shaker flavor. Animal cutouts on wooden lampshades create interesting effects. A common veranda with chairs affords lake viewing. Single $35, double $50, breakfast included. Windsurfing, mountain biking, and horseback rides arranged. (VISA only accepted.)

Hotel Tilawa, Costa Rica (506) 695-5050, fax (506) 695-5766; e-mail Tilawa@sol.racsa.co.cr; U.S. number (800) 851-8929, is an imposing two-story building above Lake Arenal, where color is key and the architecture recalls the Palace of Knossos: custom-designed floors, painted designs on walls, dining room tablecloths, and room decorations. Every room has large windows looking out on the water or attractive gardens, two queen-size beds with orthopedic mattresses, writing desk, and both tub and shower. Colorful Guatemalan bedspreads brighten the rooms. There are 24 standard rooms; single $59, double $77, breakfast included. Four junior suites have sitting area and furnished kitchenette, $148, taxes included. The restaurant is open to the public, and there is a poolside bar.

Trails take off into the forest next to the swimming pool; howler monkeys call, and guests will likely see keel-billed toucans. Guided volcano tours are available by boat or car, as are trips to the Corobicí River, Venado Caves, and Tabacón Hot Springs. The hotel offers tennis, horseback riding, and mountain bikes. Tilawa's strong suit is windsurfing: Lake Arenal is known as one of the top areas for this sport, and the lakeside WindSurf Center offers equipment for rent as well as lessons for adults and children.

The hotel offers airport pickup in San José, $120 one way for up to four people; transport via hydroplane arranged. Packages for seven days and seven nights, double occupancy, are $555 for sailors (unlimited use of equipment) and $284 for non-sailors, taxes included. Tilawa is 13 miles (21 km) northeast of Cañas and 43 miles (69 km) from Liberia.

TILARAN

Tilarán is a pleasant town 2 miles (3 km) south of Lake Arenal laid out around the traditional square, with a bank, gas stations, grocery stores, restaurants, and small hotels and cabins.

From Tilarán, take the back road to Monteverde through Quebrada Grande (unpaved) or continue on the main paved road to Cañas. From there you can go to Palo Verde National Park, go north on the Inter-American Highway to Guanacaste or south to the Tempisque Ferry that crosses over to the Nicoya Peninsula, or continue to Puntarenas. Buses run from Tilarán to San José, Cañas, and Monteverde.

Small hotels cater to those who choose to stay in town. **Cabinas El Sueño,** (506) 695-5347, is a second-floor, 12-room hotel with most rooms around an open patio. Pleasant carpeted rooms have ceiling fans. Single $10, double $16. **Hotel Naralit,** (506) 695-5393, fax (506) 695-6767, has 26 pleasant rooms with ceiling fans, reading lamps, and eclectic furnishings—an old Ideal sewing machine is the base of an attractive table. Doubles with cable TV, $21 to $25; without, $17. Lake fishing and volcano trips arranged. Ask at your hotel for restaurant recommendations.

POÁS-VARA BLANCA-SARAPIQUI ROUTE

The route from San José to the north-central region through Vara Blanca is spectacular, passing through coffee plantations and dairy farms, with Barva Volcano and Cacho Negro on one side and Poás Volcano and Cerro Congo on the other. Huge expanses of black shade-cloths shelter ornamental plants and flowers, among a growing list of nontraditional exports. Strawberries grown here are offered at roadside stands. Turnoff to Poás is just before Vara Blanca.

The winding descent after Vara Blanca passes gorgeous waterfalls, the most photographed being **Catarata de la Paz** (Peace Waterfall) between Vara Blanca and Cariblanco. The river that feeds the waterfall rises in the forests of Poás. Stop in the small parking area at the picturesque one-way bridge for picture-taking. A wet trail leads behind the falls.

POAS VOLCANO NATIONAL PARK

Location: 90 minutes from San José, 23 miles (37 km) N of Alajuela.
Size: 16,076 acres (6,506 ha).
Hours: Daily 8 a.m. to 4 p.m.
Information: Telephone hotline 192 (See Appendix A: Parks and Reserves Information), (506) 290-1927, fax (506) 232-5324.

At Poás Volcano, stand at the edge of a multicolored crater almost a mile (1.5 km) in diameter, look down 984 feet (300 m), and watch geyserlike eruptions that leave no doubt this mountain still has something to say.

Of the five craters on this 8,884-foot (2,708-m) giant, two get the most attention from visitors: the large active crater responsible for more recent lava, rocks, ash, and steam, and the extinct one that now cradles beautiful Botos Lake. The lookout at the edge of the active crater affords a spectacular view of a greenish hot-water lake. The earlier you go, the better chance you have of an unimpeded view. Clouds that drift in as the day progresses can obscure the bottom. Don't give up too easily, however, if it is socked in—glimpses come and go. While you wait for a column of mud and water to shoot into the air, notice the fumaroles and look for small measuring devices scattered around the crater. Costa Rica has fine volcanological and seismological observatories whose staffs keep close watch at Poás and other sites around the country. Depending on wind direction, you may get a good whiff of sulfur. Gas emissions sometimes damage vegetation both in the park and nearby—look for evidence of the acid rain.

Trails lead through shrubs, dwarf forest, and cloud forest covered with epiphytes. Because of volcanic activity, hunting, and deforestation outside the park, few mammals remain. Coyotes, rabbits, frogs, and toads are common, and at least 79 bird species are at home here. A park ranger told me he has seen quetzals fly over the road between the park entrance and administration building in early morning. Hummingbirds are everywhere; you might also spot an emerald toucanet, brown robin, black guan, or masked woodpecker.

The trail to Botos Lake, named for the Botos Indians who lived on the north slope when the Spaniards arrived, begins near the view point for the active crater; it's an easy 20-minute climb to the extinct crater. At this altitude, though, take your time, enjoy the tangled shrub or dwarf-forest vegetation, and hear the tantalizing song of hidden birds. Amphitheater seating beside this rain-replenished lake offers a vantage point for bird observation and for remembering that the crater walls around you, now tranquil and forest-covered, were once witness to fiery emanations.

Peace Waterfall between Vara Blanca and Cariblanco

My favorite trail is Escalonia, which begins at the picnic area. Trees soar overhead, bromeliads abound, and trail markers full of poetry salute the forest's magnificence. (I translated one for you; see sidebar.)

If you visit by tour, check to see that it gets to Poás by 9:30 a.m. at the latest and how much time it spends here. Some allow barely enough time to peer into the crater; others offer more time and a naturalist guide.

Bring a jacket and rain gear; rainfall is 138 inches (3,500 mm). Temperatures average between 50°F and 57°F (10°C and 14°C), but bright, sunny days can be 70°F (21°C).

The visitor center's first floor houses a nature shop, rest rooms, auditorium, and a snack bar operated by Cafe Britt; an outstanding insect exhibit is on the second.

Getting There
By bus: Once a day buses from San José.
By car: From Alajuela, go either through San Pedro de Poás and Fraijanes or through Heredia and Vara Blanca.
Other: Taxi from San José or Alajuela.

Where to Stay and Eat near Poás
Juan Bo Mountain Restaurant and Cabins, (506) 482-2099, is a tiny jewel at the edge of a dairy farm, just over a mile (2 km) north of Vara Blanca heading toward San Miguel. The mountain view is spectacular and the dining room warm and cozy, full of good smells and outstanding food. Two charming cabins feature polished wood floors, brightly upholstered bamboo furniture, two double beds, big windows and closets, and private baths; double $50. If you can't stay, this is a delightful stop for a meal, hot coffee or *agua*

dulce, and fresh tortillas or dessert. Restaurant open 11 a.m. to 8 p.m. Monday through Friday, earlier on Saturday and Sunday. Juan Bo is 90 minutes from San José, 9 miles (15 km) from Poás.

La Providencia Ecological Reserve, (506)232-2498, fax (506) 231-2204, (mark faxes "for Amalia") is on a farm that has 395 acres (160 ha) of primary forest. Forest denizens include quetzals, ocelots, coyotes, armadillos, emerald toucanets, peccaries, hummingbirds, and tayras. Giant ferns abound; find the huge-leafed *sombrilla del pobre* (poor man's umbrella) and magnificent oak forests, one of which is white because of acid rain from the volcano.

In clear weather the panorama is impressive: the Central Valley, Pacific, lakes in Nicaragua, and Arenal Volcano. Elevation is 8,200 feet (2,500 m). Visitors are welcome for both day tours and overnight stays. The reserve has six rustic wooden cabins (generator electricity). Four two-person cabins are $40, one for four is $53, and a *casita* for 10 is $150. In the small restaurant, meals are cooked on a wood stove; enjoy candlelight dinners. A three-hour horseback ride ($20) takes visitors on the slopes of the volcano through primary and secondary forest and to waterfalls, *páramo,* and view points, with great bird-watching along the way. Bring warm clothes and rain gear.

To get there, turn left at the green gate to Poás park and follow a gravel road for 1.5 miles (2.4 km).

Charming **Poás Volcano Lodge,** telephone/fax (506) 482-2194; e-mail poas@arweb.com; Web site arweb.com/poas, is near Vara Blanca, 10 miles

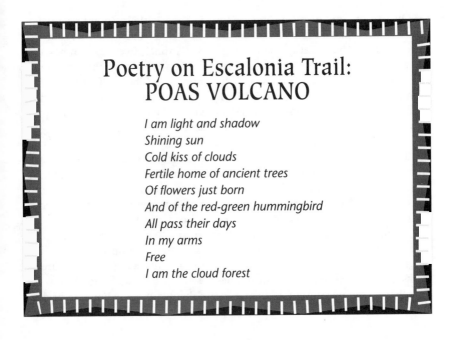

Poetry on Escalonia Trail:
POAS VOLCANO

I am light and shadow
Shining sun
Cold kiss of clouds
Fertile home of ancient trees
Of flowers just born
And of the red-green hummingbird
All pass their days
In my arms
Free
I am the cloud forest

(16 km) from the volcano and an invigorating 6,234 feet (1,900 m) high. The large farmhouse has an English-manor flavor. A sunny sitting room has a sunken conversation area and fireplace. Two rooms with shared bath and a master suite with private bath, king-size bed, and double glass doors opening onto a terrace are in the main building. Six rooms in two other buildings hint of English or Welsh cottages, private baths. Each room is different, with creative use of wood and rock walls; all windows open to a landscaped garden. Poás dominates the horizon. Rooms with shared bath $55, private bath $65, and master suite $80, including country breakfast. Light lunches or dinners served on request.

Take guided bird-watching walks in forest patches on the large farm, with a chance to observe such species as the golden-browed chlorophonia, black-faced solitaires, hummingbirds, and quetzals; epiphytes flourish. Horseback riding is available, and the lodge is 10 minutes from the three-tiered Peace Waterfall.

Where to Stay and Eat between San Miquel and Puerto Viejo de Sarapiquí

Take a winding, narrow road to the little town of **San Miguel**, where there's a large sawmill, a bank, a terrific grocery store that sells cold bottled water—Coopesarapiquí—and a popular eating spot: **Señor Tortugas**, open from 11:30 a.m. to 10 p.m., closed Monday. You have choices to make at San Miguel: roads west and north take you to Aguas Zarcas and Ciudad Quesada, destinations already discussed. To continue to Puerto Viejo, head northeast.

La Quinta de Sarapiquí, telephone/fax (506) 761-1052, a quintessential country inn, is just 3 miles (5 km) north of La Virgen and 7 miles (12 km) west of Puerto Viejo. Set in a curve along the Sardinal River, the inn has 15 rooms in bungalows surrounded by a tropical garden rich in heliconias (more than 24 species), gingers, palms, and flowering trees. The brilliant flash of hummingbirds feeding along heliconia-lined paths in the morning sun is dazzling. Each room opens onto a shaded porch with chairs so you can enjoy the flowers and birds (more than 100 species identified).

Large, inviting rooms have white tile floors, dusky-rose bed coverings, good mattresses, green and rose drapes, and ceiling fans. The bar and lounge area next to the dining room have comfortable cushioned bamboo furniture. Single or double $45. Food is delicious and nicely served: breakfast $5, lunch $7, dinner $8. You may get some delicacies from the garden. This is where I finally got to taste fried breadfruit. (Thanks, Leonardo!)

Leonardo and Beatriz are caring owners and hosts who help guests with trips: rafting or wildlife boating on the Sarapiquí, visiting La Selva Biological Station (15 minutes away) or the aerial tram, and guided nature walks at Selva Verde. On the farm, guests can swim in the Sardinal, go horseback riding or mountain biking, cross the picturesque hanging bridge to a forest patch for bird-watching (toucans, brown-hooded parrots, maybe even a great green macaw), and enjoy the butterfly garden. A small swimming pool next to the dining area has a view overlooking the river. Some groups help with a reforestation project in former pastures. La Quinta is about half a mile (1 km) of unpaved road in from the highway across an unforgettable bridge.

Rancho Leona, telephone/fax (506) 761-1019, is in La Virgen de Sarapiquí, about 8 miles (13 km) from San Miguel. The unexpected lives here: a workshop where Tiffany-style stained glass is created—visitors are welcome to watch artisans at work—as well as rain-forest jewelry. There are kayak jungle tours, a restaurant catering to vegetarians (homemade brown bread, eggplant Parmesan, French onion soup, banana splits), and a rustic rain-forest geodesic dome to bunk in. Actually Rancho Leona is the stepping-off place for the dome, which is in a secluded 80-acre (32-ha) protected forest bordering Braulio Carrillo Park. An $85 overnight tour includes transport to the forest from Rancho Leona, food, lodging, and pickup. The dome has 11 bunk beds, kitchen facilities, and a composting outhouse: no electricity here, candles and lanterns supplied. Enjoy the beautiful swimming hole in the Peje River five minutes away, walk on trails, observe wildlife. Camping allowed. Proceeds from stained-glass work and Rancho Leona's kayak tours have helped purchase this forest.

The kayak tours, famous in these parts, are $75, including equipment, guide, picnic lunch, and two nights at the Rancho Leona hostel in La Virgen. If the hostel's basic rooms are not being used by kayakers, they rent for $9 per person, shared baths. Another surprise—there's a sauna. The two creative people who keep all of this going are Ken Upcraft and Leona Wellington.

SELVA VERDE LODGE, PRIVATE RESERVE

Location: In Chilamate, 5 miles (8 km) W of Puerto Viejo de Sarapiquí.
Rates: Single $75, double $60 each, including lodging, meals, and taxes. Lodging only, $24 less.
Information/Reservations: U.S. number (800) 451-7111. In Costa Rica, (506) 766-6800, fax (506) 766-6011; e-mail travel@holbrooktravel.com; Web site www.holbrooktravel.com.

At dusk along the Sarapiquí, behind the lodge at Selva Verde, the only sound is rushing water; the green forest that gives Selva Verde its name guards the river. Brilliant blue morpho butterflies flutter along the forest's edge above the water. Dusk becomes darkness, the magic moment is gone, and yet it lives forever.

Images of time spent at Selva Verde Lodge, less than two hours north of San José, crowd in. One delightful day on a river trip down the Sarapiquí, we saw river otter, crocodile, white-crowned parrot, kingfishers, keel-billed toucans, parakeets, blue herons, aracaris, a three-toed sloth, anhingas, egrets, flycatchers, a bananaquit, oropendolas, turtles, a scarlet-rumped tanager, trees full of vultures, and iguanas draped on limbs high above the water. Children played along the river, women laundered, men rode horseback along a high bank. We passed ranches, farms, forests, and lush river vegetation.

Selva Verde has a reserve of its own, 529 acres (214 ha), across a new hanging bridge over the Sarapiquí. Well-marked trails ranging from easy to somewhat steep explore this tropical lowland forest. Go with a bilingual Selva Verde guide ($15 per person) or follow a map. Benches provide a place to rest or to wait and see what the forest reveals: a coati, sloth, raccoon, kinkajou, brocket deer, anteater, river otter, monkey, or maybe a tiny lizard. There are more than 2,000 plant species, 700 butterfly species, and 400 species of birds. Most commonly seen birds are tanagers, honeycreepers, oropendolas, trogons, toucans, and chachalacas. Wander the trails behind the lodge to the river: I recommend it—abundant birds and butterflies. Take time to smell the heliotrope. Tiny red and blue poison-dart frogs call on every side; find one in the leaf litter or the base of a tree, be still, and watch them speak. Small green and black frogs may precede you down the path.

Selva Verde's Butterfly Garden (open from dawn to dusk, free to guests at the lodge, $5 for others) is tucked among trees. The enclosed portion of the garden is marvelous: colorful rattlesnake and hot-lips plants, dozens of butterflies, and benches to sit on. Medicinal plants and endangered local species are the focus in another section.

Off-site options include a Sarapiquí wildlife trip ($25), horseback tours ($20), canoeing or river rafting ($45), or a banana plantation visit ($25).

The River Lodge consists of 40 rooms in a series of modules built on stilts and connected by thatch-covered walkways. Constructed of beautiful tropical woods, each double room has a small desk, reading lights, convenient closet space, and lots of windows with louvered shutters. Five more-rustic bungalows with fans and private baths are across the road in the forest.

A large dining room, which accommodates 100 people, shares a river view with an outdoor deck; the set menu is served buffet-style. The dining room is open to the public with prior reservation. A delightful covered outdoor lounge with hanging chairs is surrounded by flowering plants. The gift shop offers a good selection of nature books, tropical-forest posters, basketry, belts, primitive carvings, jewelry, and lots more—even slide film.

A commitment to community involvement has resulted in development of the Sarapiquí Conservation Learning Center, built on Selva Verde property for use by guests and residents. In its library, auditorium, and work rooms, local people study English, attend natural history classes, or work on handcrafts to sell in the hotel's shop.

Getting There

By bus: From San José to Puerto Viejo de Sarapiquí through Braulio Carrillo park, taxi to lodge (two hours); there's also a bus from Ciudad Quesada to Puerto Viejo.

By car: One route is via Braulio Carrillo, Las Horquetas, and Puerto Viejo; slightly longer route via Vara Blanca and San Miguel to Chilamate.

PUERTO VIEJO DE SARAPIQUI

On the banks of the Puerto Viejo River 42 miles (67 km) north of San José, (population 8,171), this small town is increasingly a destination for visitors who come to travel the rivers and explore this biologically rich area. A commercial center for surrounding villages, it has a bank, medical clinic, and gas station as well as a few restaurants, small hotels and lodges, and tour companies that specialize in wildlife river trips, rafting, and kayaking. A big natural history draw is the internationally known La Selva Biological Station, only 10 minutes away by car; from here travelers can easily move to the Arenal, Braulio Carrillo, and Poás areas.

The Puerto Viejo River flows into the Sarapiquí on its way to the San Juan River, which forms the Costa Rica–Nicaragua boundary. These waters have history: indigenous peoples, Spanish explorers, English pirates. Later some of California's Forty-niners made their way from the U.S. east coast to San Francisco via the San Juan and through Lake Nicaragua to the Pacific. Today, travelers leave Puerto Viejo for Barra del Colorado National Wildlife Refuge or Tortuguero National Park in search of a different kind of treasure.

Tour Companies

Aguas Bravas Whitewater Center, (506) 292-2072, fax (506) 229-4837; Web site www.hway.com/arenas/abravas/, specializes in rafting on the Sarapiquí River: La Virgen–Chilamate sector (class II–III, with more than 20 rapids), $40; San Miguel–La Virgen (class IV–V, only for the experienced), $50; Chilamate–Puerto Viejo (class I–II), special for bird-watching, $40. All include lunch. Aguas Bravas also has an Adventure Center in La Fortuna and runs day trips and multiday white-water excursions to Sarapiquí from San José. For example, a two-day trip is $230, including lodging, meals, transport, and rafting on the Sucio and Sarapiquí Rivers.

Transporte Acuático Oasis, (506) 766-6260, telephone/fax (506) 766-6108, offers wildlife tours on area rivers as well as boat transfers between Puerto Viejo, Barra del Colorado, and Tortuguero, a terrific way to combine the north-central portion of the country with two top natural history destinations on the Caribbean coast. A two-day trip includes the river trip to Barra del Colorado and Tortuguero, an excursion on one of the canals, and a stop at the Caribbean Corporation Association's natural history center (lodging excluded, but owner William Rojas will reserve accommodations). The popular half-day wildlife trip on the Sarapiquí is $15 per person.

Other Things to See and Do

Selva Verde Butterfly Garden, at Selva Verde (506) 766-6077, fax (506) 766-6011, is open to the public from dawn to dusk, $5 per person. A self-guided tour with a booklet that includes plant names and some medicinal uses carries you through the garden, where you'll see many birds and free-flying butterflies. The butterfly enclosure has benches where you can sit and admire these ethereal creatures—a photographer's delight. A kiosk contains natural history information.

Where to Stay and Eat in and near Puerto Viejo

El Bambú, (506) 766-6005, (506) 766-6363, fax (506)766-6132, is a pleasant 12-room downtown hotel with telephones and ceiling fans. Single or double $45, including continental breakfast. Bamboo furniture decorates pleasant rooms. A spacious restaurant and bar are on the ground floor, open on one side to the greenery of tropical vegetation. The hotel offers trips on the San Juan River to Tortuguero and Barra del Colorado as well as wildlife boat rides and visits to La Selva.

El Gavilán Lodge, (506) 234-9507, fax (506) 253-6556; e-mail gavilan @sol.racsa.co.cr; Web site www.costarica.tourism.co.cr/hotels/gavilan/, lies just outside Puerto Viejo between the Sucio and Sarapiquí Rivers. Four rooms in a two-story building adjacent to the dining room look out on a Jacuzzi in the gardens. Ten more rooms are in comfortable, simply furnished bungalows across the garden. All but two rooms have private baths and all have ceiling fans. Single $40, double $50. Lunch and dinner are $9 each.

Orchids decorate spacious grounds, along with coconut palms, fruit trees, heliconias, heliotrope, and other flowering tropical plants. Two thatched ranchos are furnished with hammocks and chairs for reading or bird-watching. Green coconuts, *pipas* in Spanish, are served as natural refreshment, along with drinks from other fruits that grow here: starfruit, oranges, guayabas, cas, passion fruit, mangos, and pineapples.

Choose from a variety of activities. Paths along the river lead to three tree decks terrific for bird-watching. A short distance away is Gavilán's almost-300-acre (120-ha) forest reserve, reached on foot or by horseback. On my most recent boat trip from El Gavilán, I saw crocodiles, sloths, turtles, iguanas, howler monkeys, long-nosed bats, kingfishers, parrots, a laughing falcon, an anhinga, mangrove swallows, and several species of heron. Plant life along the banks includes fragrant heliotrope, colorful heliconias, and vines trailing into the water.

Boat trips include the Sarapiquí ($20), San Juan ($60), and Tortuguero ($85, minimum four people). Horseback riding is $20 for three hours. Packages include transportation, meals, bilingual guide, boat rides, and hiking. The one-day trip coming through Braulio Carrillo National Park includes either a Sarapiquí boat trip ($75) or San Juan River trip. A two-day, one-night trip takes in Poás Volcano, hiking or horseback riding, and a trip to the San Juan, $199.

From Puerto Viejo, turn south at the intersection into town, next to the rural guard checkpoint and watch on the left for El Gavilan's sign.

Mi Lindo Sarapiquí, telephone/fax (506) 766-6281, in downtown Puerto Viejo has six simple, clean rooms with ceiling fans, all on the second floor;

single $9, double $18. The large open-air restaurant downstairs is popular with locals and tourists, open from early to 10 p.m. Tours arranged in the area and to Tortuguero.

LA SELVA BIOLOGICAL STATION, PRIVATE RESERVE

Location: 2 miles (3 km) S of Puerto Viejo de Sarapiquí, (79 km) from San José via Braulio Carrillo Park. From Ciudad Quesada, 37 miles (60 km) NE.
Office Hours: 7:30 a.m. to 5 p.m. for reservations.
Rates: Day visits $20 per person for half-day guided natural history walk or Birdwatching 101. For overnight visitors, single $75, double $60 each, $45 per person extra, including lodging, meals, and guided walk.
Information/Reservations: Day visitors: reserve with La Selva, (506) 766-6565, fax (506) 766-6535; e-mail recep-ls@ns.sloth.ots.ac.cr. Overnight visitors: (506) 240-6696, fax (506) 240-6783; e-mail reservas@ns.ots.ac.cr; Web site www.ots.ac.cr.

La Selva Biological Station near Puerto Viejo de Sarapiquí offers a unique opportunity to experience and learn about tropical ecosystems at one of the top two biological research stations in the Neotropics. About 250 researchers from 26 countries come each year. La Selva is owned by the Organization for Tropical Studies (OTS).

Educational natural history programs now share this marvelous reserve and the wealth of accumulated knowledge with the nonscientist. Half-day guided walks begin daily at 8 a.m. and 1:30 p.m. Groups are limited to about 10 people per guide, so reserve beforehand. These are high-quality educational experiences led by bilingual guides, either biologists or local naturalists trained by OTS in intensive courses. Overnight stays are possible if space is not filled by researchers and people enrolled in courses.

From the viewing terrace in front of reception, the panorama can include flocks of parakeets flying overhead, the red flash of scarlet-rumped tanagers, a sloth in the cecropia tree, and hummingbirds. At the start of the long suspension bridge over the Puerto Viejo River, look for the granddaddy of all iguanas in riverside trees, turtles sunning on trunks partially submerged in the water, kingfishers, and morphos. Around laboratories and researcher cabins, depending on what's in fruit, families of coatis are at home and peccaries (yes, peccaries!) feed quietly. Because of the long history of protection and research here, forest mammals such as these no longer flee at the sight of human beings.

La Selva is home to 120 species of mammals, including howler, spider, and white-faced monkeys, agoutis, jaguars, tapirs, and 60 species of bats. There are some 2,000 species of vascular plants in this tropical rain forest, 420 bird species, and 500 species of butterflies.

An inventory of arthropods (insects, spiders, crustaceans) at La Selva has already identified more than 400 species of ants alone. Known as ALAS, this long-term study involved development of innovative computer software to incorporate species information, complete with images and sounds. Think of the implications for sharing information around the world.

Guides describe the ALAS project and others underway and lead you on some of La Selva's 35 miles (57 km) of trails as they explain about tropical ecosystems. They point out the *bala*, or giant tropical ant, infamous for its powerful sting and the largest ant in Costa Rica (up to 1 inch [33 mm] long); they spot the tiny blue and red poison-dart frog and tell you its life history.

The three-hour natural history walk is a good introduction to lowland rain forest biology. Another option is half-day Birdwatching 101 for beginning birders, which combines classroom instruction with field identification. Overnight guests may explore further on their own.

On the easy, wheelchair-accessible Sendero Tres Ríos trail, a 3.7-mile (6-km) paved path, you'll encounter staff and researchers traveling by bicycle to more distant research sites. Watch for toucans, agoutis, and peccaries as you enjoy flowering bromeliads in towering trees.

Don't miss the arboretum, where a keel-billed toucan perched patiently as a group of us admired his splendor and photographed him. We spotted a purple-throated fruitcrow, collared aracari, crested owl, and yellow-billed cacique within a few yards. I have watched monkeys there. A gazebo affords a pleasant place to pause and observe. Some of the 1,000 trees are labeled.

Situated at the confluence of the Puerto Viejo and Sarapiquí Rivers, La Selva's 3,739 acres (1,513 ha) are contiguous with Braulio Carrillo National Park, which extends the protected habitat for flora and fauna to more than 120,000 acres (49,000 ha). Annual rainfall is about 152 inches, which is 13

Researchers' transportation at La Selva Biological Station

feet or 4 meters! More than 4 inches (100 mm) of rain falls even in drier months, February to April, but La Selva has some of its best weather in October, when rain falls in most of the rest of the country. Elevation ranges from 115 to 492 feet (35 to 150 m) and average temperature is 75°F (24°C)—it gets cool enough for a blanket toward morning.

Overnight accommodations are generally in ten dormitory-style rooms with bunk beds, reading lights, a ceiling fan, closet space, and a study table. The rooms were designed for researchers and students. Each two rooms shares a bath. Two rooms for up to six have private baths.

Meals are served cafeteria-style in the modern dining room, where you may find yourself rubbing elbows with leading tropical scientists, field assistants, or student researchers. Check the chalkboard there for evening talks by graduate students participating in the intensive OTS field courses or by researchers. Natural history visitors are invited.

A new Welcome Center with an exhibit highlighting research at La Selva may be completed by your arrival. A small shop in the main building has snacks, handcrafts, and a good selection of T-shirts and books.

Getting There

By bus: The San José bus to Puerto Viejo through Braulio Carrillo passes on the highway, a 10-minute walk from reception.

By car: From the Guapiles–Limón highway, turn north toward Puerto Viejo; watch for entrance on the left just past Lapa Verde restaurant. From Puerto Viejo, turn south to the La Selva entrance, just before a covered bus stop.

Other: Area hotels and lodges offer day tours to La Selva; day tour from San José.

BRAULIO CARRILLO– LAS HORQUETAS ROUTE

Braulio Carrillo National Park, the Rain Forest Aerial Tram, and Rara Avis are three marvelous natural history destinations along this route. Head north out of San José on the highway toward Limón. The park, less than 30 minutes from the capital, dominates both sides of the road. As you drop toward the lowlands, still inside the park, see the confluence of the Hondura River and the Sucio, which looks dirty (*sucio* means dirty) because of mineral content carried from its origins on Irazú. The interplay of blue and brown waters as they flow together is fascinating. For a photograph, park after you cross the bridge—but be alert. Unfortunately, both people and cars have been robbed along this highway. After leaving the park, watch for the Rain Forest Aerial Tram and then the turnoff to Las Horquetas, jumping-off place for Rara Avis.

Just three minutes from the turn off the highway toward Las Horquetas is **Efrass,** a restaurant with atmosphere alongside the San José River. The menu offers Costa Rican and international dishes. Open noon to 10 p.m., closed Monday; (506) 284-4806.

If you continue past Las Horquetas to Puerto Viejo for a loop through the north central region, you will see *pejibaye* palm, grown commercially for its fruit, which Costa Ricans love, and the heart (*palmito*). The largest heart-of-palm factory in the world is near Guapiles. Try a *palmito* salad while in Costa Rica. Near Puerto Viejo is La Selva Biological Station and other sites described in the Poás–Vara Blanca–Sarapiquí Route section.

BRAULIO CARRILLO NATIONAL PARK

Location: *N of San José on both sides of the highway to Limón.*
Size: *113,525 acres (45,943 ha).*
Hours: *Daily 8 a.m. to 4 p.m.*
Information: *Telephone hotline 192 (See Appendix A: Parks and Reserves Information), (506) 290-1927, fax (506) 232-5324.*

Braulio Carrillo is a symphony in green. Waterfalls, deep canyons, and raging rivers lend their tones. The exciting part is that the concert begins only 30 minutes from San José—and on a paved road.

While roads through virgin forest usually spell ecological disaster, this particular highway spurred creation of a national park. Braulio Carrillo was born out of a conflict between the need for a new highway to the Atlantic and the determination to preserve the largely primary forest it would travel through. The park was established in 1978, and the road through this rugged, largely untouched land opened in 1987. Most of the traffic between San José and Limón now passes on a ribbon laid down through this awesome landscape. Be alert for landslides.

The park offers many levels of enjoyment; just driving through it is a thrill. View points provide a few places to pull off. Check in at the Zurquí ranger station, 30 minutes from San José. Personnel tell you about nearby Los Niños and Los Guarumos Trails. Two trails take off from the Quebrada Gonzáles park station near the Limón end of the highway: Botarrama (which takes about two hours) and Las Palmas. See Chapter 6 for a description of the Barva sector at the upper reaches of the park, a very different habitat.

If you experience Braulio Carrillo only from the highway on your way to the Sarapiquí area or the Caribbean, try to arrive early to reduce the chance of fog narrowing the spectacular views. Dropping into the lowlands, you may see a sloth in a tree alongside the road—check the *guarumos* (cecropias) in particular. Other animals that live in the park include three species of monkey—also frequently spotted from trails at lower elevations—kinkajou, deer, jaguarundi, two species of peccaries, and five of the six species of cats in Costa Rica. In all, there are 135 mammal species here, 73 of which are bats. The bare-necked umbrella bird knows these forests, as do eagles, trogons, hawks, curassows, and guans—350 bird species total. Bromeliads and orchids adorn the trees.

This is a good place to see poor man's umbrella (*sombrilla del pobre*), a plant whose leaves grow up to 7 feet (2 m) across. People surprised by country-side rainstorms have used them for protection. If you're caught in the rain, which averages 177 inches (4,500 mm) a year, notice waterfalls that pour down the roadside; if driving, keep your eyes open for landslides. (Lowlands rainfall can be as much as 315 inches [8,000 mm].) Elevation is from 9,534 to 112 feet (2,906 to 34 m). Because of topography and the elevation range within the park, temperatures can be 59°F (15°C) at Zurquí, 37°F (3°C) at Barva, or 86°F (30°C) in the Atlantic lowlands.

Remember to stay on trails and to check in at a ranger station before setting out. Vegetation is extremely dense in this rugged region. Even experienced hikers have gotten lost; as one Costa Rican put it, the forest has eaten several small planes and a few people. Unfortunately, theft has become a threat. Don't leave items in a car parked along the road and do not park in isolated areas.

Getting There

By bus: Take the Guapiles bus from San José and ask to be let off at either Zurquí or Quebrada Honda park stations.

By car: On the San José–Guapiles–Limón highway, 7.5 miles (20 km) to the Zurquí entrance.

Other: Day visits through tour companies, lodges, and hotels.

RAIN FOREST AERIAL TRAM

Location: 32 miles (52 km) N of San José (about one hour), just past Braulio Carrillo park.
Hours: Opens at 6:30 a.m.; last tour leaves entrance at 3:30 p.m.
Rates: $47.50 for adults, $23.75 for children ages 5 to 18 and students with I.D. Children under 5 enter free but are not permitted to ride the tram for safety reasons.
Information: (506) 257-5961, fax (506) 257-6053; e-mail doselsa@sol.racsa .co.cr; Web site www.rainforest.co.cr.

Bringing ski-lift technology to the tropical forest, the Rain Forest Aerial Tram (*teléferico* in Spanish) passes through what founder Donald Perry calls "the hanging gardens of Central America," the forest canopy where it is believed two-thirds of the forest species live. As you move slowly along a 1.6-mile (2.6-km), 90-minute round trip, with brief automated pauses during the ride, you have a chance to see the plants whose flowers you find when walking on trails. Perhaps you'll see monkeys and some of the area's more than 300 bird species—or, as I did, an anteater making his way through upper branches. Guides in each of the four-to-five-passenger "aerial chariots" radio finds to other cars. "Look for the sloth in the upper branches of the tall tree to the right of station such-and-such." The highest part of the ride is on the return trip, 100 feet (30 m) above the ground.

At each end of the tram are short loop trails where the guide points out the colorful rufous-winged woodpecker, a canfin tree that exudes a flammable liquid, sleeping bats, and other forest treasures. A beautiful *bocaracá* (eyelash viper) rested in foliage near the restaurant when I was there, and the lovely *flor de un día* shared its one-day flower.

An open-air restaurant serves breakfast and lunch, each about $7 including taxes. In the information center, a video presents an introduction to canopy exploration and details on construction of the tram, which involved a Sandinista helicopter as well as banana-plantation technology.

Access is controlled: Vehicles carry visitors to the tram and visitor center area, almost a mile (1.5 km) from the entrance. Allow three hours for the visit. Bring binoculars. Entry fee entitles visitors to the tram ride, guided walks, and information-center activities.

Getting There
By bus: Frequent buses pass entrance; San José–Gaupiles buses are most convenient.
By car: Watch for sign just past the north end of Braulio Carrillo park.
Other: Tram shuttle is $17.50 round trip from San José.

RARA AVIS RAINFOREST LODGE AND RESERVE, PRIVATE RESERVE
Location: Starting point at Las Horquetas, 62 miles (100 km) from San José by way of Braulio Carrillo National Park; 120 miles (193 km) via Poás Volcano.
Rates: El Plástico Lodge: $45 per person. Waterfall Lodge and River-Edge Cabin: single $90, double $75 per person, triple $70 per person. Prices include meals, tours with naturalist guides, and round-trip transportation from Las Horquetas.
Information/Reservations: (506) 764-3131, (506) 253-0844, at hotel (506) 710-6872; fax (506) 764-4187; e-mail raraavis@sol.racsa.co.cr; Web site www.cool.co.cr/raravis/raravis.htm.

Visiting the beautiful Waterfall Lodge for the first time, a local tour operator remarked to Amos Bien, founder of Rara Avis, "You know, Amos, most people would have put the road in first." But Amos Bien is not most people, and Rara Avis is not your ordinary country inn.

Now, a few years down the line, the road has progressed quite a lot; so much so that the famous three-hour ride in a tractor-driven cart, fording rivers and lurching in phenomenal mud, is much tamer—at least as far as El Plástico, Rara Avis' hostel-like accommodations. But for the final 2 miles (3 km) between El Plástico and the Waterfall Lodge, guests still lurch in the cart or hike in on forest trails. Adventure is not dead.

Going is still slow enough that there is a chance to see the great green macaw as you bump along, to hear about a nearby achiote plantation (the plants are grown in Costa Rica as ornamentals and as a source of red dye), to observe the pasture lands clear-cut from tropical rain forest, and to see reforestation projects and secondary forest. If Amos is along, he spins tales: about a horse who died along the way and the budding student of the tropical world who later lugged the bones for miles in the belief that it was the skeleton of a giant tapir; or about Pilingo, the dog who wouldn't die.

Amos first came to Costa Rica in 1977 as a biology student. He returned to found Rara Avis, not only for nature/adventure tourism but also as a biological research center and a conservation proving ground to show neighbors they can make more money by maintaining forest than by clearing it for ranches or farms.

The road leads to Albergue El Plástico, a former prison-colony barracks rehabilitated into a rustic lodge with seven rooms containing bunk beds for 29 persons, shared baths. Guests sit at dining tables where the prisoners sent in to cut the forests once ate. Lighting is by kerosene lantern. There's good bird-watching from the upstairs porch/library, and a rushing stream down the open slope invites a dip on sunny days. At the edge of the clearing, forest beckons on all sides. A butterfly project exports these beautiful tropical denizens to zoos and greenhouses in Europe and North America.

Two miles (3 km) farther is the impressive, two-story Waterfall Lodge, built of beautiful tropical hardwoods. Each of the eight spacious rooms is a corner unit with chairs and a hammock on a wraparound balcony, and a private bath with both shower and tub. Rooms have a double and bunk beds downstairs and a double in the sleeping loft, brightly colored blankets, screened windows, and kerosene-lantern lighting.

River-Edge Cabin, up a forest trail about 10 minutes from the lodge, is terrific. In a secluded, spectacular setting above the river on the edge of a mountain, the cabin has two spacious rooms, each with its own bath, and a covered deck with a to-die-for view of forest above and below. Solar panels provide electricity. I recommend it for those who enjoy solitude and who are not reluctant to walk alone in the forest at night. Other more-rustic cabins may be available.

Meals are served family-style in a building steps away from Waterfall Lodge: plenty of food, beautiful salads, a variety of meat dishes, and well-prepared local vegetables. (The fried yuca is superb.) A reference corner has lots of good material, and the small gift shop has T-shirts and other items. An extraordinary variety of hummingbirds feed on flowers alongside the porch rail.

A short path leads to the spectacular 180-foot (55-m) double waterfall that gave the lodge its name. Miles of marked trails travel virgin rain forest, with emphasis on the rain. There is virtually no dry season at Rara Avis; rubber boots are essential. A fellow visitor, after an hour on the wet slippery trail between El Plástico and Waterfall Lodge, commented, "This must be the only trail in the world with an undertow." In a four-day period, we explored Rara Avis in 4.5 inches (114 mm) of rain; annual rainfall is about 26 feet (8 m)!

A working biologist, English-Spanish bilingual, guides visitors to such exotic birds as the slaty-tailed trogon and keel-billed and chestnut-mandibled toucans (more than 362 bird species have been identified), and the home of a tent-making bat, which cuts the leaf of a wild plantain on

Famous transport between Las Horquetas and Rara Avis

either side of the midrib and bends it to form a tent for daytime sleeping. Howler, white-faced capuchin, and spider monkeys are common, as are pacas, coatis, vested anteaters, kinkajous, and brocket deer. Tapirs, jaguars, collared peccaries, agoutis, and three-toed sloths live here, but you probably will not see them. People from 2 to 86 years of age have found their way to this remote spot, but access and trails can be rough for those not in good physical condition. There are few mosquitoes. Elevation at the Waterfall Lodge is 2,300 feet (700 m), and temperature year-round is about 76°F (24°C).

On a forest walk with Amos, you hear about the possibilities for sustainable production of forest plants that he hopes will convince neighbors to harvest rather than destroy forest. An understory plant, the stained-glass-window palm, once thought to be extinct but found here, could provide seeds for export as an ornamental plant; roots of a species of philodendron can be harvested for wicker products (the porch chairs are made of this); selective instead of clear-cutting of wood can provide income while preserving rain-forest habitat and biological diversity. Rara Avis itself protects 1,011 acres (409 ha) of primary rain forest.

Rara Avis quietly extends its commitment to education beyond student researchers and natural history tourists. Local elementary-school students and their families are invited to visit, school supplies find their way to the Las Horquetas school, and two sixth-grade students each year are sponsored to continue studies at the high school in Río Frío.

In addition to bird-watching, hiking, and river swimming, in high season guests can climb by rope and harness to the canopy. A climb to Treetop

Cabin almost 100 feet (30 m) above the forest floor is $35. Want to spend the night in it? You can: $55 for one, $45 per person for two.

Getting There

By bus: Ask Rara Avis for the bus schedule; be sure you take one that gets you to Las Horquetas before 9 a.m.

By car: From San José, take Limón highway north and turn for Las Horquetas between Braulio Carrillo park and Guapiles. From Monteverde and Arenal areas, go through San Miguel and Puerto Viejo.

Other: Rara Avis arranges taxi transfer anywhere in Costa Rica (using local taxis). An airstrip for charters is 30 minutes by taxi from Las Horquetas.

Note: All visitors to Rara Avis leave from Las Horquetas; the cart leaves the office daily at 9 a.m. Be on time—departure is. Guests may go by horseback rather than cart with advance notice, $20 each way.

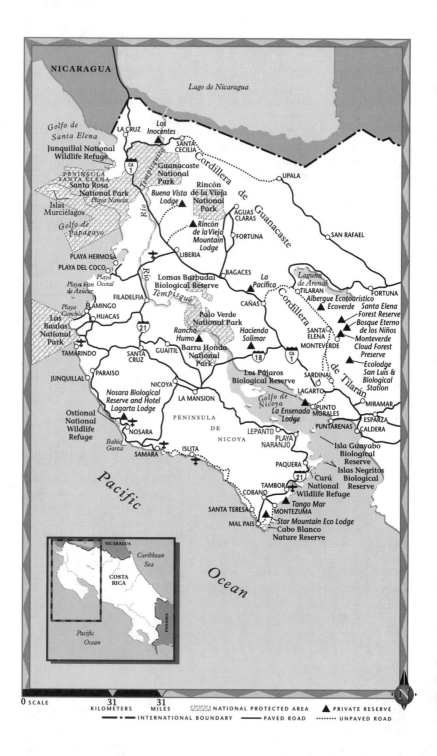

NICARAGUA

Lago de Nicaragua

Golfo de Santa Elena

Junquillal National Wildlife Refuge

LA CRUZ

Los Inocentes

SANTA CECILIA

Cordillera de Guanacaste

UPALA

Guanacaste National Park

Buena Vista Lodge

Rincón de la Vieja National Park

AGUAS CLARAS

FORTUNA

SAN RAFAEL

PENINSULA SANTA ELENA
Santa Rosa National Park
Playa Naranjo

Rincón de la Vieja Mountain Lodge

Islas Murciélagos

Golfo de Papagayo

PLAYA HERMOSA

PLAYA DEL COCO

LIBERIA

BAGACES

Lomas Barbudal Biological Reserve

La Pacífica

Laguna de Arenal

TILARAN

FORTUNA

Playa Ocotal
Playa Pan de Azúcar

FILADELFIA

CAÑAS

Cordillera

Albergue Ecoturístico Ecoverde

Santa Elena Forest Reserve

FLAMINGO

HUACAS

Palo Verde National Park

Bosque Eterno de los Niños

Playa Conchál

Rancho Humo

Hacienda Solimar

SANTA ELENA
MONTEVERDE

Monteverde Cloud Forest Preserve

Las Baulas National Park

TAMARINDO

SANTA CRUZ

GUAITIL

Barra Honda National Park

de Tilarán

Ecolodge San Luis & Biological Station

JUNQUILLAL

PARAISO

Los Pájaros Biological Reserve

SARDINAL

LAGARTO

MIRAMAR

NICOYA

Nosara Biological Reserve and Hotel Lagarta Lodge

LA MANSION

Golfo de Nicoya

La Ensenada Lodge

PUNTO MORALES

ESPARZA

Ostional National Wildlife Refuge

PENINSULA

DE

NICOYA

LEPANTO

PUNTARENAS

CALDERA

Bahía Garza

NOSARA

SAMARA

ISLITA

PLAYA NARANJO

Isla Guayabo Biological Reserve

PAQUERA

Islas Negritos Biological Reserve

TAMBOR

Curú National Wildlife Refuge

COBANO

Tango Mar

SANTA TERESA

MONTEZUMA

MAL PAIS

Star Mountain Eco Lodge
Cabo Blanco Nature Reserve

Pacific

Ocean

NICARAGUA

Caribbean Sea

COSTA RICA

PANAMA

Pacific Ocean

Rio Tempisquito

Rio Tempisque

0 SCALE   31 KILOMETERS   31 MILES   ▒▒▒ NATIONAL PROTECTED AREA   ▲ PRIVATE RESERVE

— · — · — INTERNATIONAL BOUNDARY   ——— PAVED ROAD   ········· UNPAVED ROAD

8

NORTHWEST COSTA RICA

Cloud forests, cattle ranches, long beaches, deciduous dry forests: The northwest region contains national parks, reserves, and refuges; privately owned reserves catering to the ecotourist; and more beach resorts than any other section. It's a big region.

Buses go to Puntarenas, north to Nicaragua, and down into the Nicoya Peninsula; ferries cross the Gulf of Nicoya; scheduled domestic flights go to Tamarindo, Sámara, Nosara, Carrillo, Punta Isleta, Tambor, and Liberia; and taxis in many small towns fill in the gaps. Though the Inter-American Highway opens the biggest door, some travelers come in the back way through the north central region after a visit to the Arenal area.

This huge area is organized here along transportation routes to help you get around—whether you drive, go by bus, or fly to an area.

PUNTARENAS–MONTEZUMA–MAL PAIS

PUNTARENAS

On a narrow piece of land almost 10 miles (16 km) long, Puntarenas (population 20,950) has an estuary on one side and the Gulf of Nicoya on the other. It is 71 miles (115 km) northwest of San José, and 82 miles (132 km) southeast of Liberia. Its economy is based largely on fishing and tourism. This is a laid-back coastal lifestyle: walk along the palm-lined oceanfront promenade called Paseo de los Turistas, swim in a pretty hotel pool under a warm blue sky, and watch people, ships anchored offshore, and sunsets.

Drop by the small museum downtown, **Museo Histórico Marino**, Avenida Central, Calles 3/5, for a look at Puntarenas's history. A picture of this port city's culture emerges through exhibits, terrific old photos, a video, and artifacts. Admission $2, open 9 a.m. to 5 p.m., closed Sunday.

Among popular day tours are those offering a cruise from Puntarenas to an island or beach in the gulf: good eats, swimming and snorkeling in clear waters, and entertainment. Packages include transfers from San José.

Where to Stay in Puntarenas

Friendly **Hotel Tioga,** (506) 661-0271, (506) 255-3115; fax (506) 661-0127, (506) 255-1006; e-mail tiogacr@sol.racsa.co.cr, downtown across from the beach and attractive Paseo de los Turistas, has 46 air-conditioned rooms. Hallways have a great selection of old photos. A second-floor terrace café looks out on the ocean—sunset views. No hot water in older rooms around an interior courtyard with a pool: single $32, double $41. Newer, larger rooms with hot water baths are single $44 to $55, double $55 to $66, some with private balcony; breakfast and taxes included. Staff is helpful, beach umbrellas gratis, on-street guarded parking.

Hotel Yadrán, (506) 661-2662, fax (506) 661-1944, is at the tip of the peninsula off Paseo de los Turistas with views of the estuary and sea. It has a pool, two restaurants and 42 air-conditioned rooms with telephones and satellite TV. Standard single $75, double $85; ocean-view rooms $10 more. Car rental and on-street guarded parking.

Two other options are near where the peninsula begins, 10 minutes by car from downtown. Both have pleasant tropical gardens that look onto the estuary, swimming pools, and restaurants. The beach is about a block away across the main road into town. **Hotel Porto Bello,** (506) 661-1322, (506) 661-2122; fax (506) 661-0036, has doubles for $50, including breakfast and taxes. Next door is **Hotel Colonial,** (506) 661-1833, (506) 661-1834; fax (506) 661-2969; $62, including meals.

Where to Eat in Puntarenas

Restaurants humble and fine are found downtown along the boulevard next to the beach. Try **La Caravelle** for good French food; **Steak House La Yunta,** specializing in meats; **La Casa de los Mariscos,** known for its fresh seafood; **Restaurante Aloha,** with a long-standing reputation for good lobster; **Jardín Cervecero Bierstube,** with a variety of foods and drinks; and **El Jorón,** also known for its seafood.

GUAYABO, NEGRITOS, AND LOS PAJAROS BIOLOGICAL RESERVES

Location: *Gulf of Nicoya.*
Size: *Guayabo and Negritos 355 acres (144 ha), Isla de los Pájaros 10 acres (4 ha).*

Enjoy the birdlife on these four islands through binoculars on one of the popular Gulf of Nicoya day cruises or by boat or kayak. All are havens for large populations of resident and migratory birds, mainly seabirds. No visitor facilities exist; in fact, along with protection of the birds, another reason for making them biological reserves was to avoid their "development" for tourism or other purposes, to keep some of the gulf islands in a natural state.

Guayabo welcomes peregrine falcons in winter and holds the largest of the country's four nesting colonies of brown pelicans, up to 300 individuals. Located 5 miles (8 km) southwest of Puntarenas, Guayabo is also home to brown boobies, frigate birds, laughing gulls, lizards, and crabs. It has cliffs, a small beach, and sparse vegetation.

Two islands make up the Negritos, separated by a narrow channel that harbors whirlpools. Brown pelicans, frigate birds, boobies, and gulls live here, along with parrots, doves, raccoons, and iguanas. Artifacts indicate that Indians came to the islands, either to live or to bury their dead. Coral reefs make access difficult, but the waters support dolphins, giant conch, and oysters. Stands of palm, cedar, gumbo limbo, and frangipani survive. The Negritos are 11 miles (17 km) south of Puntarenas near the shores of the Nicoya Peninsula.

Isla de los Pájaros means "island of the birds." Less than 550 yards (500 m) from the coast, 8 miles (13 km) north of Puntarenas, it has some low-growing forest and fresh water. Again, seabirds, mainly pelicans, are the predominant species.

ACROSS THE GULF TO PLAYA NARANJO AND BAHIA BALLENA

Three options exist from Puntarenas to destinations on the southern Nicoya Peninsula across the Gulf of Nicoya: car/passenger ferry to Playa Naranjo, car/passenger ferry to Paquera, or passenger launch to Paquera. Once across, you'll find the towns are small and beaches relatively uncrowded. The paved road winds through coastal mountains with occasional spectacular coastline views—24 miles (38 km) from Playa Naranjo to Tambor on Bahía Ballena. Travelers come to swim, surf, bird-watch, hike, visit islands, ride horses, scuba dive, see waterfalls, and even play golf. Curú wildlife refuge is a top natural history destination.

Where to Stay and Eat in Playa Naranjo

Oasis del Pacífico, telephone/fax (506) 661-1555, is a small hotel and marina near the dock for the car ferry. Its 36 rooms have louvered glass windows, large desks/bureaus, ceiling fans, and private baths. Single $35, double $45, taxes included. Owners Lucky and Aggie, two of the world's truly nice people, still maintain their policy: your room is free any day the sun doesn't shine.

The restaurant offers indoor or outdoor dining, with a menu enhanced by dishes from Aggie's native Singapore; homemade bread gets rave reviews.

Palms tower around two large pools. Relax under shaded ranchos at poolside to the sounds of howler monkeys, parakeets, squirrels, and family macaws and parrots. Views are of the sea, islands, and mainland. Sit at the end of the hotel's 260-foot (80-m) pier. Walk along the beach or swim in the generally clear, calm waters. Day visitors welcome; rate covers use of pool and showers. Hotel transportation meets each ferry.

Operating out of Oasis del Pacífico, Jerilin Ruhlow of **Oasis Sea Kayaking,** Web site: www.biesanz.com/jere.htm, has marvelous options for natural history visitors, from half-day ($40) and full-day ($85) kayak trips to multiday trips (camping equipment provided) that combine kayaking and hiking to destinations such as Curú, Palo Verde, Tambor and Montezuma beaches, and the Bebedero River. Equipment is good, safety gear is used, and guides have first-aid skills. She also offers mountain biking to waterfalls, villages, and river pools for swimming. Bring your own bike.

CURU NATIONAL WILDLIFE REFUGE, PRIVATE RESERVE
Location: *Coast of southern Nicoya Peninsula, 4 miles (7 km) S of Paquera, 44 miles (70 km) from Nicoya.*
Size: *208 acres (84 ha).*
Rates: *Lodging and meals $25 per day; day visit $5.*
Information/Reservations: *(506) 661-2392; operates also as fax evenings only. Advance reservations needed for day or overnight visit.*

The Curú refuge has a deserted-island kind of feeling—maybe from the coconut-strewn beach, or the mangrove swamp, or the jungled hills rising at the end of the bay. Walking through the tall forest behind the palm-fringed beach, you sense the wildness of the place. Small islands, one of them Tortuga Island, jut up in the Pacific in front of Curú Beach, one of three sand beaches in the refuge. On the distant horizon is the mainland.

Boa constrictors are at home here, as are pacas, agoutis, ocelots, white-faced and howler monkeys, rattlesnakes, iguanas, white-tailed deer, herds of peccaries, mountain lions, and margays (a small, spotted cat with a long tail). Waters along the beach host giant conch, lobsters, and oysters, and offer good snorkeling. Hawksbill and olive ridley turtles come ashore to nest. The magnificent frigate bird soars overhead. Parrots squawk. Hummingbirds, trogons, hawks, swallows, egrets, motmots, tanagers, roseate spoonbills, and fish eagles are among 223 species of birds. There are 78 mammal species, 87 of reptiles (two big crocodiles live in the river), 26 of amphibians, and more than 500 plant species. You'll see pochote trees and guanacaste trees, which indigenous peoples called *curú*, hence the name.

Creation of the Curú refuge was the doing of Federico and Julieta Schutt, who established Curú Hacienda in 1933 for commercial logging, reforestation, and agriculture. When squatters took over a chunk of the farm in 1974, the Schutts looked for ways to protect habitat and wildlife. Within a few years, the remaining forest and mangroves received protected forest status; in 1983, national wildlife refuge status was secured for the fragile marine and beach habitat. The refuge comprises 5 percent of the farm's 3,697 acres (1,496 ha): 75 percent forest and 20 percent in agricultural and cattle production.

Visitors can explore 17 trails with names like Mango, Killer, Laguna, and Río, rated from easy to difficult. On some, the plants' scientific names are marked. One-hour Finca de los Monos (Monkey Farm) Trail gets off to a picturesque start across a rustic hanging bridge over the Curú River.

Walking with Doña Julieta or her children is walking with the best guides around. Doña Julieta took me to the corral to see baby white-tailed deer. Captured by a nearby landowner on private property, they were brought here to be cared for until relocated on

*Rustic bridge to trail
at Curú Wildlife Refuge*

protected land. Doña Julieta had predicted that white-faced monkeys would be at the corral to get bananas; they were. We climbed a ladder to the second floor of a barn to see a makeshift museum of shells, bones, rocks, and research projects.

Walking with Doña Julieta's daughter, Adelina, I received an introduction to forest, swamp, and Adelina's life in this wonderland, where boas can be in bedrooms and dinner can be for family or hungry hordes of researchers. Adelina has spearheaded environmental education programs, leading more than 750 students from 16 area schools on walks and giving talks.

A spider monkey reintroduction program is off and running; this species has disappeared in many areas of Costa Rica because of hunting pressures and habitat loss. On one of my visits, a second baby had just been born. On my last visit, Blanquita, a baby howler, stole the show. Brought here from Cabo Blanco after her mother was killed by dogs, she will find her place with a group that lives at Curú.

Other conservation efforts here include an artificial reef, built of old tires, for marine species; rearing of sea turtles in captivity for release into the Pacific; reforestation of almost 500 acres (200 ha) with native tree species; and use of insect traps and natural pest predators to decrease pesticides in agricultural operations.

Though the very rustic cabins along the beach at Curú are primarily for researchers and student groups, space may be available for an overnight stay—36 beds in all. Typical meals, served family-style, are ample and tasty.

Getting There

By bus: From Paquera, take Cóbano and Montezuma buses and get off at the Curú entrance on the highway; 1.5-mile (2.5-km) walk to refuge.

By car: Entrance 4 miles (7 km) south of Paquera on main road to Cóbano. The sign is hard to see; watch on the left for a tall, gated entrance next to a house.

Other: Area hotels, lodges, and tour agencies offer day tours. Easily accessible by boat or kayak.

BAHIA BALLENA AND TAMBOR

Both a ferry and the launch from Puntarenas arrive near Paquera. The terminal building has a snack bar and clean rest rooms, small fee for use. A bus waits to meet the ferry, taking passengers as far as Montezuma.

Bahía Ballena (Whale Bay) is down the road a piece. Waters lap on a long, curved beach with a very gentle slope. At sunset one July evening several years ago, two dogs and I were the only ones on the beach near the town of Tambor. A roseate spoonbill perched in a tree at the mouth of the river, kingfishers darted back and forth, and howler monkeys sounded just out of sight. Now that tourism has increased, the chances of you, the dogs, and the wildlife having the beach to yourself are somewhat reduced, but it remains a tranquil setting. The monkeys, dogs, and birds are still there.

The tiny town of **Tambor** has growing offerings for travelers. Along with nature walks and birding, water sports attract visitors. Area lodges and hotels arrange tours. Two gift shops, Tucán Boutique and Salsa, loaded with handcrafted items, are on the main road. Both offer international phone and fax service, open daily. Tambor is 14 miles (23 km) southwest of Paquera.

Diving and Snorkeling

Tropic World Diving Station, (506) 661-2039, extension 704, fax (506) 661-2069, offers half-day excursions for snorkeling ($35) and diving ($35–$65), Diving courses run from one-day ($105, no certification) to four-day open-water certification ($450), and an advanced open-water course ($325). Ask about three- to 10-day diving packages, as well as tours to Caño Island, Coco Island, and one that takes in Cabo Blanco and Tortuga and Negritos Islands. Tropic World has offices at Playa Tambor Beach Resort and in the small beach town of Pochote on Bahía Ballena's northeast side.

Where to Eat around Bahía Ballena

In Tambor, try **Restaurant Perla Tambor** at the southern edge of town, and **Cabinas y Restaurante Cristina** near the beach. For a view of the whole sweep of the bay, stop by **Bahía Ballena Yacht Club Restaurant** for great smoothies, fruit shakes, and vegetarian fare as well as BLTs, hamburgers, and the catch of the day. Most hotel restaurants are open to the public.

Where to Stay around Bahía Ballena

Hotel Dos Lagartos, telephone/fax (506) 683-0236, is also on the beach in Tambor. The 23 rooms are neat and simple with ceiling fans—downstairs rooms seem cooler. Six have private baths, $25; rooms with shared baths are $17 to $20; no hot water. The small dining room serves breakfast; several restaurants are nearby. Dos Lagartos arranges horseback rides and boat tours. Nothing luxurious about this place, but guests give it high marks.

Tambor Tropical, (506) 683-0011, fax (506) 683-0013; e-mail tamborcr@sol.racsa.co.cr; U.S. number (503) 365-2872; e-mail TamborT@aol.com; Web site www.members.aol.com/tambort/tambor.htm, is a delightful one-of-a-kind destination on Tambor beach. Ten outstanding rooms are in five two-story hexagonal bungalows fashioned with 15 varieties of wood. The handcrafting continues inside in the breakfast bar, chairs, stools, beautiful cabinets in a blue-tiled bathroom, and lamps. Doors and polished peg-and-groove floors are of purple-heart wood. These 1,000-square-foot open rooms have a well-equipped kitchen set off by a breakfast bar, a living area furnished with cushioned bamboo sofa and chairs, and a raised sleeping area with queen-size bed. Leave screened, louvered windows open enough to see the rich hues of sunrise. Attention to detail is everywhere, down to coffee filters, napkins, and paper towels in the kitchen—no chipped five-and-dime dishes here. Double $125 to $150, including continental breakfast. Adults only.

Grounds landscaped with tropical shrubs and flowers bring hummingbirds right up to the bungalow's wraparound terrace. Coconut palms reflect in the waters of the graceful pool and Jacuzzi. The small restaurant, open to the public, serves tasty, reasonably priced light meals: cheeseburgers, chicken nuggets, and burritos, as well as local lobster. Evening dining under the stars at poolside tables is private and romantic.

Choose a boat tour to Curú wildlife refuge and Tortuga Island, including a nature walk, snorkeling, and a look at mangroves. Take a horseback tour to waterfalls and a small lagoon. Staff arranges fishing trips and visits to Mal País, Montezuma, or Cabo Blanco by taxi.

TANGO MAR, PRIVATE RESERVE

Location: Southern Nicoya Peninsula, 2 miles (3 km) SW of Tambor toward Cóbano.

Rates: Oceanfront rooms, single $145, double $160. Tropical Suites, single $160, double $175. Tiki Suites, $250. Villas, $250 to $350. Continental breakfast and taxes included. Low-season rates and packages.

Information/Reservations: In Escazú, (506) 289-9328, fax (506) 289-8218. At Tango Mar, (506) 683-0001/2, fax (506) 683-0003; Web site www.tangomar.com.

Long recognized as a deluxe destination, Tango Mar is enhancing its offerings as a natural history destination. Reforestation with native species, creation of forest corridors between forest patches, and maintenance of a small artificial lake as a sanctuary for aquatic birds are part of a well-formulated plan to make 25 acres (10 ha) of the 121-acre (49-ha) property a private wildlife refuge. The plan encompasses protection of two troops of howler monkeys and the white-tailed deer who move through here, reproduction of scarlet macaws and green iguanas in their natural habitat, and protection of olive ridley turtles who nest on Tango Mar's beach—heaviest arrivals in October and November.

Almost 2 miles (3 km) of nature trails already exist. The bird list numbers about 100, with species such as the white-fronted and yellow-naped parrot, black-headed trogon, long-tailed manakin, and turquoise-browed motmot. Water birds include the roseate spoonbill, black-crowned night-heron, northern jacana, lesser scaup, black-bellied whistling duck, and brown pelican. Mammals, in addition to howlers and deer, include white-faced monkeys, armadillos, anteaters, agoutis, coatis, porcupines, and kinkajous.

Tango Mar offers horseback riding, snorkeling, fishing, golf (nine-hole, par three and four), and tennis. A day trip goes to Tortuga Island for snorkeling, to Curú for a guided hike, and through the Pochote mangrove estuary ($70). A visit to Montezuma and its waterfalls is $45. Try the sunset champagne cruise for two, jeep jungle safaris, and massage therapy. Visit the 40-foot (12-m) waterfall; at low tide a natural pool at the bottom is great for swimming.

In a jungle setting, the hotel's pool is fed by natural mineral water. The open-air restaurant is surrounded by lush tropical plants; food and service are excellent and the evening ambiance romantic.

All accommodations have satellite TV, air conditioning, ceiling fans, and baths with big towels. Sixteen large, elegantly simple oceanfront rooms have cool floors of reddish-brown polished tiles, two queen-size beds (some king-size), rattan furniture (including desk and long benches), folk art and original paintings, fresh flowers, reading lamps, and ample closets. A private balcony faces the sea.

Twelve hillside Tropical Suites feature hand-carved four-poster canopy beds, minibars, etched-glass windows, and in-room Jacuzzis. Outdoor patios, secluded in tropical foliage, afford ocean views; monkeys pass by every day. Five Tiki Suites near the dining room are fun, with lots of glass and *caña brava* (a wild cane that resembles bamboo) as structural decoration. Cabaña-style, raised off the ground, each has an in-room Jacuzzi, king-size bed, living area, and refrigerator and light-cooking facilities. Two-bedroom, two-bath villas include kitchenettes and sitting areas. The property also has a residential area of stylish homes.

Getting There

By car: Take the ferry to Playa Naranjo or Paquera and continue past Tambor.
By air: SANSA and Travelair have flights to Tambor.

Charming Tiki Suites at Tango Mar

MONTEZUMA AND ENVIRONS

On the southern Nicoya Peninsula, 23 miles (37 km) from Paquera and 5 miles (8 km) from Cóbano is the interesting little beach town of **Montezuma**. In the past, it could not seem to decide whether to dress up and go for big-time tourism or just hang out and take what came. Some in the community organized to combat a few of the problems that did come: no more unregulated camping—now there's a specified camping area with latrines and water. You can pitch in and help with beach cleanups. New small hotels are going in, and older ones are being spruced up. Beaches are spectacular— some to the north have loads of gorgeous shells. Go horseback riding, hike to the waterfall east of downtown for a swim, snorkel, visit Cabo Blanco reserve farther down the road, bird-watch, or surf. The area attracts large numbers of European as well as North American visitors.

One of Montezuma's claims to fame is **Sano Banano**, a macrobiotic restaurant that serves delicious food with a flair. It has not only a frozen yogurt machine but also a slush machine and serves fresh popcorn. No meat here—veggie burgers, avocado sandwiches, and fresh fish. Sitting in the outdoor eating area, shaded by trees, sipping a terrific tropical fruit shake gives you another perspective on Montezuma. Open 7 a.m. to 10 p.m.; nightly movies on a large screen for patrons.

Tour Agency

Aventuras en Montezuma, telephone/fax (506) 642-0050, is a tour and information center with a helpful, friendly staff. Day tours include Curú ($20), Tortuga Island and snorkeling ($30), rafting, and horseback riding.

Transportation is arranged to Cabo Blanco as well as transfers by boat/land to such sites as Sámara, Puntarenas, Tamarindo, Arenal, and Ostional (in September/October for the turtles, $30). Here you can rent motorcycles or cars, make air arrangements and international phone calls, send faxes, and find out where to get a massage. Open 8 a.m. to noon and 2 to 7 p.m.

Where to Stay and Eat around Montezuma

Amor de Mar, telephone/fax (506) 642-0262; e-mail shoebox@sol.racsa .co.cr, is family-oriented: owners Ori and Richard Stocker welcome children. Nine rooms with private baths range from $40 to $60 for doubles; two rooms share one bath, $30 to $35. The two-story hotel has sea in front and the river on one side. Hammocks are strategically placed under palms in a pretty, grassy garden. Swim in the tide pool in front—it's a tropical aquarium. The restaurant serves full breakfasts all day—marvelous homemade bread, yogurt, and natural fruit juices.

Cabinas El Sano Banano, telephone/fax (506) 642-0068, just outside Montezuma and owned by Sano Banano restaurant owners Lenny and Patricia Iacona, is as distinctive as the restaurant. Seven romantic geodesic-dome bungalows are tucked into the forest near the beach. Each has a refrigerator and coffeemaker, ceiling fan, one or two double beds, and bathrooms with private outdoor showers (no hot water); $70 for two. A Polynesian place has a kitchen, two double beds, and an outdoor shower; $80 for up to four. Rooms in a two-story unit are $53 for two. Lighted paths through attractively landscaped grounds connect bungalows and rooms. A three-bedroom house with full kitchen is available. Getting to this secluded complex is part of the treat—no road access, about a 15-minute walk along the beach from town. Luggage can be delivered.

Finca Los Caballos Nature Lodge, telephone/fax (506) 642-0124; e-mail naturelc@sol.racsa.co.cr; Web site centralamerica.com/cr/hotel/caballos.htm, is a charming natural history destination between Cóbano and Montezuma. Owner Barbara MacGregor, from Vancouver, Canada, designed and built the lodge in 1994. Eight rooms in two Spanish ranch–style buildings have double beds (most have a single, too) with Mexican serape bedcovers, orthopedic mattresses, and fans; single $40, double $50. Hammocks and chairs on terraces extend the living space through double doors from each room. An outdoor patio dining room looks out on a small swimming pool on the edge of forever. Make a date with yourself to watch moonrise from here. The daytime vista across the mountaintops to the coast is a keeper. Watch for laughing falcons, gray hawks, toucans, hummingbirds, howler and white-faced monkeys. (A two-bedroom house with full kitchen is also available; minimum: three nights.)

Barbara serves three healthy meals a day, featuring homemade bread, jams, and sauces. I vouch for the good food, relaxing atmosphere, and good conversation.

Horseback tours are a specialty, with 12 excellent horses for riders from beginner to expert, $10 per hour. Ride through the countryside; go along forest trails and beaches to secluded waterfalls and river pools surrounded by tropical nature; choose an overnight to Mal País across the peninsula to the Pacific. Take a two-hour walk along the river to the beach. In addition to her own tours, Barbara helps guests get to Cabo Blanco or Tortuga Island, rent bicycles, hike, go diving, have a massage, and attend local fiestas. Montezuma and its beach are a five-minute drive away, or a 20-minute walk, less than 2 miles (3 km). Hear the sound of the ocean from the hilltop.

Hotel Aurora, telephone/fax (506) 642-0051, has nine rooms, six with private baths (no hot water), in a three-story house in town. Each room is cooled by a fan and has mosquito netting. A second-floor open lounge is a gathering place for guests; some take advantage of an exercise corner. Double $15 with shared baths, $30 with private bath; apartment for four $50. Only breakfast is served, but there is a refrigerator for guest use. Angela, co-owner with Kenneth, is an articulate proponent of Montezuma's special natural attractions. She can steer you to activities suited to your interests.

Hotel Celaje, telephone/fax (506) 642-0374, cellular (506) 284-7562, is about a half-mile (1 km) before the entrance to Cabo Blanco in Cabuya. This charming hideaway features seven private bungalows; a thatched, open-air restaurant (open to the public) that specializes in Italian food; and a graceful free-form pool separated from the sea by tall, picturesque palms. Candles in coconut shells glow at night along paths. Hosts and six-year residents Angelo and Erica take guests to Cabo Blanco, rent kayaks, and arrange boat or horseback excursions. Celaje is an agent for SANSA and provides transfers from Tambor airport or the bus in Montezuma. Each A-frame thatched bungalow has a fan-cooled upstairs ocean-view bedroom for up to four persons. Downstairs is a living area with hammock, hanging chair, and table with chairs. Louvered doors open up to the sand and the palms or close off for privacy. Single $30, double $40, including tax. Meal plans available.

Hotel El Jardín, telephone/fax (506) 642-0074, in Montezuma has a hillside setting. Lustrous tropical woods are dominant in nine spacious rooms. Immaculate and simply furnished, each has glass and louvered windows, a ceiling fan, and small refrigerator. From the upstairs balcony is a view of the sea; the main beach is a four-minute walk away. Hammocks hang on a long downstairs veranda. Single/double, $40 without hot water, $45 with. The restaurant, open only in high season, specializes in Italian food. Staff arrange horseback riding, hiking, sportfishing, and area tours.

At **Las Rocas,** telephone/fax (506) 642-0393, about a mile (2 km) from Montezuma on the way to Cabuya, guests find homemade bread on the table in the small restaurant, with choices of salads, sandwiches, or in the evening, entrees of chicken or fresh fish. Simple, very clean rooms are in a two-story building next to the restaurant and an open rancho for outdoor living. Rooms with shared baths are $10 per person, $15 per person with private baths. Guests have kitchen privileges. Gisella, from Italy, and Reto, from Switzerland, manage Las Rocas, which surely gets its name from rocks along the coast in front. They offer a one-day trip to a secluded beach and a birding tour to the river.

CABO BLANCO STRICT NATURE RESERVE

Location: 7 miles (11 km) SW of Montezuma, the southernmost tip of the Nicoya Peninsula.
Size: 2,896 acres (1,172 ha) of land; 4,423 acres (1,790 ha) of marine habitat.
Hours: 8 a.m. to 4 p.m., closed Monday and Tuesday.
Cost: $6.
Information: Telephone hotline 192 (see Appendix A: Parks and Reserves Information), telephone/fax (506) 642-0093.

Cabo Blanco Strict Nature Reserve is important historically as well as biologically. It was set aside as a protected area in 1963 before Costa Rica had a park service, largely through the efforts of Olof Wessberg and Karen Mogensen, both now deceased, who had come to live on the Nicoya Peninsula in 1955. Because of their love of nature and concern about rapid destruction of forest on the tip of the peninsula—plus personal commitment and a good measure of persistence with funding sources and bureaucracy—this forest and sanctuary for seabirds exists today. A memorial plaque at the entrance honors Olof and a trail is named for Doña Karen.

The reserve is a treasure. The magic begins on the path between the parking area and visitor center. Take your time and walk quietly. A white-tailed deer, framed against the greens of the forest, studied our arrival on my last visit. Further along the path, howler monkey were feeding on the yellow fruit of the jobo tree. Howlers, white-faced monkeys, and coatis eat this fruit whole, defecating the large nuts in a day or two. An agouti moved through the underbrush. Visitors often see monkeys and an admirable assortment of birds and butterflies in the picnic area next to the visitor center.

Birds are abundant. The current list has more than 130 species; one birder counted 74 species in four hours. Land species include thicket tinamou, great curassow, red-lored parrot, cinnamon hummingbird, masked tityra, scissor-tailed flycatcher, red-crowned ant-tanager, black-headed trogon, orange-chinned parakeet, blue-crowned motmot, and long-tailed manakin. Among water birds are olivaceous cormorants, bare-throated tiger-herons, American oystercatchers, and whimbrels.

The reserve claims 140 kinds of trees; predominant species are gumbo limbo, lemonwood, frangipani, dogwood, trumpet tree, and cedar. You'll pass the gumbo limbo, with its peeling bark, and the spiny pochote trees on the walk in. Rainfall in this moist forest is 118 inches (3,000 mm); average temperature, 81°F (27°C).

Cabo Blanco (White Cape) got its name from the small island a short distance off the point, though there is dispute about whether the name comes from deposits of bird guano, a white cliff, or light-colored soil. Pelicans, frigate birds, and brown boobies hang out there. The area is rich in marine life: octopus, starfish, sea cucumber, lobster, giant conch, and fish such as snapper and snook.

The small visitor center has attractive exhibits on Cabo Blanco wildlife as well as a snack stand (sometimes closed in low season), drinking water, and rest rooms. You can purchase various small publications, including a bird list with English, Spanish, and scientific names; a bilingual folder on mammal tracks; and a bilingual booklet on Cabo Blanco tree species.

A well-maintained loop trail that takes about 90 minutes goes through secondary and some primary forest, hilly but not difficult. A two-hour trek through low mountains, steep in places, leads to Cabo Blanco Beach, a sandy spot on a mostly rocky shoreline. You may still have the beach practically to yourself for a bit, except for colored crabs and seabirds. The famous English pirate Captain John Cook died off these shores in 1684 and was buried here, site unknown.

Remember as you walk through this small fragile reserve that until the 1960s, 85 percent of it was pasture and agricultural land; now it's secondary forest. Primary forest still standing when the Swedish couple mounted their conservation campaign, constitutes 15 percent of the reserve today; it provided the gene bank that allowed natural forest regeneration once the area was protected. Seeds dispersed by wind and by animals took root and grew. Some marine species on the point of disappearing are now thriving.

Getting There

By bus: Bus to Montezuma; from there go by tour, taxi, bike, horse rental, or on foot.

By car: Unpaved road from Montezuma; if the bridge is not finished, ford the usually shallow river. The reserve's parking area is a distance from the visitor center. In high season an attendant watches cars for about $1; if no one is on duty, don't leave valuables in the car, even though so far this seems to be a safe area.

MAL PAIS AND SANTA TERESA AREAS

On the other side of the Nicoya Peninsula from Montezuma is the less-visited Mal País region, which has excellent possibilities for natural history travelers. Small hotels, lodges, and restaurants cater to those who like to be off the beaten path. Dine at your lodge or ask your innkeeper for other area recommendations. Surfers, nature lovers, and fisherfolk find hosts here who love being where they are, doing what they do. Sunset is an event.

Year-round access is from Cóbano, 7.5 pleasant miles (12 km) via gravel road. At the coast, go right to Santa Teresa Beach or left to Mal País. In dry season, the route via Cabuya just north of the Cabo Blanco reserve is generally passable, which gets you to Mal País in about 15 minutes.

Where to Stay and Eat in Mal País and Santa Teresa Areas

Mar Azul in Mal País, telephone/fax (506) 640-0098, offers rustic lodging and camping. Some of the 13 rooms have private baths—no hot water; all have fans; one has a kitchenette. Owners Otto and Jeannette are hosts. Rooms $15 to $30. The restaurant serves seafood and typical meals.

Sunset Reef Marine Lodge, telephone/fax (506) 640-0012; e-mail sunreef @sol.racsa.co.cr; in U.S. (800) 388-2582, fax 544-4651; e-mail alta@grid.net, faces the long curve of Mal País Bay, within view of the Cabo Blanco reserve. Surrounded by lush gardens, 17 air-conditioned rooms of tropical hardwoods offer two double beds, desk, small table and chairs, ceiling fans, tropical flower arrangements, and big-view windows. Single $70, double $88; breakfast $7.50, lunch $12, dinner $13.50. Pretty plant-lined paths lead to a lounge area near the beach and to an intimate pool and Jacuzzi above the bay.

The lodge offers diving (starting at $35), bicycle and kayak rental ($10 for half day), boat tours, fishing, guided nature walks, and horseback riding. In a buffer zone for the reserve, Sunset Reef is no stranger to wildlife: parrots, trogons, herons, hawks, kingfishers, motmots, woodpeckers, manakins, euphonias, brown boobies, and storks are on the bird list. On a short walk you may see brocket deer, kinkajous, coatis, and monkeys. Marine life in the tidal pools is rich: starfish, oysters, octopus, colorful fishes.

To get here, turn left at the Mal País–Santa Teresa junction and continue 2.5 miles (4 km). Air/land transportation arranged to anywhere on the peninsula.

Trópico Latino Lodge, telephone/fax (506) 640-0062; e-mail tropico @centralamerica.com; Web site www.centralamerica.com/cr/hotel/ tropico.htm, has 6 miles (10 km) of white-sand beach at its front door. Go to sleep to the sound of the surf and wake up to the call of parrots and howler monkeys. Six spacious rooms have roll-up shades, screened windows, ceiling fans, and a porch with hammocks and chairs. Centerpiece of the room has to be the bed, with mosquito netting draped gracefully around its big bamboo frame. I noticed no mosquitoes, but I slept under the net—you can't tell me it's not exotic to sleep under a mosquito net. Made my day. Single $50, double $60, including taxes. No credit cards. Food is excellent; restaurant open to the public.

Marvel at the moon while relaxing in the whirlpool or swimming pool, with fireflies signaling in the garden. Surf, hike along the beach (good tide pools and rock formations to poke around in), ride horses, or fish. On Santa Teresa Beach, just 3 miles (5 km) north of Cabo Blanco, Trópico Latino has howlers, toucans, parrots, blue jays, parakeets, coatis, iguanas, big frogs, and many seabirds around. Transfers arranged from the ferry, airport, or Cóbano.

STAR MOUNTAIN ECO RESORT, PRIVATE RESERVE

Location: 9 *miles (14 km) S of Cóbano on SW end of the Nicoya Peninsula, 1.5 miles (2.5 km) from Mal País.*
Rates: Single $45, double $65, including full breakfast and taxes. Bunkhouse $25 per person. No credit cards yet.
Information/Reservations: At lodge, telephone/fax (506) 640-0101. U.S. number telephone/fax (305) 534-4851; e-mail info@starmountaineco.com; Web site www.starmountaineco.com/.

Just when I think I've seen it all, I come upon a natural jewel like Star Mountain. Tucked away in the mountains above Mal País, this secluded retreat has all the charm of a country inn set amid 200 acres (86 ha) of forest that feels primeval. A jaguar had eaten a calf not long before I arrived; the staff list anteater, margay, puma, jaguarundi, white-tailed deer, *tepezcuintle*, coati, armadillo, kinkajou, coyote, raccoon, skunk, and howler and white-faced monkeys among mammals they have seen.

The growing bird list has 120 species, such as long-tailed and red-capped manakins, both fiery-billed and collared aracaris, squirrel cuckoos, laughing falcons, black-headed and violaceous trogons, and several species of hummingbirds, herons, and woodpeckers.

You want trails? You've got 'em, from short and easy (with arrows for self-guiding) to a six-hour adventure trek though the forest where, depending on time of year, you encounter several waterfalls. A steep two-hour walk affords an expansive view of both the Gulf of Nicoya and the Pacific. Go horseback riding. I recommend a leisurely walk back down the road you came in on to watch the birdlife along the stream and the blue morpho butterflies.

With easy access to the beach, Star Mountain offers a boat tour to Cabo Blanco Island to see mantas, turtles, and birds. A day trip to Tortuga Island in a local *panga* (small boat but equipped with life jackets) is $150 for up to four. Snorkeling, fishing, and sea kayaking arranged.

The colorful open-air dining room with its rustic tree-trunk tables offers some international cuisine surprises, influenced by the manager Bernard, who is a multilingual French chef. Imagine crepe flambé in the forest. Expect light lunches and dinner menus that include a vegetarian choice.

The four rooms—owner Bill Clay of Florida has more planned—open through double doors onto a long porch (with great Costa Rican leather rocking chairs) looking out on the landscaped grounds and down to a sun deck, pool, and Jacuzzi. All rooms have big showers (with shampoo/conditioner/soap dispenser!), ceiling fans, desks, and original Costa Rican artwork. Choose your room by color. The pink room has two double beds, a watermelon painting, and a big dressing area off the bathroom separated by a bamboo curtain. The gray room has a king-size bed. For a group or family, a two-room bunkhouse accommodates up to nine.

Getting There
By bus: Get to Cóbano; transfer provided.
By car: Head to Mal País from Cóbano; watch for signs at the Mal País–Santa Teresa junction. The dirt road passes through a couple of streams: in rainy season ask if four-wheel-drive is necessary.
Other: Transfers from Tambor airport or Paquera ferry. Arrival by helicopter arranged.

INTER-AMERICAN HIGHWAY TO LIBERIA AND POINTS NORTH

Excellent private nature reserves and national parks and reserves are accessible along this route. Note the vegetation changes as the Inter-American Highway winds between the coastal zone and the mountains to the east. In dry season, flowering red, white, pink, and yellow trees decorate a browner landscape. In any season the national tree, the guanacaste, spreads its branches like a great fan: horses and cattle seek shade under its mimosa-like leaves in pasturelands.

The road to Monteverde described in the next section, takes off from here, and 11 miles (18 km) past the Lagarto River bridge is the Tempisque ferry turnoff, which carries cars and passengers to the Nicoya Peninsula—see the Pacific Northwest Beaches and Upper Nicoya Peninsula section.

Though there are a number of good restaurants along here, a favorite is **Garabito Restaurant**, at km 125. Order ceviche, fried yuca, shrimp, fish, and lots more.

Where to Stay between Puntarenas and Tempisque Ferry
Hotel Vista Golfo de Nicoya, telephone/fax (506) 639-8303, cellular (506) 382-3312, is perched on a hillside 3 miles (5 km) beyond the town of Miramar. As its name implies, the place has a commanding view of the gulf and Chira Island, Isla de los Pájaros, and San Lucas Island. There's forest and farmland before and behind you, birdsong, tranquility, beauty. Enjoy a cold glass of perhaps the best tropical fruit punch in existence as you relax in the shade of an enormous fig tree on the deck next to the restaurant/bar. There's an aviary, a pool filled with natural spring water, Jacuzzi, and a nature trail or two on this 173-acre (70-ha) former cattle ranch. In addition to a wealth of birds, you're likely to see coatis, white-faced monkeys, morpho butterflies, agoutis—I saw a gorgeous green snake.

The 14 rooms look down on pool and garden. Each is a bit different; most have private baths; one is two-story with a living area. Furnishing are simple but comfortable with fans and decorator touches; generally smallish rooms have a big view from the balcony. Single $26 to $45, double $30 to $45.

Activities include horseback rides to a nearby river ($25) and mountain biking; tours visit a gold mine—see panning for gold in the old style—Cedral Lagoon, and a cloud forest. Staff arrange Tortuga Island tours and transfers around the country. Day packages are available: a tour including guided hike to the river and visit to mine, lunch, and use of pool or trails is $35; with horseback riding, $40. See pineapples, sugarcane, coffee, 400 tropical fruit trees, and some 3,000 coconut palms.

The hotel is about two hours from San José or Liberia airports. Turn off the Inter-American at a big gas station, about 4 miles (6 km) past the Puntarenas exit. From Miramar follow hotel signs.

LA ENSENADA LODGE, PRIVATE WILDLIFE REFUGE

Location: 87 miles (140 km) NW of San José, 56 miles (90 km) SE of Liberia, mainland side of Gulf of Nicoya N of Punta Morales.
Rates: Single $31, double $25 per person, no credit cards.
Information/Reservations: (506) 228-6653, (506) 289-6653, fax (506) 289-5281.

La Ensenada Lodge is a delightful surprise at the end of a dirt road through rural landscapes. The 865-acre (350-ha) property is registered as a private wildlife refuge. Guests can enjoy water- and land-based birds—more than 140 species, including white ibis, tricolored heron, purple gallinule, double-striped thick-knee, parrots, parakeets, bellbirds, trogons, and kingfishers. With luck, you might see a jabiru. Crocodiles, coyotes, howler and white-faced monkeys, sloths, agoutis, and iguanas are about. A freshwater and salt-water lagoon add to mangrove, river, and forest habitats.

Hotel Vista Golfo de Nicoya

Also a working farm, Ensenada offers a chance to participate in Costa Rican farm life: cattle, horses, and various fruit crops, including watermelon. Ride native criollo horses ($15) to explore refuge trails, visit a salt flat (January to April see salt produced much the way indigenous peoples did it), and go to a freshwater lagoon and through forest to a hilltop view of the gulf at sundown.

Boats carry guests on a two-hour island and mangrove tour to see roseate spoonbills, hawks, black-bellied whistling ducks, and egrets, along with crocodiles and howler monkeys, $26 each for two. A three-hour boat trip to Palo Verde National Park is $46 each. Marked hiking trails go through dry forest, mangroves, and wetlands. Tennis, swimming in the pool, water-skiing, and windsurfing are other options, but be sure to leave time to relax in the hammock on your front porch.

Lodging is in wooden bungalows facing gulf waters (*ensenada* means cove or small bay). Eight cabins have two rooms, each with its own bath, while four larger cabins are ideal for families; one has a ramp for wheelchairs. Meals are served in a large thatched rancho with checkered tablecloths: breakfast $3.50, lunch $8.50, dinner $10.

Getting There

By bus: From San José, take the bus to Punta Morales and catch the afternoon bus to Abangaritos, where lodge staff picks you up with advance notice. By car: From San José, take the Inter-American to Punta Morales turnoff and continue for 12 miles (19 km) on gravel road (watch out for the chickens); from Liberia, take the Inter-American to the Costa de Pájaros turnoff and continue 9 miles (15 km).

HACIENDA SOLIMAR, PRIVATE RESERVE

Location: Between the Inter-American and the Tempisque ferry.
Rates: Hacienda house $85 per person including lodging, meals, guided birding tour, and taxes; guest house, $75. Credit cards accepted with prior payment; at ranch only cash or traveler's checks.
Information/Reservations: San José, (506) 238-3890, fax (506) 237-0196; Solimar (506) 669-0281; U.S. number (800) 295-2222, fax (607) 729-2904; e-mail solimar@sol.racsa.co.cr; Web site www.birdcostarica.com.

Madrigal Estuary one late afternoon is a memory I will keep. Light filtered through trees along the riverbank; water hyacinths covering the winding water glowed green; the still air carried sounds of hundreds of ibis and egrets settling in communal roosts, herons, kingfishers, wood storks, and roseate spoonbills. So many birds in this secluded setting . . . and in rainy season! What must this must be like in dry season when other water sources around here dry up?

A glimpse comes from the Solimar visitor book back at the hacienda house. Former guests repeatedly report sighting more than 100 species of birds in a three-day stay: the double-striped thick knee, which lays its eggs on the bare ground; squirrel cuckoo; black-headed trogon; violaceous trogon; tricolored heron; collared forest-falcon; and euphonias, parrots, and jays galore.

The estuary is not all of this almost 5,000-acre (2,000 ha) hacienda: eight habitats are home for 317 species of birds, including 32 species of raptors and six of owls. Most frequently seen mammals are howler and white-faced monkeys, lesser anteaters, armadillos (my Texan sister-in-law was not impressed), coatis, collared peccaries, jaguarundi, and white-tailed deer; other common fauna are snakes, frogs, and iguanas. Walk with Pedro or Dimitri, fantastic local guides, to seek the resident jabiru. The Tempisque basin is Costa Rica's only breeding area for these tall, elegant-looking birds with white bodies, black heads, and red "necklaces." Ask about nine- to 14-day guided birding tours from Solimar to the Caribbean rain forest and the highlands, available for groups or individuals.

Trails and ranch roadways offer opportunities to stroll at one's own pace and discover the abundant life here. Guests can go horseback riding, $10 per hour, or mount up with the cowboys for a morning's work on the ranch, $25. Climb the short, steep trail back of the house to the *mirador*, where you can see forever: Palo Verde National Park, Miravalles and Tenorio Volcanoes, the Tempisque River. Sit there on a bench in the shade of a tree.

A cool dip in the pool at the house after a hot day of travel or birding is heaven. A wraparound deck and a large covered outdoor lounging area with marvelous leather Costa Rican rocking chairs look out at the pool and bright red- and orange-blossomed trees called *malinches* in Spanish (poincianas).

Hearty, delicious meals (Marlene was the cook during my visit) are served family-style in the screened-in dining area that adjoins a spacious living room. Lower walls are of river rock. This house, the center of hacienda life for the Pacheco family since 1957, now offers gracious country living for natural history visitors. Ardent birder Oscar Pacheco enthusiastically oversees this aspect of the property, which continues to function as a working cattle ranch and reforestation project. Some 865 acres (350 ha) have been reforested with native species, and 1,000 acres (400 ha) more has been under natural regeneration for up to 27 years, enriched with some wood-producing native species.

The two-story hacienda house has five rooms, most with private baths and no hot water. Rooms have screened, louvered windows; big closets; simple furnishings. Six rooms are in a nearby guesthouse.

Part of the pleasure of spending time at places like this is getting to know local staff—guides, cooks, cowboys, cleaning personnel. I think you'll enjoy that at Solimar—I did. (Save some of your souvenir money for Pedro's hand-painted gourds.)

Getting There

By car: From the Tempisque ferry turnoff on the Inter-American, go 8 miles (13 km) and take the unpaved road that slopes down to the right; continue 4 miles (7 km) to ranch headquarters.

Other: Ask about transfers.

CAÑAS

An important junction on the Inter-American 107 miles (172 km) northwest of San José, Cañas offers gas stations, banks, a clinic, pharmacies, and small restaurants and hotels. From here travelers can go northeast by paved highway to Tilarán for access to Arenal and other north central destinations. The town (population 17,075) can be a base for day trips into Lomas Barbudal Biological Reserve and/or Palo Verde National Park. About 4 miles (6 km) northwest of Cañas is a paved road to Upala, a gateway to the western side of Caño Negro wildlife refuge (see Chapter 7).

Big ditches in this area are part of the government's ambitious Arenal–Tempisque irrigation project (SENARA) to supply Guanacaste farms with water. By the time the water gets to the lowlands, it has already generated electricity three times: at Arenal, Corobicí, and Sandillal hydroelectric plants. The project benefits more than 1,000 farm families, providing water to almost 45,000 acres (18,000 ha) that would otherwise be dry for half the year. Main agricultural crops are rice, sugarcane, sorghum, and cotton; cattle ranching is also important to the economy.

River Trips
Cata Tours, (506) 296-2133, fax (506) 296-2730, telephone/fax (506) 674-0180, offers a grand river trip on the Bebedero to Palo Verde and the Tempisque River. See crocodiles and birds galore, and probably monkeys, too. Three hours on the river with a bilingual guide is $39 from Cañas, $75 from San José.

Watch for **Safaris Corobicí,** telephone/fax (506) 669-1091; e-mail safaris@sol.racsa.co.cr; Web site www.nicoya.com/, at km 193, about 2.5 miles (1.5 km) north of Cañas. The company offers a bird-watcher's special on the Corobicí: $35 for a two-hour float trip. A three-hour trip to the Catalina entrance of Palo Verde is $45, and a five-hour family float trip is $60 per person. Children under 14 accompanied by an adult are half-price on all trips. A half-day saltwater estuary trip ($50) goes to the border of Palo Verde, into the Tempisque River.

Other Things to See and Do
Las Pumas, (506) 669-0444, off the Inter-American just before La Pacífica, is an animal sanctuary operated for many years by Werner and Lily Hagenauer. Here are 15 cats representing all six species found in Costa Rica: jaguar, puma, margay, jaguarundi, ocelot, and *oncilla* (little spotted cat), along with peccaries, scarlet macaws, and other animals that have been brought here by individuals or wildlife agencies. Open 8 a.m. to 5 p.m. daily; no charge, but donations needed and gladly accepted.

Where to Stay in and near Cañas
Capazuri Bed and Breakfast, telephone/fax (506) 669-0580, is just past Cañas at km 191; the Gamboas give a warm greeting. They have five bright,

pleasant rooms with bamboo furniture and private baths but no hot water. Single $11, double $22, breakfast included. Campers are welcome, $3 per person, and camping facilities include a bath and access to the large rancho in the garden, furnished with a refrigerator and hammocks. Breakfast for campers is $3. A swimming pool should be finished by your arrival, set among many flowers and tropical fruit trees. The Gamboas keep lots of information on hand for guests and offer helpful travel tips.

Nuevo Hotel Cañas, (506) 669-1294, fax (506) 669-1319, in Cañas is a pretty little place in a quiet area half a block east of the Inter-American, one block past the main intersection into town. Ten spic-and-span rooms, with cable TV, telephones, and ceiling fans, open onto a garden and small swimming pool, even a whirlpool. Nothing fancy, but rooms are comfortable and ambiance pleasant. Single $19, double $33. Though the staff doesn't speak English, service is with a smile. The hotel has a restaurant 1½ blocks away. Be sure to ask for the *Nuevo* (new) Hotel Cañas.

Where to Eat near Cañas
On the banks of the Corobicí River just 2.5 miles (4 km) north of Cañas is **Restaurant Rincón Coribicí,** (506) 669-0303, a delightful pause in the journey. Whether dining indoors or on the open terrace, the view of the river and Tenorio volcano is fabulous. Take binoculars in and appreciate why birders like this area. Food is good—get a side order of fried yuca if you haven't yet tried it. Pleasant rest rooms; public phone outside. The gift shop is loaded with handcrafted items, natural history books, cards, and jewelry. Open 8 a.m. to 10 p.m. It may be closed briefly in September or October.

LA PACIFICA, PRIVATE RESERVE
Location: From Cañas, 3 miles (5 km) N on the Inter-American; 108 miles (173 km) NW of San José; 30 miles (48 km) SW of Liberia.
Rates: Single $60, double $70.
Information/Reservations: (506) 669-0050, fax (506) 669-0555.

Pacífica means peaceful or tranquil, and indeed the traveler who pulls into La Pacífica senses a serenity to the place. Actually it was named for the wife of a former president of Costa Rica who once lived here, but why quibble? The name fits.

La Pacífica was set up as a model for economic self-sufficiency and protection of natural resources, combining agricultural activities, tourism, and research. Scientific researchers have been coming to "Finca La Pacífica" since the 1960s. The rich diversity of habitats that draws scientists— tropical dry forest, river habitat, swampland, pastures—also makes the area attractive to natural history visitors.

Accommodations are in 33 pleasant rooms grouped in buildings on spacious grounds. Interiors of those nearer the swimming pool—what a treat that pool is on a hot Guanacaste day—reflect cool earth tones, from the tile floor to striped, woven bedspreads. Sliding wood and glass doors open onto small terraces; the rooms are cooled by ceiling fans. Older cabins have been completely remodeled: there's lots of light now and convenient modern baths.

The restaurant has a pretty patio on one side and garden and fish pond on the other. One wall is "art in pottery" from Nicoya. The food is excellent. Dining is a la carte or buffet: breakfast buffet $6; lunch and dinner $12. Open to the public 6:15 a.m. to 10 p.m.

Guests can follow roads and trails on their own or with a bilingual naturalist guide, go by horseback with a local guide ($10 per hour), or bicycle. Two hiking trails are nearby: Las Garzas is a short walk in forest along the Corobicí, good for catching a glimpse of water birds and turquoise-browed motmots, black-headed trogons, yellow-naped parrots, and orange-chinned parakeets. The 2-mile (3.5-km) Chocuaco Trail, named for the boat-billed heron, has both riparian and deciduous forest. My guide shared fascinating tidbits about trees and plants. Did you know that the monkey ladder vine is used to treat diabetes? Keep your eyes open for the chewing-gum tree, the water vine, and the *bejuco* (vine) used locally as sandpaper. Seen here are long-tailed manakins, howler monkeys, Jesus Christ lizards, great egrets, and iguanas.

The beautiful Corobicí River, popular with rafters, forms part of the ranch's boundary. Rafting trips and river trips on the Bebedero to Palo Verde Park are arranged. You can also visit Doña Pacífica's house, accessible by car or horseback, now a museum. Several archaeological sites on the property have been excavated.

About 40 percent of Hacienda La Pacífica's almost 5,000 acres (2,000 ha) is covered with natural forest, windbreaks, and reforested areas, including tree species such as the increasingly rare *cocobolo* (rosewood), *caoba* (mahogany), and spiny pochote. Birdlife is abundant, with 26 percent of the country's species seen here; 68 species are migratory. The lagoon and rivers lure water birds—bird and tree lists available. Forest animals include armadillos, squirrels, *tamandus* (anteaters), deer, and monkeys. Studies on the howler monkey at Pacífica go back more than 20 years.

Visitors may tour agricultural operations, including a modern dairy and organic garden. In addition to beef and milk products, the ranch produces mangoes, pepper, sugar, rice, and heart of palm.

Annual rainfall is 66 inches (1,674 mm); average high temperature is about 91°F (33°C) and average low 73°F (23°C).

Getting There

By bus: Take the San José–Liberia bus and ask the driver to let you off at La Pacífica, or get off in Cañas and take a taxi.

By car: On the Inter-American Highway, La Pacífica is just north of Cañas before the Corobicí River.

BAGACES

This town on the Inter-American Highway 120 miles (194 km) northwest of San José, is the junction for trips to Palo Verde National Park, about 45 minutes away, and to Miravalles Volcano. A bit farther north is the road to Lomas Barbudal Biological Reserve. All are wonderful natural history destinations. For good directions and information on either Palo Verde, Lomas Barbudal, or Barra Honda, stop at Tempisque Conservation Area office in Bagaces, a white house on the highway next to the gas station, just across from the road to Palo Verde.

Mud pots at Miravalles Volcano north of Bagaces

What to See and Do

Palo Verde and Lomas Barbudal are described in following sections. A back road that connects the two is basically unmarked. When I tried it, the beginning was marvelous; roseate spoonbills dotted the rice fields. Farther along, however, as night approached and muddy ruts got deeper on what became little more than a track through isolated fields, I kept thinking, "This *cannot* be the road to Lomas Barbudal." It wasn't. Perhaps you follow directions better than I did.

Miravalles Geothermal Project is northeast of Bagaces. Follow "Miravalles" signs passing through Fortuna. A small gate in the fence along the road is a public entrance to see bubbling mud pots, small geysers in gray pools, steam, and the powerful natural energy found here. The sign is small; ask for *las hornillas* if you get lost. Notice the signs that warn you not to leave valuables unprotected in your car. The thermal site, not far from the road on a trail through open grassy ground, is awesome, with the underground forces rising to the surface in front of you and majestic Miravalles Volcano reigning on the horizon. Taxis are available from Bagaces.

Where to Stay and Eat in Bagaces

Albergue Bagaces, (506) 671-1267, fronts on the highway. Thirteen simple, clean rooms (no hot water in baths), each with desk, reading lamps, high wood ceilings, and fans, are built around a large lounge and TV room (local channels). Stop by and meet Cliff, the new owner from the United Kingdom, who will be making changes in months to come. Single $13, double $19, no credit cards yet at this modest, friendly place. The rooms are back of a large restaurant, open to the public from 10 a.m. to 10 p.m., though hotel guests can have breakfast early. Live music at Friday night *rancheras* gives a chance to mix with local folks—music stops about 1 a.m.

PALO VERDE NATIONAL PARK

Location: From Bagaces, 17 miles (28 km) SW on unpaved road; from Liberia, 34 miles (54 km) S.
Size: 48,936 acres (19,804 ha).
Hours: Daily 8 a.m. to 4 p.m.
Cost: $6.
Information: Telephone hotline 192 (see Appendix A: Parks and Reserves Information), telephone/fax (506) 671-1290, (506) 671-1062. Bagaces office, Tempisque Conservation Area: staff can arrange for a local guide to accompany you (some bilingual).

Palo Verde National Park lies along the east bank of the Tempisque River above where it flows into the Gulf of Nicoya. The area encompasses lakes, swamps, grasslands, savanna woodlands, and forest, probably 15 habitats in all. It is one of the most important sanctuaries for migrating waterfowl in Central America and is habitat for many resident species. About 280 bird species have been counted.

Herons, ibis, ducks, storks, and jacanas are among those that descend on the lowlands to feed and mate. The rare, endangered jabiru nests here, most commonly seen from November to January. The largest stork in the world, the jabiru has a white body, gray neck and head, and a rose-red necklace. The only scarlet macaws left in the tropical dry forest of the Pacific live in this area.

In the rainy season, flooding of the plains is widespread. In the dry months of November through April some waterholes disappear; those that remain attract birds and other wildlife, allowing the patient visitor a good chance to see them. An observation tower open to visitors is near the large marsh.

A trail system takes visitors into the forest past flowing springs that attract wildlife, past a natural cactus garden, to a superb lookout over the Tempisque floodplain, through a marsh (a printed guide recommends this as the best place to see a tropical rattlesnake or boa constrictor), through second-growth forest that is reclaiming pastureland, and to virgin tropical dry forest.

From the entrance it is 7.5 miles (12 km) to Puerto Chamorro on the bank of the Tempisque, where huge iguanas forage. On the way, pass trailhead signs: Sendero Pizote (Coati Trail) and Sendero Venado (Deer Trail), a 2.5-km (1.5-mile) loop. Near the station operated by the Organization for Tropical Studies (OTS) are mango trees; approach quietly for a chance to see some of the 145 mammal species that make their home in the park. Peccaries, iguanas, deer, monkeys, and coatis feed on the fruits. The white-tailed deer who watched me while I watched him did not seem the least bit frightened.

In dry season the Catalina sector can be reached by car (about 7.5 miles or 12 km), but rainy season is another story. The Manigordo Trail takes off from the station there, as does a trail to a viewpoint on Cerro Pelón, the highest place in the park, 774 feet (236 m).

The Tempisque River has a 13-foot (4-m) rise and fall with the tide. Sometimes it flows backward. River trips are a popular way to see some of the park's wildlife. Crocodiles and caimans can often be seen on its banks, along with howler monkeys and a multitude of birds. Tours pass by Isla de los Pájaros in the Tempisque, part of Palo Verde. An important nesting site, the small island at times seems covered with birds. You can generally see the lovely color of the roseate spoonbills as they nest and fly overhead. There are wood storks, glossy ibis, anhingas, and great egrets. Many boas inhabit the island, feeding on bird eggs and nestlings.

Park rangers at the entrance can give you information. On one visit, the friendly guard on duty rushed from the forest to urge me to come with him quickly—he had just come across a snake eating a frog and wanted me to see it.

You may see cattle grazing inside the park, part of a controversial management plan to keep marshes open for waterfowl, free of invasive cattails, as well as to control jaragua grass as a fire-prevention measure. Forest fires are a threat in this dry forest.

Park relations with neighbors are important; nearby rice farmers lose more of their crops than they like to birds, who do not recognize boundaries. Some have automatic cannons whose sounds help keep birds from the fields.

Annual rainfall is 90 inches (2,295 mm); average temperature is 81°F (27°C), though it can reach 105°F (41°C) at midday. Nights and early mornings are generally cool. While it's windy in the dry season and insects are scarce, the rainy season brings humidity, little breeze, mosquitoes, and gnats.

In dry season most trees lose their leaves to conserve water, but many wear bright flowers. The *palo verde* tree, which gave the park its name, has pretty yellow flowers that adorn its green, thorn-clad branches.

Getting There

By bus: Tak a bus to Bagaces; take a taxi from there.

By car: In Bagaces, turn west at the Palo Verde sign. Pavement ends but the road is generally passable year-round. Keep binoculars and cameras handy; birds are everywhere.

Other: Tour companies and lodges offer both land and water trips. Boat trips on the Tempisque usually include Isla de los Pájaros.

Where to Stay at or near Palo Verde National Park

Palo Verde Biological Station San José, (506) 240-6696; fax (506) 240-6783; e-mail reservas@ns.ots.ac.cr; Web site www.ots.duke.edu or www.ns.ots.ac.cr, is a possibility within the park. The station is operated by OTS; designed primarily for researchers and student groups, it is also open to natural history visitors. A new screened dining room, where guests are served tasty, family-style meals, and a new four-room, two-bath building with a small sitting area are backed by tropical vegetation. Next to the main road are older rooms with new shared baths, and a small gift shop. Solar energy is an important source of electricity at this remote spot. Overnight visitors may have a chance to talk to researchers during mealtimes and can arrange for a guided walk. Lodging and meals are $55 per person. OTS also invites day visitors to the station; $17 including lunch and a guided walk. Day and overnight visitors must also pay the park entrance fee.

Other lodging possibilities nearest Palo Verde park include **Rancho Humo**, across the Tempisque (described elsewhere in this chapter), and lodging in Bagaces, Cañas, and Liberia.

LOMAS BARBUDAL BIOLOGICAL RESERVE
Location: W of the Inter-American between Bagaces and Liberia.
Size: 5,631-acres (2,279 ha).
Hours: Often unstaffed.
Cost: $6.
Information: Telephone hotline 192 (see Appendix A: Parks and Reserves Information), telephone/fax (506) 671-1290, (506) 671-1062. Bagaces office, Tempisque Conservation Area: staff can arrange for a local guide (some bilingual).

My first impression of Lomas Barbudal (Spanish for "bearded hills") was birds everywhere: so many binocular stops that we hardly made progress driving along the dirt road. The quantity was overwhelming, representing some of the more than 180 species here. Because they are disappearing in other areas, three of these species are particularly important: king vulture, great curassow, and yellow-naped parrot. The man on the street will tell you that yellow-naped parrots are the best talkers in the parrot family, so trapping for the pet trade is a factor in their disappearance, along with loss of habitat. Curassows make for good eating.

Enthralled with the birds, we had little time for the bees—one of the reserve's claims to fame. About 250 species are thought to live here, some endemic species. About 60 species of moths, butterflies, and wasps are also abundant. Congo and white-faced monkeys move about the reserve, as do coatis, peccaries, white-tailed deer, armadillos, and raccoons.

Deciduous forests make up 70 percent of the reserve. One of the species that flowers profusely in the dry season, when its branches are bare of leaves, is the *cortesa amarilla* (yellow cortez). A curious tree is the cannonball. You'll know it when you see it: the fruit looks like big balls hanging on strings down the trunk and lower branches.

Rainfall in this region, classified as tropical dry forest, averages 59 to 79 inches (1,500 to 2,000 mm). Rivers such as the beautiful Cabuya flow year-round; its natural, sandy-bottomed pools are ideal for a swim under the big trees along its banks, where monkeys and birds also escape afternoon heat. Students from Bagaces High School constructed a trail that begins between a small center (nobody around except a troop of howler

What Is That Yellow Tree?

In this area it may well be a yellow cortez, corteza amarilla (Tabebuia ochracea). In dry season, this tree loses its leaves and is ornamented with a profusion of yellow blossoms. From a distance it resembles a giant bouquet. All trees in this species tend to flower on the same day, so the countryside can be studded with bouquets. Flowers in a single tree last only about four days, but the tree may bloom two or three times during the dry season. Its wood is hard and durable, favored by farmers for fenceposts, and the bark has been used medicinally for malaria and chronic anemia.

monkeys, on my most recent visit) and the river pools. The reserve has more than 20 natural springs.

Getting There

By bus: A San José-to-Liberia bus passes the turnoff on the Inter-American, leaving a 4-mile (6-km) walk.

By car: Easiest route is from Bagaces: continue north on the Inter-American 6.8 miles (11 km), then 4 miles (6 km) west via unpaved road.

LIBERIA

Capital of Guanacaste Province Liberia (population 34,099), is sometimes referred to as the White City because early adobe houses got a coating of the area's abundant lime. Some old houses have the unusual architectural feature of two doors on their northeast corners, offering views of the rising sun and twilight and giving long hours of natural daylight inside.

An information center at **El Sabanero Museum: Casa de la Cultura,** is in a house with these *puertas del sol* (corner doors). Signs direct you to the 150-year-old building 3 blocks from the park, open 8 a.m. to noon and 1:30 to 4 p.m., closed Sunday. A small museum contains memorabilia related to the cowboy (or *sabanero*) and early life in this "Wild West" region. Friendly staff members have photos of most area hotels and lodges and can make reservations. Telephone/fax is (506) 666-1606.

Liberia, located 154 miles (248 km) northwest of San José, is a commercial center and transportation hub. Scheduled national and international flights and charters land at Daniel Oduber Quirós International Airport about 11 miles (17 km) west of town. The main road west is a principal gateway to the Nicoya Peninsula, beach resorts, and northern Pacific coast.

The Inter-American continues north to the Nicaraguan border, 48 miles (77 km) away. Wherever you are headed, fill up with gasoline here.

Liberia can be a base for day trips to several national parks and reserves, including Rincón de la Vieja, Santa Rosa, Palo Verde, and Lomas Barbudal, as well as beaches such as Ocotal, Hermosa, Coco, and Tamarindo.

Getting There

By bus: From San José, Puntarenas, Nicoya, and some beach sites.
By car: Liberia is four hours from San José on the Inter-American Highway.
By air: Domestic flights, both SANSA and Travelair, international charters, and LACSA serve Liberia.

Where to Stay and Eat in Liberia

Hotel El Sitio, San José (506) 290-2238, fax (506) 290-5909, Liberia (506) 666-1211, fax (506) 666-2059, has 52 large, attractive rooms opening onto landscaped grounds and courtyard, and an open-air restaurant, pool, gift shop, exercise room, parking, children's playground, and thatched bar. Rooms have air conditioning and ceiling fans (windows that open), satellite TV, a large desk/dresser, and direct-dial telephones; single $50, double $65. A car-rental agency is on-site. Explore the hotel's 12 acres (5 ha) of property on foot or horseback with a real Guanacaste *sabanero*. Transfers available to nearby beaches and the Liberia airport.

Hotel Las Espuelas, Las Espuelas (506) 666-0144, San José (506) 239-2000; e-mail hherradu@sol.racsa.co.cr; Web site www.costasol.co.cr; U.S. and Canada numbers (800) 245-8420, fax (506) 225-3987, has 44 rooms with private baths; single $53, double $68. Polished floor tiles gleam along covered walkways leading from the lobby and restaurant/bar areas through landscaped grounds to wings of rooms named for nearby parks and reserves. Rooms are bright and air-conditioned, with satellite TV. There is a large pool in the garden, and tennis courts. Tours to area attractions are available. The hotel is on the Inter-American Highway about 1 mile (2 km) south of Liberia.

Nuevo Hotel Boyeros, (506) 666-0995, fax (506) 666-2529, has 70 air-conditioned rooms built around a courtyard, adults' and children's pools, a rancho-style bar, and a 24-hour restaurant. Upstairs rooms have balconies, downstairs have small verandas; single $27, double $38, including taxes.

RINCON DE LA VIEJA NATIONAL PARK

Location: NE of Liberia; Santa María sector through Liberia, Las Pailas sector through Curubandé, each about 16 miles (25 km) from Liberia.
Size: 34,801 acres (14,084 ha).
Hours: Enter anytime, but entrance stations attended 7 a.m. to 5 p.m.; hikes to crater must begin before noon.

Cost: *$6, camping $2.*
Information: *Telephone hotline 192 (see Appendix A: Parks and Reserves Information), telephone/fax (506) 695-5577, (506) 695-5598; e-mail acginves@sol.racsa.co.cr; Web site www.acguanacaste.ac.cr.*

From the porch of the century-old ranch house in Rincón de la Vieja National Park, I watched a doe and fawn walking without fear at the edge of the clearing. On the way up the mountain, a morpho butterfly fluttered across the road; four species of this brilliant butterfly live in the park. Tapirs roam here, as do howler, capuchin, and spider monkeys. The armadillo is so abundant it could practically be the symbol of the park. Peccaries are common, and there's evidence that jaguar and puma stalk this preserve.

The white-fronted Amazon parrot and spectacled owl are among 257 species of birds. Doves are everywhere; at lower elevations is the curassow. There are kites, toucans and toucanets, redstarts, and motmots. A small cicada with the voice of a frog lives underground.

The park, in the Guanacaste Mountain Range, is the source of 32 rivers. As much as 197 inches (5,000 mm) of rain falls at higher elevations. The park's forests are important not only in maintaining water in rivers in the lowlands in dry season but also in flood prevention in rainy months.

Two volcanoes crown this mountain mass: active Rincón de la Vieja, and dormant Santa María. In fact, Rincón de la Vieja has two craters; the dormant one has a crystal-clear cold-water lake, while the lake in the other crater steams. Rincón erupted again in 1995, spewing ash and sending hot mud into area rivers. The best time to climb to the craters is in the driest months, February through April—subject, of course, to volcanic activity.

Visitors have access to the park's scenic beauty and geologic attractions through two entrances, both on bad roads, especially in rainy season. The ranch house, or *casona*, is the administrative center for the Santa María sector. The Enchanted Forest Trail begins here. A walk through that fairyland of tall trees, ferns, mosses, and delicate orchids touches a primeval chord within. The national flower, the guaria morada orchid, thrives here. A small waterfall makes it picture-perfect.

A shorter Sendero Colibrí (Hummingbird Trail) or a walk to a *mirador* with a view of Liberia and Miravalles Volcano are other possibilities. Less than 2 miles (3 km) away are sulfur waters that many say are medicinal. A 5.6-mile (8-km), three-hour trek takes you to the other park entrance, at Las Pailas, a magic land of bubbling mud pots, hot-water pools, and steam and gas vents.

Travelers who enter the park via the Las Pailas sector should check in at the ranger station. Various trails exist, including the climb to the craters and to waterfalls. The principal loop trail here leads to fumaroles and mud pots bordered by verdant forest and a pretty waterfall. Hanging bridges now cross the river, so no more wading through knee-deep water. A pool in the Río Blanco is only a short walk from the ranger station. Camping permitted in designated areas. Average temperature is 59°F to 79°F (15°C to 26°C), and it can get cold at night in both sectors. Elevation is from 2,133 to 6,286 feet (650 to 1,916 m).

Getting There

By bus: Take a bus to Liberia, then go by jeep taxi to either entrance.
By car: Santa María entrance: take the unpaved road toward Colonia Blanca and follow signs to park. Beware: an unbridged river on the outskirts of Liberia can be a problem after a hard rain. Las Pailas entrance: turn east about 3 miles (5 km) north of Liberia and continue 12 unpaved miles (20 km) through the village of Curubandé to the park. (A ranch along the way charges a right-of-way fee, 300 colones).
Other: Hotels, lodges, private reserves, and tour companies offer day trips. See below for a description of a backdoor entrance.

Where to Stay near Rincón de la Vieja

Though Liberia is the closest large town, day visits are possible from La Cruz to the north and Cañas to the south, as well as from beach areas to the west.

Santa María Volcano Lodge, (506) 381-5290; e-mail santa@arweb.com; fax (506) 666-2313, (506) 383-3004, offers a backdoor entrance to the Santa María sector of Rincón de la Vieja, accessible through Bagaces north to Aguas Claras and Colonia Blanca, a fantastically beautiful drive in a land of volcanoes. The lodge is a small place at the edge of a tiny town at the base of a big mountain. Its wooden A-frame cabins somehow look like playhouses from the outside, though inside they have plenty of room for beds, closet, and table and stools. Some have sleeping lofts, some have walls of river stone in the bathroom; all have porches. Two rooms are in the main house. Each is $43 per person, including room, meals, and laundry service; no credit cards.

Meals are served family-style in the dining room, featuring fruits of the land. Trees in the garden include papaya, starfruit, grapefruit, guanabana, passion fruit, and macadamia. There is also *palmito* (or heart of palm) and banana. All this brings birds—one visitor counted 20 species in the same tree. Also in the main house is a small, rustic bar.

Owner/manager Rosalba de Vargas invites guests to see the milking if they like. She offers a range of excursions: to Rincón de la Vieja by horseback (about 9 miles [15 km]), to hot springs and fumaroles (a 2.5-mile [4-km] trek), to a nearby hacienda for a Negro River swim, to see pre-Columbian petroglyphs in primary forest, or to Miravalles Volcano. The lodge is actually between Miravalles and Rincón de la Vieja Volcanoes. Local guides are available for hiking tours ($25), and horses rent for $20 to $30, depending on tour length. Though the lodge is not in the forest, it's near enough that howler monkeys are neighbors.

The human neighbors who live down the road in Colonia Blanca are modern-day pioneers. So bring your frontier spirit and discover the charm of this simple, out-of-the-way place. It's not so out of the way, however, that it cannot be reached by intrepid Costa Rican buses. Those for Colonia Blanca leave Liberia twice a day for the 2½-hour trip. By car, Santa María Volcano Lodge is 90 minutes from Bagaces.

RINCON DE LA VIEJA MOUNTAIN LODGE, PRIVATE RESERVE

Location: 16 miles (26 km) NE of Liberia.
Rates: Singles $40, doubles $51. Breakfast $9, lunch or dinner $11. A three-day package is $170 per person, double occupancy for lodging, meals, horse tour to mud pots, and full canopy tour. Others available.
Information/Reservations: Telephone/fax (506) 695-5553; e-mail rincon@sol.racsa.co.cr; Web site www.guanacaste.co.cr/rincon.

I almost didn't get past the Colorado River at the entrance to Rincón de la Vieja Mountain Lodge. Cicadas were singing, a morpho floated above the river, shafts of sunlight sparkled on the rushing water, tall trees created a cathedral effect—sheer enchantment.

Enchantment might also be the best word to describe what awaits here on the slopes of Rincón de la Vieja Volcano, just outside the national park that protects it. You can visit bubbling mud pots and geysers, hike to hidden waterfalls, bathe in mountain streams or hot springs, ride horseback through pristine forest, and visit a mountain lake. As well as visiting the nearby national park, lodge guests may explore 30 miles (48 km) of trails in the ranch's 740 acres (300 ha) of primary forest, in elevations from 2,100 to 6,000 feet (640 to 2,520 m), visit a hot spring or a Chorotega archaeological site, and return to the Río Colorado to watch for birds and butterflies and soak up the energy and beauty of the place. A full day of horseback riding and hiking takes in the gurgling mud pots as well as a lake and 90-foot (27-m) waterfall, colored a spectacular blue from copper in the water.

Traverse an exhilarating trail through the treetops, moving among 16 platforms via strong steel cables. Top Tree Trails offers a four-hour forest canopy experience for $50, including horseback ride to platforms and lunch, or a full-day naturalist tour that adds bathing in thermal sulfur springs, $77. Nighttime in the canopy is another option.

Owner Alvaro Wiessel's family has a history of more than 100 years in the area; the lodge was the family home. Today it contains a living area, dining room, kitchen, and rooms for guests. Alvaro has brought the number of rooms to 27 by adding guest cottages with private baths (some with hot water); front porches have hammocks and chairs. Furnishings are simple but comfortable; some rooms have bunk beds. The newest group of rooms is built in rich forest beside a small stream. A small swimming pool and rancho/bar are in front of the lodge.

Among the showier of 257 species of birds on the ranch are violaceous, elegant, and orange-bellied trogons; crested caracaras; red-lored, mealy, yellow-naped, and white-fronted parrots; toucans; motmots; and the three-wattled bellbird. Mammals include howler and white-faced monkeys, deer, coatis, peccaries, and pacas. Tapirs live here but are not often seen.

Guests may accompany ranch workers, helping with milking or herding cattle. The lodge rents horses; working cowboys give riding instruction. Hikes can be with people who have grown up here or with bilingual naturalist guides.

Getting There

By car: North of Liberia, turn east through Curubandé and follow lodge signs; last 7 miles (11 km) unpaved. A small passage fee is levied by a ranch along the way.

Other: Transfers available from Liberia ($25 for up to five), San José ($140), Monteverde, and beaches.

BUENA VISTA LODGE, PRIVATE RESERVE

Location: About 19 miles (31 km) NE of Liberia.
Rates: Doubles with shared baths $30 to $35; with private baths, $40 to $45; bunk-bed rooms with private bath $15 per person. Ten percent discount if you have this book and reserve directly with Buena Vista. Breakfast $6, lunch and dinner $8 each. Day visit $35.
Information/Reservations: Telephone/fax (506) 695-5147, (506) 666-2069.

A cold mountain stream rushes; mud pots bubble; steam escapes from open fissures in the earth and drifts up from pools of hot water to play hide-and-seek with the tall trees of the primary forest. Standing here you can't help but think of the Earth in formation, of creation, of beauty, of the power of natural forces.

Here on the slopes of Rincón de la Vieja Volcano, next door to the national park, Gerardo Ocampo, his wife, Amalia, and their four children share and conserve nature's bounty. Buena Vista is both a private nature reserve and a working farm. Visitors are invited to hike forest trails, bird-watch, help ranch hands with the cattle, bathe in thermal waters or mountain streams, and walk or ride horseback to waterfalls—six large ones to choose from (half-day horseback waterfall trip, $25). Day visitors are welcome to come for a horseback ride to the spring, trail walk, and lunch.

All of this is on the 3,950-acre, (1,600-ha) farm, but there's also the option of a tour to Rincón de la Vieja National Park less than 2 miles (3 km) away, $35. Gerardo suggests March to May and July or August as best months to climb the crater.

At an intriguing spa about 30 minutes by horseback from the lodge, enjoy a natural sauna, a simple wooden house built over one of the *pailas* (mud pots): steam rises through the floor. A concrete and stone "hot tub" is fed by a mix of hot mineral waters and cold water from the mountain stream alongside, set in the rain-forest verdance. Along the trail, notice the rich pink

▲ Serenity at Bosque de Paz in North Central Costa Rica
(Ree Strange Sheck)

▲ Orchids at Excazú oxcart parade (Ree Strange Sheck)

▲ Gran Hotel Costa Rica, downtown San José (Ree Strange Sheck)

▼ Costa Rica's blue morpho butterfly (Ree Strange Sheck)

▲ Colorful ponciana tree (*malinche*) against seasonally dry landscape at Ocotal Beach (Ree Strange Sheck)

▲ Decked out for Independence Day (Ree Strange Sheck)

▲ Three-toed sloth (Ree Strange Sheck)

▼ Oxcarts still add color to the Costa Rican landscape. (Ree Strange Sheck)

Arenal Volcano and Lake Arenal (Ree Strange Sheck)

Exotic bromeliads abound in lush vegetation. (Ree Strange Sheck)

▲ Steam rises from hot waters at Tabacón, near La Fortuna.
(Ree Strange Sheck)

Bring binoculars to see the amazing flora and fauna of Costa Rica. (Ree Strange Sheck)

Infinity pool at Hotel Punta Islita (Ree Strange Sheck)

▲ Author explores canopy—try it! (Jack Ewing)

▲ Bridal veil mushroom at La Selva Biological Statio (Ree Strange Sheck)

▼ An agouti enjoys dinner. (Ree Strange Sheck)

Buena Vista Lodge near Rincón de la Vieja Volcano

fruit of the pitaya, a cactus-looking plant. Guided spa tours are $15 by horse-back, $5 on foot.

Forest trails behind the lodge are well maintained and easy to walk. Five trails wind through the almost 100 acres (40 ha) of primary forest. A troop of white-faced capuchin monkeys fussed at me as I explored at dusk. You might see a paca, peccary, deer, river otter, macaw (either the scarlet or the rarer green), toucan, oropendola, or agouti. Perhaps you'll hear a coyote concert or sounds of the howler monkey. One of the forest trails displays tree names. A half-day hiking tour is $10; a canopy tour among 10 platforms is $30.

On one of my Buena Vista visits, a pregnant peccary named Gerardina helped my sister hurry between the dining room and our room. That night, a friendly skunk nosed around my Jeep and waddled off. The resident scarlet macaw is always around, and now a toucan and two parrots have joined the menagerie. I must report that Gerardina is no longer around—my sister is glad.

On the drive up to the lodge, keep a lookout just past a wooden bridge. In that magnificent forest, I have spotted a spider monkey in roadside trees, golden red hair shining on its back, while a motmot posed for pictures nearby. I've also seen quail, cuckoos, and morpho butterflies here.

Buena Vista has 47 rooms, all but four with private baths. Rooms in the rustic main lodge are around a tropical patio; others are grouped in cabins near the forest, in the landscaped gardens, and near a small lake. A creative mix of wood and river stone decorates some rooms, some have wooden ceilings, and all have shared verandas or private porches. Perhaps you'll sleep on a bed with a river-stone base.

On weekends, cowboys present some local customs of the Guanacaste *sabanero*; marimba music may accompany a nighttime meal in an open-air rancho/bar, especially when groups are present. Music or not, you're likely to see large frogs in the rancho. Breakfast is served in the main house, where cooking is on a wood stove. Meals are ample, varied, delicious, and visually pleasing. Drinking water comes from a spring, and electrical energy comes from a hydroelectric plant.

Buena Vista means "good view," and there are quite a few: an almost-touchable one of the Rincón volcano, a more-distant look at Orosi Volcano and the Pacific, and on a clear night, lights of Bagaces and Liberia below. Rainy season, May 15 to November 30, brings some 6.5 feet (2 m) of rainfall. Lodge elevation is 2,592 feet (790 m). Temperatures average 82°F to 86°F (28°C to 30°C), but early on December mornings it can be 64°F (18°C).

Getting There

By car: From the sign at km 247 on the Inter-American Highway north of Liberia, continue 12 miles (19 km); paved to Cañas Dulces, mainly gravel afterward.

Other: Ask about transfers from Liberia.

SANTA ROSA NATIONAL PARK

Location: N *of Liberia between the Inter-American Highway and Pacific.*
Size: 122,352 acres (49,515 ha) of land, 193,000 acres (78,000 ha) of marine habitat.
Hours: Enter anytime, but booth at main entrance open 7:30 a.m. to 4:30 p.m.
Cost: $6 entrance, lodging in Tropical Research Station $15 per person, camping $2 per person.
Information/Reservations: Telephone hotline 192 (see Appendix A: Parks and Reserves Information), telephone/fax (506) 695-5598, (506) 695-5577; e-mail acginves@sol.racsa.co.cr; Web site www.acguanacaste.ac.cr.

In times past, Indians have walked this land; hunters, woodcutters, cowboys, and soldiers, too. Footprints today belong mainly to researchers, park rangers, and nature lovers. What had been virgin tropical dry forest, cleared pastures, and a battlefield now is Santa Rosa National Park, a piece of property where history is still being written.

Santa Rosa's historical significance was the primary reason it was protected by the government, first as a national monument and then a national park. Soon, however, the ecological importance of its flora and fauna and of the habitats that exist in this dry Pacific region was recognized. It is the ecological battle that's making history now, an effort not only to protect but also to restore some of these habitats. Research at Santa Rosa sheds light on plant and animal interrelationships and how forests regenerate themselves.

A young park ranger told me that most Costa Ricans who visit Santa Rosa National Park come initially because of its history, but they leave excited about the intricacies of nature. She carries the park's environmental education program to nearby village schools, and walks with the children when they come on tour.

The main historical drawing card is the site of the Battle of Santa Rosa (March 20, 1856), which pitted a well-trained, well-armed invading army against a ragtag band of Costa Rican peasants who had become soldiers overnight. The patriots won, routing adventurer William Walker's forces in 14 minutes. The battle took place around La Casona, the house at Hacienda Santa Rosa. Visitors today can walk through the big house and see historical displays, stand on the wide wooden veranda and look toward the 300-year-old stone corrals, or step into the kitchen and see where cheese was preserved by hanging over the woodstove.

A stately guanacaste, Costa Rica's national tree, stands nearby. Its wood is good for construction; its ear-shaped fruit, which gives the tree its English name of ear fruit, has been used to wash clothes and is food for horses, cows, and small forest mammals.

At the entrance booth 4 miles (7 km) from the Ranch House (*casona*), park maps are for sale; the ranger can help you decide what to see in the time you have. Climb the short trail behind La Casona to see a monument to battles and heroes and a panoramic view of volcanoes and Guanacaste countryside. Take the short, well-marked nature trail called Indio Desnudo, identifiable by its reddish-brown trees. Keep your eyes open: I was within spitting distance of a handsome 5-foot (1.5-m) boa constrictor before I noticed it draped over a

Wind and the Frigate Bird

Winds seem to be an important factor in determining where frigate birds build nests. They need help landing and becoming airborne because of their small bodies, short feet, long wings, and deeply forked long tails. A nesting site for the magnificent frigate birds (Fregata magnificens) is on Bolaños Island in Salinas Bay near La Cruz, administered as part of Santa Rosa National Park. Wind during dry season—nesting time—is consistent and strong there. The only other nesting site in Costa Rica is on a small island in the Gulf of Nicoya. During mating season, the male blows out his bright red throat pouch to attract a female, who lays a single egg. The birds are called tijeretas (pronounced tea-hay-RAY-tahs) in Spanish because of their scissorlike tails (tijeras is Spanish for scissors).

tree root by the path.Some trees are labeled. Look also for Indian petroglyphs at Quebrada Duende on the delightful, well-maintained trail. Sendero Los Patos and the trail to the Playa Naranjo Mirador offer other hiking options.

Two of Santa Rosa's beaches are famous as sea-turtle nesting sites: Naranjo, about 8 miles (12 km) from park headquarters, and Nancite, 11 miles (17 km) away. Though three species come ashore to lay eggs, it's the hundreds of thousands of Pacific or olive ridley turtles on small Nancite Beach that get the most attention. From July to December, mass nestings (*arribadas*) occur periodically, while single turtles come ashore every night. The other two species are green and leatherback turtles. Camping is permitted at both beaches, but since Nancite is a study area a permit from the research center is required.

The Murciélago section of Santa Rosa is farther north. Ask about conditions of the unpaved road and rivers that must be forded to reach the ranger station. Murciélago ("bat" in English) belonged to Anastasio Somoza when he was president of Nicaragua. Talk to station staff for stories from those days. Go to the coast at Playa Blanca (11 miles, 17 km) or at Santa Elena or El Hachal Bays, or take the trail to Pozo del General, which has water year-round and is important for animals in the dry season.

Santa Rosa National Park has capuchin, howler, and spider monkeys, deer, armadillos, coyotes, coatis, raccoons, and cats—115 species of mammals, about half of them bats. Studies have identified more than 3,000 species of moths and butterflies among more than 30,000 insect species. Magpie jays and parrots make lots of noise, while some of the 253 species of birds get attention with their coloring: look for orange-fronted parakeets, elegant trogons, and crested caracaras.

The park has a pronounced dry season from November to May. Rainfall is about 63 inches (1,600 mm). Average temperature is 79°F (26°C).

Bolaños Island in Salinas Bay west of La Cruz is also part of this park. Rising 266 feet (81 m) from the Pacific, this rocky mound protects seabirds. Magnificent frigate birds and American oystercatchers nest here, and this is one of the country's four nesting sites for brown pelicans. No visitor facilities exist, but watching through binoculars at a tactful distance is not against the rules. The island is 3 miles (5 km) from Puerto Soley.

Camping is possible near the administrative center at Santa Rosa, at Naranjo and Nancite beaches, and at Pozo del General. Beds are sometimes available at the Tropical Dry Forest Research Center in Santa Rosa's administrative area, though priority goes to researchers and students for its dorm-style rooms and shared baths. Soft drinks and snacks are available at the cafeteria; meals only with advance notice.

Getting There

By bus: From San José, take the Peñas Blancas or La Cruz bus to main park entrance, leaving a 4-mile (7-km) walk to La Casona and headquarters. Or take buses from Liberia that go north.

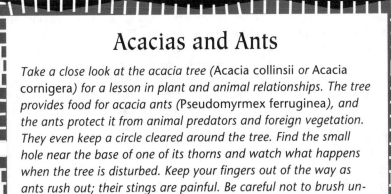

Acacias and Ants

Take a close look at the acacia tree (Acacia collinsii or Acacia cornigera) for a lesson in plant and animal relationships. The tree provides food for acacia ants (Pseudomyrmex ferruginea), and the ants protect it from animal predators and foreign vegetation. They even keep a circle cleared around the tree. Find the small hole near the base of one of its thorns and watch what happens when the tree is disturbed. Keep your fingers out of the way as ants rush out; their stings are painful. Be careful not to brush unwittingly against an acacia branch along a trail.

By car: Main entrance 22 miles (35 km) north of Liberia; Murciélago entrance 6 miles farther (10 km) via Cuajiniquil.
Other: Tourist agencies, hotels, and private nature reserves offer day trips. Taxis available in Liberia.

Where to Stay near Santa Rosa
Though Liberia is the closest large town, day visits are possible from La Cruz and Cañas areas as well as from beach areas to the west and private reserves.

GUANACASTE NATIONAL PARK
Location: N of Liberia on the E side of the Inter-American Highway.
Size: 80,337 acres (32,512 ha).
Hours: Always open, but trails limited to use by overnight visitors at research stations.
Cost: Lodging at biological stations $15 per person, camping $2 per day.
Information/Reservations: Telephone hotline 192 (see Appendix A: Parks and Reserves Information), telephone/fax (506) 695-5598, (506) 695-5577; e-mail acginves@sol.racsa.ac.cr; Web site www.acguanacaste.ac.cr.

Established in 1989, Guanacaste encompasses dry tropical forest and rain forest stretching from lowlands along the northern Inter-American Highway to the mountains of the Guanacaste range. Preservation and restoration of one of the last remaining tropical dry forests was an impetus for forming Guanacaste National Park. Tropical dry forests once stretched along the Pacific from central Mexico to Panama, but most have fallen to agricultural and residential use. At adjoining Santa Rosa park, studies on the forest's seasonal patterns, distinct life forms, and interactions between plants and animals help determine the size and habitats necessary to sustain healthy populations of species. Seasonal migration of some of the animal life from Santa Rosa to rain forests in mountains on the east meant protecting those forests as well.

In addition to protecting remaining forest, regeneration is underway on large areas cleared earlier for agriculture and pasture. Environmental education programs for visitors, who range from local schoolchildren to foreign travelers, share what is being learned in this restoration process.

The good news for nature lovers is that biological stations offer accommodations for tourists as well as researchers, on a space-available basis. The trails are limited to overnight visitors—no day visits.

Cacao Biological Station sits in cloud forest at 3,609 feet (1,100 m). Cacao Volcano, at 5,443 feet (1,659 m), looms above. Sleeping quarters are in one of the station's three wooden buildings: four rooms for eight people each, blankets provided. A panorama of forest and distant coastline unfolds from a long, covered porch. The station is rustic: no electricity, cold-water showers. Other small buildings house a kitchen and a laboratory or meeting space. Bring your own food. Virgin forest behind the buildings holds tapirs, cats, bellbirds, orchids, and bromeliads. Howler monkeys announced daybreak when I was there. Hiking in the afternoon, we saw howler, spider, and white-faced monkeys within 300 feet (90 m) of each other. There is a trail to the Maritza Biological Station, about three hours away by foot, and one to the top of Cacao. A local guide is recommended for getting to Cacao—when the bad road ends, continue on a not-well-marked trail by foot or horseback.

Maritza is accessible by a road best traversed in four-wheel-drive vehicles. I can attest to that, having slid the entire 11 miles (18 km) after a serious downpour. Maritza lies on the skirts of Orosi Volcano in a windier, cooler area. A more modern facility, the station can house 32 tourists and researchers; shared baths, bring your own food.

In forests around the rivers, wildlife is abundant: toucans, bellbirds, peccaries, sun bitterns, monkeys. Jaguars have been known to kill cattle in the area. I arrived too late to see a band of 15 peccaries that had appeared on the trail near the laboratory that morning. Coatis frequently visit the station. Less than 2 hours from Maritza by foot is Llano de los Indios, an open pasture with petroglyphs carved in volcanic stone. More than 80 pieces of rock art are both abstract and representational.

In the Atlantic watershed, **Pitilla Biological Station** houses 32 persons (shared cold-water baths; bring your own food). Both the facilities and the road leading to it are rustic; there's no electricity, and four-wheel-drive is necessary. (Enter via Santa Cecilia.) Views from Pitilla include the Lake of Nicaragua and Orosi Volcano.

A research station is on **Murciélagos Islands**—Institute of Biological Investigations San José, on San José Island. Scientists study the abundant marine flora and fauna as well as land species. Ask about visiting or camping.

Getting There

Contact Guanacaste Conservation Area. Access limited to overnight visitors at the biological stations.

Where to Stay near Guanacaste National Park

Though Liberia is the closest large town, day visits are possible from La Cruz to the north and Cañas to the south as well as from beach areas and private reserves.

LA CRUZ

La Cruz (population 8,737) is the last town of any size before the border with Nicaragua. This pleasant, unpretentious place is on hills overlooking beautiful Salinas Bay and Bolaños Island. Make your way to the *mirador* for a cliffside panorama of sea, coastal hills around the bay, and sky. In daytime, it's like looking at a relief map of the area; at sunset, phenomenal. Until recent years La Cruz was a stopover primarily for those coming or going from the border. Now it's also a base for travel to unspoiled beaches such as Rajada and Jobo, for a boat trip around Isla Bolaños, or for a visit to Santa Rosa National Park (especially its nearby Murciélago sector). Heading east from La Cruz through Upala, travelers reach the western side of Caño Negro wildlife refuge and continue on to Lake Arenal and Arenal Volcano via San Rafael. La Cruz is 12 miles (19 km) south of the Nicaraguan border.

Try Restaurante Ehecatl near the Mirador, or ask your innkeeper for other area recommendations.

Getting There

By bus: San José–Peñas Blancas buses pass daily.
By car: 36 miles (58 km) north of Liberia on the Inter-American.
By air: The nearest airport is in Liberia.

Where to Stay and Eat in and near La Cruz

Amalia's Inn, telephone/fax (506) 679-9181, in La Cruz looks over the blue waters of Salinas Bay from its cliffside setting, a panorama of coastline in both Costa Rica and Nicaragua. Doña Amalia graciously receives guests in her attractive two-story house. Each of eight comfortable rooms is different. The third floor has larger rooms great for families. A second-floor balcony and a patio area by the swimming pool afford a top-of-the-mountain view, where you look down on birds in flight. Double $35; breakfast $5 per person. No smoking here. Amalia knows the area well because of her family's history and their big ranch you see below. From the inn, it's 4 miles (7 km) to Puerto Soley on the bay.

Two-story **Hostal de Julia,** telephone/fax (506) 679-9084, is about a block (125 m) east of the Red Cross in La Cruz. It has 12 rooms with private baths. Brick floors and nice use of wood in wardrobes, desks, fans, and bathroom accessories make rooms inviting. Single $21, double $30. Julia arranges kayak and boat trips and horseback riding; the beach is 20 minutes away.

Hotel Colonias del Norte, telephone/fax (506) 679-9132, is 4 miles (6 km) north of La Cruz. The two-story main building has a pretty dining room with large windows looking out on Guanacaste countryside. A pool and thatched ranchos have forest as a backdrop. Each of the 24 comfortably simple rooms has a ceiling fan; double $40.

The 618-acre (250 ha) property offers guests opportunities to hike or ride horseback in primary forest where there are toucans, at least 31 butterfly species, and 50 mammal species, including bats. Guided walks are available. The hotel offers trips into Nicaragua and tours to Santa Rosa (Murciélago sector) and Rincón de la Vieja. Italian fare joins Costa Rican dishes on the table—lots of tropical fruits and fresh cheese. The bus to Peñas Blancas gets you to the turnoff, a short distance from the hotel.

LOS INOCENTES

Location: 9 miles (14 km) E of La Cruz near the border with Nicaragua.
Rates: Lodging and meals $59 per person. Day trip $30, including lunch.
Information/Reservations: (506) 679-9190, (506) 265-5484, fax (506) 265-4385, U.S. number telephone/fax (504) 895-5130 (Jaime's sister); e-mail orosina@sol.racsa.co.cr; Web site www.arweb.com/orosi.

There's something special about waking at dawn's early light to the bass-toned barks of howler-monkeys. When you open the big windows of your south-facing room at Los Inocentes, Orosi Volcano looms big enough to touch. Teak floors, polished wood, wide L-shaped verandas both upstairs and down—the hacienda is so inviting that nothing less than those intriguing barks from the forest down by the river spur you to get dressed and leave it for an early morning horseback ride.

Los Inocentes is a working ranch as well as a naturalist lodge. Perhaps that accounts for horses that are a pleasure to ride. Don't worry if you're not an expert rider; Dennis Ortiz, your nature-tour guide, will have you riding like a pro. We found the howlers and white-faced monkeys. Dennis patiently tracked the more shy spider monkeys three times so I could get a perfect camera angle. He and the horses tried not to laugh when a tree and I got tangled up while I was juggling cameras, lenses, reins, and binoculars. On an earlier visit he found not one but two sloths for me, and we saw deer, howler and spider monkeys, coatis, and—a highlight for me—a black-headed trogon. The three-hour guided horseback tour is $18. If horses are not your thing, manager Jaime Víquez has a tractor-driven trailer to take you to the forest (minimum: five). Day visitors are welcome for the guided nature tour.

The forest generally follows the *quebradas* (ravines) and riverbeds. Birdwatching is excellent in open pastures; I heard the laughing falcon before I

Los Inocentes

saw it. Both white-fronted and yellow-naped parrots are common, flying overhead in pairs or flocks. The elusive king vulture is among 119 species of birds officially recorded on ranch property. Orange-fronted and orange-chinned parakeets, several species of hummingbirds, Montezuma oropendolas, and *pauraques* (nightjars) are among birds seen regularly. Animals to watch for include white-tailed deer, coatis, raccoons, sloths, and peccaries in this premontane moist forest, elevation 1,000 feet (280 m). All nature tours are escorted: the guide knows not only where and what to look for in flora and fauna but also the ranch boundaries. Bird-watchers who want a solitary trip can go to the nearby river, and the veranda offers good viewing for those who can't tear themselves away from the charm of the house. Try a guided night walk in the forest.

To the south is Guanacaste National Park. Maybe you do want to touch 4,879-foot (1,487-m) Orosi Volcano; sign up for a trip that explores its slopes. Transportation arranged for day trips to beaches on the bays of Salinas and Santa Elena, to Murciélago in Santa Rosa park, to Las Pailas and its bubbling mud at Rincón de la Vieja park, and to Santa Rosa. Kayak tours are $65 including lunch and transport.

Guests can also enjoy a small pool at the lodge or swim in natural pools in the river. At night back at the lodge, turn your eyes to the heavens for a bit of stargazing; there may be constellations visible in Guanacaste's vast sky that you've never seen. Lodge meals are something to look forward to, including fresh fish and fruit from trees near the house: limes, mangoes, guavas, *nances*, star fruit, and others.

For a different kind of tour, with advance notice, visit a two-room school on the property for children of ranch workers and of neighboring families. Local children perform traditional dances if requested beforehand.

The hacienda was built in 1890 and remodeled in 1982 with an eye to maintaining its architectural integrity. Stone corrals, like those at Santa Rosa, testify to the age of the property. The main house has 11 nicely decorated rooms with large closets: some baths do not adjoin the rooms, a necessary adjustment to preserve original architecture. All baths have solar hot water. Five small worker houses have been redone as cottages for visitors.

Getting There

By bus: A direct San José–Santa Cecilia bus passes in front; on the San José–Peñas Blancas bus, get off in La Cruz, and take a taxi ($6).

By car: South of La Cruz, turn right toward Santa Cecilia; continue 9 miles (14 km) on paved road. From Upala, head east toward La Cruz.

MONTEVERDE AREA

Monteverde is not only the name of a village but the name that describes the whole zone. There are three communities in the "urban area" of about 3,700 persons: largest is Santa Elena, with bank, shops, and the local high school; next along the road is Cerro Plano; and finally, Monteverde, where even the gas station has a view.

Travelers are drawn to this other-worldly place in search of its most famous denizen, the quetzal; to experience the magical cloud forest; and frankly, to see what all the hullabaloo is about: Monteverde is still the single internationally best-known destination in Costa Rica.

Even before Costa Rica was a top tourism destination, natural history travelers made their way up the mountain, lured by articles, television specials, and word of mouth about golden toads and resplendent quetzals, about scientific research in a remote mountaintop setting, about community efforts to save tropical forest, and about friendly, peace-loving Quakers who settled here. Today several private reserves and tourism businesses oriented toward natural history offer a chance to learn about the biological richness of this place.

The sound of birds and wind in the trees is not the only music to be heard here. The Monteverde Music Festival, mid-January to mid-March, brings professional musicians for memorable nighttime performances. Contact the Monteverde Institute for information, (506) 645-5053, fax (506) 645-5219; e-mail mviimv@sol.racsa.co.cr.

The tiny, progressive community of Monteverde is itself worth a visit. Quakers came here in 1951 from the United States, drawn by Costa Rica's demilitarized environment. They put down roots, formed a community, and set up a business that now makes some the finest cheeses in the country. The Quakers bought milk from neighboring farmers and invited them to become shareholders in Productores de Monteverde, still the largest single employer in the area. The Quaker way of consensus, participatory decision-making, and working together for the common good has strongly influenced the way things are done in the area.

Most areas this size are pleased to have one protected area. The Monteverde region has five private reserves plus other top nature attractions. Let's start with the reserves.

MONTEVERDE CLOUD FOREST PRESERVE, PRIVATE RESERVE

Location: Less than 4 miles (6 km) from Santa Elena; 113 miles (182 km) NW of San José.
Hours: Daily 7 a.m. to 4 p.m.
Rates: Entrance $8 per person, $4 for students with I.D., children under 12 free. Walks led by bilingual guides $23, including admission and slide show. Use of shelters on backpacking trips, $3 per night. Lodging and meals in the rustic field station (casona), $21 per person.
Information/Reservations: For guided natural history walks, (506) 645-5112 or make arrangements through a hotel; for lodging in the casona (506) 645-5276; for overnight in the shelters (506) 645-5122; fax (506) 645-5034; e-mail montever@sol.racsa.co.cr; Web site www.cct.or.cr.

The flash of a quetzal above a waterfall made every bump on the road to the Monteverde cloud forest worthwhile. It was a rainy day, and the guide's search for the bird at familiar haunts had turned up nothing. Then suddenly, appearing almost turquoise against the rich, dark green of the forest, the red and emerald bird with its magnificent tail swooped across a picture-postcard setting. It took my breath away.

The desire to see what many consider the most beautiful bird in tropical America brings thousands of people every year to this biological reserve. But the Monteverde reserve is more than quetzals: some 400 species of birds, 490 butterfly species, 100 mammal species, 120 species of reptiles and amphibians, and 2,500 plant species live here. It is the only known home of the golden toad, a brilliantly colored 2-inch amphibian: males are orange, females yellow and black with patches of scarlet. None have been seen since 1989; only time will tell if this species has disappeared. The preserve also protects the tapir (with a greater chance of seeing tracks than the wary, once-common, now-endangered animal itself), ocelot, olingo, and three species of monkeys. From March to August, hear the booming call of the three-wattled bellbird. At any time of year, the fantastic variety of epiphytes covering cloud-forest trees is dazzling: there are 420 identified species of orchids and 200 of ferns. The preserve has checklists of birds and mammals, an informative nature trail guide, and a trails map.

Monteverde Cloud Forest Preserve, within the Arenal Conservation Area, is not a national park. It's managed by the Tropical Science Center (TSC), a nonprofit scientific research and education organization based in

San José. Founded in 1972, the reserve encompasses some 27,181 acres (11,000 ha) on the Continental Divide in the Tilarán Mountain Range, protecting both Atlantic and Pacific watersheds and containing eight ecological life zones.

Temperature ranges between 56°F and 64°F (16°C and 18°C); average annual rainfall at the *casona* is about 118 inches (3,000 mm), but the reserve can get up to 236 inches (6,000 mm). Bring rain gear and rubber boots, or rent boots at the preserve; trails can be muddy. Though little rain falls December through March, mist rolls in on strong trade winds from the Atlantic and moisture forms on the abundant forest vegetation, dripping from the canopy to the ground. This "indirect rain" is a striking demonstration of the importance of forest conservation. Without trees and forest plants to collect and disseminate this water, the mist would vaporize in hot dry air to the west, and rivers that flow to the lowlands would carry less water. Watershed protection was why the small group of dairy-farming Quakers who settled here put aside 1,369 acres (554 ha) of forest. That parcel is now part of the reserve, leased to TSC for management.

To protect habitat and ensure visitors a worthwhile experience, limits are placed on the number of people allowed on almost 8 miles (12.4 km) of trails—seven trails, in all. Priority is given to those taking the natural history walks, led by bilingual naturalist guides. A slide show is part of the tour. Make reservations; heaviest visitation is December through April. In addition to public areas with marked trails and longer trails for backpackers, the preserve has areas where almost no use is allowed and others that are restricted to scientific investigation.

The cloud-forest preserve has an environmental education program with area schools, bringing students to the forest as well as working with teachers. Volunteers assist with many activities at the preserve, one-week minimum. Contact the preserve for more information.

Overnight accommodations at the preserve's field station are limited to dorm-style rooms for 40 people, sometimes filled by researchers and students. Baths are shared. A snack bar and gift shop are at the entrance.

Getting There
See directions for Monteverde. Once there, taxis and a twice-daily bus are available for trips to the reserve; some hotels provide shuttle service. Walking at least one way, about 1.5 miles (2.5 km) from the cheese plant, carries the reward of terrific bird-watching.

BOSQUE ETERNO DE LOS NIÑOS, SAN GERARDO SECTOR, PRIVATE RESERVE
Location: 5 miles (8.5 km) N of Santa Elena.
Rates: Lodging and meals $30.
Information/Reservations: (506) 645-5003, fax (506) 645-5104; e-mail acmmcl@sol.racsa.co.cr; Web site www.monteverde.or.cr.

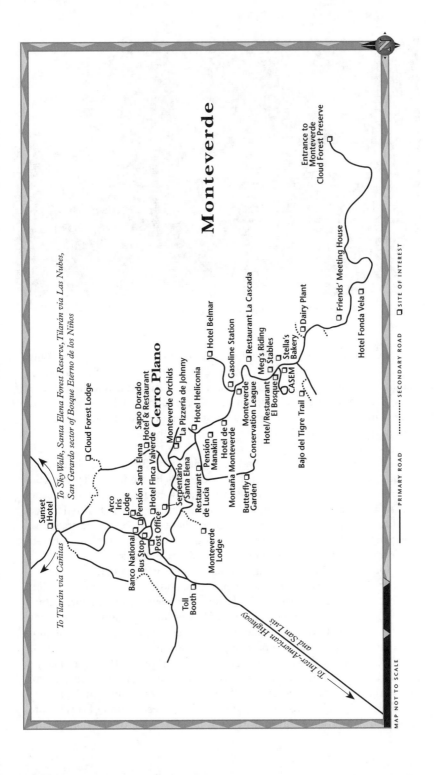

Monteverde

To Tilarán via Cañitas

To Sky Walk, Santa Elena Forest Reserve, Tilarán via Las Nubes,
San Gerardo sector of Bosque Eterno de los Niños

Cloud Forest Lodge

Sunset Hotel

Arco Iris Lodge

Pensión Santa Elena

Sapo Dorado Hotel & Restaurant

Hotel Finca Valverde

Monteverde Orchids

La Pizzería de Johnny

Cerro Plano

Hotel Heliconia

Banco National

Bus Stop

Post Office

Serpentario Santa Elena

Restaurant de Lucía

Pensión Manakin

Hotel de Montaña Monteverde

Monteverde Lodge

Toll Booth

Monteverde Conservation League

Butterfly Garden

Hotel Belmar

Gasoline Station

Restaurant La Cascada

Meg's Riding Stables

Hotel/Restaurant El Bosque

Stella's Bakery

CASEM

Dairy Plant

Bajo del Tigre Trail

Friends' Meeting House

Hotel Fonda Vela

Entrance to Monteverde Cloud Forest Preserve

To Inter-American Highway and San Luis

MAP NOT TO SCALE

——— PRIMARY ROAD   ·········· SECONDARY ROAD   □ SITE OF INTEREST

Casona and exhibit area at Monteverde Cloud Forest Preserve

The adventure of staying at San Gerardo begins with getting there. Where vehicles leave off, guests start a 2-mile (3.5-km) trek to the San Gerardo Field Station. It's a terrific walk. Lush vegetation, fantastic views, and birdlife along the way make up for the often-muddy track. Then you round a bend and Arenal Volcano is on the horizon and Lake Arenal's waters glisten. As you come off a forest trail into a clearing, the two-story wooden station welcomes.

It's somehow a surprise to find such a facility in this remote place. Rustic, yes; but well done. Six upstairs rooms, each with four beds (two bunks) and private bath, open onto a wonderful veranda great for bird- and volcano-watching. When Arenal rumbles, all eyes look for the thin molten-red lines flowing down the sides: a natural sound-and-light show. This field station was built primarily for researchers and student groups, so there is a large laboratory and lecture space on the first floor, along with the dining area.

More than 3.7 miles (6 km) of hiking trails wind through the forest. Epiphyte-laden trees, ferns, vines, heliconias, and other tropical vegetation abound. Among 200 species of birds are black guans, hummingbirds, toucans, tangers, and swallow-tailed kites. Howler monkeys announce the day, and you can also find white-faced monkeys, agoutis, coatis, and armadillos. The margay is here, but you probably won't see it.

The San Gerardo sector is part of the 46,089-acre (18,652-ha) children's rain forest operated by the Monteverde Conservation League, a private nonprofit organization with offices in Monteverde and La Tigra. Children and adults have contributed to allow preservation of this rich resource for tomorrow's children. Here at San Gerardo, one of the reasons for protecting these forests is crystal clear. Sources for Lake Arenal's water are here, waters that feed a hydroelectric plant that produces almost half of the electricity in Costa Rica and then flow into the Guanacaste lowlands to be used for irrigation.

Volunteers are sometimes needed at San Gerardo and for other projects managed by the league. Donations are always welcome.

Getting There
From Santa Elena, follow signs to the Santa Elena Forest Reserve (this part by vehicle). From here, take a 1.6-mile (2.5-km) walk down an old forest road and another half-mile on a forest trail. Get to the reserve by taxi or horseback.

SANTA ELENA FOREST RESERVE, PRIVATE RESERVE
Location: 3 miles (5 km) NE of Santa Elena.
Hours: Daily 7 a.m. to 4 p.m.
Rates: Admission $5, free for children under 12. Guided walks $19, including entrance fee.
Information/Reservations: (506) 645-5390, fax (506) 645-5014.

The Santa Elena Forest Reserve protects cloud-forest habitat. It has about 8 miles (12 km) of trails at an elevation of 5,600 feet (1,700 m). Arenal volcano, some 7 miles (14 km) away, can be seen from Sendero del Bajo and Youth Challenge Trail when weather cooperates. Observation platforms are ideal spots to take in the verdant landscape and watch the ever-changing patterns of sunlight and mist. Flocks of mixed species of birds move through the forest, howler monkeys sound off, small streams gurgle softly, and epiphytes and dangling roots and vines help weave a magical spell as you walk in this hushed atmosphere.

Two trails have self-guiding booklets ($1), and most involve loops ranging from less than a mile (1.4 km) to almost 3 miles (4.8 km) long. Guided walks are available, and rubber boots and ponchos are for rent. Visitation is limited to 80 people at a time, so it's best to make reservations, especially January through March.

The visitor center has a gift shop and exhibits made by students of the local high school, which manages the reserve. Visit the small café is at the entrance. The center and trails were built with assistance of many volunteers.

Volunteers are always needed at the Santa Elena Reserve—minimum age 16, minimum time three days. Housing is provided. Contact Santa Elena High School Cloud Forest Reserve, Apartado 90-5655, Santa Elena, Monteverde, Puntarenas, or call or fax.

Getting There
From Santa Elena, taxis and horses available. Hotels offer tours.

ECOLODGE SAN LUIS & BIOLOGICAL STATION, PRIVATE RESERVE

Location: San Luis Valley in NW Costa Rica, 30 minutes from Monteverde.
Rates: Cabins $90 per person, bungalow $70, bunkhouse $55, including meals, lodging, nature guides, access to trails, activities, and taxes.
Information/Reservations: In Monteverde telephone/fax (506) 645-5277, in San Luis telephone/fax (506) 380-3255, in U.S. telephone/fax (615) 297-2155, (800) 699-9685; e-mail smithdp@ctrvax.vanderbilt.edu; Web site www .greenarrow.com/nature/san_luis.htm.

Ever dream of what it would be like to be a researcher in the tropical rain forest? Do you like to take part in village activities or meet local folks when you travel? Ever want to pick coffee or help reforest? Well, here's your chance to have a hands-on experience in a rain-forest setting that mixes biological station research and education and activities on a working tropical farm with natural history tourism.

Ecolodge San Luis was designed by tropical researchers Diane and Milton Lieberman to provide a rich mix of guests, scientists, students, staff, and members of the San Luis community, fostering interaction in as many ways as possible. The rustic dining room is one place where this happens. Researchers and visitors sit elbow-to-elbow at long tables for meals, served family-style. They run into neighbors who drop by for coffee and a bite to eat and share resources in the corner reference library.

Guests can participate in studies on seasonal migration of birds or seed dispersal by birds and mammals, help with research on living fenceposts, work in the greenhouse with tree seedlings, plant trees, take daily weather data, or help with whatever research project is underway. You are welcome to sit in on lectures or slide shows when student groups are present. There's an orchid garden (help collect plants for it), medicinal plant garden, and organic garden, plus coffee fields and a small dairy operation.

Hike in a stupendous forest, either alone or accompanied by guides who are active researchers. The ecolodge property, 162 acres (66 ha), borders Monteverde Cloud Forest Preserve and the International Children's Rain Forest, Bosque Eterno de los Niños. More than 225 species of birds have been seen here, along with mammals such as howler and white-faced monkeys, coatis, kinkajous, sloths, tayras, pumas, and agoutis. A resident long-tailed weasel is often seen near the kitchen.

Night walks, bird-watching (see 60 species before breakfast), horseback riding, swimming in the San Luis River, hiking to a waterfall—many options. You really can pick coffee and even help take it by horseback to the local processing plant. Harvest bananas. Join cooks in the kitchen to learn how to make tamales and *gallo pinto* or, as I did, learn how to cook eggs on a banana leaf. Cooking is in the traditional way, on a woodstove. Take part in local fiestas, soccer games, and dances. Go on a day trip to Monteverde.

For those who have dreamed of being a researcher, sign up for a seven-day tropical biology experience—biology background not important. Study a different topic every day via field lectures, hikes, lab work, and small-group activities. Spend a day studying something of particular interest to you. The program is $130, added to lodging costs.

Accommodations come in three types. The four-room research bunkhouse (formerly a milking barn) has bunk beds, shared baths, and varnished mahogany walls. A four-room bungalow of varnished hardwoods offers wide verandas with hammocks; one room is wheelchair accessible. Spacious, lovely cabins a short walk up the hill are in two six-room wings joined by a large covered deck. High-ceilinged rooms have a double and single bed, closet, and glass doors onto a balcony with panoramic views of forest, mountains, and countryside.

Getting There

By bus: From San José, take the Monteverde bus; from there taxi to San Luis (taxi about $30).

By car: Same directions as to Monteverde, but turn off for San Luis at the orange bus stop and continue to San Luis school; turn right to ecolodge.

ALBERGUE ECOTURISTICO ECOVERDE, PRIVATE RESERVE

Location: *About 4 miles (6 km) NW of Santa Elena in Monte los Olivos.*
Rates: *$29 per person, lodging and meals included. Packages available.*
Information/Reservations: *(506) 385-0092, (506) 645-5059, fax (506) 645-5131.*

Monte los Olivos is a small mountain village that could serve as a case study for how communities in areas around national parks and reserves can become involved in local conservation projects. This group of families who struggled together to form a community, build a one-room school for their children, find a teacher, and buy textbooks, have gone on to build Albergue Ecoturistico Ecoverde. Until now their livelihood has depended largely on dairy farming—the goal is for the lodge to open up additional opportunities.

Set within the Arenal Conservation Area, the lodge is operated by the town's Ecological Association. Members do construction, cook food, clean cabins, maintain trails, and guide visitors, in addition to dairy farming. The idea of the project is to share not only the biological richness of the place but also a way of life.

Guests can participate in dairy farming, walk on cloud-forest trails, sit in the pavilion surrounded by a small lake to watch wildlife, climb to a lookout with an expansive view of Arenal Volcano and Lake Arenal, ride horses, and get to know the community, many of whom share the last name of Barquero. Villagers accompany guests on hikes to the lake or waterfalls at

Río Chiquito. Expect hummingbirds here, and quetzals, monkeys, and other cloud-forest flora and fauna, but without a crunch of crowds.

A day visit includes lunch, guided trail walk, visit to the viewpoint on horseback or by cart, and transportation. A three-day package offers tours both on the property and to Monteverde attractions, starting from $111, including lodging, meals, horseback ride to the volcano lookout, transportation to two Monteverde reserves, visit to the dairy, and two trail walks at Ecoverde.

Eight cabins, four with private baths, were built largely with wood from fallen or diseased trees. Facilities are rustic but comfortable. Typical food is served in the small restaurant, also open to the public: breakfast $3, lunch or dinner $5.

The project incorporates recycling, organic gardening, and forest management. Support has come from Arenal Conservation Area (ACA), World Wildlife Fund-Canada, and Canadian International Development Fund.

Getting There
From Santa Elena, take the road toward Tilarán to Cabeceras; at the junction choose the road to Las Nubes and watch for the lodge sign.

Other Things to See and Do in the Monteverde Area
Art galleries. Visit Sarah Dowell's studio (up the hill from the cheese plant), and see Meg and Stella Wallace's work at Stella's Bakery, across from CASEM. Don't miss Galeria Extasis and the beautiful creations of Marco Tulio Brenes; his workshop/gallery is south of La Cascada, tucked back into the forest.

Bajo del Tigre Trail is part of Bosque Eterno de los Niños, the largest private reserve in Costa Rica. Operated by the Monteverde Conservation League, this International Children's Rain Forest is open daily from 8 a.m. to 4:30 p.m. A short loop trail and extensions off of the loop go through forest and around an emerging arboretum (60 tagged native species) to *miradores* with fantastic vistas of river canyon, forest, and the Gulf of Nicoya. The 2-mile (3.3-km) system of trails is named for manakins, monkeys, bellbirds, and bats, all of which are found here along with emerald toucanets, coatis, swallow-tailed kites, agoutis, sloths, and vegetation different from the nearby cloud forest. This type of lower-elevation forest and its wildlife has become rare in Costa Rica as a result of deforestation and agriculture. Buy a copy of the artistic, informative self-guiding trail booklet. A Children's Nature Center provides a place for kids to explore rain-forest wonders, and there is a children's trail.

The league's information center is here. A nonprofit organization founded in 1986, its activities include research, education, protection of flora and fauna, and habitat rehabilitation. Pick up material on league programs and gift items, and ask about visiting other sectors of the reserve. Follow signs off the main road, about half a mile (1 km) west of the cheese factory. Adults $5, children free. Volunteers are often needed to help out at Bajo del Tigre.

The Canopy Tour in San José, telephone/fax (506) 257-5149, in Monteverde (506) 645-5243; e-mail canopy@sol.racsa.co.cr; Web site www.canopytour.co.cr/, provides a two-hour adventure in the upper layers of the cloud forest, starting with a short hike and then a climb on a rope ladder through a strangler fig to a platform for viewing the forest. From here, visitors slide to two more view points and then rappel to the forest floor. Platforms are between 66 and 98 feet (20 and 30 m) above the ground. The tour is $45, students with I.D. $35, children $30.

Balconies onto the forest at Ecolodge San Luis & Biological Preserve

CASEM gift shop sells locally hand-crafted items, many with intricate embroidery or weaving. Hand-painted cards and stationery make beautiful, easy-to-carry gifts. Designs used on textiles and paper goods are drawn from the area's rich biological diversity: quetzals, bellbirds, golden toads. The women's craft cooperative, whose sales directly benefit local residents, is open from 8 a.m. to 6 p.m. Monday through Saturday; 10 a.m. to 4 p.m. on Sunday. Next door is Coope Santa Elena's **coffee-roasting operation**; stop in and try Café Monteverde.

Chunches, (506) 645-5147, in Santa Elena just south of the bank has books in English and Spanish (good selection of natural history material), newspapers, and magazines. The area's only Laundromat is here. In a coffeehouse corner, owners Wendy Rockwell and Jim Standley serve homemade desserts and light meals along with espresso or other coffees. Closed Sunday.

Hummingbird Gallery, (506) 645-5030, displays spectacular natural history photographs as well as wooden objects local artists make from fallen wood. A gift shop has jewelry, textiles, original T-shirts, and loads of natural history books. Hummers put on a show-stopping performance as they zoom in to the many feeders in the garden. Open 8:30 a.m. to 4:30 p.m. daily.

Monteverde Butterfly Garden, (506) 645-5512; e-mail wolfej@sol.racsa .co.cr; Web site www.whispercom.com/monteverde/monteverde.html, open 9:30 a.m. to 4 p.m. daily, $6 for adults, $3 for children, offers a glorious experience with butterflies. The guided walk with well-trained bilingual guides goes through three botanical gardens that provide different habitats:

forest understory, mid-elevation, and highland forest-edge. Afterward, you can have as much time as you like to walk along the paths or sit alone to watch or photograph the free-flying butterflies. It is a magical place.

Owner Jim Wolfe, a biologist, has lived in the area for years and is glad to share fascinating tidbits about insects, plants, and their relationships. The nature center includes displays of butterflies and other insects—look at butterfly wings under a microscope. You may get to see a butterfly emerge from its pupal case. A small reference library and a video are available to visitors, along with a colorful pamphlet ($1.30) chock full of butterfly ecology: feeding, defense, migration, and life cycle. Ask for the plant guide, which gives scientific and family names of labeled plants in the gardens and on the trail, along with brief information about them.

An added feature of the garden is the inside view of an active leaf-cutter ant nest. You must see how Jim and the ants created this marvel. Visitors can also walk a self-guided trail to see medicinal plants. One of the prettiest small gift shops in the country is here, with its melodious fountain, stained glass window, and mural. Shirts with elegant butterfly designs are the work of Marta Iris, the other owner.

Monteverde Cheese Factory, known as La Lechería, is open Monday through Saturday from 7:30 a.m. to 4 p.m.; on Sunday, it closes at 12:30 p.m. Watch cheesemakers through a glass partition beside the sales room, and buy cheeses, ice cream, sour cream, bread, marmalades, and tasty goodies made locally by Rockwell's.

Monteverde Orchids, telephone/fax (506) 645-5510, near Cerro Plano showcases some 400 of the 500 orchid species found in the Monteverde region. The terraced garden has miniature orchids so tiny that owner Gabriel Barbosa hands out a magnifying glass with each admission ticket so visitors will be able to appreciate the beauty of even the tiniest specimen. At least 40 species will be in bloom at any time of year. The display, also part of a research project, is organized into 22 family groups with signs pointing out group characteristics. Gabriel, who has a species of orchid named after him, investigates orchid pollinators and is working on an inventory of Monteverde's orchid species. Open 8 a.m. to 5 p.m. Admission $5.

Serpentario Santa Elena, telephone/fax (506) 645-5238, (506) 645-5772, has more than 20 species of snakes on display as well as poisonous frogs, the giant marine toad, turtles, and basilisks. Open daily 8 a.m. to 5 p.m. Admission $3.

Sky Walk, telephone/fax (506) 645-5238, offers a chance to experience a cloud forest from a different perspective. Don't miss it! The loop walk through mostly primary forest passes over trails, platforms, and five hanging bridges: the highest 121 feet (37 m) above the ground, the longest almost 400 feet (120 m) long. No more than 10 people per group; a limit of three groups per hour guarantees 20 minutes to visually explore the canopy from each bridge. Admission $8 adults; $4 children from 6 to 12 years. For a three-hour guided natural history walk add $10; no guide fee for children under 10 years. Open 6 a.m. to 5 p.m. daily. Reservations recommended: office open from 9 a.m. to 8 p.m. The Sky Walk is 2 miles (3.5 km) north of Santa Elena, just before the entrance to Santa Elena Reserve.

Tropical rain-forest slide shows. Images captured by internationally known Patricia and Michael Fogden are presented year-round in the auditorium next to the Hummingbird Gallery, usually at 7:30 a.m., 11 a.m., and 4:30 p.m. daily; $3, by reservation: (506) 645-5212. Another show is presented nightly at 6:15 at the Monteverde Lodge, with excellent photos by Richard Laval and Luis Saenz, $5: (506) 645-5057.

Getting to Monteverde
By bus: Direct buses from San José twice a day. For night arrivals, have a flashlight handy to get from the main road to your hotel. The bus stops in Santa Elena before proceeding to Monteverde. Some hotels pick up from bus with advance notice. Public buses available from Puntarenas and Tilarán to Santa Elena; taxis available to hotels.

By car: Two routes are off the Inter-American Highway: one, near km 134, goes through Sardinal (paved for a short distance); the other, near km 149, is at Río Lagarto bridge. The two join near Guacimal. Count on 90 minutes for either route. A bumpy road gives occasional breathtaking views of the lowlands below as you climb on roads that seem to hang by grace along the edge of the mountains. As you wind through thin clouds, cows across deep valleys look like brown or white dots scattered on the steep pastures. A route from Tilarán is mostly unpaved, through Quebrada Grande to Santa Elena.

Other: Tours by boat, horseback, or car leave from La Fortuna; see Chapter 7.

Where to Stay in Santa Elena Sector
Albergue Santa Elena, (506) 645-5051, (506) 645-5298; fax (506) 645-5147, is near the bank in downtown Santa Elena. It has 11 clean, simple rooms, eight with private baths. Single $15, double $25, no credit cards. Vegetarian dishes are available in the restaurant, which is open to the public. Owner Mireya Salazar Méndez arranges horseback tours, including one- or two-day trips to San Gerardo Abajo and its view of Arenal Volcano, as well as to the volcano itself.

Arco Iris Lodge, (506) 645-5067, fax (506) 645-5022; e-mail arcoiris@sol. racsa.co.cr; Web site www.bbb.or.cr/Lodges/ArcoIris/ArcoIris.htm, with its hillside setting. It has a first-class view of spectacular rainbows that grace this high land (*arco iris* means "rainbow"). Owners Haymo Heyder and Susanna Stoiber continue to work toward making the lodge a model of ecologically sound development—they use natural concoctions rather than insecticides, separate garbage for recycling, and tend an organic garden, whose harvests contribute to fare served in the small restaurant. Breakfast (always with homemade bread, marmalade, and granola) and dinner are available with advance notice.

Seven cabins are of wood or concrete and wood; my favorite is Honeymooners' cabin next to forest and a small stream. It's intimate—windows on three sides and a porch facing the forest. The newest addition is a two-room cabin with a small sitting room. Double $45, $10 per person in bunk-bed cabin, no credit cards. Haymo and Susanna help plan excursions and arrange tours with naturalist guides or accompany guests on scenic horseback rides. The lodge is a two-minute walk from downtown Santa Elena.

Cloud Forest Lodge, San José (506) 292-1233, fax (506) 292-1233; Monteverde (506) 645-5058, fax (506) 645-5168, is about a mile (2 km) from Santa Elena. The 18 rooms are on a 70-acre (28-ha) farm. Rooms have natural-tone tile floors, a private terrace, and high wooden ceilings. Single $45, double $55. The main lodge building, of wood and stone, contains a dining room and lounge; panorama from a grand covered balcony is of the Gulf of Nicoya and surrounding forest. Explore 2 miles (3 km) of forest trails, no charge for ponchos and boots. Climb in the forest canopy for $45. No smoking is allowed in buildings or on trails. Transfers available from San José and elsewhere in the country. (VISA only accepted.)

El Sapo Dorado, (506) 645-5010, fax (506) 645-5180; e-mail elsapo@sol .racsa.co.cr; Web site www.q.co.cr/usr/sapodorado/, features 20 charming rooms in 10 bungalows tucked among fruit trees and gardens in a clearing surrounded by forest. Each room has a quiet, spacious feel to it, with a pretty table and chairs and two queen-size beds. Classic suites have corner fireplaces; wood supplied. Sunset terrace suites have dynamite views of the Gulf of Nicoya, stained-glass window panels, and a small refrigerator. The restaurant, open to the public, offers gourmet dining (better to have a reservation in high season). Daily specials may include sailfish Niçoise, beef in peppercorn sauce, or chicken in olive sauce. A vegetarian dish is always available. Desserts are scrumptious. Classic doubles $70, sunset terrace doubles $80, no credit cards. Private cloud-forest walks arranged. Located just outside Santa Elena on the road to Monteverde.

Hotel Finca Valverde, (506) 645-5157, fax (506) 645-5216, has two-room wooden cabins set on a forested hillside, close to downtown Santa Elena but with a feel of seclusion. Each of 18 pleasing rooms can comfortably sleep up to four (sleeping loft). Single $35, double $50. The restaurant/bar is open to the public. On a short forest trail on the property, one naturalist saw 60

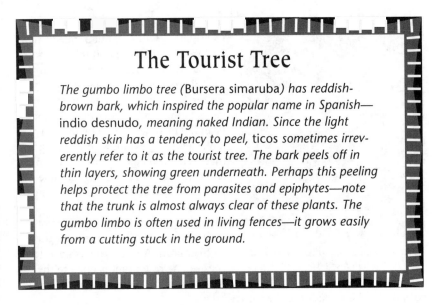

The Tourist Tree

*The gumbo limbo tree (*Bursera simaruba) *has reddish-brown bark, which inspired the popular name in Spanish—*indio desnudo, *meaning naked Indian. Since the light reddish skin has a tendency to peel,* ticos *sometimes irreverently refer to it as the tourist tree. The bark peels off in thin layers, showing green underneath. Perhaps this peeling helps protect the tree from parasites and epiphytes—note that the trunk is almost always clear of these plants. The gumbo limbo is often used in living fences—it grows easily from a cutting stuck in the ground.*

species of birds in two days; tours go to the Santa Elena Reserve. Guests can help pick coffee on the farm at harvest time. Five Valverde brothers and one sister have a hand in this endeavor, which is on the farm where they were raised. The Serpentarium next door is also in the family. Transport arranged to anywhere in the country.

Monteverde Lodge, San José (506) 257-0766, (506) 222-0333, fax (506) 257-1665; e-mail costaric@expeditions.co.cr; Web site www.crexped.co.cr, is a short walk from downtown Santa Elena. It has the feel of a secluded, upscale mountain lodge. The gardens were designed to attract hummingbirds and other wildlife, complete with small stream and waterfall. Here in the tranquility of its forest setting, the lodge offers guests distinctive architecture and some out-of-the-ordinary features: a 15-person solar-heated indoor Jacuzzi in a glassed-in alcove, an impressive freestanding fireplace in the spacious, open bar/restaurant area steps up from the lobby, chandeliers, and wonderful vistas of surrounding forest.

The 27 forest-view rooms are bright and comfortably furnished, with sitting areas next to high windows and baths with both tubs and showers: single $80, double $93, taxes included. Breakfast $13, lunch $19, dinner $22; meal plans available. A two-night tour is $399 per person (double occupancy) including lodging, meals, transportation, taxes, and guided walks in the reserve.

Transportation is available to Monteverde and Santa Elena reserves; San José transfer $40. Rubber boots available. Monteverde Lodge is owned by Costa Rica Expeditions.

Young anteater found on a farm and released in Monteverde forest

Sunset Hotel, (506) 645-5048, fax (506) 645-5344, is about a mile (1.6 km) from Santa Elena off the road to the Santa Elena Reserve. Seven comfortable rooms have private baths, orthopedic mattresses, and wonderful views of the Gulf of Nicoya and Chira Island. The dining room, with pretty tablecloths, has windows on three sides that look out on a manicured garden and the spectacular sunsets. Double $36, breakfast and taxes included; no credit cards. Carmen and Vitalis Mengel and their children orient you for area tours and rent horses for trips on their farm. A forest trail is open to guests. The restaurant is open to the public for dinner, reservation required; go early for the splendor in the western sky.

Where to Stay in Cerro Plano Sector

Hotel Belmar, (506) 645-5201, fax (506) 645-5135; e-mail belmar@ sol.racsa.co.cr, has 28 rooms in two Swiss chalet-type buildings with a commanding view of the slopes of the Tilarán Mountains and Gulf of Nicoya. Guests report seeing monkeys and quetzals from the balconies. Rooms are large and tastefully furnished, with matching comforters and upholstered armchairs. Singles $50, double $60. Meals are served family-style in a large dining room. The hotel arranges transportation, horseback riding, and guided tours to the forest (rubber boots for rent). Belmar is up the road from the gas station.

Hotel de Montaña Monteverde, Monteverde (506) 645-5046, fax (506) 645-5320, San José (506) 224-3050, fax (506) 222-6184; e-mail monteverde @ticonet.co.cr; Web site ticonet.co.cr/monteverde.html, has 31 rooms, an indoor Jacuzzi with a great view of forested mountains and the Gulf of Nicoya, sauna, TV room, bar, and a lounge area with balcony and rocking chairs. Room doors are decorated with painted butterflies and birds, and each room opens onto a terrace and pretty gardens with flowering plants. Single $45, double $65, junior suites $78. A honeymoon suite has its own Jacuzzi and balcony, $110. The dining room is open to the public. The hotel has a nature trail to a small lagoon, rents horses, has guided tours to the reserve, and offers San José transfers.

Hotel Heliconia, (506) 645-5109, (506) 645-5145, fax (506) 645-5007; e-mail heliconi@sol.racsa.co.cr, started out as a small pensión, but its growth to 22 rooms has not diminished the friendly atmosphere. Curtains hand-painted with designs of local flora and fauna grace each room. Floor-to-ceiling glass in the Jacuzzi room gives it a forest setting. Single $64, double $66. The dining room/bar is open to the public, by reservation. Afternoon and evening tours to Arenal Volcano offered. Transport provided to anywhere in the country. A three-day, two-night package includes lodging, meals, several tours, and round-trip San José transfer, $288 per person, double occupancy.

Pensión Manakin, (506) 645-5080, fax (506) 645-5516, has 11 rooms, three with private tiled baths. Windows make rooms bright, and they are very clean. Mario and Yolanda and their four children are caring hosts. Good typical food is served in the dining room. Single $6, double $12 with shared bath; with private bath double $20. (VISA only accepted.)

Where to Stay in Monteverde
El Bosque Hotel and Restaurant, (506) 645-5158, fax (506) 645-5129; e-mail elbosque@sol.racsa.co.cr, is near the CASEM gift shop. The 23 rooms are in buildings curved around a clearing off the main road, surrounded by trees. Each opens onto a covered porch and has tile floors, rough white-plaster walls, and a high wooden ceiling. Bright bedspreads add color. Single $25, double $35. The hotel has a short nature trail plus the Bosque Restaurant, a Monteverde favorite. Reception is in the restaurant, on the main road.

Hotel Fonda Vela, San José (506) 257-1413, fax (506) 257-1416, Fonda Vela (506) 645-5125, fax (506) 645-5119; e-mail fondavel@sol.racsa.co.cr; Web site www.worldheadquarters.com, is past the cheese factory going toward Monteverde Cloud Forest Preserve. Set on hills of the 35-acre (14-ha) Smith farm, the 28 rooms are in buildings situated to give guests maximum privacy, surrounded by forest, flowers, and small landscaped areas. Most are spacious and have gleaming wood floors with area rugs and rich-colored comforters; all are lovely—wheelchair accessible. Some suites have refrigerators, sitting areas, and a sleeping loft. The forest offers ample opportunity for bird-watching without leaving the hotel. From my balcony on my last visit, I watched morpho butterflies, an agouti, and a turquoise-browed motmot.

Enjoy hiking trails through forest on the farm and guided horseback rides ($8 an hour). Through the dining room's enormous glass windows, watch hummingbirds feed, mists roll in, and sunlight sparkle. A small stage hosts evening musical performances by both local and visiting artists. An impressive wood-railed ramp leads to the second-level bar area. Artwork by Paul Smith (father of Stephen and Pablo, who manage the hotel) adorns walls. Single standard room $50, double $59, junior suites from $66, double occupancy, mountain suites $74.

Where to Eat in the Monteverde Area
El Bosque Restaurant, (506) 645-5158, described in the hotel listing, is a tradition with visitors and residents alike. Food is good and prices reasonable.

El Sapo Dorado's, (see hotel listing) intimate restaurant, (506) 645-5010, is known for its excellent food and quality service.

La Pizzería de Johnny, (506) 645-5066, serves good pizza and more, located in Cerro Plano next to the Monteverde Orchids. Gift shop and outdoor dining.

Restaurant De Lucia, (506) 645-5337, in Cerro Plano on the road to the Butterfly Garden, offers good atmosphere, delicious food nicely served, candlelight at dinner, wines. José and Lucia are attentive hosts. Open daily 11:30 a.m. to 9:30 p.m.; reserve in high season.

Rocky Road Cafe is in downtown Santa Elena above Jiménez Bakery. People-watch from the balcony. U.S.-style hamburgers and Pacific Northwest jo-jos are specialties. Open 8 a.m. to 4 p.m., closed Sunday.

Stella's Bakery and Coffee Shop, (506) 645-5429 is across from CASEM. Besides seeing Stella's artwork, visitors get good food and, if Stella's around, interesting conversation.

PACIFIC NORTHWEST BEACHES AND UPPER NICOYA PENINSULA

Popular beach and natural history destinations are here. Swim, surf, watch turtles nest, hike, descend into caves, take an estuary tour, or visit national reserves, including Las Baulas, Barra Honda, and Ostional. Access off of the Inter-American Highway is across the Tempisque River by ferry or west from Liberia. You may also cross the Gulf of Nicoya from Puntarenas to Playa Naranjo and head northwest on the Nicoya Peninsula, but that's slower going. Scheduled airline service from San José on Travelair or SANSA quickly moves travelers to Liberia or Tamarindo, Nosara, Sámara (Carrillo), and Punta Islita, while international flights now arrive at Daniel Oduber Quirós airport near Liberia.

An increasing number of road signs now make travel in this area less by-guess-and-by-golly, and hotel advertisements also help direct drivers.

Plan to dine at your hotel—some have all-inclusive rates—or ask your innkeeper for other area recommendations.

GULF OF PAPAGAYO AREA

In the works since 1974, the ambitious, government-directed Gulf of Papagayo project encompasses 17 beaches—mainly on Culebra Bay—and almost 5,000 acres (2,000 ha). The plan calls for thousands of hotel rooms, a marina, golf course, vacation homes, and shopping centers on land leased to developers. The project is a king-size measuring stick for the government's commitment to environmentally responsible tourism.

Head west out of Liberia to just south of Comunidad; before Playa del Coco, turn toward Playa Hermosa and follow the signs. For these beaches, the Liberia route is quicker than the Tempisque route. Approximate driving time from San José is 4½ hours by car, 30 minutes from Liberia.

Where to Stay and Eat in Gulf of Papagayo Area

Costa Smeralda, (506) 670-0042, fax (506) 672-0079; e-mail smeradla @sol.racsa.co.cr, has spectacular Mediterranean-style architecture. Its 64 rooms are terraced on gentle hills that front Playa Buena. Bright white walls and red roofs of the resort hotel accent a landscaped lawn and beautiful plantings of palms, crotons, and other colorful tropical vegetation. The multilevel main building is arches, wide verandas, and pretty railings on terraces and stairways. Views are of artistically curved swimming pools below, thatched ranchos, and hills across the blue bay. The restaurant, with Italian and French specialties, is open to the public; reservations preferred.

Large, glass-fronted rooms open onto individual tiled porches. Each room has satellite TV, telephone, colorful matching drapes and bed coverings, reading lamps, big closets, air-conditioning, and original watercolors on the wall. All-inclusive rates (lodging, meals, drinks, taxes) are single $170, double $250. Lodging and meals only are single $135, double $170. Suites available.

On-site Swiss Travel offers snorkeling, diving, kayaking, bird-watching, and horseback riding, with trips to Miravalles Volcano, Palo Verde and Rincón de la Vieja, and private reserves at Buena Vista and Los Inocentes. Car rental available.

Small patches of forest remain around the hotel, so howlers are present, along with iguanas, raccoons, coatis, hummingbirds, and many other bird species. Transfers available from Liberia or San José airports.

Malinche Real Beach Resort, San José (506) 233-8566, fax (506) 221-0739; Malinche (506) 670-0033, fax (506) 670-0300; e-mail costarica@ bluebayresorts.com; Web site www.bluebayresorts.com, spreads out over a hill sloping down to the curve of the beach. Attractive bungalow-type buildings nestled among the trees hold 100 rooms, each with its own deck for enjoying spectacular ocean sunsets. Each room has a small refrigerator, telephone, cable TV, air conditioning and ceiling fan, and king- or two queen-size beds. Single $150, double $110 per person, including meals, all drinks, nonmotor sports, and health club and fitness facilities.

Restaurants offer casual and formal dining, including Italian and macrobiotic specialties. The health club has indoor and outdoor Jacuzzis, sauna, lap pool, wave-resistance pool, exercise machines, aerobic classes, massage, and weights.

About 60 acres (24 ha) of the 100-acre (40-ha) development are in forest, where guests enjoy guided walks on five trails. There's horseback riding along the beach and in the forest as well as snorkeling and kayaking. Two-person sailboats, mountain bikes, water bikes, diving, and tennis are available. Tiered swimming pools offer a shallow area for children. A tour desk arranges visits to area attractions, and car rental is available.

PLAYA HERMOSA

The mile-long (1.5-km) Hermosa Beach is on a bay with hills at both ends. It's not uncommon to see dolphins in the bay or howler monkeys moving through trees along the shore, especially in dry season. *Hermosa* means beautiful, and indeed it is. Daily express bus from San José. Turn right just before Playa del Coco and follow signs.

Diving/Water Sports

Bill Beard's Diving Safaris, telephone/fax (506) 672-0012, e-mail diving@ sol.racsa.co.cr; Web site diving-safaris.com; U.S. number (800) 779-0055, is in Sol Playa Hermosa Resort. Two-tank dive trips are $60, 8:30 a.m. and 1 p.m. daily departures. Night dives are $45, and long-range dive trips, available year-round, are $80 to Catalina Island and $110 to Bat Island. Snorkeling trips are $26. Stop by the dive center, which hums with activity, or call to check on certification courses, including PADI and NITROX. Bill has been diving off of Costa Rica's shores for more than 27 years. Some of his tips: best months for manta rays at Catalina Island are December to May; whale sharks are seen year-round.

Where to Stay and Eat in Playa Hermosa

Condovac La Costa, (506) 256-3420, (506) 221-2264; fax (506) 221-4619; e-mail condovac@sol.racsa.co.cr; Web site www.loria.com/condovac, is on Playa Hermosa. The 101 air-conditioned villas feature bedroom, living area, bath, equipped kitchen, cable TV, telephone, and a terrace overlooking the bay, $110. The complex includes restaurants, bars, minimarket, two large pools (one for children), and tennis courts. Go mountain biking, scuba diving (including classes), snorkeling, sportfishing, Jet-Skiing, waterskiing, sailboating, kayaking, windsurfing, and hiking. Check with on-site tour agency for trips to national parks, reserves, and volcanoes, or to a secluded beach to swim, explore, and enjoy a barbecue. Motorized carts transport guests around the hillside complex. Transfers from San José.

Villa del Sueño, telephone/fax (506) 672-0026; e-mail delsueno@sol.racsa .co.cr, is near the first entrance to Playa Hermosa. This "house of dreams" (its name in Spanish) was created by owners Claude, Silvia, and Robert. Travelers receive a warm welcome in the large, open lounge (cushioned wicker furniture) next to the dining room. The beach is about 200 m away; the sparkling pool is a few steps from the veranda.

Twenty large rooms in the main villa have decorator touches, rocking chairs, ceiling fans, shuttered windows, and pretty bedspreads. Standard double $45; superior double, with two double beds and a seating area, $55.

Next door are condominiums for rent: one-bedroom apartments $95 for two, efficiencies for two $75. No small children.

Meals are a highlight, from breakfast that can be crepes, French toast, fresh fruit, or eggs to lunch with something Italian generally included. Dinner is a four-course affair. The restaurant is open to the public— reservations recommended.

Area excursions include transport, meals, and English-speaking guide. Visit Rincón de la Vieja for $75. Take a horseback nature tour at Los Inocentes, raft the Corobicí, or visit Santa Rosa National Park. Go to Palo Verde, Arenal, Las Baulas (turtles nesting), and Gauitil (pottery-making).

PLAYA DEL COCO

On a horseshoe-shaped bay that opens into the Gulf of Papagayo, the town of Playa del Coco is small, eclectic, and tied to the sea. It's easily reached by bus from San José and Liberia, and is about 30 minutes from the Liberia airport. Small sodas (cafes) and restaurants are scattered along the road into town and close to the park. Find French, Italian, and Mexican restaurants along with fresh seafood and typical fare. Water sports and tour companies arrange activities.

Where to Stay and Eat in and near Playa del Coco

Hotel Villa Flores, telephone/fax (506) 670-0269, is a 10-room bed-and-breakfast in Coco Beach 1½ blocks from the beach. Single $40, double $50, $55 for two in larger air-conditioned upstairs suites; full breakfast. Set in an ample garden, it has an open dining and lounge area downstairs; the restaurant specializes in pastas. There is also a bar, small gym, and swimming pool. A full-day boat tour takes in secluded Gulf of Papagayo beaches, and staff arranges other tours. Owner Gianfranco Nichilo is a skin-diving aficionado and sometimes goes with guests on dive trips to Santa Catalina, Murciélagos Island, or other spots in Culebra Bay.

Hotel Resort La Flor de Itabo, (506) 670-0011, (506) 670-0292, fax (506) 670-0003, is less than a mile (1.3 km) from downtown and the beach. It has eight air-conditioned rooms in the main building, with phone, satellite TV, and private baths: single $50, double $55. Four apartments (for up to four) have kitchenettes and air conditioning, $70. Ten bungalow rooms are $40. Taxes included. The restaurant, with views of the tropical gardens, specializes in seafood and Italian dishes. A pool is set in tropical gardens.

The hotel runs its own tours: boating on the Tempisque River ($65), horseback to Rincón de la Vieja and hot springs, a barbecue at Zapotal Beach, and a visit to Lomas Barbudal reserve. A two-day, one-night trip to Arenal Lake and Arenal Volcano includes Las Pumas animal refuge, Arenal Botanical Garden, Tabacón Hot Springs, and a mountain hike, $150 per person, minimum four. Sportfishing is a specialty, from $380 per day.

Longtime Italian management. Car rental available, both standard and four-wheel-drive.

La Villa del Sol, telephone/fax (506) 670-0085; e-mail Villasol@sol.racsa. co.cr; Web site www.amerisol.com/costarica/lodging/villasol.html, is a charming seven-room house built around an atrium. The inn is set amid tropical grounds studded with palms and flowering shrubs. A second-floor terrace has a view of the beach and of sailboats and fishing boats in the bay, less than 300 feet (80 m) away. The bright, open living area is furnished with pretty cushioned bamboo furniture. Spacious rooms have cathedral ceilings, large windows, and ceiling fans. Five rooms have private baths and two share a bath, double $35, breakfast included. In front of the house is a pool and sunning area. This end of the beach is away from weekend and holiday crowds, about half a mile (1 km) north of downtown.

French Canadian owners and gracious hosts Jocelyne and Serge Boucher arrange sailing, fishing, diving, horseback riding, cycling, kayaking, and area tours. Transfers arranged. They also rent air-conditioned houses with pools and ocean views.

Rancho Armadillo, (506) 670-0108, fax (506) 670-0441, e-mail armadil @sol.racsa.co.cr; Web site www.lasirena.com/coco.html; U.S. number (817) 453-4658, is a 25-acre (10-ha) retreat in the mountains with a view of the coastline stretching in the distance. Actually, the hotel is only a mile (2 km) from the beach, shuttle provided. Owner Jim Procter offers six air-conditioned rooms, one with a sitting area, some stained-glass accents: $125 per person, including lodging, meals, and beverages, prebooking recommended. Ask about the availability of a beautiful house, with wooden pegs in the floors and dovetail joints in windows.

The ocean-view restaurant attracts locals as well as visitors, with a menu not found elsewhere in these parts: Cajun shrimp or blackened chicken, Texas hamburger, chile without beans, foot-long subs, and more.

If you tire of relaxing in the pool and bird-watching, Jim is pleased to set up horseback riding, hiking, boating to nearby beaches ($35 per hour), windsurfing, or diving ($55 for a two-tank dive); fishing and diving packages available. Other options are tours to explore the canopy near Rincón de la Vieja or to Arenal Volcano and turtle-nesting sites. Go by boat to pre-Columbian sites. Look for signs on the way into Playa del Coco (near the boatyard).

OCOTAL BEACH

Just 2 miles (3 km) from Playa del Coco is Ocotal Beach, small and beautiful, a personal favorite. The tide pools are fascinating. At the north end of the beach, caves shoot the water from incoming tide back out with tremendous force. Big Guanacaste iguanas are almost always moving about at the edge of the sandy beach, parrots squawk. Turn left coming into Playa del

Coco and follow the meandering road through countryside and small settlements; watch for signs.

Diving/Water Sports

Hotel Ocotal, (506) 670-0321, fax (506) 670-0083; e-mail elocotal@ sol.racsa.co.cr; Web site www.centralamerica.com.cr.hotel/ocodiv.htm, has a complete dive shop renting equipment for water sports, including cameras for underwater photography, and offers diving instruction. A two-tank boat dive is $55; a night dive, $40. A $485 dive package includes five days and four nights (double occupancy) at the hotel, two days of boat diving, tanks, weights, guide, and breakfast. Ask about sportfishing packages.

Where to Stay and Eat at Ocotal Beach

Hotel Ocotal, (506) 670-0321, fax (506) 670-0083; e-mail elocotal@sol .racsa.co.cr; Web site www.centralamerica.com/cr/hotel/ocores.htm, www.elit.com/cr.ocotal/, has a spectacular view of coastline and sea from its rooms and restaurant on the cliff above the beach. Sunset from here is an unfolding piece of art. Each of 20 cliffside rooms and one suite opens onto a terrace with an unforgettable sea view. Make time to enjoy it from your terrace, from the pretty tropical swimming pool area at the end of the path, or from the Jacuzzi. Rooms have bamboo accents, air conditioning, ceiling fans, telephones, satellite TV, small refrigerators, coffeemakers, and double or king beds with pretty comforters. In addition, eight rooms and two suites are along the beach below, and six high-ceilinged duplex bungalows on the hillside contain 12 spacious rooms. A pool is located by each area. Standard single $70, $80 double, suites $145, bungalow rooms $105.

The restaurant serves buffet or a la carte meals either inside or on a covered terrace. Notice the great timbers in the dining room's remarkable roof structure. Meal plan $49, open menu, including tips and taxes. Father Rooster Bar on the beach has a "barefoot atmosphere" for informal dining and drinks. A shuttle for beach, restaurant, and rooms is available with a phone call.

The tour desk arranges trips to see turtles, parks, and a volcano or to climb into the canopy. Other activities include sportfishing, horseback riding, mountain biking, surfing, and boat cruises along isolated beaches and coastal islands. Scuba diving is a specialty here. On-site are an exercise room and lighted tennis court. Car rental available.

Hotel Villa Casa Blanca, telephone/fax (506) 670-0448; e-mail vcblanca @sol.racsa.co.cr; Web site www.worldheadquarters.com, is a charming 13-room inn. Owners Janey and James Seip often join guests for breakfast on the large covered terrace in a tropical garden setting. Both the company and the breakfast are delightful. Besides the typical *gallo pinto*, find Belgian waffles, fruit, breads, and some of the best pancakes around. The Spanish-style villa, practically hidden in a tropical garden, is a short walk from the beach and has its own small swimming pool.

Splashes of color abound in the unique rooms: comforters, drapes, stool or chair cushions, shower curtains, artwork, and plants. Staying here is like being a guest in a nice home. Each room has a private bath, air conditioning, and ceiling fans; single $49, double $59, including breakfast. The second-floor blue-and-white honeymoon suite has a canopy bed, breakfast corner, high wood ceilings, view of the sea, and a bathroom with a raised tub on a tile platform, $85. Also upstairs is a condo with canopy bed, living area, kitchen, breakfast nook, and a balcony overlooking the back garden, $95 for two. A smaller suite has a Jaccuzi, cable TV, and access to a private garden, $95. No smoking here.

Though lunch and dinner are not served, restaurants are within walking distance, or staff will help you order from menus of restaurants in Playa del Coco, food delivered. Tours to Arenal, Tempisque River, Palo Verde, Santa Rosa, and turtle-nesting sites arranged. Horse or kayak rental, $10 per hour. The Seips handle rental of several neighboring houses, some with pools and Jacuzzis.

FLAMINGO, SUGAR BEACH, CONCHAL

These three curved beaches are lovely to look at. Flamingo is a fishing and yachting center with its own marina and upscale summer homes. For a more secluded, natural setting, try special Sugar Beach. Conchal's shell-strewn beach draws olive ridley turtles February to April and only recently has been developed for upscale tourism. All are accessible off the main road between Liberia and Santa Cruz, turning west at Belén and northwest at Huacas. Lots of signs. The good news is that most of these roads are paved. Buses run daily to Flamingo and Conchal; the nearest airport is in Tamarindo.

Where to Stay and Eat at Flamingo Beach

Flamingo Marina Hotel and Club, San José (506) 290-1858, fax (506) 231-1858, Flamingo (506) 654-4141, fax (506) 654-4035; e-mail hot-flam@sol.racsa.co.cr; U.S. number (800) 276-7501, has standard rooms, double $78; suites and apartments from $120; condos at $200—more than 40 in all. All have air conditioning, ceiling fan, satellite TV, telephone, refrigerator, and ocean view. Check out suites with Jacuzzi, wet bar, and private terrace. The restaurant looks across two pools to coastline and sea. Enjoy a large outdoor Jacuzzi and tennis court. Tours include national parks, diving, fishing, horseback riding, and bird-watching. Transfers from San José ($25 one way); round trips to Tamarindo ($20) and Liberia ($50).

Hotel Aurola Playa Flamingo, San José (506) 233-7233, fax (506) 255-1036; Flamingo (506) 654-4010, fax (506) 654-4060; e-mail aurola @sol.racsa.co.cr; U.S. number (800)-2AUROLA, is the grandam of Flamingo. It has 125 rooms, suites, and apartments in two complexes, pools, swim-up bar, restaurants, gym, sauna, boat charters, tour agency. Large rooms have air conditioning and fans, satellite TV, minibar, and telephones. Single or

Ocotal Beach from Hotel Ocotal

double from $75 in bay-view rooms, $100–$120 for beachside rooms; suites from $150. Diving lessons. Transfers from San José.

Hotel Fantasias Flamingo, San José (506) 222-9847, fax (506) 257-5002, at hotel (506) 654-4350; e-mail flamingo@sol.racsa.co.cr; Web site www.multicr.com/fantasias/, is cliffside above the bay: 21 rooms finished, 21 more to go. Expect air conditioning, ceiling fans, full-length mirrors on sliding closet doors, telephones, and terrace or balcony. Poolside rooms $120, others $110 for up to two, breakfast included. The air-conditioned dining room features an international menu. Stairs descend to a small secluded beach; a shuttle goes to the main Flamingo Beach, six blocks away. Staff books tours: diving, fishing, horseback riding, national parks and reserves. Transfers available.

Stop by **Marie's Restaurant**, meet Marie, and sample everything from Mexican food and fresh fish to milkshakes. **Amberes** is another local favorite.

Where to Stay and Eat at Sugar Beach
Hotel Sugar Beach, (506) 654-4242, fax (506) 654-4239; e-mail info @sugar-beach.com, Web site www.sugar-beach.com; U.S. and Canada number (800) 458-4735, is the only hotel on Pan de Azúcar beach. The curve of the small bay, the rocky headlands, the forest, and the peace provide a lovely setting. The uncrowded white sand beckons. Hear monkeys and see iguanas, raccoons, coatis, and armadillos. Birding is good both on the grounds, beginning with the resident green macaw, and in surrounding forest. Trails go to

another beach or up the mountain: the property encompasses 24 acres (9.7 ha). Swim on the beach or in the pool. Ranchos on the beach offer terrific places to relax. Enjoy boat excursions to other secluded beaches, surfing trips to Witches Rock, and sightseeing trips. There are sea kayaks, canoes, surfboards, snorkeling equipment, boogie boards, etc. Fishing, scuba diving (Catalina Island is right out front), turtle tours, horseback riding, and estuary tours arranged.

The hotel's large open-air restaurant invites leisurely dining. Chefs prepare nightly specials—no fixed eating hours here. Meals reasonably priced.

All accommodations have both air conditioning and fans. The 16 spacious rooms in duplexes fronting the beach have windows on three sides, high native-hardwood tongue-and-groove ceilings, Spanish tile floors, hardwood or wicker furniture in the sitting area, and two double beds: doubles $110 to $138. Six smaller versions are $100. Four double rooms in a hexagonal building with wraparound balcony are charming: $90. A honeymoon suite is $165. Furnished apartment and three-bedroom beach house available.

Round-trip pickup service from Tamarindo, accessible by bus and air, is $20, $30 for Liberia.

Where to Stay and Eat at Conchal Beach

Hotel Condor Club, (506) 654-4178, fax (506) 654-4050, on a hill above Conchal Beach has bungalows containing 30 rather small but pleasant rooms with air conditioning, ceiling fans, satellite TV, and telephones. Single $35, double $45, including continental breakfast. A restaurant and bar in the main building open to a pretty pool, sundeck, and panoramic view.

Down the hill is Condor's private beach club with pool, plus tennis courts—shuttle service. Aquatic sports include diving, snorkeling, windsurfing. Horseback ride, mountain bike, or tour to Las Baulas in turtle-nesting months. See ridleys here, and monkeys and parrots, too. No, those aren't condors, as one visitor thought: they're buzzards. But it's nice to be in a place where even the buzzards seem regal. Transfers available. Get to hotel via Matapalo.

Meliá Playa Conchal Beach and Golf Resort, hotel (506) 654-4123, fax (506) 654-4181; San José (506) 293-4915, fax (506) 293-4916; e-mail mconchal@sol.racsa.co.cr; U.S. and Canada number (800) 336-3542, fax (305) 530-1626, has 308 suites, Robert Trent Jones-designed golf course, lighted tennis courts, free-form swimming pool as big as a lake, Jacuzzis, health club, restaurants and bars, small shopping center, travel agency, and more. Suites $165 for up to two; master suites $400.

Monkeys and parrots live here, and turtles come ashore during the year. Besides wildlife watching on the property and along the beach and nearby estuaries, choose from a full range of natural history tours to parks and reserves.

PLAYA GRANDE

The white sands of Playa Grande north of Tamarindo stretch almost 2 miles (3 km). Visitors come to see turtles nest, including the largest of them all, the leatherbacks; to surf; to sun; and to explore in and along the estuaries.

El Mundo de la Tortuga, telephone/fax (506) 653-0471, a small turtle museum near the beach, offers audiocassette, self-guided 30-minute tours in English, Spanish, French, or German. Superb photographs and drawings illustrate facts about turtles, answering common questions: Why do turtles come here? Where do they come from? When will they come back? The 20-minute audiovisual experience covers the nesting process, what goes on inside the nest, emergence of baby turtles and the dangers they face, impact of humans on turtle survival, and protection measures at Playa Grande. Admission $5. Transfers from key area locations.

The museum is open from 4 p.m. until two hours after high tide, October 1 to March 15. A private initiative, the museum aims to help protect endangered sea turtles through environmental education. Area teachers and school groups get free tours. Browse in the turtle souvenir shop, with some items made by neighbors to Playa Grande.

Where to Stay and Eat at Playa Grande

Hotel Las Tortugas, (506) 653-0423, telephone/fax (506) 653-0458; e-mail nela@cool.co.cr; Web site www.cool.co.cr/usr/turtles, is a few steps from the beach where giant leatherbacks nest from October to March, and turtles can be seen year-round. Owners Louis Wilson and Marianela Pastor work to protect this important wildlife area and educate guests about turtle-watching. Because turtles are sensitive to light, none of the 11 rooms or suites has views to the south where the nesting beach is.

Each of the comfortable rooms is different in size and decor, all with air conditioning; from $60 to $85. Larger suites with king-size beds and living areas, $125, taxes included. A covered deck for outdoor dining or a sunset drink surrounds the main restaurant, which serves typical and international dishes. Next to the small, turtle-shaped pool is a thatched rancho with hammocks, and the Jacuzzi is heated.

A short distance away five attractive apartments (one that looks like a lighthouse) rent for $30 to $125 in high season; an upscale house is also available.

Choose among deep-sea fishing and estuary excursions by canoe or boat, and horseback riding. Tide pools are great for snorkeling, bathing, or exploring; there's a beach trail to the north, and a surf break is in front of the hotel. Owners do not recommend ocean swimming here, however. Masks and snorkels, boogie boards, and surfboards can be rented. Trips to destinations around the country arranged with a local employee-turned-entrepreneur who now has his own tour-transport business.

The express bus from San José to Santa Cruz is an option for those without car who do not want to fly. Taxi from there to Playa Grande about $25.

Villa Baula, San José (506) 257-7676, fax (506) 257-1098, Villa Baula (506) 653-0493, fax (506) 653-0459; e-mail hotelvb@sol.racsa.co.cr; Web site www.costaricainfo.com/baula.html, is on the beach, a five-minute walk to the estuary. Twenty rooms and five bungalows are in thatched wooden structures, with ceiling fans, and screened windows. Rooms are in two two-story buildings, $54 for up to two persons. Bungalows, raised off the ground, have two bedrooms, small refrigerator, and a covered porch area, $82. Furnishings are simple.

The restaurant, open to the public, has a varied menu: breakfast $5, lunch $9, dinner $12, plus taxes; meal plans available. Swim in the pool (children's pool also), tour the estuary with a local guide from a Tamarindo cooperative ($20), ride a horse on forest trails, or visit other beaches. Rent kayaks for a solo estuary, $6 an hour; mountain bikes are $5 an hour. Sportfishing offered. At the park station on the beach, register and pay at night for turtle-viewing. Hear and see howler monkeys here; observe birds of the tropical dry forest on the hotel grounds and in forest along the estuary.

By car, take the road from Huacas to Matapalo and follow signs for Villa Baula. Don't try to find it in the dark. Transfers available from Tamarindo airport, bus stops, and San José.

LAS BAULAS NATIONAL MARINE PARK, TAMARINDO NATIONAL WILDLIFE REFUGE

Location: Playa Grande on Pacific NW coast, near Tamarindo.
Hours: Open 24 hours; register after 6 p.m.
Information: Telephone hotline 192 (see Appendix A: Parks and Reserve Information), at Playa Grande (506) 653-0470.

Fortunately, the mangroves and big leatherback turtles (*baulas*) that this area was set up to protect don't care what the place is called. It began life as a government-protected area under the name of Tamarindo National Wildlife Refuge, but in 1991 the area was enlarged and decreed to be Las Baulas de Guanacaste National Marine Park to give it a higher status of protection under the law. The legislative assembly did not approve the decree: the issue was complicated by the fact that the expanded area includes expensive private lands difficult for the government to purchase. National parks, theoretically, are government owned, while wildlife refuges can be mixed ownership. So the area became a wildlife refuge again. Guess what? It was declared a park again. So let's just use both names here and get on with it.

Whatever its name, it encompasses beaches that attract one of the largest leatherback turtle populations in the world. Peak nesting months in the refuge are October through January, when as many as 200 females may come ashore per night. Smaller but noticeable numbers continue to arrive until March, but there are actually turtles here year-round. Each nest contains from 70 to 100 eggs, and the babies hatch in about 70 days. Warmer temperatures in the nest produce females; cooler temperatures, males.

The *baula* is the largest sea turtle living today. Females can be 6 feet (1.8 m) long and weigh more than 1,300 pounds (590 kg). The species has a tough skin or hide instead of a true shell—hence its English name.

Major obstacles to survival for these sea creatures are not only loss of habitat, egg-poaching, and accidentally being caught by fishermen, but also plastic pollution. Plastic in the water resembles jellyfish and may be ingested by the turtles, who love the jellyfish most sea animals steer clear of: the Portuguese man-of-war.

Olive ridley turtles also sometimes come ashore to lay eggs, though not in the massive *arribadas* experienced at Nancite in Santa Rosa park or the Ostional refuge.

To see the protected mangrove, take a boat along one of the estuaries. All five species that live in Costa Rica thrive here: black, white, buttonwood, tea, and the red, with its stilt or prop roots. You may be surprised to see the decorations on these woody plants: orchids, bromeliads, termite nests. The American crocodile lives here.

Las Baulas is a good bird-watching area. Lowlands attract the wood stork, white ibis, jacana, roseate spoonbill, and American egret—at least 174 species have been identified. There's also a fragment of tropical dry forest. Crabs abound: ghosts, hermits, and garish crabs with black bodies, orange legs, and purple pincers.

Boats can be rented in Tamarindo or Playa Grande for trips in the estuaries: local tour operators and hotels arrange guided estuary tours. Park personnel oversee nighttime tours to see nesting turtles. A small subregional office of the Tempisque Conservation Area, Ministry of Natural Resources and Environment, is located just before the beach. Stop by for information.

Getting There
By bus: Direct San José–Tamarindo bus.
By car: Access from Tamarindo and Playa Grande. To reach Playa Grande from the south, go through Villarreal to Matapalo; from Liberia through Belén and Huacas to Matapalo. Then follow signs to Playa Grande.
By plane: The nearest airport is Tamarindo, daily service from San José.

TAMARINDO
The town (population 2,997) has grown in a long, narrow strip along Las Baulas Estuary and Tamarindo and Langosta Beaches, with fingers of development into the low-lying coastal hills. Though Tamarindo is booming, most hotels are still small and streets unpaved, though on my latest visit decorative blocks for the streets and main town circle were stacked, ready to be placed.

Tamarindo, 43 miles (69 km) southwest of Liberia, draws beach lovers, nature lovers, fisherfolk, and surfers. Travelers come to see turtles nest, especially on Playa Grande across the estuary. Local boatmen charge less than a dollar apiece to ferry people across the estuary. Estuary tours to see birds, crocodiles, and the life of the mangroves are another attraction. A local cooperative offers a two-hour tour—guides have good eyes but not much English, $12 per person. Telephone (506) 653-0201 for details.

Concern that light from development in the area would keep turtles at sea resulted in night lighting designed to minimize impact on the beach.

The Tourist Information Center on the right side as you enter town, open daily 8 a.m. to 4 p.m., has a handy town map and information on lodging, restaurants, tour agencies, area parks and reserves, and medical attention. Make reservations, get photocopies, and buy cold drinks. Proceeds from this private effort by local tourism businesses go toward much-needed road repair; telephone/fax (506) 653-0337.

Getting There
By bus: Daily express bus from San José.
By car: From Liberia southwest through Filadelfia, Belén, Huacas, and Villarreal, mostly paved road.
By air: Daily domestic flights to Tamarindo, 40 minutes. The Liberia airport is 45 minutes away by car.

Tour Companies
Iguana Surf, telephone/fax (506) 653-0148; e-mail iguanasurf@aol.com; Web site www.tamarindo.com/iguana; U.S. fax (619) 788-9437, rents Jet-Skis, surfboards, Hobie cats, ocean kayaks, snorkeling equipment, and boats. Tours include a two-hour kayak estuary tour ($25), snorkeling tour to Capitán Island by kayak ($25) or boat ($30, minimum: five), transfers to other beaches in the area, and a Culebra Bay cruise. Main office has a nice gift shop: on the road to Langosta Beach, turn off before town circle.

Mary P. Ruth's **Papagayo Excursions,** (506) 653-0227, fax (506) 653-0254; e-mail papagay@sol.racsa.co.cr; Web site www.papagayo.racsa/co.cr, was a pioneer tour company in the area. Papagayo offers professionally trained, bilingual guides for nature safaris, deep-sea fishing, coastal cruises, scuba diving, horseback riding, and land trips to national parks. Examples are a two-hour jungle boat safari ($20), Las Baulas turtle safari ($25), four-hour tour to beaches such as Conchal and Flamingo with time to snorkel and relax on the beach ($35), day trip to Palo Verde and Guaitil ($40), visit to Ostional ($80), and day visits to Arenal Volcano and Rincón de la Vieja. Two offices: one as you enter town at the estuary; the other at the Papagayo Boutique in Tamarindo Commerical Center.

Where to Stay in Tamarindo
Bella Vista Village Resort, telephone/fax (506) 653-0036; e-mail belvista @sol.racsa.co.cr; Web site www.tamarindo.com/bella, welcomes guests with six

Touring the mangroves

thatched octagonal bungalows that have a million-dollar view of turquoise Tamarindo Bay. Under each high conical roof is a kitchen, comfortable living area (with fold-out bed), and sleeping loft with single and double beds. Charming, fanciful murals outside and tasteful fabrics, hand-painted kitchen tiles, and artifacts inside give each a theme: choose the Butterfly Room, Jungle Room, Fanta-Sea Room, or Indian Room. Single $80, double $90, $15 per person extra. Spaced at varying levels around a pretty pool, the bungalows look like a tiny, planned village, with the light colors of their walls brilliant against rock wall terracing and greens of the garden. A short walk down a gentle slope goes to town and beach.

Owners and hosts Gabe and Judy Bettinsoli seek to provide a balance of serenity and service; they arrange nature trips, horseback riding, scuba, snorkeling, boating and canoeing, or sportfishing—even dinner reservations.

Cabinas Zullymar, (506) 226-4732, (506) 653-0140, fax (506) 653-0028, is at the center of town, with a beachside restaurant and rooms across the street. All 43 rooms are simply furnished and clean, with pretty carved doors, some hot-water baths, and ceiling fans. Single or double $28 to $49. Tours of estuary, surfing, and snorkeling arranged and car rental available. Manager Edwin Martinez is a happy, helpful man.

El Jardín del Edén, (506) 653-0137, telephone/fax (506) 653-0111; e-mail hotel2jardineden.com, is on a hill above town, a complex of five

To Observe Turtles at Las Baulas

It's first come, first served for the privilege of watching turtles nest on the beach—no advance reservations. From October 1 to March 15, two park huts (one near Hotel Las Tortugas and another near Hotel Villa Baula) open at 6 p.m., where the hopeful sign up. A maximum of 60 people per night are admitted through each of these stations. When a turtle comes ashore, a local guide takes no more than 15 people to observe the process; 15 more observe the next turtle, and so on. Obviously, there's no guarantee on the number of turtles that may come ashore in any given night. At the station near Hotel Las Tortugas, entrance fee and guide is $5; the one near Hotel Villa Baula is usually reached from Tamarindo in a $12 package that includes boat transport, entrance, and guide.

From the $5 amount, Las Baulas receives about a dollar fee for the wildlife refuge. Of the rest, 30 percent goes to the guide and 70 percent to the local guide association to be used in community projects at Matapalo, Langosto, and Tamarindo. Matapalo's new community center is one tangible result.

Guides are housewives, former turtle egg-hunters, local folk who are still learning how to present information to visitors, so bear with them. Their work in conservation and turtle protection counts. Only a few speak English, but language training is in the works. As a program that involves community members who live around a protected area, bringing added income to individuals as well as towns, it merits recognition and support.

Mediterranean-style villas, two swimming pools, restaurants, and Jacuzzi. The beach is a three-minute walk away. Each of 18 rooms has ocean views, air conditioning and ceiling fans, refrigerator, minibar, pretty bamboo furniture, telephone, and satellite TV. Most have a terrace or balcony. Single $80; larger single $105, double $120, buffet breakfast included. Apartments with kitchen, dining room, and large terrace, double $140. Owners are Italian and French; their heritage is reflected in the restaurant menu. Herbs are grown on the property. Tours arranged; fishing packages.

Hotel Capitán Suizo, (506) 653-0075, fax (506) 653-0292; e-mail
capitansuizo@ticonet.co.cr; Web site www.tamarindo.com, exudes quiet
excellence and good service. To enter the door is to leave behind the heat,
noise, and workaday world. Twenty-two rooms with balconies or private
terraces look onto a lush tropical garden and sea views. Paths lead to a
large, cloth-tablecloth, open-air restaurant, which has a glassed-in kitchen
that lets you watch the European chef and his assistants at work; and to the
free-form pool with one end banked like a beach and a Tarzan-like rope
hanging from the tree over the water.

Eight thatched bungalows feature two walls of sliding wood-and-glass
doors, original works of art, fresh flowers, sitting area with upholstered sofas
and chairs, a raised bedroom alcove, and a huge bathroom with sunken tub
and private outdoor shower: $130 double occupancy, including breakfast.
Rooms are equally attractive: $95, with air conditioning $110. All have telephones, ceiling fans, screened windows and doors, ample closets, and pretty
Italian tile floors. The restaurant is open to the public, set hours for meals; a
select international dinner menu.

Located at the southern end of Tamarindo, Capitán Suizo has easy access to both Tamarindo and Langosta beaches. Activities include snorkeling
($25 half day), diving, kayaking, estuary tours with a naturalist guide ($20),
horseback riding, and sportfishing. After all that, relax with a massage. Own-
ers/managers are Ruedi and Ursula Schmid of Switzerland. Capitán Suizo is
affiliated with Small Distinctive Hotels of Costa Rica.

Hotel El Milagro, (506) 653-0042, (506) 653-0043, fax (506) 653-0050, is
across the road from the beach. The 32 rooms have high wooden ceilings, tile
floors, and wooden, louvered double doors that open onto porches. The dining
room is open to pool and gardens. Staff arranges turtle-watching tours, estuary
trips, horseback riding, surfing, and trips to Santa Rosa and Arenal Volcano.
Single with fan $55, double $60, buffet breakfast included; air conditioning
$10 more.

Hotel Pasatiempo, (506) 653-0096, fax (506) 653-0275; e-mail passtime
@sol.racsa.co.cr; Web site tamarindo.com/pasa, is downtown, about two
blocks from the beach. Ten rooms in thatched bungalows are in landscaped
gardens, each with its own private terrace. Each has reading lamps, ceiling
fan or air conditioning, and private bath, some bidets. Double $59, including
continental breakfast and taxes. A pool is near the restaurant and bar area—
come for sunset happy hour. In high season, some evenings find live music
or satellite sports specials. Staff set up guided nature tours, horseback riding,
snorkeling, or scuba diving. Bicycles available.

Where to Eat in Tamarindo

It would take you days to eat your way through Tamarindo. Don't miss **Sunrise Cafe** on the town circle. The waffles (Belgian-style) with strawberries

and cream for breakfast are to die for; cappuccino here, too. For fine Italian dining, try **La Meridiana**: handmade pasta, fresh-baked bread, spices and cheeses from Italy, and hospitality of owners Fabio and Vittoria, open for lunch and dinner. Stop by **Johann's Bakery** on the way into town, goodies galore. Also try **La Terraza Restaurant**, **Fiesta del Mar** on the circle, and **Blue Maxx Cafe**.

NICOYA

A pretty town (population 23,326) with a picturesque colonial church, Nicoya is a major crossroads that most tourists pass through on their way to somewhere else. (Nicoya is 33 miles [53 km] from the Tempisque ferry on the Nicoya Peninsula and 52 miles [83 km] from Liberia.) It's a pleasant place with the flavor of small-town life on the Nicoya Peninsula.

The church, a national monument, originated in the 1500s, with construction of this building completed in 1644. Damaged by an earthquake, it was restored in 1831. Walk inside and feel its history.

Across the street is a subregional office of Tempisque Conservation Area, open 8 a.m. to 4 p.m. weekdays; visitors welcome. Contact this office for reservations to visit Barra Honda caves (506-685-5667, 506-686-6760). Staff provide information about other area parks and refuges.

From Nicoya, head northwest for the ferry across the Tempisque River or a visit to Barra Honda National Park and some private nature reserves. The road southeast heads for Playa Naranjo; when the pavement stops, it's slow going—plenty of time to take in the countryside and a character or two. One rainy afternoon, I noticed an old, bearded man on the bank along the road, half-hidden as he squatted in tall grass. As the car approached, he rose slightly, carefully aimed his machete, and chopped. In the rear-view mirror, I watched as he resumed his station, presumably waiting for the next passerby. Near Lepanto, notice the salt beds, then continue to Playa Naranjo and the dock where the car ferry from Puntarenas arrives. Find descriptions of the southern peninsula in the Puntarenas–Montezuma–Mal País section.

Where to Stay in Nicoya

Hotel Curime, (506) 685-5238, fax (506) 685-5530, is at the edge of town toward Sámara, four blocks from the bus stop. Its 26 modest rooms have air conditioning or fans, small refrigerators, TV, and private baths; larger units have living area. Single $21 to $30, double $30 to $42, taxes included. The open-air restaurant is closed in low season; there is a large swimming pool.

BARRA HONDA NATIONAL PARK

Location: 14 miles (22 km) NE of Nicoya on the Nicoya Peninsula.
Size: 5,671 acre (2,295 ha).
Hours: December–April, daily 7 a.m. to 4 p.m. (last tour leaves at 1 p.m.); May–December, 7 a.m. to 1 p.m.

Cost: $6 entrance; camping $1.50 per person per day; guided tour rates below.
Information/Reservations: Telephone hotline 192 (see Appendix A: Parks and Reserves Information), telephone/fax (506) 659-9039, (506) 659-9194.

The main attraction at Barra Honda is a network of caves through a peak that once was a coral reef beneath the sea. Located just west of where the Tempisque River flows into the Gulf of Nicoya, Barra Honda still holds many secrets. Of the 42 caves discovered, only 19 have been explored. The human remains and pre-Columbian artifacts discovered have yet to yield their stories, but exploration has revealed several large caverns adorned with stalactites, stalagmites, pearls, soda straws, columns, popcorn, and other intriguing formations. Nature's underground artistry is most profuse in the Terciopelo (fer-de-lance) Cave, so named because early speleologists found a snake of this species smashed on its floor. Terciopelo contains the Organ, a columnar formation that resounds with different tones when gently tapped. This is the only cave open to the public. The deepest cave, Santa Ana, is almost 790 feet (240 m) beneath the surface.

Shafts into these caves are mostly vertical; no elevators to carry you down or caverns lit with colored lights. Descent is down a metal ladder almost 90 feet (27 m) and back up the same way, not for the fainthearted or infirm. Cave visits are permitted only with trained guides from communities around Barra Honda. Reservations are necessary for groups, recommended for individuals; call (506) 685-5667. Cost of equipment is $5 per person; for guides, $21 for up to four people, $24 total for five to eight people. Allow a minimum of three hours, including the walk to and from the cave entrance. Below-ground wildlife includes bats, insects, blind salamanders, fish, and snails.

For noncavers, the park offers trails that lead to a view point overlooking the Gulf of Nicoya and Chira Island, a tall evergreen forest, and waterfalls over natural travertine dams. The summit of Barra Honda Peak, pocked with large and small holes and decorated with sculptured rock, hints of the artistry in the caves below. Los Laureles Trail is 3.5 miles (5.5 km) long. The first 40 minutes are uphill, but then it levels off. Fauna you may see include white-faced and howler monkey, Amazonian skunk, long-nosed armadillo, white-nosed coati, coyote, magpie jay, and orange-fronted parakeet. The vegetation of the tropical dry forest to moist premontane forest transition zone is mostly deciduous. Average annual rainfall is 78 inches (1,970 mm); average temperature, 81°F (27°C). Highest elevation in the park is 1,385 feet (423 m).

Guided walks led by neighboring community members are $9 per person. Bring water, and if you choose to go without a guide, buy the inexpensive trail guide and stay on the trail. Two tourists became lost and died here in 1992.

In addition to offering tours, community guides work as park volunteers, helping with trail maintenance as well as park protection and fire-fighting.

This park/community cooperation is an example of how people who live in a buffer zone around the park can receive direct financial benefit while at the same time the park receives a helping hand.

Camping is allowed near the ranger station: showers and toilets.

Getting There

By bus: From Nicoya, take the Santa Ana bus, which is about a mile (2 km) from the entrance—no Sunday bus.

By car: Turn off the Inter-American for the Tempisque ferry; once across the river, continue 10 miles (16 km) to the sign for Barra Honda. Road unpaved from the village of Barra Honda.

Other: A taxi from Nicoya is about $10. Hotels, tour companies, and private reserves on the peninsula and even Liberia and San José offer tours.

Where to Stay near Barra Honda

Since the park is a day trip from many destinations in this chapter, as well as from San José, lodging is not a problem. One modest, nearby option is at Santa Ana: **Albergue de Montaña Las Cavernas,** (506) 279-5383, operated by the Campos family, Luis Guillermo and Estela. The nine rooms are clean, no hot water, doubles $17. Typical Costa Rican food is served in an open-air restaurant. Only Spanish spoken.

RANCHO HUMO

Location: Near town of Puerto Humo on Tempisque River, Nicoya Peninsula.
Rates: Single or double $78.
Information/Reservations: San José, (506) 255-2463, fax (506) 255-3573; Rancho Humo, (506) 385-0387; e-mail ecologic@sol.racsa.co.cr; Web site www .arweb.com/bird.htm.

Located across the Tempisque River from Palo Verde National Park, Rancho Humo offers a marvelous opportunity to enjoy the rich birdlife that lives in or migrates to this habitat. Birds such as the roseate spoonbill, anhinga, jabiru, northern jacana, stork, and egret are among 279 species of birds identified in the area. Sounds of howler monkeys, who hang out along one of the trails near the hotel, reverberate here. Iguanas are guaranteed; other wildlife of the area includes crocodiles, boas, coatis, raccoons, and collared peccaries. Some 148 species of trees are known to exist on this 2,470-acre (1,000-ha) reserve.

With the sun still low in the eastern sky and parrots moving noisily from tree to tree, an iguana and I once watched rays of light travel over the green of Palo Verde to shimmer on the waters of the Tempisque. Guests don't have to go outside and sit with an iguana for this early morning treat; it can be savored from one of 24 attractive air-conditioned rooms on a bluff above the river. Sliding glass doors open from each onto a terrace with treetop views of the forest and the river below.

Large picture windows in the spectacular rancho-style restaurant give an almost 360-degree view. Meals are served buffet-style: breakfast $6.50, lunch or dinner $10, plus taxes. Meal plan available. The skeleton of a crocodile head on the circular bar in the middle of the restaurant bares phenomenal teeth.

Don't miss early morning and late afternoon flights of birds along the river—watch for roseate spoonbills. Take time to enjoy the sunset's magic. Rancho Humo has boats, covered to protect travelers from sun or rain and equipped with life jackets. A short trail from the hotel goes through forest to the dock at Puerto Lapas. *Lapas?* It's Spanish for "macaws"—scarlet macaws are found here, along with big magpie jays, parrots, orioles, flycatchers, and parakeets.

Visit Isla de los Pajaros and Palo Verde park ($62) or the Bebedero mangroves. Boat service is available to various points, including Tempisque ferry and Puerto Chamorro at Palo Verde. Mountain-bike rental, $5 an hour, offers another option for seeing Palo Verde and for exploring Rancho Humo's forests and floodplains. Rent horses, $5 per hour. A day trip to Gauitil and San Vicente visits pottery makers, $57; the tour to Barra Honda National Park includes descent into the caverns, guides, and lunch, $100.

Getting There

By car: From the Inter-American, cross the Tempisque by ferry, turn at Quebrada Honda for Puerto Humo; from Nicoya, head through Corralillo to Puerto Humo; from Santa Cruz, go through Guaitil. Watch for hotel signs.
By plane: Charters to hotel airstrip, $375 for up to four.
Other: Boat transfers from Tempisque ferry, Palo Verde, or the Bebedero; San José transfer $150 for up to four.

SANTA CRUZ

Santa Cruz is a picturesque town 14 miles (23 m) northwest of Nicoya and 35 miles (56 km) southwest of Liberia with streets of paving stones. Fill the car with gas if you're heading to beach areas such as Tamarindo, Playa Grande, Junquillal, or points south. A subregional office of the Tempisque Conservation Area, with information about Ostional wildlife refuge, is here, telephone (506) 680-1820, (506) 680-0761. Santa Cruz is a crossroads (population 17,083), with routes to Barra Honda (via Santa Barbara), to pottery-making villages of Guaitil and San Vicente, to top beach destintions, and to Ostional or Las Baulas.

The villages of **Guaitil** and **San Vicente** are worth a visit for Chorotega Indian–style pottery. See artisans at work in the largely cottage industry. Pottery is sold in front of potters' houses and in shops. Cerámica Chorotega in San Vicente has a bilingual brochure on the history and process of this pottery-making, with many pieces styled after pre-Columbian pottery excavated nearby. The increase in tourism helped move local residents from producing utiliarian pieces for domestic use to making forms and designs their ancestors once used. U.S. Peace Corps volunteers organized workshops on marketing and business procedures.

Breeding programs release iguanas in the wild.

Getting There

By bus: Several buses a day run from San José, some via the Tempisque ferry, others from Liberia.

By car: There are paved roads either from Liberia or Tempisque ferry.

Where to Stay and Eat at Playa Blanca and Junquillal

These beaches are accessible by car even in rainy season. Buses from San José, Nicoya, or Liberia to Santa Cruz, Junquillal, and Paraíso get you close. Most hotels arrange pickup from the closest stop. By car from Santa Cruz, go through Ventisiete de Abril about 10 miles (16 km), and continue another 10 miles to Paraíso, unpaved but generally good. Turn left after the soccer field in Paraíso and follow hotel signs.

Secluded **Hotel Antumalal**, telephone/fax (506) 680-0506; e-mail antumal @sol.racsa.co.cr; Web site www.westnetcom/costarica/lodging/antumalal, is beautifully situated in lush tropical gardens. The open-air restaurant has an international menu, and the lovely, palm-fringed pools (one for children) are steps away from a long, uncrowded beach. Restful rooms are in bungalows on a gentle slope down to the sea. The 23-high-ceilinged standard rooms are large, with red brick floors and rough-plastered white walls. Windows on two sides provide good ventilation, and there are ceiling fans. Each room has a porch with hammock and table and chairs for dozing, reading, or watching birds. Single $75, double $85. Seven suites, each with king-size bed, small refrigerator, private balcony, and living area are $100.

Guests can get to an estuary for good birding either on a hike around a rocky headland at low tide or on a road through dry forest. I was delighted to spot a colorful member of the trogon family. Tide pools invite exploration. Hear howler monkeys, some of whom spend most of the day in trees near the dining area and upper rooms. I photographed a troop, including several babies, dozing and playing there from breakfast to lunchtime. Excursions can be arranged to Palo Verde, Caño Negro, Ostional, and Las Baulas. There's tennis, horse rental, and from November to May, diving. The San José–Junquillal bus stops at the entrance.

Hotel Guacamaya, telephone/fax (506) 653-0431; e-mail alibern@sol.racsa .co.cr; Web site crica.com/hotels/guacamaya, owned by Swiss brother and sister, Alicia and Berni, has a hillside setting back from the beach with great ocean and coastal mountain views. A nice breeze plays across the landscaped garden and through the large rancho-style restaurant, which has an international menu and is open to the public. Six rooms are large and comfortable: double $50 including taxes. Enjoy the pool (one for children), go horseback riding, take a boat ride along the coast or on an estuary, and go diving or deep-sea fishing. The young owners provide customized tours to wherever in their vehicle (maximum four). House available for rental.

Hotel Iguanazul, telephone/fax (506) 653-0123, (506) 653-0124; e-mail iguanazul@ticonet.co.cr; Web site www.ticonet.co.cr/iguanazul.html or www.paradise.co.cr, is a friendly place on Playa Blanca, 19 miles (30 km) west of Santa Cruz. The 24 rooms have a Southwestern United States flavor with white plaster walls, red brick floors, and exposed beams in high ceilings, decorated with folk-art rugs and wall hangings. Single with fan $50, double $65; with air $60 and $72, including continental breakfast.

The hotel sits on a bluff above the beach like an oasis, with nothing else around (well, there is the field of echinacea as you come in). Impressions are of sky and sea. The hub of activity is the dining room/bar/pool area, which has a grand view of the Pacific. The setting sun is spectacular—view it from ranchos on the path to the ocean, complete with *bancos* and hammocks. On a clear night, see the Milky Way and constellations galore, a natural planetarium. Snorkel in a clear, low-tide lagoon; kayak on a nearby estuary ($20); mountain bike ($20 for half-day rental); visit Ostional or Las Baulas to see nesting turtles come ashore; go panga fishing with a local fisherman; ride horses; surf; or visit a nearby private nature reserve ($15). Beach walks from the hotel may bring you face to face with coatis, armadillos, iguanas (yes, there are blue ones), or monkeys. Marvel at the fantastic multihued rocks along the shore—geologists are intrigued by them. Tide pools beckon.

Visiting French Canadian chefs have passed along recipes to local staff— excellent sauces, great pasta. Ask for a full-service picnic and enjoy it on the secluded white sands of Playa Blanca. Transfers from Santa Cruz or San José.

OSTIONAL NATIONAL WILDLIFE REFUGE

Location: *40 miles (65 km) SE of Santa Cruz; 21 miles (34 km) from turnoff before Sámara.*
Size: *790 acres (320 ha) of land; marine portion, 19,768 acres (8,000 ha).*
Hours: *Open daily 24 hours. After 6 p.m. register at administration.*
Cost: *$1.*
Information: *Telephone hotline 192 (see Appendix A: Parks and Reserves Information); contact the subregional office of the Tempisque Conservation Area (ACT in Spanish) in Santa Cruz, (506) 680-1820, (506) 680-0761, or the main ACT office in Bagaces, telephone/fax (506) 659-9039.*

The night was very dark. A young man led us across the beach of the Ostional refuge to the high-tide line, where a Pacific or olive ridley turtle was patiently digging a hole in the sand with her back flippers. She dug as far as the flippers would reach, flinging sand out behind her shell.

As soon as the flying sand had settled, soft eggs began to drop into the hole—one, two or three at a time, plopping on top of each other until there were about 100. Once the egg-laying began, the guide could use his flashlight briefly without disturbing the creative process. The whishing of sand off to the left signaled another hole begun.

Within 25 minutes, the digging and laying were finished and the turtle began methodically pushing sand back in, using both front and back flippers. Then she pounded her body against the surface to pack it down and moved around in a circle, scattering sand, leaves, and beach debris over the spot to obliterate any evidence of her buried treasure. Within an hour of emerging from the sea, she was back in it.

Nesting turtles can be found on this beach practically any night of the year, though massive arrivals, called *arribadas*, peak from July to December, when as many as 120,000 ridleys nest over four- to eight-day periods. *Arribadas* are usually about two weeks apart, but the interval can stretch to a month.

Harvesting of turtle eggs for food (there's a popular notion that they are aphrodisiacs), along with the killing of adults for meat or leather, threaten these and other sea-turtle species around the world. The Ostional refuge was set up to protect the nesting sites of ridleys, leatherbacks, and the green turtles that occasionally come ashore.

In an innovative program, local residents (who once plundered the nests and now live mainly off subsistence agriculture) harvest eggs from the first arrivals on the beach and then patrol it to prevent illegal egg-taking. About 30 percent of the eggs deposited during an *arribada* are lost anyway when turtles dig up eggs laid earlier. In the first 36 hours of each *arribada*, members of the development association collect about a million eggs to sell nationally; over the course of the last decade this has come to be a major income source for villagers. If you're here during the day you may see the egg collection, or horses with sacks of turtle eggs slung over them tied up at the local cantina.

Driver's Alert

From Junquillal to Playa Carrillo, some stretches are gutbusters; count on many 25-mph (40-kph) stretches. Parrots and parakeets are among the many species of birds that help travelers forget the rough and dusty (in dry season) routes from one beach area to another. Howler monkeys rest in tree branches hanging over the roads. Four-wheel-drive is advisable in rainy season. There are two large, as-yet-unbridged rivers—the Rosario between Junquillal and Ostional, and the Montaña between Ostional and Nosara—plus smaller ones. I had to turn back once. Ask if the road is passable. Places along this route may be reached more easily from Nicoya and Mansión.

Signs on back roads anywhere in the Nicoya Peninsula are far too sparse for strangers. If you drive these roads at night, which I don't recommend, have a flashlight handy: the voice of experience. When you finally spot a sign hung on a fence or attached to a tree in what feels like the middle of nowhere, you may have to get out of the car and use the flashlight to read it.

Ridley eggs hatch in about 50 days, with many hatchlings picked off on their way to the water by vultures, crabs, or frigate birds, while others become food for predators in the water, including other turtles. Survival rates, needless to say, are low, about 2 percent, extremely—in fact—making the protection of eggs all the more important. Ostional and Nancite in Santa Rosa National Park are the major nesting sites for olive ridleys in Costa Rica.

A few patches of forest contain howler monkeys, kinkajous, coatis, and basilisks. The Ostional River estuary offers good bird-watching—190 species have been identified. Rainfall averages almost 67 inches (1,700 mm) a year; temperature averages 82°F (28°C).

Visitors who come for the nesting should join a guide from the local development association at the rancho at the upper edge of the beach. An administrative station for the refuge is scheduled to be built.

Getting There
By bus: Forget it.
By car: Accessible from Sámara, Nosara, Nicoya, Santa Cruz, and Tamarindo. See Driver's Alert.

Other: Best bet for a night visit is an organized tour, leaving the driving to others.

NOSARA

Nosara is a quiet, rural village (population 3,496) that has had contact with foreign tourists and residents for years. There are a number of small grocery stores now, but if you need gas you still get it from a barrel via a plastic container and a funnel. The many byways make it difficult to give directions to particular hotels; just follow the signs and ask. Nosara is on the Pacific side of the Nicoya Peninsula, 224 miles (361 km) from San José.

Getting There

By bus: Daily express bus from San José, bus from Nicoya.
By car: From Nicoya, take paved road to Sámara, turn north on unpaved coast road; a secondary road exists from Nicoya to Nosara, but you're less likely to get lost going through Sámara.
By air: Daily scheduled flights from San José.

RESERVA BIOLOGICA NOSARA AND HOTEL LAGARTA LODGE, PRIVATE WILDLIFE REFUGE

Location: Nosara.
Rates: Single $50, double from $55, two-room bungalow $75.
Information/Reservations: (506) 682-0035, fax (506) 682-0135; e-mail lagarta@sol.racsa.co.cr.

A terrific option for natural history visitors is the new Hotel Lagarta Lodge, set on a hill 130 feet (40 m) above the Pacific with views of the coast to Ostional and of the Nosara River twisting and turning its way to the sea. Nature trails lead through a 125-acre (50 ha) private wildlife reserve of mangroves and forest established by the hotel's Swiss owners, the Roths. So far the bird list includes 170 species, including toucans, motmots, manakins, and a wealth of seabirds. You may see a jaguarundi, monkeys, frogs, colorful crabs, and perhaps even snakes. Five main trails offer short and longer options to the river's mouth and across a tributary to the rich world of mangroves and humid tropical forest.

Some of the eight attractive rooms are in the main lodge; others are through landscaped grounds up a flight of stairs. Meals are served in an open-air restaurant. Explore the reserve, swim in the pool, go horseback riding or biking (bike rental $10 per day), or take excursions to Guaitil, Ostional, or San Juanillo for diving or snorkeling. A two-hour river trip, with an ornithologist guide, is $20. The hotel is a 10-minute walk from a white-sand beach and five minutes from the mouth of the Nosara River. Day visitors welcome.

Getting There

See directions for Nosara. Lagarta Lodge offers pickup from the town of Nosara for a fee.

Where to Stay and Eat near Nosara

Café de Paris, (506) 682-0087, fax (506) 682-0089; e-mail cafedeparis @nosara.com; Web site nosara.com/cafedeparis, encompasses a charming French bakery, open-air restaurant, and small hotel. Some 3.7 miles (6 km) from the center of Nosara town on the road to Sámara, the place offers the unexpected: Thai and Swedish massage, coconut macaroons to die for, champagne dinners. Ten rooms, some air conditioned and others with ceiling fans, some with kitchenettes, are in a tropical garden; all have high ceilings, screened windows, and a small outdoor rancho and hammock. There is a swimming pool. In each bungalow the smaller room is $25 for a double; larger, $45; entire bungalow $65. Tours include Ostional, Guaitil, kayaking on the Nosara River, and fishing.

Estancia Nosara, telephone/fax (506) 682-0178, a short walk from the beach, has eight rooms around a kidney-shaped pool. Single with air conditioning $35, double $56; with fans, $25 and $46. Each sleeps up to four people and has a kitchenette and dining nook. Rooms have high wooden ceilings and Spanish tile floors. There's a large restaurant, rancho bar, pool, and tennis court; horses are available, and tours include an Ostional tour and a Nosara River crocodile/bird tour.

Hotel Playas de Nosara, telephone/fax (506) 680-0495; e-mail nosara@sol .racsa.co.cr; Web site www.nosara.com/nosara/, is one of those gracious beach hotels in harmony with its natural surroundings. Though rooms offer a view of the sea, it's hard to spot the hotel among the trees from the beach just below. Expansive vistas of sky, sea, and shoreline from the open-air dining room would surely bring a bit of balance to even the most restless mind. From a spectacular observation area above the dining room, you have an even greater panoramic vista of coastline, the pretty swimming pool below, and forest and gardens. It's one of my favorite places.

Rock outcroppings on the beach create wonderful low-tide pools for exploring, swimming, and snorkeling. The hotel arranges turtle-nesting tours, river trips for birding, and horse rentals. There are nature trails on the property and birding is good. Don't miss sunset on the beach.

The 16 rooms are in several buildings set among flowered gardens. Each is large, with brick floors, a ceiling fan, louvered doors to the balcony, decorative wall hangings, table and chairs, and private bath: $95.

The hotel is an intriguing work in progress. Don't be discouraged by perennial signs of construction when you arrive in the parking area. See what Greek owner, John Fraser, is creating—and re-creating.

Laid-back Hotel Playas de Nosara

Rancho Suizo Lodge, (506) 682-0057, fax (506) 682-0055; e-mail aratur@sol.racsa.co.cr, has 12 bright, high-ceilinged rooms in thatched bungalows, each with its own porch. Single $40, double $57, a double-deluxe bungalow $82, taxes and breakfast included. Swiss owners René and Ruth are gracious hosts. The restaurant, open to the public, includes dishes from their homeland; flags of Swiss cantons hang in the pleasant, thatch-roofed dining room. The beach is only steps away, close enough to hear the surf.

Tours go to Ostional for turtle-watching and to Nosara for birding. Other options include hiking, snorkeling, and horseback riding; guests have free use of boogie boards and mountain bikes. A garden whirlpool and the bar near Playa Pelada beach, complete with a beer garden and barbecue, are gathering places for guests.

Where to Stay at Bahía Garza
Villaggio La Guaria Morada Hotel, (506) 680-0784, (506) 233-2476, fax (506) 222-4073, stands between the coastal hills and the sea, with forest along the beach stretching to Punta Guiones. Here, thatched bungalows and a towering rancho-style restaurant lend an exotic, romantic flavor. Sounds of howler monkeys drift to the bungalows at night and in early morning. A large swimming pool is next to the restaurant/bar, and there is a small library and TV room. Gone are the casino and disco; emphasis now in this tranquil setting is on enjoyment of the natural world.

The 30 rooms are in well-ventilated bungalows with French doors that open onto private terraces. Rooms have rough white plaster walls, red-clay tile floors, dressing-room areas, louvered windows, large closets, fans, and kitchenettes. Single $50, double $85, including breakfast; children under 12 years free, maximum two. Tours to Ostional, horseback riding, and sport-fishing arranged. Transfers available from Nosara airport. San José–Nosara bus passes in front.

SAMARA

This small Pacific town (population 2,761) is booming with tourism, mostly tied to the beach experience. On streets and in restaurants, you'll hear languages from around the world. On the highway into town is a modern gas station, and there are a growing number of lodgings, restaurants, and tourism-related businesses. Sámara is 22 miles (35 km) from Nicoya, via paved road and 206 miles (331 km) from San José.

Getting There

By bus: Daily bus from San José, several daily from Nicoya.
By car: Paved road from Nicoya.
By air: Daily scheduled flights to Sámara/Puerto Carrillo.

Where to Stay and Eat from Sámara South to Islita

Guanamar, San José (506) 239-2000, (506) 239-4500, fax (506) 239-2405; Guanamar (506) 656-0054, fax (506) 656-0001; U.S. and Canada number (800) 245-8420, is 4 miles (7 km) south of Sámara on Playa Carrillo. The 39 rooms and two suites are set in villas on a bluff above the majestic blue Pacific and the white-sand, mile-long (1.5-km) beach. Broad, shaded wooden walkways with clean white railings connect the pool and other areas of the resort. White wicker furniture with bright cushions stands out against the rich wooden floors and ceiling of the restaurant/bar, open to the public, which also looks out on sea views and forest-covered hills.

Spacious, airy rooms are carpeted, with balconies or terraces, satellite TV, telephone, room service, air conditioning, fan, and fresh flowers. Double with sea view $102 for up to two; without $94. Two-bedroom, two-bath suites are $134. (Children under 12 sharing room with adults are free.) Some balconies are at treetop level for a close-up view of canopy wildlife. Monkeys drop by.

The resort, which has more than 1,000 acres (470 ha) of land, offers trail walks with local guides, horseback riding, mountain biking, kayaking, snorkeling, waterskiing, boat rental, and sportfishing (catch and release). Free beach shuttle. Packages and boat or air transfers. Located five hours by car from San José.

Hotel Giada, (506) 656-0132, fax (506) 656-0131, at the entrance to Sámara, has 13 attractive rooms with wicker furniture, two full-size beds (some king), matching print sheets and drapes, ceiling fans, and double louvered doors that open to a private terrace or balcony. Rooms surround a tropical garden, no pool (quieter rooms at the back). Single $30, double $40, including breakfast and taxes. SANSA agent. Take a dolphin tour, swim or snorkel on the island in front of Sámara ($5), see turtles at Ostional ($35), observe crocodiles ($75), tour beaches by boat, kayak, ride horses, or go diving. The hotel is 1½ blocks from the beach.

Hotel Isla Chora, San José (506) 257-3032, fax (506) 256-9378; Isla Chora (506) 656-0174, fax 506-656-0173; e-mail hechombo@sol.racsa.co.cr, in Sámara has style, from the rooms to the Italian restaurant to an outdoor theater and gardens. Ten rooms have interesting angles, decorator couches in painted rattan and wicker, colorful spreads on the two full beds, a small desk, ceiling fans, and air conditioning. Single $60, double $70. Four two-room apartments feature equipped kitchenettes and balconies, $121 for up to four. Dining is a treat: scallopini, gnocchi in gorgonzola sauce, pizzas, etc. Italian ice cream is made on the premises—no need to look any further for cappuccino or espresso. My breakfast was served to the sounds of Vivaldi.

Behind a carved garden gate is a kind of amphitheater. On Thursday nights in high season, Costa Rican groups perform on the stage; Friday nights are for concerts or disco. Not to worry: music ends no later than 1:30 a.m. Besides, the rooms have thick security windows designed to keep out 75 percent of exterior noise.

Tours go to secluded white-sand beaches, Ostional, Palo Verde, Barra Honda, Rincón de la Vieja, Las Baulas, and other natural history sites. A two-minute walk from the beach, the hotel also offers dolphin tours ($25), snorkeling, fishing, horseback riding, and car rental.

Hotel Las Brisas del Pacífico, (506) 656-0250, fax (506) 656-0076; Web site www.guiarica.co.cr/brisas, in Sámara has 36 rooms, some in bungalows close to the ocean; others on the hillside, with fantastic sea views. Pleasant, bright bungalows have louvered doors to porches, ceiling fans, and table and chairs, single or double $60 to $75. Large hillside rooms have balconies and air conditioning, $95. If you don't get one with its own Jacuzzi, enjoy the whirlpool beside the swimming pool. The open restaurant/bar is surrounded by trees and tropical plants. Las Brisas rents horses, boats, and waterskiing equipment.

Hotel Punta Islita, (506) 231-6122, (506) 296-3817, fax (506) 231-0715; e-mail ptaisl@sol.racsa.co.cr; Web site www.nacion.co.cr/netinc/puntaislita; U.S. and Canada number (800) 525-4800, south of Carrillo, is an extraordinary experience: unforgettable ocean views, secluded beaches, fine dining, rooms with Santa Fe–style elegance. A tall, impressive thatched roof covers a huge, circular, open dining room made intimate by good service, the right music, and decorator touches. Food is excellent and attractively served— a French chef presides over the kitchen. The infinity pool, which appears to flow off into the ocean below, is connected to a sun-warmed Jacuzzi.

Twelve thatch- and red-tile-roofed bungalows contain 20 rooms and four suites. Rich earth tones and marvelous blues predominate. All have air conditioning and ceiling fans, bed frames of teak logs harvested from the property's plantation, cushioned bamboo chairs, mini-refrigerators, and a private patio with hammock and chairs. Single or double $132. Suites have a sun-heated Jacuzzi on the patio, wet bar, sunken living area, and cane ceilings. Each two villas share an open-thatched kitchen and living area and a small outdoor Jacuzzi: $175 for up to two. Breakfast included. Each two-villa/rancho complex is $350. Ask about a three-bedroom villa with kitchen.

The beach is a 10-minute walk away, where a rancho-style Beach Club offers hammocks, beach chairs, and a bar for drinks and snacks. Take a guided walk or horseback ride to the forest or along the coast. Fish with local folk, hunt oysters, or, at low tide, pass through a tunnel in the rocks of Punta Islita to discover yet another secluded beach. Snorkel, play tennis, or hit a few on the driving range. Listen to the howler monkeys.

In season, join a turtle-nesting tour to adjacent Camaronal Wildlife Refuge. Boat tours go to Carrillo and Sámara, and sportfishing is offered. Guests can rent four-wheel-drive Kawasaki mules to explore roads on the 75-acre (30-ha) property, 70 percent of which is forested or to get to Norman's, a neighbor's charming bar down the road to watch the sunset. Visit the village of Islita.

Most travelers arrive by air (Travelair or charter to local landing strip). When the river is down and the road dries up, the adventurous can come from Carrillo by four-wheel-drive vehicle. Check with the hotel about road conditions; routes also through Coyote and San Pedro. Hotel Punta Islita was selected as a member of Small Luxury Hotels of the World (small independent luxury hotels and resorts in 50 countries), the only member in Central or South America.

Sueño Tropical, (506) 656-0151, fax (506) 656-0152; Web site www. novanet.co.cr/tropical, operated by three brothers from Italy, is a charming spot near Playa Carrillo. Twelve rooms with bamboo motifs, deep red-tile floors, ceiling fans (some air conditioning), and large louvered windows open onto terraces and an expansive tropical garden. Single $35; double $40. There are two pools, one for children. A bougainvillea-lined stairway curves up to the restaurant, which specializes in Italian dishes and enjoys a reputation for good food—open to the public. Tours go to Barra Honda, Palo Verde by boat from the Tempisque ferry ($60), Las Baulas ($55), and Arenal, Ostional, and Guaitil. Diving and horseback riding arranged.

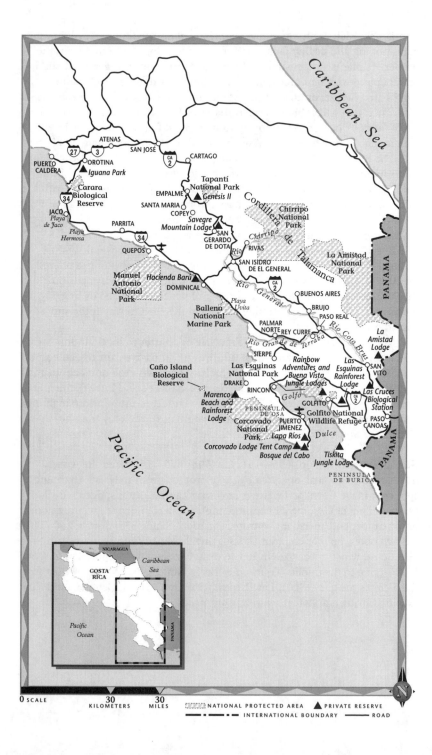

9

SOUTHERN COSTA RICA

The Talamancas, the highest mountains in the country, are here, along with beautiful mid- and southern-Pacific beaches; plantations of pineapple, African palm, and bananas; reforested pastures; virgin forest; rice fields; cattle ranches; and some lands that knew only indigenous peoples and a trickle of pioneers until the Inter-American Highway to Panama pushed back the frontier in the 1950s.

Road travel into the region from San José is via three routes: along the Inter-American Highway through the highlands; the old Spanish road through Orotina and the coast; or the Inter-American to Puntarenas, then south for Puerto Caldera and Orotina. Scheduled flights go to Quepos, Golfito, and Puerto Jiménez. Some of the largest and smallest national parks are here, along with biological reserves, wildlife refuges, and private nature reserves.

HIGHLAND ROUTE ALONG THE INTER-AMERICAN HIGHWAY

An early start is recommended for a trip on the Inter-American Highway south from San José. Fog or rain become likely at higher elevations as hours pass. As you approach the colonial capital of Cartago, watch for highway signs for San Isidro de El General and head south. Ahead are premier natural history destinations: peaks to climb, rivers to raft, forests to explore, small beaches to have to yourself, and bird-watching par excellence.

A word of caution: the Inter-American shows signs of damage from various tropical storms and a major hurricane. Repairs are ongoing, so damage and road work slow traffic, especially south of San Isidro.

FROM CARTAGO TO SAN ISIDRO DE EL GENERAL

One of the most spectacular drives in the country, this road winds up through Cerro de la Muerte and descends to the General River Valley. From the highest point on the Inter-American Highway, 10,938 feet (3,334 m), the road drops to 2,303 feet (702 m) in 28 miles (45 km). The constantly changing scenery is full of beauty. The highest point is near km 89: when conditions are right (not often), see both oceans.

As the road climbs out of the Central Valley after Cartago, fields of agave plants called *cabuya* (hemp) cover the hillsides; then small farms with dairy cows dominate the landscape. Elevation increases and temperature drops. Enter the recognizably different stunted vegetation of the *páramo*, then pass into forest once dominated by tall oaks, whose remaining specimens are adorned with red bromeliads shining in the sun or shrouded in mist. Next come tree ferns, vines, and *sombrilla del pobre* (poor man's umbrella)—walls of greenery on both sides of the road. Lower, the vista of the General Valley opens up and you may catch the perfume of heliotrope along the road.

Things to See and Places to Eat

Casa Refugio de Ojo de Agua is a small historic refuge near km 73 that sheltered early travelers and settlers who made the difficult journey over

Striking páramo landscape of Cerro de la Muerte

Cerro de la Muerte by foot or horseback. The two-room adobe has been partially restored. Walk into the room where travelers stopped to rest and escape the cold; see where the fire was made for cooking. A plaque commemorates the pioneers of the southern zone; an exhibit reports that the route was built in 1869, serving settlers until the highway was built in 1945.

Cerro de la Muerte got its name, Mountain of Death, because crossing it involved danger from storms and frigid nighttime temperatures. This is the northernmost true *páramo* in the hemisphere; its plants and temperatures are associated with Andean climes.

Restaurants offer *gallo pinto, papusas, gallos* (tortillas filled with practically anything—usually meat, potatoes, or *arracache*), or cheese or bean empanadas. Top a meal off with a glass of stout Costa Rican coffee or *agua dulce*. At km 60 and km 77, rub shoulders with local folks at **Chesperitos**. **Las Georginas** (km 95) also has good food, buffet-style.

GENESIS II, PRIVATE WILDLIFE REFUGE

Location: 39 miles (62 km) S of San José, near village of Cañon.
Rates: $85 per person for lodging and meals. Some guided tours, rain gear available. Multiday packages include transfer from San José. No credit cards.
Information/Reservations: (506) 381-0739, fax (506) 551-0070; e-mail genesis@yellowweb.co.cr; Web site www.yellowweb.co.cr/genesis.

Walking through the cloud forest at Genesis II is like moving through a hanging garden in the mist. Bromeliads crowd every inch of space on stately oaks. Mosses and mushrooms abound. I counted four orchids blooming on the same tree branch. Fallen blossoms from the canopy high above decorate the forest floor.

In the Talamanca Mountains, more than 7,500 feet (2,286 m) high, this forest has an air of eternity about it, calling for quiet observation. Bird songs echo through the trees. It seemed appropriate that a collared redstart, known as the "friend of man," followed as we walked on the trail. Five mixed feeding flocks passed by.

Birds bring many visitors to this 95-acre (38-ha) private reserve. The current bird list has more than 153 species. The resplendent quetzal is no stranger here—easily seen from March to June. Canadian owners Steve and Paula Friedman report seeing nine quetzals one day from the balcony.

Distinctive sounds of the three-wattled bellbird are sometimes heard here. There are collared trogons, black guans, emerald toucanets, silvery-fronted tapaculo, and hummingbirds—fiery-throated, magnificent, volcano, purple-throated, and gray-tailed mountain gems. Mammals are not as flashy but include sloths, armadillos, tayras, squirrels, and rabbits. Tracks of the tapir have been seen, probably visiting from the Río Macho Forest Reserve next door. Butterflies abound. More than 12 miles (20 km) of well-maintained trails and dirt roads facilitate exploration. The Genesis II forest now has the status of a government-recognized private wildlife refuge.

Lodging is in the main house, which is like an aerie nestled in the trees. Five simply furnished rooms share two baths. Facilities are humble, but attention is first-class. Paula turns out marvelous meals served family-style, featuring garden-fresh fruits and vegetables grown on the property. She uses many recipes published in her *Quetzal Cookbook*, everything from typical Costa Rican dishes to lemon chicken, lasagna, and corvina with a lemon, dill, and butter sauce. A tent platform is available for campers.

An optional side trip could include a visit to Dominical or perhaps to Los Cusingos, the farm of Alexander Skutch, well-known naturalist and ornithologist.

Steve directs young people in a volunteer program. Activities include trail work, reforestation of cleared land, sometimes even research or artwork for Genesis projects. The program attracts people from around the world who pay to spend vacations on conservation-related work here—four week minimum. In spare time, volunteers have taught English to adults and children in a school down the road.

The name, Genesis II? Steve and Paula chose it to signify a "second beginning," where they would attempt to live on the land in a more proper, peaceful way.

Getting There

By bus: San José to San Isidro de El General bus—get off at yellow Cañon church; pickup with advance notice.

By car: 90 minutes south of San José on the Inter-American, 2.5 miles (4 km) east on unpaved road from the turnoff at Cañon.

Other: Transfer from San José $50 for one person, $70 for two.

Where to Stay along the Inter-American Highway between Cartago and San Isidro

Albergue Mirador de Quetzales, (506) 381-8456, (506) 534-4741, is near km 70. This is a rustic retreat where the Serrano Obando family—parents and eight children—give a warm welcome. The small lodge has six rooms with bunks of rough-hewn wood: two shared, very clean baths. Four A-frame cabins, private baths, have been added. Lodging, dinner, breakfast, and guided walks are $34 per person. No credit cards. Good smells emanate from the kitchen, with fresh milk, cheese, blackberries (*mora*), and rainbow trout from the farm, along with homemade bread.

Eight trails wind through the farm's 106 acres (43 ha). Son Jorge says quetzals are seen here year-round, along with about 100 other species of birds. The guided walks are also open to day visitors, $12. Rubber boots available. The lodge is 700 m from the Inter-American turnoff.

Avalon Lodge and Private Reserve, (506) 380-2107, telephone/fax (506) 771-7226; e-mail smiller@sol.racsa.co.cr, is 2 miles (3.5 km) west of the Inter-American at Division, just past km 107. What awaits is 375 acres

(152 ha) of cloud forest, fantastic mountain views, lodging, hiking trails, hot tub, and, on Sundays with advance notice, a certified masseuse. Owner Scott Miller reports 80 species on a growing bird list: see the collared trogon, quetzal, three-wattled bellbird, sulfur-winged parakeet, black-faced solitaire, and yigüero. If you give Scott prior notice, he will arrange an expert bird guide to help you find these and more, $60 a day. Expect to find beautiful orchids and butterflies in this high land. Guests can mountain bike from Avalon to San Isidro de El General along mountain roads and through small towns, choose a horseback adventure from Cerro de la Muerte to Avalon (minimum of four for either), and hike on Avalon trails, one of which is an adventurous five-hour trek to a waterfall.

Two cabins with private baths are $35 and $45, double occupancy; four rooms with shared bath, $22 for two. All have heat. Ask about low-budget packages in shared rooms and about volunteer opportunities. Meals served family-style: breakfast $4, lunch $5, dinner $7. Camping $6 per person per day; day visits $3. No credit cards. The 2 miles (3 km) of unpaved road is accessible year-round.

Where to Stay in San Gerardo de Dota

Turn off at km 80 for San Gerardo de Dota, famous among natural history travelers for its cloud forests and the quetzal who lives there. The road down into the valley is narrow, with a few hairpin curves and unforgettable vistas. I enjoy walking along the road in this valley for the scenery, birds, friendly people, and peace.

Trogon Lodge, San José (506) 223-7490, fax (506) 255-4039, lodge (506) 771-1266; e-mail mawamba@sol.racsa.co.cr; Web site www.crica.com/mawamba/, has mountain air, a rushing river, forest, flowers, cabins, and trout ponds, creating a living landscape painting. Nights can be chilly at 7,000 feet (2,134 m), so each room has an electric heater and the dining room has a cast-iron woodstove that radiates warmth. Ten rooms are in cabins on slopes above the beautiful Savegre River. Striped comforters, reading lamps, built-in closet and luggage space, and glass windows with louvered shutters make for comfort in this highland retreat. Single $42; double, $58. Meals served family-style: breakfast $7, lunch or dinner $9. While eating, watch five species of hummingbirds feed outside the windows. Kitchen staff told me what time quetzals would feed in a tree near the dining room, and they did.

A walk on the trails may allow glimpses of the acorn woodpecker, Baird's and elegant trogons, black guan, emerald toucanet, or flame-colored tanager. A two-hour guided walk is $24 for guests or day visitors, $5 unguided. Horseback riding is $10 an hour. Fishing is allowed in trout ponds. A one-day package from San José is $72; two days and one night, $166: three days and two nights, $237. All include transportation, meals, guided walks; multiday tour adds lodging. Day visitors $20. Trogon Lodge belongs to Grupo Mawamba.

SAVEGRE MOUNTAIN LODGE (CABINAS CHACON), PRIVATE RESERVE

Location: *San Gerardo de Dota, between Cartago and San Isidro de El General in Talamanca Mountains, 6 miles (10 km) from the turnoff on the Inter-American.*
Rates: *$65 per person including lodging, meals, taxes; three-day/two-night package $315, including round trip from San José, lodging, meals, bird-watching and waterfall tours, horseback riding, and fishing. A one-day tour, including breakfast and lunch, $19.*
Information/Reservations: *Telephone/fax (506) 771-1732; e-mail ciprotur @sol.racsa.co.cr; Web site www.ecotourism.co.cr.*

At Savegre Mountain Lodge, they don't talk about "if" you see a quetzal, they say "when." Roland Chacón, one of owner Efraín Chacón's 11 children, told me we would see one on our early morning tour. We drove up the mountain, and there it was, sitting in the tree where he expected it. The red, white, and green bird, so elusive in some places, seemed to appear as if on cue. Best months to see them are February through May, but they are here year-round.

The Chacóns' place is famous for quetzals and for hospitality. Efraín, who has lived here for more than 40 years, began a dairy farm. People started coming to fish for trout in the Savegre River that flows through his property. At first, Efraín and his wife took overnight visitors into their home. Eventually, they built a cabin for them; in 1980, ecotourists began to arrive in search of the quetzal.

The lodge, also known as Cabinas Chacón, now has 20 comfortable, simply furnished rooms, some with sitting rooms. A spacious restaurant/bar is popular not only with overnight but also day visitors and local folks. Bring your appetite: food is good and plentiful; fresh trout is on the menu. A bright lounge next to the dining room has lots of glass looking out to the river and a dazzling display of hummingbirds at feeders. Most nights a fire blazes in the fireplace. Look at the guestbook in the lounge—entries since 1973. A small gift shop sells T-shirts, sweatshirts, photos of quetzals, and the farm's coffee, canned trout, and trout pâté.

There is a small dairy, and guests can visit the extensive apple, peach, and plum orchards and packing plant on the farm. All up and down the valley, fruit trees are replacing pastures on steep slopes.

About three-fourths of the 740-acre (300-ha) Chacón farm is in primary forest. There is a 5-mile (8-km) trail that takes two to three hours to hike (fabulous views of forest canopy), a 2.5-mile (4-km) trail, and a half-mile (1-km) trail. For real hikers, a trail goes from the farm to Cerro de la Muerte. Local bilingual guides well-versed in natural history lead lodge bird-watching tours and a waterfall tour. Horseback riding and fishing in the Savegre River are options.

A walk along the country road in front affords a look at flowering trees, the rushing river that flows alongside, and a variety of birds. I watched a woodpecker gathering nuts, and I once happened upon a pair of quetzals right by the roadside. Many of the more than 160 species of birds here can be seen from the cabin area. The quetzal is not the only flashy bird in the Dota Valley: trogons, emerald toucanets, and iridescent hummingbirds lend color. Animals you might see include rabbits, porcupines, white-faced monkeys, white-tailed deer, frogs, squirrels, and foxes.

Trout fishermen and ecotourists have been joined by scientists and students in this special place. The Quetzal Education Research Complex is Southern Nazarene University's tropical campus.

The lodge is at 6,890 feet (2,100 m). Rainiest months are October and November—generally little rain December to June. Precipitation is 120 to 150 inches (3,046 to 3,807 mm) per year; temperatures rarely exceed 76°F (24°C). Bring insect repellent for hiking on higher trails and a jacket.

Getting There
By bus: Get off the San José–San Isidro bus at km 80; the Chacóns can pick you up, $17 round trip.
By car: Heading west off the Inter-American, continue 5.5 miles (9 km) on an attention-getting road with hairpin curves and beautiful views.
Other: One-way San José transfer $70 for one person, $35 each for two. Transfers arranged throughout the country.

SAN ISIDRO DE EL GENERAL
In San José province, **San Isidro** lies in the intermontane valley between the awesome Talamanca Range and the coastal mountains 85 miles (137 km) southeast of San José. A center for shopping and transportation in a largely rural landscape of dispersed settlements, it is a pleasant place for wandering and absorbing the flavor of a small Costa Rican town (population 42,794). I stumbled onto a double wedding in the church on the plaza one evening. Shortly after, a dog ambled in through the open door and made its way down the aisle, sniffing and looking, and ambled out again. Nobody seemed to mind. Since church doors often stand open in this country, it's not uncommon to see a bird flying above the altar, to hear chirping from the ceiling in the quiet of the day.

Significant population spilled over into this rich region only in the last half of this century. The very mountains that formed a barrier are an attraction for today's travelers. Chirripó National Park brings the hardy hikers, while the abundance of birds delights others. Some visit this area on the way to or from the Dominical–Uvita area and lovely Pacific beaches (see the Coastal Route section, later in this chapter), allowing travelers to make a loop that combines mountains and sea.

Things to See and Do near San Isidro
Santuario de Aves Neotropicales Los Cusingos, the farm of naturalist, ornithologist, and author Alexander F. Skutch, is 30 minutes from San Isidro in Quizarrá—visit by reservation. In 1993 this 178-acre (72-ha) farm was

purchased by the Tropical Science Center (TSC) under a commitment to maintain it as a bird sanctuary and protect its flora and fauna, especially birds—both Neotropical migrants and resident endemic species. Dr. and Mrs. Skutch still live on the farm and he continues his bird research. You will recognize his name as coauthor of *A Guide to the Birds of Costa Rica*. Read about the farm in his *A Naturalist in Costa Rica* (see Recommended Reading in Appendix B). Trails lead through a forest that somehow radiates the special energy of the man who has protected it since 1942. Entrance $8 per person. Area lodges and hotels arrange visits, or reserve through TSC in San José: (506) 253-3267, fax (506) 253-4963; e-mail cusingos@cct.or.cr.

Getting to San Isidro

By bus: Frequent buses run from San Isidro, plus there's a bus from Dominical. By car: Travel the Inter-American through Cartago and head south.

Where to Stay and Eat in and near San Isidro

Hotel del Sur, (506) 771-3033, fax (506) 771-0527, is 2.5 miles (4 km) south of San Isidro on the Inter-American Highway. On clear days you can sit by the large pool and gaze at the impressive Talamanca Mountains above the trees. The 47 rooms are on two floors around a pretty garden with a fountain; ten cabins for up to five persons each are farther back on the property. Each of the 20 deluxe rooms has two queen-sized beds, TV, reading lamps, desk, and lounge chairs (two are handicapped accessible). A carved wooden door, white tile floors, and pretty watercolors say welcome. Solar hot water. Some have air conditioning and ceiling fans; others, fans only: single/double occupancy $35 to $50. Carpeted standard rooms, plainer, have ceiling fans, and double and single beds, $25. Buffet breakfast included. Cabins, with refrigerators, $50.

In addition to swimming pools, there are tennis and volleyball courts and bicycles for rent. Tropical plants abound on the ample grounds. A hotel minibus takes guests to Dominical, Los Cusingos, or other local attractions. Bilingual naturalist guides arranged. Airport pickup available.

Hotel Iguazú, (506) 771-2571, in front of the old Banco Nacional, is a block from the bus stop. The second-story hotel has 21 clean modest rooms, from $8 with shared bath; with private bath, single $12, double $20. No credit cards.

Talari Mountain Lodge, telephone/fax (506) 771-0341 is 5 miles (8 km) east of San Isidro via paved road; heading south, turn left at the first road after the Jilguero River—the same road that goes to Chirripó. Each cabin is named for a different area bird, with a painting of that bird decorating the outside wall. More than 150 species of birds have been identified on Talari's 20 acres (8 ha). The eight rooms are light and comfortable: single $35, double $48, including breakfast and taxes. Walk-ins with this book get 10 percent off. Hosts Pilar and Jan—they describe themselves as a *tica*-Dutch blend—are gracious and attentive.

The swimming pool has an area for children; the main building includes a nice lounge area. Big windows in the pleasant restaurant offer expansive views along with good food, some grown at Talari: corn, beans, yuca, and a variety of fruits including star fruit and cherimoya (*anona*). Don't miss the guava ice cream. On Friday evenings, enjoy music with dinner—Jan plays their Russian piano. The restaurant is open to the public for dinner Thursday to Saturday from 6 to 9 p.m. and Sunday and holidays from noon to 7 p.m.

Trails on the property go to the General River, through interesting secondary forest, and to an area being reforested with native species. A day trip to San José de Rivas by horseback includes lunch at a 33-foot (10-m) waterfall; another combines horseback and hiking to Cerro Paraguas near Pueblo Nuevo, close to 6,900 feet (2,100 m) elevation. Jan and Pilar offer tours to Chirripó (30 minutes away), including all equipment, guides, and bearers. A four-day, five-night package, including two nights at Talari, is $182 each for four to eight people. A three-day, two-night horseback trip through forest to a waterfall is $160 for one person, $95 each for two to four. Free shuttle service to Talari from San Isidro.

CHIRRIPO NATIONAL PARK
Location: 94 miles (151 km) S of San José, ranger station 9 miles (15 km) NE of San Isidro de El General, through San Gerardo de Rivas.
Size: 123,921 acres (50,150 ha).
Hours: Open daily at 5 a.m., latest departure to Crestones at noon.
Cost: $6; overnight in lodge $6.
Information/Reservations: Telephone hotline 192 (see Appendix A: Parks and Reserves Information), (506) 771-3297, telephone/fax (506) 771-3155.

Geologists, botanists, mountain climbers, biologists, adventure-seekers, and just plain nature lovers make their way to Chirripó National Park. The park contains the country's highest peak (Chirripo Peak at 12,529 feet [3,819m]), glacial lakes, rivers, and habitats ranging from mixed forests, fern groves, and swamps to oak forests and *páramo*.

On a clear day, visitors can see both oceans from the peak. There are cloudy and clear days throughout the year, but the driest time is February and March. Annual rainfall is between 138 and 197 inches (3,500 and 5,000 mm). Some longtime visitors say they cannot resist trips in rainier times, when the exuberance of the vegetation defies description.

At whatever time of year, take warm clothes. Though maximums in the 80s are possible, count on cold nights. There can be strong winds. Extremes between day and night can vary by 43°F (24°C); lowest temperature recorded is 16°F (–9°C). You may wake up to a frosty world, finding ice on lakes and stream banks.

Trails are marked. A new lodge for up to 60 persons offers bunks, a kitchen, and lounge area; bathrooms are close by (cold water showers). Bring a warm sleeping bag and carry enough liquids. While ascent to the summit appears daunting, it's not so difficult if taken slowly and carefully. Allow at least 10 hours to get to the top. Tent camping is not allowed unless you are hiking a loop; no open fires.

Endangered species protected at Chirripó include the margay, puma, ocelot, jaguar, tapir, and quetzal. Birds and animals are more abundant in the forest zones, though there are hummingbirds even in the high *páramo*. Plants seem to cover every inch of trees in the cloud forest: orchids, bromeliads, mosses, and ferns. The way to the summit passes through seven distinct forest types. The higher you climb, the more stunted the vegetation.

Names like Savanna and the Lions, Valley of the Rabbits, and Moraine Valley hint of what early explorers found when they scaled these heights (lions were pumas). Discovery also awaits today's visitor to Chirripó, a place where you can look down on rainbows.

Independent travelers must call the conservation area for information about guides or pack horses and to reserve lodge space. The hardy inhabitants of nearby San Gerardo de Rivas are often sought out as guides—it's rumored that some can run up the mountain.

Getting There

By bus: From San Isidro de El General, take the bus to San Gerardo de Rivas, 6 miles (9 km) from the ranger station.

By car: From San Isidro, go to San Gerardo de Rivas and continue on unpaved road to the ranger station.

Other: Area lodges arrange treks, along with some San José tour agencies (see Chapter 4 for details on a three-day adventure offered by Camino Travel).

FROM SAN ISIDRO TO GOLFITO

From San Isidro the Inter-American Highway passes through farm and ranch country and then mile after mile of pineapples. Past the cutoff at Paso Real (the route to San Vito), the road winds along the Térraba River—beautiful scenery. Palmar Sur, where both SANSA and Travelair flights land daily, is often the jumping-off place for travelers to the Sierpe River or Drake Bay (described in the Osa Peninsula section).

Things to See and Do

A few miles past El Brujo, with its checkpoint where you may be stopped by guards looking for contraband, watch for a lovely waterfall on the **Río Catarata**. Indian healers from the area purportedly have used its waters in medicinal preparations. Less than an hour from San Isidro is **Buenos Aires** and pineapple country—stop to taste the fresh fruit at a roadside stand.

At the Indian village of **Rey Curré**, pull off for a visit to the local craft cooperative across from the school. If it's closed, go to the house next to the school. Children and adults carve plants, animals, and indigenous designs on gourds. Each gourd has the name of the person who made it. Sometimes there are woven purses for sale. If you buy at the house by the school, where the chickens have more bravado than feathers, check to be sure no ants live in the gourds. You don't want to be cooped up in a car when the creatures decide to come out—take it from me.

LAS ESQUINAS RAINFOREST LODGE, PRIVATE RESERVE
Location: *Just NW of Golfito.*
Rates: *Single $115, double $170, including lodging, meals, taxes, and guided walk. No credit cards.*
Information/Reservations: *Golfito office (506) 775-0515, fax (506) 775-0631, lodge telephone (506) 382-5798; e-mail reserve@sol.racsa.co.cr; Web site www.powernet.co.cr/reservecr/esquilod.htm.*

As a steady rain fell in the Rainforest of the Austrians, a sector of Piedras Blancas National Park north of Golfito, I felt blessed to walk with guides from nearby La Gamba. They work for Las Esquinas Rainforest Lodge, part of a commendable project that involves park neighbors in ecotourism activities.

Together the three of us experienced the rain as well as the magic and mystery of this rich forest, letting the wet soak our hair and clothes and drip off our noses. These guides, whose roots are here, showed me a tree that exudes a flammable liquid. They explained the medicinal qualities of trees and other plants, pointed out miniature orchids and kingfishers and hummingbirds, and let me name two pristine waterfalls. My choices? Inocencia (Innocence) and Vida (Life). The guides then named the trail between the two Inocencia de la Vida. I hope you get to name them, too.

The lodge was built with the aid of the Austrian government to offer people in the La Gamba Valley an alternative to destroying the forest. It provides employment, and part of the lodge profits go to finance projects that benefit the community.

The spectacular main building is set in a former cattle pasture surrounded by forest. Its immense conical thatched roof covers reception, gift shop, lounge area, and open dining room, with a second-level library and VCR-viewing space tucked under the roof. In the dining room Tiffany-style stained-glass hanging lampshades, tablecloths, and bamboo chairs with brightly colored cushions provide a pleasant setting for delicious meals served buffet-style. Angela, the personable chef, not only excels in the kitchen but also is becoming an expert on flora and fauna.

Ten rooms in five bungalows are a short distance away. Built of natural rock and wood, with curtained windows on three sides, rooms have bamboo furniture, reading lamps, and ceiling fans. Each room has a veranda with comfortable furniture (even a rocking chair) to lounge in. Watch in the landscaped gardens for golden-hooded tanagers (in Spanish called *siete colores*, seven colors); scarlet-rumped tanagers, and hummingbirds. Parrots and toucans abound. Perhaps you'll see the flash of orange and blue as a Baird's trogon flies by. Hear howler monkeys.

Guests can walk in the botanical garden to find many tropical fruit trees—

Las Equinas Rainforest Lodge near Golfito

guanábana, cas, papaya, star fruit, three kinds of mamones, water apples—and banana and cacao plantings are nearby. The guide will probably cut one of the cacao pods so you can try the tasty pulp around the chocolate bean. Harvests find their way to the table. Perhaps you will be treated to fried yuca, breadfruit, lemongrass tea, or a heavenly chocolate dessert. A stream meanders through the grounds, flowing into a naturally filtered swimming pool. Lodge elevation is 787 feet (240 m), average temperature 91°F (33°C).

Marked trails (three to five hours long) move through the park, which adjoins lodge property: guided walks $15. Guests choose from a variety of excursions: to El Chorro Waterfall, the Esquinas coast, and a visit to Casa Orquídeas; to Río Coto to see the mangroves; to Wilson Botanical Gardens at Las Cruces; or horseback riding in Valle Bonito.

The sector of Piedras Blancas Park next to the lodge is called Rainforest of the Austrians to recognize donations from the people of that country to purchase more than 3,000 acres (1,200 ha) of endangered forest, which was then turned over to Costa Rica to be included in the national park system.

Getting There

By bus: Take the bus to Golfito, ask the lodge about transfers.
By car: On the Inter-American, turn west at km 37 and follow signs, about 2.5 miles (4 km); four-wheel drive not necessary. About 4 miles (6 km) from Golfito, go to La Gamba and follow signs; ask about road conditions.
By air: SANSA and Travelair have flights to Golfito; airport pickup is free with reservations.

GOLFITO

A port town, Golfito (population 14,537) was a busy center for banana exportation when the Bananera Company, a subsidiary of United Brands, operated in the area from 1938 to 1985. African palms have replaced bananas on much of the land, though bananas are being planted again.

In recent years Golfito has developed another kind of commerce: a "duty-free" shopping complex (the *depósito*), which opened in 1990. People come from around the country to shop, especially on weekends. Now, with improvement of the port, Golfito expects another shot in the arm from cruise ships.

The town itself is along a narrow strip of about 4 miles between water and mountains. Approaching by air, you may wonder where there is enough level land for a runway. Once in Golfito, getting around is no problem. Taxis constantly run the major street from one end of town to the other, picking up passengers for about $1; the public bus is even cheaper. Water taxis at the public dock near the gas station can get you around in the gulf. Golfito is located 211 miles (340 km) south of San José and 14 miles (22 km) from the Inter-American on the Golfo Golfito, which opens into the Golfo Dulce.

Golfito National Wildlife Refuge practically surrounds the town on its landward side. Piedras Blancas National Park, private reserves, and beaches draw natural history travelers. Just across the Golfo Dulce lie Puerto Jiménez, Corcovado park, and other destinations on the southern Osa Peninsula. A daily launch leaves Golfito at 11:30 a.m.; the $3 trip takes less than 90 minutes. Passengers sometimes watch dolphins that keep company with the boat.

If kayaking is your thing, or you would like it to be, contact **Yak Yak Kayaks**, telephone/fax (506) 775-1179. No experience necessary. Multiday tours arranged. Owner Ani Mac also has a couple of beachfront cabins just 10 minutes from Golfito.

A private botanical garden, **Casa Orquídeas**, is on Playa San Josecito, north of Golfito, access by boat only. Ask about a trip at your hotel or at the local dock. Open Sunday through Wednesday morning.

Plan to dine at your hotel restaurant, if there is one, or ask your innkeepers for other area dining recommendations.

Getting There

By car: About eight hours from San José. Take the Inter-American Highway south, turn west at Río Claro for the last 14 miles (22 km).
By air: Flight less than an hour, daily on SANSA and Travelair.

Where to Stay and Eat in and near Golfito

Cabinas Los Cocos, telephone/fax (506) 776-0012; Web site www.zancudo .com, on Zancudo Beach, has four cabins with kitchens, fan, and a deck with hammock and chairs. Choose either a quaintly restored banana company house, $30, or a thatched bungalow with polished tropical hardwood floor, $35. If you don't want to do your own cooking, owners Susan and Andrew Robertson can suggest one of the several restaurants on Playa Zancudo.

They also operate **Zancudo Boat Tours**, which provides taxi service to and from Golfito and Puerto Jiménez and a number of half-day tours in the $30 to $35 range. One is a Coto River (Río Coto) wildlife trip; another, a Golfo Dulce boat trip to a botanical garden. Transfer available from Golfito to Cabinas Los Cocos or guests can take the local daily ferry between Golfito and Zancudo. Zancudo is accessible by car from Golfito.

Golfo Dulce Lodge, in San José (506) 222-2900, fax (506) 222-5173; e-mail aratour@sol.racsa.co.cr, is a 30-minute boat ride away from Golfito on San Josecito Beach. Looking somewhat like a tiny village, five bungalows and thatched restaurant are set in landscaped grounds against a backdrop of forested slopes. At the edge of Piedras Blancas National Park, the lodge offers jungle hikes through lodge property (enjoy the wildlife lookout) as well as in Piedras Blancas and the Golfito National Wildlife Refuge. Boat excursions go to Río Esquinas or Río Coto for birding and animal observation, as well as across to Puerto Jiménez. A beach walk visits a privately owned botanical garden. New is a small biological station where release of birds and cats into the wild is the focus.

Bungalows have large covered verandas with hammocks and comfortable cushioned bamboo furniture. Bamboo is also the dominant decor inside the spacious, light-filled rooms, each with a sitting area. Family-style meals in the restaurant have a European touch contributed by Swiss owners/managers Esther and Marque Greter.

Hydropower supplies the electrical energy; a natural spring, water for the pool. Minimum stay is two nights: a three-day, two-night package is single $190; double $380, including lodging, meals, boat transfers from either Golfito or Puerto Jiménez, meals, and taxes. Ask about packages with tours included.

Las Gaviotas, (506) 775-0062, fax (506) 775-0544, is on the main road coming into Golfito. There are pleasant open-air restaurants; swimming pools for children and adults are next to the gulf. Each of 18 rooms and three bungalows is set in tropical gardens. Rooms, a bit dark because they open onto covered individual porches, are brightened by quilted bedspreads. Each contains a desk and chair: room with fan $36; with air conditioning $42. Bungalows have two bedrooms and a living room/kitchen area with a hot plate and refrigerator, $84. All have telephones and local TV. Near shore are remains of a World War II minesweeper, which now serve as a picturesque roost for land and sea birds.

Samoa del Sur, (506) 775-0233, fax (506) 775-0573, with its huge, distinctive, thatched-roof restaurant/bar, is north of downtown next to the water. The 12 rooms and one suite are large and airy with two double beds, desk, and ceiling fan: double $38. See the shell museum and enjoy the book-exchange library. Restaurant open to the public from 7 a.m. to midnight.

GOLFITO NATIONAL WILDLIFE REFUGE

Location: *Golfito.*
Size: *5,683 acres (2,300 ha).*
Cost: *Currently no fee is collected.*
Information: *Telephone hotline 192 (see Appendix A: Parks and Reserves Information), (506) 789-9092*

Virgin forest covers about half of Golfito National Wildlife Refuge, important not only for the species of plants and animals that live there, some endangered, but also for the Golfito community. The tall evergreen forest on this rugged terrain safeguards water sources for today's population and future generations, while it also reduces the danger of landslides that would affect the town.

Though a number of short and long trails crisscross the refuge, access is largely limited to views from the edge, walking along the road to view incredible trees and birdlife. Plans exist to open up the trails again for visitation, but I hesitate to say when it will be done. Check with the Osa Conservation Area at the number above.

Rainfall is heavy, almost 196 inches (4,976 mm) a year, and temperatures are warm, averaging 82°F (28°C). The combination creates a marvelous tropical wet forest where mosses, lichens, bromeliads, and 31 species of orchids make a greenhouse on the limbs of a single tree. Heliconia plants splash their exotic, showy flowers of red, orange, and yellow against vibrant greens of the understory. Eleven of the 30 or so species of heliconia in the country are here.

Some tree species reach almost 165 feet (50 m) high. The purple heart tree grows at Golfito; you see its beautiful purple wood made into salad bowls and earrings in souvenir shops. There is manwood, whose wood can lie on the ground for more than 30 years without decomposing; ceiba; and the bully tree, whose red leaves stand out against the canopy.

Among 146 bird species are the endangered scarlet macaws, great tinamous, parrots, herons, pelicans, ibis, owls, parakeets, and trogons. All four species of monkeys in Costa Rica live in the refuge, as do cats such as jaguarundi and margay, anteaters, bats, pacas, and agoutis. You can sometimes see the monkeys on the road past the airport; they come to eat exotic fruits planted by the banana company years ago—great spot for birders, too.

The driest months are January through March; bring rain gear even then.

RAINBOW ADVENTURES AND BUENA VISTA JUNGLE AND BEACH LODGES, PRIVATE RESERVE

Location: *N of Golfito on the Golfo Dulce.*
Rates: *At Rainbow Adventures: lodge rooms, single $185, double $255; penthouse, single $200, double $270; beach cabins, single $215, double $285. At Buena Vista: beach house, single $155–$165, double $220–$230; jungle house, single $145–$155, double $210–$220. Included are round-trip transfer from Golfito, meals, snacks, snorkeling gear, jungle tour, nonalcoholic drinks, beer at meals, and taxes.*

Information/Reservations: *Reserve via U.S. number if possible: (800) 565-0722, (503) 690-7750; fax (503) 690-7735. The Costa Rican number is in Golfito, faxes checked on trips in: telephone/fax (506) 775-0220.*

Travelers take a 45-minute boat ride north of Golfito along shores where steep forest meets the sea, past small unpopulated beaches, to find two small lodges with loads of character and a private reserve of 800 acres (324 ha). The lodges are a half-mile apart on Cativo Beach, with primary and secondary forest behind.

On arrival at Rainbow Adventures, I spotted my very first green honeycreeper moving through tree branches next to my room. During my stay I witnessed a continuing, stubborn battle between a red-lored parrot and a yellow-naped woodpecker over a hole in a nearby tree trunk. The brilliance of the scarlet-rumped tanager flashed in the landscaped gardens around the lodge and two cabins. Five chestnut-mandibled toucans perched in a single tree just off the trail during the free introductory jungle walk. A growing bird list is now at 260 species. I regret to report that the resident scarlet macaw who posed for pictures met his demise in an unexpected encounter with an ocelot.

Pleasant surprises are more often the order of the day at the Rainbow Adventures. Would you expect to find stained-glass windows and turn-of-the-century antiques in the main lodge? The first floor of the wooden structure has a lounge and dining room open to gardens, plus an air-conditioned library with more than 3,000 books related to natural history. The second has three double rooms that open onto a large veranda. The third, the penthouse, is open on three sides, with stained-glass panels suspended between the waist-high wall and the roof. All have solar-heated or on-demand propane hot water and bidets. Antiques throughout were collected by owner Michael Medill of Oregon. Two secluded cabins have open living areas (with handwoven silk rugs) and two bedrooms. Furnishings are handmade by resident craftspeople. You'll find a tropical flower on your pillow when you arrive. A swimming pool lies between the lodge and the palm-lined beach.

Meals with herbs and vegetables from the organic garden are generally served buffet-style. Staff provide nice touches: when a drink made of *guanábana* is served, they have a guanábana fruit on hand to show guests. The garden provides produce such as pineapples, papayas, bananas, plantains, water apples, avocados, star fruit, *anona*, *mamón chino*, chestnuts, and edible hibiscus. Guests, me included, rave about the food.

Buena Vista Jungle and Beach Lodges, also owned by Medill, has two stories, with four double rooms partly open to a panorama of palms, tropical plants, and the blue waters of the gulf—no antiques, more of a classy treehouse feeling looking out from the rooms. Tropical woods are lovely. A single-story lodge with kitchen, dining, and lounge areas has the same standards and services as Rainbow Adventures. From the 200-foot-long (60-m) dock in front there's a terrific gulf view; the dock sports a diving board.

If you can tear yourself away from the lodges or the warm, usually gentle beach waters, you can fill your days with a variety of activities. Hikes with a local guide include a two-hour trek to a 50-foot (15-m) waterfall, through the forest to the small hydro project that supplies electricity; a jungle and vanilla grove tour; or customized jungle hikes—perhaps to a big swimming hole above the waterfalls. Guided tours $4 per hour, boots provided. Animals commonly seen include agouti, banded anteater, coati, kinkajou, raccoon, tayra, iguana, Jesus Christ lizard, armadillo, collared peccary, and howler, spider, and white-faced monkeys. On my last visit, Rainbow manager John Lovell and I saw the biggest, most beautiful fer-de-lance (snake) either of us had ever seen.

Boating activities include a birding trip on the Esquinas River (Río Esquinas) through mangroves and primary and secondary forest (30 species counted on my tour, including a tree full of exotic king vultures), a dolphin tour, fishing, and snorkeling at a number of sites, where you may see parrot fish, angelfish, triggerfish, starfish, moray eels, octopus, sharks, sea turtles, or dolphins. Boat rental for tours is $35 an hour, including guide, snorkeling gear, and safety equipment. Kayaks rent for $25 for three hours. A $25 half-day boat trip visits Casa Orquídeas botanical garden.

A portion of the profits from these properties goes to the local school. A short video about Rainbow Adventures can be rented.

Getting There

By bus: San José-to-Golfito bus.
By air: Flights to Golfito via SANSA, Travelair, or charter.
Other: Rates include round-trip boat transfer from Golfito to Rainbow Adventures and Buena Vista.

TISKITA JUNGLE LODGE, PRIVATE RESERVE

Location: 37 miles (60 km) S of Golfito on the Pacific coast.
Rates: Single $125, double $100 each, including lodging, meals, guided walk, and taxes. A two-day, two-night package leaves on Monday and Saturday: $495 per person (double occupancy) including meals, lodging, ground and air transfers from San José, and some guided walks. Some packages include Corcovado or Manuel Antonio.
Information/Reservations: San José (506) 255-3418, (506) 221-0303, fax (506) 255-4410; e-mail suntours@sol.racsa.co/cr; Web site www.greenarrow.com /travel/tiskita.htm.

Two flashy, fiery-billed aracaris perched along the road and small squirrel monkeys cavorting through tree branches introduced me to Tiskita Jungle Lodge before I even reached the main building. The guide explained that this subspecies of tití monkey appears only in southern Costa Rica.

Birders and nature photographers can have a field day without leaving the lodge's landscaped grounds. Hundreds of tropical fruit trees draw birds like a magnet. I watched three chestnut-mandibled toucans casually eat a

Tiskita Jungle Lodge dining room

fruit breakfast. In the same tree were blue-crowned manakins, a lineated woodpecker, and blue-gray and scarlet-rumped tanagers. A bird book is left handy to help identify what you spot, and a bird list of more than 300 species lets you know if anyone has seen it before you. Ask for the illustrated booklet on tide pools and the printed nature-trail guide.

Since 1980 manager Peter Aspinall, who owns the lodge with brother John, has been using about 62 acres (25 ha) of this almost 440-acre (180-ha) property to grow exotic tropical fruits gathered from around the world. His experimental station has the most extensive collection of tropical rare and exotic fruits in the country. Birds and guests alike can have their fill of more than 100 varieties, tasting such delicacies as star fruit (*carambola* in Spanish), passion fruit (*maracuyá*), guava, guanábana, custard apple (*anona*), jackfruit, araza, abiu, and dozens of others that are not yet household words. Once, he reminds you, bananas and pineapples were considered rare and exotic fruits.

Animals come out of a primary forest that covers more than 300 acres (120 ha) to savor the fruits. You may cross paths with four species of monkeys, coatis, pacas, white-lipped peccaries, anteaters, or cats such as the ocelot, jaguarundi, and margay. Well-marked trails go through farm and forest, and to the beach at the bottom of the hill. Choose a guided fruit walk through the orchards or a rain-forest walk. The trail map facilitates exploration on your own. A short walk leads to a pristine waterfall whose waters flow into small, protected pools; bathe in the company of kingfishers and hummingbirds underneath a natural canopy of giant forest trees (feel the tickle of fresh-water shrimp). Ocean swimming and snorkeling is best at low tide, which also reveals tide pools with colorful fish, anemones, and other sea creatures. Night walks and early morning birding walks are options, and horses can be rented. Fishing and surfing are options. Nearby is the longest left-breaking wave in the country, a 1,600-yard (1,440-m) run at Punta Pavones.

An Indian reserve borders Tiskita, which is the Guaymi name for fish eagle. A visit to the Indian settlement can be arranged. Dashing hats and attractive bags made by Guaymis are for sale in the gift shop. Profits from sale of cards and T-shirts go to the Tiskita Foundation, which has purchased nearby endangered forest. Tiskita's work with the nearby community of Punta Banco has facilitated a local clinic, with a new community center and library in the works.

Electricity has arrived at Tiskita. The cabins have fans, reading lamps, and an electric plug in bathrooms. Each cabin is a bit different, constructed of wood and natural stone. Semi-outdoor bathrooms allow bird-watching while you bathe: no hot water. The Aspinalls refer to Tiskita as five-star rustic. Support columns in rooms are polished tree trunks; door handles are pieces of naturally sculptured wood. Screened windows and outdoor terraces are common features of the 14 cabins—some are individual, some share a common veranda. No smoking allowed in lodge facilities.

From a covered lookout furnished with forest-green lounging chairs and surrounded by heliconias and palms, sounds of sea and land mix—lots of parakeets and hummingbirds. Look out across the Pacific to the Osa Peninsula. Watch the sun slide into the ocean in the evenings. A new swimming pool has the same spectacular views.

The original farmhouse, built in 1979, has a small reference library, lounging chairs, and a dining room. Meals are served buffet-style—delicious, varied, and generous.

Telephone has not yet arrived, but the lodge has radio contact with the outside. Though it's remote, it is possible to drive in; an interesting 2½-hour trip through farm and ranch leads into a frontier region, crossing the Río Coto by ferry and sometimes fording small streams. A bridge now spans the Río Claro; I am sorry, in a way, that you'll miss the adventure of fording it, especially in rainy season.

Though fireflies sparkle in the evening, bring a flashlight for nighttime walks. Boots and umbrellas are available for guests. Tiskita is closed in October because of heavy rain.

Getting There

By bus: Daily bus between Golfito and Punta Banco passes Tiskita entrance. It leaves Punta Banco at 5 a.m. and Golfito at 2 p.m.; about $3 for the three-hour trip (pay a small amount at the ferry).
By car: Check with Tiskita about road conditions in rainy season.
By air: Most packages include round trip via charter plane.

SAN VITO

San Vito is a small place (population 13,529) with some big names around it: La Amistad National Park and the private nature reserves of Las Cruces

Biological Station (with its Wilson Botanical Garden) and La Amistad Lodge. Italian immigrants helped settle the area around San Vito, arriving in the early 1950s to clear and farm the land. You will find several Italian restaurants (try **Lilliana** or **Mamma Mía**) and hear Italian spoken on the streets. For other places to dine, try the restaurant at your hotel or ask at your hotel for other area recommendations. Find banks, gas stations, and interesting little shops. San Vito is 168 miles (271 km) south of San José.

Outside San Vito on the way to Las Cruces Biological Station, look for **Cántaros**, a marvelous gift shop chock-full of the unusual—Boruca Indian masks, primitive wood carvings, books, carved gourds, embroidered and silk-screened T-shirts, ceramics, jewelry, and more. Also inside this colorful farmhouse, owner Gail Hewson has created a library for local young people. Cántaros is open from 8 a.m. to 4 p.m., closed Monday; (506) 773-3760.

Where to Stay and Eat in San Vito
Hotel El Ceibo, telephone/fax (506) 773-3025, has 40 modest rooms with private baths and hot water. Ask for one of the 28 newer rooms with individual terraces and cable TV: single $15, double $24; older rooms about $3 less. There is a pleasant restaurant/bar and ample parking.

Getting There
By bus: Direct San José–San Vito bus.
By car: From the north, turn just before the Inter-American Highway crosses the Río Grande de Térraba at the junction for Paso Real and San Vito. Drive carefully: cowboys and cattle travel the paved road, along with the usual menagerie of bicycles, dogs, chickens, and pedestrians. Accessible from Golfito and Ciudad Neily via a road with dramatic views.
Other: Check whether SANSA has begun flights.

LA AMISTAD COSTA RICA-PANAMA INTERNATIONAL PARK
Location: Southern Costa Rica, entrances between Paso Real and San Vito.
Size: 479,199 acres (193,929 ha).
Hours: Tres Colinas sector daily 6 a.m. to 6 p.m.; Altamira sector daily 5 a.m. to 5 p.m.
Cost: $6, camping $2 per day per person.
Information: Telephone hotline 192 (see Appendix A: Parks and Reserves Information), Buenos Aires office (506) 730-0846, in San José telephone (506) 771-3297, fax (506) 771-3155.
Amistad means "friendship," and this international park was created in connection with a sister park established across the border in Panama to protect a vast corridor of forested land in these two countries. A gigantic national park, La Amistad is big enough to sustain a healthy population of animals that require large areas for hunting and reproduction, such as tapir, jaguar, puma, and harpy eagle.

Probably the largest population of quetzals in the country resides in this refuge of rain forest, cloud forest, and *páramo*, along with at least 400 other bird species. Epiphytes abound in cloud forests, where you see oak, elm, magnolia, and sweet cedar. More than 130 varieties of orchids have been found in the southwest corner of the park alone. There are 263 species of amphibians and reptiles. Spread across the rugged Talamanca Mountain range, Costa Rica's highest, the park protects not only endangered plants and animals but also important watersheds. Within the Amistad Biosphere Reserve, it's administered through the Amistad Pacific Conservation Area.

Though much of this fantasy land of geology and wildlife has yet to be explored, trails for hardy visitors do exist, principally at two entrances well off paved road; camping allowed. In the Tres Colinas sector, hikers can tackle Cerro Kamúk in a three- to four-day trip, elevation 11,660 feet (3,554 m). In the Altamira sector, one long trail requires up to three days (leading into the Valle del Silencio), while another trail can be hiked as a day trip from camping facilities (showers, baths, covered cooking area). Cooking must be done on a gas stove—no wood fires allowed. Get more information and arrange for local guides through the Buenos Aires number above.

Temperatures vary according to elevation, with upper altitudes rainy and sometimes cold. Come prepared.

Getting There
By car: Four-wheel-drive vehicle necessary in rainy season for the unpaved roads to either entrance. For Tres Colinas sector, turn east shortly after taking the Paso Real turnoff from the Inter-American, proceed toward Potrero Grande, and continue 14 miles (23 km) to the park station. For Altamira sector, turn east toward Colorado about 16 miles (26 km) from Paso Real; continue 14 miles (23 km) to the campsite.

Where to Stay Near La Amistad
See hotels and private nature lodges mentioned in this section.

LAS CRUCES BIOLOGICAL STATION (WILSON BOTANICAL GARDEN), PRIVATE RESERVE
Location: 3.5 miles (5.6 km) S of San Vito near Panama.
Rates: Overnight rates: single $75, double $60 per person, including lodging, meals, and taxes. Day visit $16 including lunch and self-guided garden walks; without lunch $8.

Information/Reservations: Reservations for overnight or day visit with lunch: (506) 240-6696, fax (506) 240-6783; e-mail reservas@ ns.ots.ac.cr. No reservation necessary for day visit without lunch.

Sunshine, mountain mists, tropical birds, a tapestry of color that only nature can weave, a sense of peace—all of this is at Las Cruces Biological Station plus terrific food, tasteful rooms, and caring attention from official hostess/associate director Gail Hewson.

Nature travelers have made pilgrimages to the botanical garden here since it was established by Robert and Catherine Wilson in the 1960s. The 25-acre (10-ha) Wilson Botanical Garden contains an internationally known collection of tropical plants, some 5,000 from the tropics and subtropics. The palm collection is one of the largest in the world; many are on delightful Tree Fern Hill Trail. More trails await: Heliconia Loop Trail; Bromeliad Walk (see birds drinking from the big bromeliads in dry season); Orchid Walk (with more than 200 native and exotic species); Fern Gully (Costa Rica has 800 species of ferns); Maranta Trail; and Bamboo Walk. The Natural History Loop winds through Hummingbird Garden, with plants to attract this amazing creature. Costa Rica has 54 species of hummers; the garden has 24. This self-guided trail has 15 stations; the trail booklet, on sale in the gift shop, is packed with interesting facts and explanations. Another booklet describes uses of 75 species in the medicinal plant garden. Guided walks with a bilingual naturalist are $35 per group. The garden is open daily.

Since the Organization for Tropical Studies (OTS) purchased the property from the Wilsons and established Las Cruces Biological Station, nature travelers and local folk have been joined by scientists from Costa Rica and around the world and by graduate and undergraduate students, further enriching the environment for learning. Guests have a chance to mingle with students or get a glimpse of leading-edge research going on here and in the surrounding rural landscape. Station director Luis Diego Gómez is himself internationally recognized for his botanical research.

The 580-acre (235-ha) biological station includes a forest reserve with trails that allow appreciation of orchids and palms and heliconias growing in their natural habitat. The Las Cruces Forest Reserve has some 2,000 species of flowering plants, 330 species of birds, 80 species of reptiles and amphibians, and 80 species of mammals, including bats. The garden and forest reserve are habitat for more than 326 species of birds (including local aquatic species) and more than 3,000 kinds of moths and butterflies.

Out of the ashes of a devastating fire that destroyed the old lodge (and library and laboratories) in November 1994 rose beautiful accommodations for natural history visitors. Twelve light-filled rooms have hardwood floors and a glass wall onto a balcony with garden and mountain views. Each room, named for a different flower, is furnished with a cushioned bamboo chair, bamboo nightstands, twin beds, a desk, and in-room telephone. One is handicapped-accessible. You are practically guaranteed to see fiery-billed aracaris from your balcony, and birding from a large terrace near the dining room is terrific.

Meals to look forward to are served either inside the dining room or on a covered outdoor terrace with fantastic views of distant mountains. Student groups and researchers have separate quarters, but everybody comes together at mealtimes for interesting conversation. A small gift shop has marvelous publications about the garden and Las Cruces, pretty T-shirts, calendars, tropical playing cards, natural history books, posters, and Boruca Indian handcrafts.

Las Cruces is located in a mid-elevation tropical rain forest. There's little or no rainfall January through March, but the rest of the year brings heavy fog and afternoon rains. Rainiest months are August through November. Annual rainfall is 158 inches (4,000 mm). Year-round temperatures stay in the 70s (21°C to 26°C) in daytime and the 60s (15°C to 21°C) at night. Las Cruces is part of the Amistad Biosphere Reserve recognized by UNESCO.

For more information about OTS, a private nonprofit organization that provides leadership in education, research, and wise use of natural resources in the tropics, check out its Web site: www.ots.duke.edu.

Telephone at Las Cruces is (506) 773-3278, fax (506) 773-3665, but reservations are through the San José OTS office, see above.

Getting There

By bus: Daily direct San José–San Vito buses (advance ticket purchase advisable), taxi to Las Cruces.

By car: From San Isidro, continue 9.3 miles (15 km) past El Brujo; watch for sign: San Vito is 45 km. From Golfito, go to Ciudad Neily, turn north on Route 16 to Agua Buena.

Other: Taxi from Golfito. Check whether planned air service from San José to San Vito via SANSA is a reality yet.

LA AMISTAD LODGE AND RAINFOREST RESERVE, PRIVATE RESERVE

Location: At Las Mellizas, about 16 miles (26 km) NE of San Vito, 7 hours S of San José near Panamanian border.

Rates: Single $80, double $65 per person, including lodging, meals, guided tour, taxes. Packages available.

Information/Reservations: San José (506) 290-2251, (506) 220-2331; fax (506) 232-1913. Lodge number is (506) 773-3193.

The bird list for this place tells the story of incredible biodiversity here—almost 400 species so far: more than 20 species of hummingbirds alone. On a short walk before breakfast with the resident naturalist, I saw crimson-fronted parakeets, fiery-billed aracaris, acorn and lineated woodpeckers, a double-toothed kite, white-ruffed manakin, boat-billed flycatcher, green hermit, Vaux's swift, boat-billed flycatcher, blue-grey tanager, and rufous-collared sparrow.

La Amistad Lodge is on Hacienda La Amistad, with elevations from 4,100 to 7,218 feet (1,250 to 2,200 m). It includes thousands of acres of rain forest within the Las Tablas Protected Zone. On the Pacific slope of the Talamanca Mountains, Las Tablas was declared part of the Amistad Biosphere Reserve by the United Nations and a World Heritage site by UNESCO for its rich biodiversity. Sixty percent of the flora and fauna in Costa Rica is thought to exist here.

I watched a quiet Belgian arthropod specialist practically in ecstasy as he collected from the forest floor tiny creatures not yet described in scientific literature. He confirmed that the 3-inch (7.6-cm) grasshoppers on the balcony were not just the largest I have ever seen, they are the largest in existence.

To walk in this forest is to walk in a sacred place; one of the trails even has a cathedral—an immense, awe-inspiring fig tree. More than 37 miles (60 km) of trails are suited to different energy levels and physical abilities. Watch for dead man's finger among the incredible variety of mushrooms along the paths. Howler monkeys, white-faced monkeys, and peccaries live here, among an estimated 215 mammal species.

Owner Roberto Montero, whose grandfather owned this land, can relate area history, how Las Tablas became a protected area, and how he believes conservation through sustainable development is the key to preserving natural resources. At La Amistad Lodge, guests get more than rain-forest ecology; they also see almost 400 acres (160 ha) devoted to organic farming: coffee, vegetables, cardamom, sugarcane, fruit orchards. It has been more than 10 years since any kind of agrochemicals were applied to this land, including pasture for cattle. The La Amistad brand name is now on coffee, hot sauces, chips, refried beans, and other organic products for export. Fruit pulp from coffee is composted for organic fertilizer. Guests can see the coffee-processing plant from the lodge.

The lodge is a three-story marvel of tropical woods. In the downstairs dining room, delicious buffet-style meals are served by friendly local people. Beautiful pre-Columbian pieces from the property are on exhibit (petroglyphs can be seen on some trails). The huge, high-ceilinged lounge area on the second floor has comfortable seating in front of a big stone fireplace and opens onto an ample balcony. Five rooms, shared baths, are off the living area. Across a walkway in back are five additional rooms with ceiling fans and private baths. Radio, computer, and telephone operate on solar power, and a hydroelectric plant provides other electricity.

Optional guided tours on the hacienda include half-day and full-day adventures, mostly in the $20 to $35 range: natural history walks, horseback riding, bird-watching, trout fishing, a hardy hike to the Río Negro waterfall, a tour of the hacienda. Though there is much to do at the hacienda, day tours are offered to Wilson Botanical Garden at Las Cruces ($70) and to Bambito in Panama ($100).

*Mushroom artistry
on the Osa Peninsula*

Guests may choose to stay at campsites deep inside the forest reserve. Cotoncito, with six rustic cabins, shared baths, and a dining/common room, is the first of several planned inside the huge 37,000-acre (15,000-ha) forest reserve. With Cotoncito as a base, guests venture out on tours or simply delight in this secluded retreat's surroundings: forest, the fauna, and nearby Coton River. Cotoncito is an hour from the lodge via four-by-four pickup. Don't miss this high adventure.

Getting There
By bus: San José–San Vito bus; arrange transfer from there with lodge.
By car: From San Vito continue through Sabalito (pavement ends here) and Las Mellizas, following lodge signs.
Other: La Amistad offers transfers to and from San José as well as to destinations such as Tiskita, Golfito, and Jacó.

OSA PENINSULA

The Osa Peninsula has Corcovado National Park, private nature reserves, lodging from rustic to tropical elegance, rivers and coastline, and spectacular wildlife. Access is by air, boat, bus, or car. An unpaved road goes from Puerto Jiménez to Rincón to join the Inter-American, opening up the eastern and southern parts of the Osa to road travelers. Access to the western shores of the peninsula is by air, boat from other Pacific ports, or road for 7 miles (11 km) from Palmar (where SANSA and Travelair land) to Sierpe and then by boat on the Sierpe River to Drake Bay and points south. This section contains information on Caño Island Biological Reserve and Coco Island National Park.

PUERTO JIMENEZ AND SOUTH COAST
Puerto Jiménez (population 7,064), across the Golfo Dulce from Golfito, is the jumping-off place for exceptional natural history/adventure destinations. The Osa Conservation Area has an office here to help you with visits to Corcovado National Park. South of town toward the tip of the peninsula are private nature reserves well worth a visit.

You'll find small, modest hotels in town as well as restaurants and tour businesses. While the big attractions are further along the southern end of the peninsula, if you need a place to stay in Puerto Jiménez try friendly 10-room **Hotel Manglares,** telephone/fax (506) 735-5002; $13 per person. It has a restaurant, thatched rancho with hammocks, and pleasant gardens. Boat trips in the gulf and Corcovado and Caño Island tours arranged.

Getting There
By bus: San José–Puerto Jiménez bus, twice daily.
By car: Take the Inter-American south through San Isidro de El General and

Palmar Norte; turn west at Chacarita (north of Golfito) and go around the gulf to Puerto Jiménez.

By boat: Passenger launch between Golfito and Puerto Jiménez, once a day each way.

By air: Daily flights on Travelair and SANSA, plus charters.

CORCOVADO NATIONAL PARK

Location: Osa Peninsula on Pacific side.

Size: 103,258 acres (41,788 ha) of land; 5,930 acres (2,400 ha) of marine habitat.

Hours: Park open daily; office in Puerto Jiménez 8 a.m. to 4 p.m. Monday through Friday.

Cost: $6, camping $2 per person per day.

Information/Reservations: Telephone hotline 192 (see Appendix A: Parks and Reserves Information), (506) 735-5282, telephone/fax (506) 735-5036; advance reservations essential for camping or meals at stations.

Corcovado, on the Osa Peninsula in southwest Costa Rica, is a remote park. It is big. It is marvelous. A park administrator told me he once counted 150 scarlet macaws flying in two groups near the Madrigal River. I sat at the Sirena station one morning and watched two of these large members of the parrot family preen their brilliant red, yellow, and blue plumage; eat; and glide gracefully from treetop to treetop.

Five hundred species of trees live here, including probably the tallest in the country, a ceiba or kapok tree that soars to 230 feet (70 m). Eight habitat types exist: montane forest, cloud forest, alluvial plains forest, swamp, palm forest, mangrove, and rocky and sandy vegetation.

You may encounter scientific researchers studying everything from how jacamars know not to eat toxic butterflies and the life habits of the squirrel monkey to why some South America species are found here but not in Panama or on Costa Rica's Atlantic side. Researchers often work out of the Sirena station.

Trails link four major park stations: Sirena, La Leona, and San Pedrillo, on the Pacific coast; and Los Patos, inland near the Rincón River. They range from 4 to 15 miles long (6 to 24 km). Two popular routes are Los Patos to Sirena, 11 miles (18 km), and La Leona to Sirena, 10 miles (16 km). The hike from San Pedrillo to Sirena is not advisable except from December to April (drier months, when rivers are lower). Shorter trails fan out from stations. At Sirena, seven trails offer half-mile to 3-mile (1- to 5-km) forays into the forest. With advance notice, visitors can eat at ranger stations: breakfast $4, lunch or dinner $7.

Many visitors experience Corcovado on day trips to the San Pedrillo entrance by boat from the Drake Bay area and to La Leona from the southern end of the peninsula, about a 2-mile hike (3-km) from Carate. Some charter flights make Sirena a day-visit possibility. From Puerto Jiménez, visitors enter through La Leona or hike to Los Patos.

The Pacific adds a marine component. Sperm whales pass by, marine turtles nest on its beaches, and there's a live coral reef at Salsipuedes. Among endangered species protected at Corcovado are five species of cat (including the jaguar), giant anteaters, sloths, and the harpy eagle, the largest bird of prey in the world. Identified so far are 367 species of birds, 500 of trees, 104 of mammals, and 117 species of amphibians and reptiles. Herds of white-lipped peccaries have been known to tree visitors along the trails.

Though its remoteness and heavy vegetation protected areas now encompassed by the park, Corcovado does have an interesting human history. Local lore holds that Cubans trained along its beaches before the Bay of Pigs landing, and that Sandinistas sought its isolation for training for a brief period before President Anastasio Somoza of Nicaragua was overthrown in 1979. Miners invaded its confines to pan for gold in the 1980s but were evicted in 1986. Again in 1995, park personnel evicted miners. Small farms and forestry operations had made inroads in the virgin forest before the park was established in 1975.

Much of the terrain is hilly, rising from deserted coastal beaches. Elevation is from sea level to 1,932 feet (782 m). Mid-December to mid-April is the driest period; average annual rainfall in the mountains is 217 inches (5,500 mm). Average temperature is 79°F (26°C).

Obtain information about Corcovado at the Osa Conservation Area office in Puerto Jiménez across from the landing strip. Camping is permitted in designated areas next to park stations, by reservation only. Mosquito netting recommended.

Getting There
See directions for getting to Puerto Jiménez. From there, the closest ranger station is Los Patos, which involves getting to La Palma and then a two-hour trek by foot. For the southern Pacific area, continue by taxi or car to the end of the road for the trek to La Leona. Boat access from Drake Bay. Area lodges and private reserves arrange tours; San José agencies offer packages.

Where to Stay near Corcovado
Several private nature reserves and lodges in the area offer day tours to Corcovado.

LAPA RIOS, PRIVATE RESERVE
Location: Osa Peninsula, 10 miles (16 km) S of Puerto Jiménez.
Rates: Single $238, double $164 each, including lodging, meals, taxes.
Information/Reservations: (506) 735-5130, fax (506) 735-5179; e-mail LapaRíos@centralamerica.com; Web site www.centralamerica.com/cr/hotel /laparios.htm.

The brochure for Lapa Ríos asks, "Who says wilderness and luxury can't mix?" Owners of this 1,000-acre (405-ha) private reserve, John and Karen Lewis, thought it could be done and set out to protect this piece of rain forest through a small, upscale ecotourism project designed to have minimal impact on the environment and to contribute to local development, education, and employment.

Lapa Ríos is the result of their dream. The luxury wilderness resort has a spectacular main lodge that houses reception, restaurant, bar, and an outdoor terrace. Guests look up at the underside of the 50-foot (15-m) thatched palm roof. The intrepid can climb a hardwood circular stairway that makes four complete turns to an observation walkway three stories high. A 360-degree view encompasses forest and the sea 350 feet (107 m) below. The cliffside swimming pool next to the lodge has a dynamite ocean view.

Fourteen bungalows are on three ridges below the main lodge. The first two are accessible to the lodge and pool by wheelchair ramp. My secluded bungalow was 100 steps down. Each has a peaked thatched roof and gleaming floors of tropical hardwood. One wall is white stucco and cane; the other three are largely open, low wooden walls with screens above, bamboo rollups for privacy. Double louvered doors open onto a large private deck and small patio garden with an outdoor shower. The tiled bathroom has two sinks set in tropical hardwood and a large shower, open to a view of the forest, solar hot water. Furnishings are primarily of bamboo. Each room contains two double beds draped with mosquito netting, desk, luggage racks, chairs with bright cushions, and ceiling fans.

Carbonara Beach down from the lodge is safe for swimming and has tide pools. Surfers find good waves nearby. Lapa Ríos uses local charter boat services for fishing, tours to Sirena Station at Corcovado and to Caño Island, or a cruise on the Golfo Dulce.

A self-guided trail free for guests features 18 points of interest described in a booklet. Bilingual naturalist guides lead tours in the reserve, most $20 to $30 per person. Beach Walk focuses on marine biology, and a three-hour Rain Forest Ridge Walk along a fairly level trail through primary forest is a nice introduction to the biodiversity of tropical rain forests. Among the species that live here are small green-and-black poison-dart frogs, leaf beetles, army ants and the birds that follow their marches, Costa Rica's four species of monkeys, and boa constrictors. The Wild Waterfalls adventure combines forest hiking with pristine waterfalls and the Carbonara River— this one for the hardy.

Other options include an easy Medicine Walk (led by shaman guide) or an Early Birds Tour to see some of the more than 320 species of birds found here. A night walk reveals forest secrets not visible during the day. Bring a flashlight to see the eyeshine of nocturnal creatures. Ride horses, surf, fish, snorkel, or have a massage in a private forest overlook.

Guests can plant a tree on 250 acres (100 ha) of regenerating forest. The $25 fee goes into the Lapa Ríos reforestation program and the donor receives a certificate. On Tuesdays and Thursdays interested guests accompany Karen to the local school to share songs, stories, photos, or readings with the children. Lapa Ríos received the 1995 Tourism for Tomorrow

Award for the Americas, given by British Airways to recognize responsible ecotourism and sustainable development, and was a runner-up for the Condé Nast Eco-tourism Award in 1997.

Area tours include a visit to Corcovado National Park via charter flight to Sirena for a hike to Río Claro ($600 for four people), snorkeling in the Golfo Dulce (half-day for two, $155), sea kayaking ($45), or a trip across the gulf to visit a botanical garden or to enjoy birding on the Esquinas River.

Meals are a treat; they look and taste great. Though food is included in the rate, there is no fixed menu: guests choose from several selections. Desserts are scrumptious. Restaurant staff members are well-trained and friendly. The restaurant is open to the public.

Getting There
By car: From Puerto Jiménez, south 10 miles (6 km) via unpaved road.
Other: From Puerto Jiménez, Lapa Ríos offers transfers, $20 per person.

BOSQUE DEL CABO, PRIVATE RESERVE
Location: Osa Peninsula, about 10 miles (16 km) S of Puerto Jiménez.
Rates: Standard bungalows, single $95, double $75 per person, meals included. Deluxe bungalows single $105, double $85 per person, including meals. House $675/week for two, $775 for four, meals not included. Prefer no credit cards.
Information/Reservations: In Puerto Jiménez telephone/fax (506) 735-5206, fax (506) 735-5043; e-mail boscabo@sol.racsa.co.cr.

If you like nighttime by candlelight, scarlet macaws flying overhead, a private outdoor shower with water heated only by the sun on the pipes, and the sound of the sea as you drop off to sleep, then Bosque del Cabo is for you.

Perched above Matapalo Beach on the tip of the Osa Peninsula, this small wilderness lodge has perhaps just the right amount of comfort and adventure. The naturalist in me thrilled at the continuous parade of tropical birds so easily seen. The explorer reveled in the horseback ride through a tropical storm, an encounter with a snake, and tracking howler monkeys on a forest trail. The romantic in me relished the thatched bungalows above the sea, mosquito netting draped gracefully over the beds, and a private outdoor shower with a forest for a backdrop. Four scarlet macaws flew over in perfect formation as I showered my first morning there.

I confess that I appreciated the modern bath with a flush toilet, the good food, and the comfortable beds. I enjoyed experiencing the bungalow at night with only candles or a kerosene lantern to warm the darkness. Doors fold back to open the front of each of the seven bungalows to sea and forest. Three are deluxe bungalows with king-size bed, wraparound deck, and solar electricity, but you can still choose candlelight. An attractive two-bedroom house with furnished kitchen is available.

As I stood on my veranda, I counted a feeding flock of 15 chestnut-mandibled toucans while the sounds of howler monkeys mixed with the

Bosque del Cabo on the Osa Peninsula

sounds of the surf and a hummingbird whispered by my ear. Scarlet macaws are regular visitors.

If you can tear yourself away from bird-watching and ocean-gazing (whales sometimes pass by), take an hour's hike to the gulf side of the peninsula to swim in gentler waters, walk the trail down to the small river, or go on a horseback ride to the ocean side of the peninsula to visit the tide pools along a deserted beach and walk up to the 30-foot (9-m) waterfall. There are also other horseback tours. During high season, a resident naturalist guide can accompany you. Owner Philip Spier and staff are pleased to help arrange for surfing, sea kayaking, deep-sea fishing, and sailing.

Dining-room hours are flexible to meet needs of both bird-watchers and late sleepers. Local fruits and vegetables are incorporated in the meals, which include both typical Costa Rican and North American dishes. Special dietary needs can be met with advance notice. Solar power provides electricity in the dining room in the evenings.

Getting There
By car: From Puerto Jiménez, about 10 miles (16 km) south.
Other: Taxi from Puerto Jiménez, about $24.

CORCOVADO LODGE TENT CAMP, PRIVATE RESERVE
Location: Near Carate, SE Pacific coast of Osa Peninsula.
Rates: Single $76, double $67 per person, including lodging, meals and taxes. Meal plan available. A three-day/two-night package is $949 per person, double occupancy, including round-trip transfer from San José, lodging, meals, bilingual naturalist guide, hikes in lodge reserve and/or Corcovado, and day visit to the platform.
Information/Reservations: *(506) 257-0766, (506) 222-0333, fax (506) 257-1665; e-mail crexped@ sol.racsa.co.cr; Web site www.crexped.co.cr.*

Fantasies of camping in the rain forest? Here's a chance to do it with enough adventure to satisfy a vigorous spirit and the surprise of some earthly comforts. The trip in usually involves air time in a small plane to Puerto Jiménez, taxi ride over unpaved road to Carate, and a 30- to 45-minute walk along a beach on the southern Pacific coast of the Osa Peninsula to the tent camp.

Then new arrivals at Corcovado Lodge Tent Camp, owned by Costa Rica Expeditions, discover the campsite and roomy 10-by-10-foot tents (with straight walls for plenty of headroom) pitched on wooden platforms. Each is furnished with two single beds and has a covered front porch. A screened-in, thatched dining room, bath houses, and a thatched hammock house and bar complete this jungle complex, with forest behind and palm-fringed beach in front. Neighbors include magnificent scarlet macaws. Electricity from a small generator is limited to certain hours in dining area and bath houses, so this is flashlight country after dark—along with moon-light, of course.

A self-guided loop trail is free to guests. On the two- to three-hour, mainly easy hike through the lodge's 400-acre (162-ha) private reserve, you may come face to face with coatis, tayras, scarlet-rumped tanagers, snakes, hermit hum-mers, or colorful poison-dart frogs. Since the reserve is contiguous to mam-moth Corcovado National Park, cats and tapirs that live there could wander by, or perhaps you will see evidence of their having passed this way.

Other hiking tours range from easy to hard. Two take trekkers into Cor-covado: one a strenuous four-hour hike through the La Leona entrance to the Madrigal River and beach ($25 plus park fee); another two hours farther through forest and along beach to Salsipuedes ($40 plus park fee), where vis-itors relax in tidal pools and sometimes see flocks of scarlet macaws.

An afternoon horseback ride to the tip of the peninsula offers breathtak-ing views of macaws squawking in flight overhead or feeding in almond trees, as well as of roosting sites for egrets, herons, and roseate spoonbills. Top it all off with sunset on the Pacific ($35).

If the tent doesn't offer enough adventure, spend the night on a platform 120 feet (50 m) above the forest floor. Observe diurnal creatures winding down and nocturnal ones moving onto the stage. Maximum is two people plus the guide for this extraordinary experience ($125 per person).

If you are more of a diurnal creature yourself, ascend into the canopy by day to enjoy its incredible biodiversity—still a frontier for scientific research ($69). The platform is in a 200-foot (61-m) *ajo* tree. Birds and monkeys fre-quent the neighborhood, which almost always has at least one tree in fruit. The *ajo* itself, which got its name from the garlic smell of its yellow flowers, has fruits in April and May, fruits favored by scarlet macaws, honeycreepers, toucans, and tanagers. Spider monkeys swing noisily through the trees to feed. Participants in the canopy expeditions are hoisted to the platform and brought back to the forest floor in a bosun's chair—plenty of adventure with a level of comfort.

Getting There

By car: From Puerto Jiménez, continue around the southern end of the peninsula and north to Carate, where cars stop and hiking begins.
Other: Taxi from Puerto Jiménez to Carate. Packages include air charters and ground transport.

THE SIERPE RIVER AND DRAKE BAY

The Sierpe River region is a destination in itself, as well as a gateway to Drake Bay, named for Sir Francis Drake, who sailed these waters more than 400 years ago. The Sierpe River trip can be fascinating, with the chance to see kingfishers, tiger-herons, crocodiles, turtles, parrots, monkeys, blue herons, muscovy ducks, perhaps even a roseate spoonbill. But how much you see may depend on the speed at which you travel. Some boat captains seem to view the river pretty much as a highway, a means of getting from one place to another as quickly as possible. I had the good fortune to travel once with Mike Stiles, owner of the Río Sierpe Lodge, who slows down for wildlife viewing and explores some of the estuaries. A hard rain in the mountains had brought an avalanche of water hyacinths downriver on my return trip, transforming the water into a floating garden—beautiful but tricky for navigation. The mouth of the Sierpe can be treacherous at times: be sure to go with a seasoned boatman.

Though the Drake Bay area is remote, accessible by charter flights or boat, a growing number of nature tourism sites exist from the Sierpe to Corcovado National Park. A road inching its way from Rincón now reaches as far as Drake's small landing field but not yet to the town. Some see the road as a benefit to allow easier access; others fear it will increase logging. Time will tell. In the meantime, mountain bikers are taking advantage of it.

Remember that boat landings on beaches will be wet, so come prepared with suitable shoes and clothes. Only a few sites have docks.

Corcovado National Park, Caño Island Biological Reserve, rich forests, mangroves, rivers, and wildlife are major attractions. However you initially get to the area, you can move about by boat and hiking. From Drake there is a path through forest and along beach that connects town and areas south. I walked as far as Marenco, a nice alternative to seeing this area from the ocean. The hanging bridge over Agujitas River near the town of Drake is not to be missed.

ISLA DEL CAÑO BIOLOGICAL RESERVE

Location: *12 miles (20 km) W of Drake Bay on the Osa Peninsula.*
Size: *494 acres (200 ha) of land; 6,672 acres (2,700 ha) of marine habitat.*
Hours: *Open daily 8 a.m. to 4 p.m.*
Cost: *$6.*
Information/Reservations: *Telephone hotline 192 (see Appendix A: Parks and Reserves Information), (506) 735-5282, telephone/fax (506) 735-5036.*

Caño Island (Island Caño) is interesting both as an archaeological site and for its marine life. Rising above the Pacific, the land contains tall evergreen forest, a prehistoric cemetery, and mysterious round stones sculpted by the Indians who once walked here. Unfortunately, many graves were plundered before the island came under protection. The most abundant pottery dates from A.D. 220 to 1550.

Crystalline waters are a snorkeler's delight. Five coral reefs, containing at least 15 species of stony coral, create a marine wonderland that almost made me forget my fear of being so far from shore in deep waters. Lobster and giant conch live here, as do eels, octopuses, sea urchins, brittle stars, and countless fish—jacks, grunts, and triggerfish. Manta rays, sailfish, sea turtles, humpback whales, and dolphins have been seen near the island. Snorkeling and diving are limited to the sea in front of the ranger station.

Island wildlife is scarce, consisting mainly of pacas, opossums, boa constrictors, a few species of bees, moths, butterflies, beetles, frogs, bats, rats, lizards, and ants. Among the birds are ospreys, brown noddies, brown boobies, terns, and egrets. The forest is largely made up of locusts, wild figs, rubber trees, wild cacaos, and milk trees, which exude a white latex that can be drunk as milk.

A trail climbs through the forest to points of archaeological interest. High cliffs rise from the coastline, with only a few small, sandy beaches that largely disappear at high tide. Maximum elevation is 361 feet (110 m).

Most visitors to Caño Island arrive as part of a tour. Prior reservation is necessary; independent travelers should contact the Osa Conservation Area office at the numbers above.

Getting There
By boat: Lodges and tour agencies bring visitors from sites on the Osa Peninsula and Golfito area as well as from Dominical and Quepos.

Where to Stay and Eat in the Sierpe River and Drake Bay Area
Aguila de Osa Inn, telephone/fax (506) 296-2190, (506) 232-7722; e-mail aguila@centralamerica.com, is an upscale, 14-room complex of guest rooms, open-air restaurant, and dock on a bluff overlooking Drake Bay. Attractive rooms have hardwood floors, screened windows, ceiling fans, and carved doors. Some bathrooms have sunken tubs, and a classy two-bedroom suite with a conical roof has windows on three sides. Single $145; double $110 per person, suites from $242, including meals. Land and water transfer from Palmar to the inn is $130 for two. A horseback tour of beach and forest is $55, a jungle hike in Corcovado $65, snorkeling at Caño Island $65, kayaking free for guests. Ask about diving and sportfishing.

Casa Corcovado Jungle Lodge, (506) 256-3181, fax (506) 256-7409; e-mail corcovado@sol.racsa.aco.cr, is a 170-acre (69-ha) private reserve adjoining Corcovado National Park, with a pristine half-kilometer of white-sand beach to explore—experience the magic of being under a waterfall. Attractive individual bungalows, surrounded by rain forest, have private baths, light-colored tile floors with decorative patterns, lots of windows, and beds gracefully draped with mosquito netting. Electricity in this remote place comes from hydropower and solar systems; drinking water, from a mountain spring. Meals are good, and there is a thatch-roofed open-air bar.

In addition to guided walks on the property, guests take tours to the park and to Caño Island, kayak, and scuba dive or sportfish. A three-day, two-night package is $527 per person, double occupancy, including air from San José, land and boat transfers, lodging, meals, tours, park fees, and taxes. Ask about rates from Palmar Sur or Sierpe.

Corcovado Adventures Tent Camp, telephone/fax (506) 258-1751; e-mail sobervac@mail.multicr.com; Web site www.multicr.com/sobervacations/, is an alcohol-free site facing the beach with rich forest behind. Each tent, on a base that also provides a private porch, is furnished with a single and double bed, nightstand, and battery-powered lamp: $75 per person for lodging and meals, tours extra. Dining room and itchen are powered by solar panels. A communal bath has five toilets and showers. The camp holds 18 people. A three-night, four-day tour from either San José or Quepos is $578, all inclusive. Guided tours include a day in Corcovado and a day at Caño Island plus use of kayaks and time for snorkeling, fishing, hiking, and swimming. Hammocks hang among palm trees. Wildlife is abundant—the owner says this is the place where monkeys come to see you.

Drake Bay Wilderness Camp, reservations telephone/fax (506) 284-4107, (506) 256-7394; lodge (506) 771-2436; e-mail hdrake@tico net.co.cr, is a relaxing, laid-back kind of place. You soon settle into tropical time, pausing to delight in antics of three squirrel monkeys who cavort in the fruit-laden gardens, making a date with a spectacular sunset, and lounging in hammocks. An inviting natural tide pool beckons at low tide.

Part of the wilderness camp is on the point between the river and the Pacific; the rest faces the ocean, backed by forest. Twenty rooms, most with solar hot water, are in seven buildings. All are simply furnished and have ceiling fans, luggage racks, even washcloths, $68 per person. Four 10-by-10-foot oceanfront tents (with electricity) offer an alternative, with occupants sharing a two-shower, two-toilet communal bath; $48 per person double, meals included. Good food is served family-style in a separate dining room, with complimentary *bocas* at 5 p.m. in the thatched, open-air lounge.

Guests can choose horseback riding, mountain biking, kayaking, diving, night fishing, offshore fishing, and tours to Corcovado or Caño Island. Scuba diving and kayaking packages available. I treasure a memorable morning on a Río Claro tour. Walking on beach and forest trails with Fernando, the knowledgeable naturalist guide, was a treat. We saw 12 scarlet macaws feeding in distant trees and a white hawk—Fernando explained that these hawks follow white-faced monkeys, waiting for the chance to take a young monkey, and then we saw the monkeys. We watched a spectacular blowhole and a "walking beach" alive with hermit crabs. River otters played in the Río Claro. Guests swim up the beautiful river, outfitted with life vests and fins, and float back down with the gentle current. Tall trees are on both banks; kingfishers fly by. You can snorkel in a lagoon or visit a waterfall above the river.

Owners and hosts at Drake Bay Wilderness Camp, Herbert and Marleney (Marleney's family homesteaded this land), offer an exiting new option: tent camping in their 740-acre (300-ha) Drake Bay Bio Preserve. Surrounded by the tropical jungle, guests sleep in comfortable 10-by-10-foot tents (twin beds) and relax on their own front porch; solar-powered electricity. Dining room and shared baths are in a central building. Breeding and release programs are underway for butterflies, iguanas, and deer, and native tree species are being grown for reforestation of cut-over areas. Lodge guests can visit the preserve on a day trip. Volunteers are needed to help with preserve projects.

La Paloma Lodge, (506) 239-2801, telephone/fax (506) 239-0954; e-mail lapaloma@lapalomalodge.com; Web site www.lapalomalodge.com, is a delightful hilltop retreat. Spectacular views of the Pacific and landscaped gardens provide a rich setting for the tropical birds that abound here. Fiery-billed aracaris were feasting regularly on *almendro* trees when I was there. Their calls mixed with those of chestnut-mandibled toucans, parrots, and macaws in jungle melodies, blending with distant sounds of the sea.

The centerpiece of the complex, owned and managed by Mike and Sue Kalmbach, is a large, thatched-roofed structure that contains dining room, bar, lounge, a small library with reference books and magazines, and a marvelous veranda along the ocean side with lots of chairs for sunset-watching at complimentary *boca* time before dinner. Excellent food is served family style.

Hanging bridge over the Agujitas River, near Drake

Homemade bread is on the table at every meal, and nighttime brings rich desserts. Don't be surprised if Mike sits down with you at dinner. Sue is generally the one who helps with arrangements by phone or fax. A swimming pool near the clubhouse has a dramatic ocean view.

Five standard rooms are in a lodge near the clubhouse and five thatched, two-story deluxe ranchos down a forested path. Comfortable, spacious lodge rooms open onto private verandas with hammocks. Deluxe ranchos have private porches, a downstairs living sleeping area and bathroom, and a marvelous, spacious bedroom upstairs, open between the waist-high walls and the overhang of the tall thatched roof. Views are of forest and sea. Rooms and ranchos have solar hot water, ceiling fans, and orthopedic mattresses. Electricity is a combination of solar and generator power.

A four-day, three-night package is $625 per person in the lodge, $725 for a rancho, including round-trip air and boat transportation from San José, meals, and a choice of daily tours. Other packages available.

Accompany La Paloma's experienced naturalist guide to see and learn about toucans, manakins, scarlet macaws, parrots, monkeys, sloths, herons, and iguanas. Guided day trips go to Corcovado and Caño Island. Guests can kayak in the bay and the Pacific as well as the Agujitas River—no charge for kayaks. Horseback riding and sportfishing are other options. The beach is only a short walk away. I highly recommend a gentle canoe trip on the Agujitas River: take a dip in the cool water—a contrast to the warmer water of the bay—and enjoy the birds.

Rio Sierpe Lodge, cellular telephone (506) 284-5595, fax (506) 788-8111; San José (506) 257-7010, fax (506) 257-7012; e-mail escapes @sol.racsa.co.cr, is 15 miles (24 km) from Palmar by boat. At that point the river is more than a half-mile (1 km) wide and 50 feet (15 m) deep. Along the opposite shore are some of the tallest mangroves in the world. The lodge, on a narrow bluff between the river and the mountains, consists of 11 rooms with private bath, some in the main house and others a few steps away, as well as three new two-story rooms. All have private tiled baths with passive-solar hot water. Furnishings are simple but comfortable. Windows are screened, and there is a wall fan; double from $65 per person, including lodging, meals, soft drinks, transfers from Palmar, and taxes. Guests can be picked up at Quepos, Dominical, or Playa Piñuela at added cost.

Electricity is from a generator, and battery-powered reading lamps function after the generator goes off at night. Water is from a mountain spring. Food is plentiful and tasty, with lots of fruits, vegetables, and seafood—Mike, the owner, serves a mean spaghetti.

Guests can hike on trails from the lodge and enjoy the beaches at Boca Sierpe at no cost. From the dock, expect to see crocodiles, sea turtles, manta rays, and a wonderful variety of fish. The lodge has a reference library, including bird books to help identify the myriad you will see. Some 175 species are spotted regularly, including the mangrove hummingbird (which Mike says often shows up at breakfast), Baird's trogon, the black-cheeked ant-tanager, yellow-billed cotinga, and black hawk.

Tours with local naturalist guides include Corcovado or Caño Island ($55); an adventure that includes horseback riding, hiking, swimming, and snorkeling ($75); a Laguna Sierpe boat trip ($50); or half-day excursions to beaches ($25). Mike also offers scuba diving and estuary and ocean fishing trips, and there are archaeological ruins to visit; at the nearby beaches you can swim, snorkel, or marvel at huge sand dollars and other sea shells. Rubber boots and snorkeling equipment provided.

From the lodge guests look directly over Violin Island and the Térraba/Sierpe Mangrove Reserve. A six-day, five-night kayaking package explores not only the mangrove reserve and Violin Island but goes to Guarumal Bay (brown booby and frigate bird rookeries) and San Josecito beach in Corcovado, $1,055, including round-trip air from San José, land and water transfers, lodging, meals, and kayaking guide and equipment. A three-day, two night naturalist tour is $345 each, double occupancy, including transport as above, meals, lodging, and excursions to Corcovado, Caño Island, or mangroves as time permits. Diving packages start at $550 each for two persons, three days, two nights.

MARENCO BEACH AND RAINFOREST LODGE, PRIVATE RESERVE

Location: Pacific coast of Osa Peninsula, between Drake Bay and Corcovado.
Rates: Room $60 per person, bungalow $91, meals included. All-inclusive packages include airfare, ground and boat transfers, meals, lodging, and specified tours: two-night package with Corcovado tour $390 per person; three-night $540, including Corcovado and Caño Island.
Information/Reservations: (506) 258-1919, fax (506) 255-1346, U.S. and Canada number 800-278-6223; e-mail marenco@sol.racsa.co.cr; Web site www .crdirect.com/corcovado.

There are no roads to Marenco. This remote, tropical wilderness lodge and reserve is set in a hillside clearing amidst lush premontane wet forest. Explore the miles of beach and forest trails on the reserve's 1,977 acres (800 ha). Sit on your room's balcony and watch a parade of exotic birds—parrots, toucans with their outrageous beaks, scarlet macaws, brightly colored tanagers. Humpback whales are among the 20 whale species that pass by year-round in the ocean below, the most in December and January.

On forest trails you may encounter a slow-moving sloth or catch the scent of white-lipped peccaries. The resident naturalist will tell you about the subspecies of squirrel monkey, called tití, that's endemic to southern Costa Rica and northern Panama. Watch for motion in the trees to spot them and the other three monkey species that live here: howler, white-faced capuchin, and spider. So far at Marenco, 140 species of mammals and 376 species of birds have been counted.

Rent one of the reserve's horses to go along the beach or forest trails, and walk to the cool waters of the Río Claro and take a dip beneath towering forest giants. It's possible to walk on the beach and forest trails all the way to the tiny community of Drake Bay.

A nighttime visit to the tide pools reveals sea creatures you may never have seen before. Daytime snorkeling is good at coral gardens along Marenco's coastline, where you may see parrot fish, tangs, puffers, and angelfish. On a boat tour to Caño Island, 11 miles (17 km) west of Marenco, you'll probably see dolphins, and you may be startled by a manta ray. Diving safaris at Caño Island expose an underwater wonderland of octopus, lobster, moray eel, jack, damselfish, and triggerfish. Marenco does PADI dive certification.

A highlight for most is a day trip to nearby Corcovado, entering at San Pedrillo and hiking along the beach and into the forest, enjoying a jungle waterfall. Plant and birdlife is outstanding. A bilingual naturalist guide explains intricate biological relationships and points out what you might overlook. You are treading the turf of Corcovado's animal kingdom: the jaguar, giant anteater, tapir, agouti, ocelot, and kinkajou.

Marenco is a buffer zone that protects the park, employs local people, and offers travelers a chance to taste the richness. Eight cozy rooms along the edge of the hillside have balconies open to a priceless view. The 17 larger bungalows of wood and bamboo have shining hardwood floors, two double beds, and floor-to-ceiling screened windows that let in lots of light and forest colors. Meals are served buffet-style in a large, open dining room.

Marenco now has electricity 24 hours a day, but bring a flashlight anyway. A radio telephone is powered by solar energy. The small reference library with some preserved local flora and fauna is worth a visit. Crafts made by local people are available in the Rain Forest Shop.

Getting There
Package rates include round-trip transportation from San José. Non-package travelers should contact Marenco about land, sea, and air possibilities.

ISLAND DEL COCO NATIONAL PARK
Location: In the Pacific 331 miles (532 km) SW of Cabo Blanco; latitude 5 degrees N, longitude 8 degrees W.
Size: 5,930 acres (2,400 ha) of land; 240,268 acres (97,235 ha) of coastal waters.
Hours: Open daily 24 hours.
Cost: $6.
Information/Reservations: Telephone hotline 192 (see Appendix A: Parks and Reserve Information), (506) 233-4533, telephone/fax (506) 256-0365.

This beautiful green island in the Pacific off Costa Rica was an early haven for explorers, privateers, pirates, and whalers because of its abundant fresh water, wood, fish, and coconuts; *coco* is Spanish for coconut. Today, it attracts treasure hunters, divers, scientists, and natural history travelers.

More than 300 expeditions have uncovered only a few tantalizing pieces of three treasure caches believed to lie hidden somewhere on Coco Island (Isla del Coco). Some believe that stories of these treasures fired the imagination of Robert Louis Stevenson for his *Treasure Island*.

Scientists and tourists come in search of other riches: many endemic species—those that occur nowhere else—have evolved on this isolated piece of land. Its wild beauty encompasses spectacular inland waterfalls and others that plunge into the sea, dense vegetation, and underwater caves and coral gardens. Seventy of the 235 plant species identified so far are endemic, two species of lizards, 64 of the island's 362 species of insects, and three of the 97 bird species. An endemic palm is named for Franklin D. Roosevelt, who visited the island four times. Coco Island is an important nesting site for seagulls, noddies, and boobies. Another nesting bird is the Espíritu Santo, or Holy Spirit. A small white bird, it often hovers in the air, unafraid, a few feet above a visitor's head. Its more prosaic name in English is white tern. Eleven species of shark move through the island's waters, including huge whale sharks, hammerheads, and white-tips, among 200 species of fish. Other underwater riches include 18 species of coral and 118 species of marine mollusks.

The rugged coastline of high cliffs makes access possible at only two bays, Chatham and Wafer. Inscriptions dating to the 1600s on the rocky coast at Chatham provide evidence that early sailors sought safe harbor here. The rugged terrain and dense vegetation call for caution—a tourist who became separated from her group in 1989 has never been found.

Rainfall averages 276 inches (7,000 mm) a year. The highest point is Iglesias Peak, 2,087 feet (636 km), and upper elevations are covered by cloud forest; epiphytes abound. Of volcanic origin, the island contains rocks that are 2 million years old.

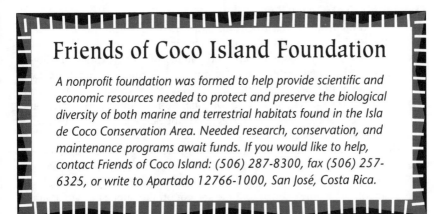

Friends of Coco Island Foundation

A nonprofit foundation was formed to help provide scientific and economic resources needed to protect and preserve the biological diversity of both marine and terrestrial habitats found in the Isla de Coco Conservation Area. Needed research, conservation, and maintenance programs await funds. If you would like to help, contact Friends of Coco Island: (506) 287-8300, fax (506) 257-6325, or write to Apartado 12766-1000, San José, Costa Rica.

A fragile environment maintains this living laboratory for the study of evolutionary processes. Introduced species, such as pigs, deer, rats, coffee, and papaya, endanger the delicate ecological balance. Fishing and increased tourism also affect this special place, as does its popularity with divers. Historically, the island's isolation minimized human impact; its inclusion in the park system is aimed at protecting it. An international commission has been set up to work for conservation of this resource, with Jean-Michel Cousteau a member. In 1997, it was named a UNESCO World Heritage Site.

A park station on the island has radio contact with the mainland. Permission is necessary for a visit. Most travelers come as part of an organized tour; private yachts must have prior permission—contact Isla del Coco Conservation Area at the above fax. No overnight facilities for visitors.

Getting There
See Chapter 4 for companies that offer diving tours; see Appendix A for a seaplane option.

COASTAL ROUTE

Two of the most visited national parks and biological reserves in the country—Manuel Antonio and Carara—are here, along with popular beaches, ranch retreats that combine beach with mountains, and small hotels and lodges that offer a full range of natural history adventures as well as delightful places simply to relax surrounded by tropical nature. From the Central Valley, follow the Inter-American Highway west of the international airport to the turnoff for Atenas and Orotina. (See Chapter 6 for a description of the Atenas area.) From Puntarenas and Liberia, head south for Puerto Caldera, Orotina, and points south.

OROTINA TO CARARA
Part of the route from Atenas to Orotina was the old Spanish trail from San José to the Pacific. The mountain road to Orotina passes through picturesque villages, farms, coffee fields, and patches of forest. Notice the "living fences." Other trees with bright blossoms on this route are the *llama del bosque*, "flame of the forest" (red flowers), and *cortesa amarilla* (yellow flowers). On the dramatic descent toward Orotina, notice almost perpendicular hillsides cleared for pastures. The terrace-like appearance is created by the horizontal trails of grazing cows.

Area attractions include Carara Biological Reserve and Iguana Park private reserve. Only about two hours from San José, Carara has become a popular day tour for natural history visitors. Seeing it with a guide is recommended. One disappointed young woman told me she got off the public bus at Carara and walked on trails without seeing anything spectacular. I think she expected the birds and animals to come out and greet her. Guides know animal territories, which trees are in fruit, and what to look for. They point out orchids that a novice would miss.

Get out binoculars for a stop near the bridge over the Tarcoles River near Carara. Crocodiles bask in the mud along its banks; birds enjoy the waters. You might see a wood stork, blue heron, or American egret. Watch for scarlet macaws flying overhead: see them between 5 and 6:30 a.m. and between 4 and 5:30 p.m. Dozens of these gorgeous red, blue, and gold members of the parrot family fly between the reserve and nighttime resting places in mangroves along the ocean. Truly these birds are a spectacular sight.

CARARA BIOLOGICAL RESERVE
Location: 56 miles (90 km) SW of San José near Tarcoles River, 16 miles (25 km) SW of Orotina.
Size: 11,614 acres (4,700 ha).
Hours: Daily 7 a.m. to 5 p.m., offseason 8 a.m. to 4 p.m.
Cost: $6.
Information/Reservations: Telephone hotline 192 (see Appendix A: Parks and Reserves Information), (506) 416-6576, fax (506) 416-7402, telephone at park (506) 383-9953.

The green forest of the Carara reserve stands tall against eroded hillsides—land whose soil, once the trees were cut, tired out quickly when turned into fields for crops or pastures for cattle. In a transition zone between the dry north Pacific and the more humid south, Carara has an average rainfall as high as 126 inches (3,200 mm) in the interior and as low as 79 inches (2,000 mm) near the coast. A large lagoon, rivers, and streams supply life-giving moisture.

Most of the reserve is primary forest, with regal giants that spread their branches in a tall canopy. Some plants that live in the trees send their roots to the ground; vines wind up trunks toward the light. Epiphytes, ferns, and palms soften the setting.

Because of lush vegetation and relative ease in seeing wildlife, Carara can be an excellent choice for a traveler's first tropical-forest experience—especially when accompanied by a naturalist guide. For example, in three hours we saw: a fiery-billed aracari, blue-gray tanager, spectacled owl, boat-billed heron, crested guan, anhinga, brown jay, white-tailed kite, wood stork, blue heron, orange-bellied trogon, roseate spoonbill, yellow-headed caracara, chestnut-mandibled toucan, dotted-winged antwren, blue-crowned motmot, great kiskadee, scarlet macaws, crocodiles, white-faced monkeys, iguanas, squirrels, leaf-cutting ants, and lizards. We didn't see the resident snakes, or the morpho butterfly, sloth, coati, agouti, peccary, porcupine, anteater, coyote, or howler or spider monkey. Perhaps you will.

In early morning and late afternoon, flocks of scarlet macaws fly overhead between the reserve and roosting sites in the mangroves. You may see them in the reserve during the day, feeding in fruiting trees. Some 300 macaws live around here.

Go first to Quebrada Bonita ranger station to pay admission and arrange for a guided walk, $15 per person for two hours. Las Aráceas Trail leaves from there; allow at least an hour for the walk through transitional evergreen forest. Laguna Meándrica Trail starts between the Tarcoles River and Quebrada Bonita, offering habitat different from the other trail. Visitors are advised not to go down to the Tarcoles River or to the lagoon on the Meándrica Trail—large crocodiles live in both. Stay on trails. No camping is allowed, but there are picnic areas, latrines, and water for day visitors.

Dry season is from December to April. Terrain is hilly and humidity is a factor—you may find yourself huffing and sweating. Elevation is 2,087 feet (636 m), and average temperature is 82°F (27.8°C). Take it easy.

Parataxonomists working with the National Biodiversity Institute collect insects at Carara. I once saw cases of insects so tiny they can barely be seen, as well as flashy butterflies and bizarre-looking beetles.

Getting There

By bus: Buses to Jacó and Quepos pass by.
By car: From San José, go through Atenas to Orotina, continuing to Carara. From Jacó, go 11 miles (17 km) north.
Other: Travel agencies offer tours, as do hotels and lodges from Guanacaste to Quepos.

IGUANA PARK, PRIVATE RESERVE

Location: 6 miles (10 km) from Orotina.
Rates: $13, including entrance, guide, and lunch.
Hours: 9 a.m. to 5 p.m., closed Monday.
Information/Reservations: (506) 240-6712, fax (506) 235-2007; e-mail *iguverde@sol.racsa.co.cr.*

This 1,000-acre (400-ha) private park is administered by the Pro Iguana Verde Foundation, whose goals include conservation and restoration of tropical forest; restoration of populations of green iguanas and, more recently, scarlet macaws; and education programs to train local communities in sustainable use of forest and wildlife.

Dagmar Werner, president of the foundation, began breeding iguanas in Costa Rica in 1988. Iguanas have traditionally been a protein source for local peoples. Here they are reproduced, raised in captivity, and released into the forest at about seven months of age. They can be harvested two years later to provide meat and leather. The philosophy is that permanent release programs guarantee perpetual use of the species as well as its survival in the wild. To date, more than 250,000 iguanas have been released.

At the visitor center, learn about this project through audiovisual and printed materials. In a garden enclosure are dozens of iguanas of various

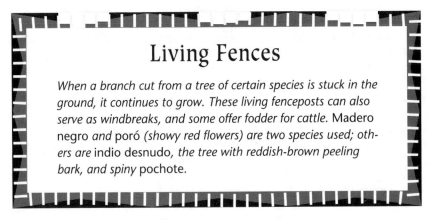

Living Fences

When a branch cut from a tree of certain species is stuck in the ground, it continues to grow. These living fenceposts can also serve as windbreaks, and some offer fodder for cattle. Madero negro *and* poró *(showy red flowers) are two species used; others are* indio desnudo, *the tree with reddish-brown peeling bark, and spiny* pochote.

sizes: a guided walk on a forest trail reveals iguanas in the wild as well as other forest creatures, including birds such as trogons, toucans, tanagers, tityras, motmots, and scarlet macaws.

The foundation branched out to do research on captive breeding of scarlet macaws in 1995, and now works in a pilot project with the Ministry of the Environment and Energy (MINAE) that has already resulted in release of macaws in the vicinity of Carara. Releases have been hatchlings from captive-bred parents that could not be reintroduced into the wild, hatchlings from confiscated eggs or baby birds, and those from nests considered high risk because of poaching or because a chick is the second or third in a nest. Parental care focuses on the first chick. At a later stage of the program, which is being closely watched as the first of its kind for Central America, the macaws will be released in areas that previously had populations of these birds.

A gift shop in the visitor center has items made locally from iguana leather, as well as posters, T-shirts, and books. The Mama Iguana restaurant features—what else?—iguana meat, though other dishes are available.

For another view of Iguana Park, join The Canopy Tour to climb into the upper layer of the forest, moving from tree to tree and platform to platform via cables. Make reservations with The Canopy Tour, telephone/fax (506) 257-5149. Their tour with transportation (from San José, Puntarenas, or Jacó), lunch, park fee, and guides is $89; without transport or lunch, $50 for adults, $35 for children.

For more information about Iguana Park, write to Fundación Pro Iguana Verde, Apartado 692-1007, San José, or contact the telephone and fax numbers given above.

Getting There
By car: At Orotina, bear left about 1,312 feet (400 m) after crossing railroad tracks (don't take the road to Jacó). When the road dead-ends, turn right for almost 2 miles (3 km) more—some signs. A memorable one-lane suspension bridge along the way is proof you're on the right road.

Where to Stay and Eat in the Orotina-Carara Area

At **Dundee Ranch Hotel and Adventure Resort,** (506) 428-8776, fax (506) 428-8096; e-mail tirolcr@sol.racsa.co.cr, horses are in, cattle are out, pastures are regenerating, forest is protected in a nature reserve, and guests have some unusual activities to choose from. A working horse ranch and resort, Dundee offers horseback riding tours, including one in the Valley of the Monkeys; birding in the forest and nearby lagoons; and hiking and photography in its own forest reserve in Machuca River Canyon. Guests can also visit the reserve via a safari in Cricket (a tractor tram). See the tropical landscape from an ultralight plane, sign up for a workshop on pre-Columbian pottery, or take a tour to nearby Orotina.

Back at the ranch, swim in the pool next to the large restaurant bar. A wooden walkway leads to a small conference room/bird observation point in a shallow lagoon. Colorful northern jacanas, egrets, and black-bellied whistling ducks enjoyed the water when I was there. The hotel has two bird lists: one for those observed at the ranch; one for birds at nearby estuaries. Lists give scientific, English, and Spanish names. At Dundee you may see crested caracaras, hummingbirds, trogons, scarlet macaws, kingfishers, hawks, and cuckoos. Other animals include monkeys, crocodiles, coatis, colorful frogs, anteaters, and lots of butterflies, including the blue morpho.

The 23 bright, comfortable rooms have red clay tile floors, colorful bedspreads, big closets, table and chairs, air conditioning and ceiling fans, and TV. Single or double $70, including breakfast.

Transportation from San José is $15 each. By car, access is west from Orotina on a back road; or, from Puntarenas and Caldera, take the turnoff to Cascajal and follow signs. Dundee is associated with Hotel Chalet Tirol in the Central Valley.

Hotel Villa Lapas, (506) 220-2412, (506) 663-0811, fax (506) 232-9597, (506) 663-1516; e-mail fiesta@sol.racsa.co.cr, is next door to Carara on a former cattle ranch whose pastures have been returning to forest for more than ten years. The modern, 48-room hotel is in forest along the Tarcolitos River. A flock of scarlet macaws may squawk in a nearby tree as you eat in the pretty, open-air dining room, and a toucan will probably drop by. One birder spotted more than 75 species of birds in 30 minutes.

Large rooms with high ceilings face the river. Features include a desk with storage drawers and ample closet; some rooms have ceiling fans, some air conditioning. There is a gift shop, library, TV and video room, swimming pool, and mini golf.

A guided three-hour walk in the Villa Lapa forest is on well-maintained trails. An optional trek goes to a nearby spectacular three-tiered waterfall. Guests enjoy the butterfly garden, with species such as the morpho, monarchs, zebras, and "crackers," which get their name from the sound they make. Tours to Carara, five minutes north, and to Manuel Antonio, 90 minutes away, are available. Call about day visits.

Service and food are good in the dining room, also open to the public. Rates are inclusive, covering lodging, meals, taxes, drinks, some activities, and taxes: single $150, double $100 per person.

Rancho Oropendola, telephone/fax (506) 428-8600, is at San Mateo, just before Orotina. Five cabins are spaced around a pretty tropical garden with a river out back. Ceiling fans keep the comfortable rooms cool; one has air conditioning. Beds with orthopedic mattresses are double, queen-, or king-size. Rooms $45; suites, with living area and large screened in porch, from $55. Owner/manager Ted Woodford is proud of the swimming pool; water is cleaned by the system used in space shuttles—no chlorine needed. Visit the gold mine at nearby Desmonte, where you can enjoy a waterfall, pools, and rocks, or enter the mine itself. Rancho Oropendola is 20 minutes from Carara, near Iguana Park.

Tarcol Lodge, telephone/fax (506) 267-7138, U.S. number (800) 593-3305, Tarcoles near Carara, is geared to birders and naturalists. At high tide, the five-bedroom, two-bath lodge at the mouth of the Tarcoles River is almost surrounded by water. At low tide, guests may see as many as 2,000 birds on the sand flats. Rooms in the 30-year-old, two-story house are simply furnished; $99 includes round trip from San José, lodging, meals, guiding, and taxes—four-day minimum if lodge provides transportation. Good food.

Through binoculars in the evening, see 30 to 40 pairs of scarlet macaws in trees across the river. Possible tours include Carara, horseback riding on the beach, turtle-watching at Playa Hermosa, or an estuary trip. Some tours are included in your stay, depending on its length. Owners of Tarcol Lodge, the Erbs, also have the private nature reserve Rancho Naturalista near Turrialba (see Chapter 6). Reservations necessary.

THE COAST SOUTH TO QUEPOS

From Carara, the road drops to the coastal lowlands with tantalizing views of the Pacific. **Jacó** is the only town of any size along this stretch; its beach is popular with surfers and weekenders from the Central Valley. For a town of 3,128, Jacó seems to have a lot of activity. I prefer the less-crowded southern end of town. *Please read the tips on water safety; riptides are not uncommon.*

South of Jacó the highway passes through large cattle ranches and then waving fields of rice; near Parrita, groves of African palm appear. Be alert for one-lane bridges. Roadside signs along the way advertise lodging on beaches such as Playa Hermosa (a favorite with surfers and a sea-turtle nesting site), Esterillos beach, and Palo Seco.

Tour Agency
J.D.'s Watersports, San José (506) 257-3857, fax (506) 256-6391; Punta Leona (506) 669-0511, fax (506) 661-1414; e-mail PHoyman@aol.com; Web

site www.centralamerica.com/cr/tours/jd.htm; U.S. number (970) 356-1028, fax (970) 352-6324, based at Punta Leona 10 miles (16 km) north of Jacó. The company offers Jungle River Cruises on the Tarcoles and through a mangrove estuary, with chances of seeing crocodiles, scarlet macaws, parrots, roseate spoonbills, herons, pelicans, ibis, and Jesus Christ lizards. No, this group doesn't feed crocodiles to lure them close to the boat. The tour includes lunch at the company's riverside farm and a swim in the pool. Day trip from San José is $79, $49 if you arrive on your own. Take a sunset cruise for $30.

A PADI-certified center, J.D.'s offers certification courses; diving trips for beginners and experts are $65 half-day, including two tanks, weights, and guide. Owner Pat Hoyman recommends January and February as the best months for viewing giant mantas and, for the adventurous, a white-tip shark dive.

Ask about a multiday package that includes Arenal and Poás Volcanoes as well as Punta Leona, Jungle River Cruise, a day of snorkeling, and lodging. Sportfishing is $150 per person; packages available. Equipment rental includes kayaks, boogie boards, and snorkeling and scuba gear.

Where to Stay and Eat on the South Coast

Hotel Club del Mar, telephone/fax (506) 643-3194; Web site www.jacobeach .com, is tucked away on a peaceful cove at the south end of Jacó Beach. Light, nicely furnished rooms nestle among trees and tropical gardens, with the Pacific steps away. The view of the surf and headland is fantastic. The 18 rooms offer a cool, soft respite from the coastal sun—all have ceiling fans, some have air conditioning. Carved wooden lintels, floor-to-ceiling louvered doors, rattan furniture with deep cushions, and balconies or porches are among attractive features of superior rooms. Standard and economy rooms have equipped kitchenettes and colorful cushioned furniture. Doubles are $90 for superior rooms, $77 for standard, $64 for economy, taxes included. Prefer no credit cards. There is a sparkling swimming pool and a library.

Philip and Marilyn Edwardes, gracious owners and hosts, along with son Simon, help guests with custom trips. The hotel offers turtle walks during egg-laying season (August 15 to October 15), a horseback trip into forested mountains with a member of the Madrigal family, a hidden-waterfall picnic, massages, snorkeling (with guide), surf lessons, and family fishing. As agent for Fantasy Tours, Club del Mar arranges volcano and park visits, boat trips, and rafting. If you can't stay at Club del Mar, treat yourself to a gourmet meal at its Las Sandalias restaurant.

Punta Leona Hotel and Club, San José (506) 231-3131, fax (506) 232-0791; Punta Leona (506) 661-1414; e-mail puntaleona@sol.racsa.co.cr; Web site www.Amerisol.com/costarica/lodging/leona.html, is set amid 740 acres (300 ha) of forest and beach. From the entrance on the highway, a 2.5 mile (4 km) drive passes through exquisite forest. Some of Punta Leona's forest is now a government-recognized private wildlife refuge. This is scarlet macaw country—artificial nests placed here protect chicks from nest-robbers who sell macaws on the black market, with the goal of increasing numbers of these beautiful birds in the wild.

Rooms, chalets, bungalows, and condos—total of 180 rooms—offer lodging options. At pretty Selvamar sector, set among the trees, a single room is $72; double, $82. Chalets are $80 to $125. A shuttle from these lodging areas goes to white-sand beaches on either side of the rocky outcrop known as Punta Leona and to restaurants.

The newest development, Leona Mar Condominium Hotel, stands on a cliff above the ocean: gorgeous views of the Pacific from rooms and pool. Steps lead to the white sands of Playa

Club del Mar on Jacó Beach

Blanca. Units have furnished kitchens open to a living area. There's cable TV, air-conditioning, roomy bedroom, washer and dryer, from $135 for up to four. When I stayed, a coati appeared on the terrace regularly at breakfast time, parrots flew overhead, and iguanas were at home on the beach.

The complex has three pools, miles of nature trails, three restaurants, tennis and basketball courts, game room, small store, and gift shop. Equipment rental for water sports is available, as is horseback riding. Visit the on-site water sports company as well as the tour company, which arranges visits to Carara, volcanoes, and parks.

Villa Caletas, (506) 257-3653, fax (506) 222-2059; e-mail caletas@ mail.ticonet.co.cr, is 2 miles (3 km) south of Punta Leona, 56 miles (100 km) southwest of San José, and 7 miles (11 km) south of Carara. More than 1,000 feet (350 m) above the sea, the hotel has a commanding view of coastline from the Nicoya Peninsula to Jacó. Tones of French colonial and Victorian architecture lend distinction. The main building has two restaurants, bar, elegant hallways and conversation areas, and eight guest rooms with queen or twin beds, single or double $130.

Twenty villas are tucked among tropical gardens down the slope, each with bedroom, living room with sofa bed, and private terrace, from $160. Art and antiques decorate rooms and villas, almost all with sea views. No telephones or TVs here. Fans and sea breezes quietly cool. Fixed prices for the breakfast buffet and lunch and dinner (a la carte).

The swimming pool seems to float on the edge of forever. A small Greek-style amphitheater, which hangs on the side of the cliff—not for those with a

African Palm

In 1945, the Bananera Company started the first commercial palm plantation between Parrita and Quepos, replacing banana plantations that had been badly affected by Panama disease. By 1965, African palm plantations reached as far south as Golfito. Palm oil is used not only for fat, margarine, and cooking oil, but also in soaps and perfumes.

fear of heights—is the site of concerts and weddings. Sunsets and scarlet macaw fly-bys are spectacular. The property includes 250 acres of forest (100 ha), so wildlife is around, especially birds and small mammals. Beach transfers provided, and trips are arranged to Manuel Antonio, Carara, Tortuga Island, and Manantial Waterfalls. Water sports, horseback riding, and bicycle riding are options. Villa Caletas is affiliated with Small Distinctive Hotels of Costa Rica.

QUEPOS AND MANUEL ANTONIO

Though Manuel Antonio National Park brings thousands of visitors a year to the area, it is not the only attraction. Travelers can mountain bike, horseback ride, take off on jungle jaunts or estuary tours, waterski, parasail, snorkel, or sea kayak; sportfishers discovered the rich waters here years ago. Don't let the activities crowd out peaceful time for conversations with nature.

Hotels, restaurants, and tourism-related businesses are along the hilly 5 miles (7 km) between Quepos and Manuel Antonio. Though a proliferation of small *sodas*, as the road nears the park, detracts from the beauty of place and raises questions about pollution, Manuel Antonio park itself continues to be a small jewel. Visitors must wade across an estuary to reach the entrance, an adventurous introduction to a special experience. Frequent, inexpensive bus service between Quepos and Manuel Antonio facilitates getting around. Hotels have considerably reduced rates during "winter" months of May to November.

Quepos was named for the Quepo Indians. Quepo artifacts often turn up in surrounding pastures and fields. Mogote Island, a sheer-sided land with a crown of thick vegetation, visible from Cathedral Point in Manuel Antonio National Park, was Quepo ceremonial ground. Today Quepos is the center of an agricultural area where cattle are raised, and rice, beans, sorghum, African palm, papayas, and mangoes are grown. A bustling town, it has lots of small shops that serve area residents as well as tourists with a population of 13,833; the town is 110 miles (177 km) southwest of San José.

Things to See and Do

Buena Nota gift shop, telephone/fax (506) 777-1002; e-mail buennota@sol
.racsa.co.cr, on the road to Manuel Antonio between Karahé and Piscis Hotels,
has clothing and beachwear designed by owner Anita Myketuk, pottery, jewelry, film and batteries, handcrafted wooden items, books, maps, newspapers,
and more. It serves as an informal information center for the area; Anita answers questions with amazing patience. She and husband Donald, who have
lived here almost 24 years, have worked hard on beach safety and environmental issues. Donald does talks on area history and archaeology by prior request.
La Buena Nota is open from 8 a.m. to 7 p.m. daily.

Ask about availability of the upstairs two-bedroom apartments ($100
per night) or two fully furnished houses for rent past the Mariposa Hotel—
gorgeous views of Cathedral Point, the beach, and forest. The one-bedroom
is $400 per week; the two-bedroom, with a front deck where one could sit for
a few years, is $600.

Jardín Gaia, (506) 777-0535, telephone/fax (506) 777-1004; e-mail wildlife
@cariari.ucr.ac.cr, near Manuel Antonio is a wildlife rescue center that receives animals confiscated by wildlife officials as well as injured animals; it
attempts to rehabilitate them for release in the wild. Begun by Dario Castel-
franco in 1991, the center has taken in more than 400 birds and 100 other
animals, some on the endangered list. Visitors receive a guided tour with explanations of ongoing research and education projects and see the fauna in
residence at the time: perhaps a crocodile, a squirrel, howler or white-faced
monkey, sloth, macaw, opossum, coati, scarlet macaw, toucan, or hummingbird. The center is largely supported by donations (both funds and volunteers who come from around the world), with some reimbursement for food
and medicine for animals brought by wildlife officials. Guided walks at 11
a.m., 2 p.m., 4 p.m., $5 for adults, children up to 12 free.

La Botánica, Calle 5, telephone/fax (506) 777-1223, sells organically
grown spices raised on the family farm of owner María Ester Bekins. She
has medicinal herbs and does consultations. The spices, marketed under the
Especias Ceilán label, make good gifts. Open 8 a.m. to 5 p.m. Monday through
Friday, closed Sunday. María Ester usually offers a refreshing glass of mint tea.
Ask about agroecological tour of spice farm and wildlife refuge, $15.

Tour Companies

Iguana Tours, in Quepos next to the soccer field, telephone/fax (506) 777-
1262; e-mail iguana@sol.racsa.co.cr, offers white-water rafting on the Parrita
River (class II–III during rainy season) $70. From April to November, raft
the Naranjo River (class III–IV) with rapids like Robin Hood and Twister,
$55. Sea kayak at Damas Island to explore mangrove and see wildlife, $65; a
coastal trip passes near islands where boobies and frigates nest, $65.

A mangrove boat tour is another option, $55 including lunch. A half-day dolphin-watch boat tour cruises by caves, limestone cliffs, and blowholes, with a chance to encounter dolphins, turtles, and sea birds beyond offshore islands, $45. For hiking, choose a guided walk at Rainmaker, north of Quepos, $39, or accompany a nature guide in Manuel Antonio on a two-hour walk—$35 includes entrance fee, guide, and hotel transfer.

Equus Stables, (506) 777-0001, between Quepos and Manuel Antonio, has guided horseback tours. Its beautiful stables make it a kind of horse heaven.

Lynch Tourist Service, telephone/fax (506) 777-0161, (506)-777-1170; telephone (506) 777-1571; e-mail lyntur@sol.racsa.co.cr, in downtown Quepos offers a range of eco-adventure tours, including bird-watching, rafting, and horseback tours. A four-hour Manuel Antonio park tour is $45. Guides carry spotting scopes for close-up looks at wildlife. A horseback ride to a waterfall is $65. Lynch offers a water taxi to Drake Bay, crossing in three hours: $60 one way, round trip $99. Lynch is a SANSA and Travelair ticket agent.

Getting There
By bus: Express buses from San José, about 3½ hours. Get off at Quepos and make return-trip reservations if continuing on to Manuel Antonio. Also buses from Puntarenas and San Isidro de El General.
By car: About 3½ hours southwest of San José via Orotina and Jacó.
By air: Several daily flights on Travelair and SANSA, 30-minute flights. Car rental available.

MANUEL ANTONIO NATIONAL PARK
Location: 4 miles (7 km) S of Quepos.
Size: 1,687 acres (683 ha) of land; 135,905 acres (55,000 ha) marine habitat.
Hours: 7 a.m. to 5 p.m., closed Monday.
Cost: $6.
Information/Reservations: Telephone hotline 192 (see Appendix A: Parks and Reserves Information), (506) 777-0644, fax (506) 777-0654.
White-faced monkeys leap from tree to tree along the beach in dazzling displays of aerial skill. Shyer squirrel monkeys, an endemic subspecies found only in this area, peek from behind leaves along trails. Slow-moving sloths give a lazy look at visitors from their high vantage points. I had my first close-up look at a coati and an agouti in the wild on the forest trail in Manuel Antonio. Large iguanas rustle through leaves on the forest floor or sun themselves on beach logs.

The warm Pacific waters are home to a variety of marine life; snorkelers, divers, and even watchers at tide pools see brightly colored fish. Don't miss the tiny bright-blue ones in pools among rocks at the western end of Manuel Antonio Beach. Whales pass by, and dolphins swim offshore. There are 10 species of sponge, 17 of algae, 78 of fish, 19 of coral, and 24 of crustaceans.

Researchers have identified some 200 species of birds and 109 species of

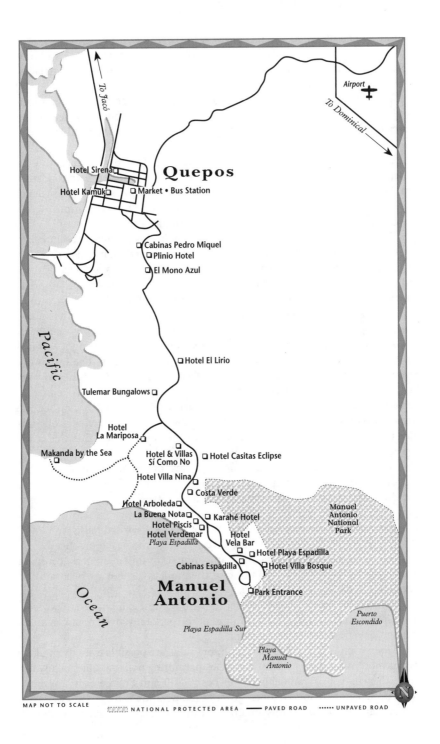

To Jacó

To Dominical

Airport

Hotel Sirena
Quepos
Hotel Kamuk
Market • Bus Station

Pacific

Cabinas Pedro Miquel
Plinio Hotel
El Mono Azul

Hotel El Lirio

Tulemar Bungalows

Hotel
La Mariposa
Makanda by the Sea
Hotel & Villas
Sí Como No
Hotel Casitas Eclipse
Hotel Villa Nina
Costa Verde
Hotel Arboleda
La Buena Nota
Hotel Piscis
Hotel Verdemar
Playa Espadilla
Karahé Hotel
Hotel
Vela Bar
Hotel Playa Espadilla
Cabinas Espadilla
Hotel Villa Bosque
Park Entrance

Manuel
Antonio
National
Park

Ocean

**Manuel
Antonio**

*Puerto
Escondido*

Playa Espadilla Sur

*Playa
Manuel
Antonio*

N

MAP NOT TO SCALE   NATIONAL PROTECTED AREA   PAVED ROAD   UNPAVED ROAD mammals, half of which are bats rarely seen by visitors. Among marine birds are brown pelicans, magnificent frigate birds, and brown boobies. Land birds include parrots, Baird's trogons, green kingfishers, gray-headed chachalacas, and golden-masked tanagers.

The fun begins by wading across an estuary to the park entrance; water can be waist-high on a short adult at high tide, or barely cover the feet at low. Carry in what you want to eat or drink; cold drinks are now available inside.

Once inside the park, go along a wide trail through tall forest or walk along South Espadilla Beach. Toward the far end of the beach, enter the forest and cross over to gentler Manuel Antonio Beach or take a path to Cathedral Point, which separates the two beaches. From there, see Mogote Island rising up sharply from the sea, its high cliffs crowned with vegetation. Both Mogote and Cathedral Point are prehistoric Indian sites.

These two white-sand beaches are lined with lush vegetation almost to the high-water line. The clear waters are warm. Espadilla is steeper, with bigger waves. Farther down a trail through low mountains is Puerto Escondido, rockier and not as kind to the feet. Its beach disappears at high tide; check with rangers before you start out. Guided walks to Puerto Escondido and a lookout point are limited to 15 per group. Allow time for a leisurely walk along short Perezoso Trail, named for the sloths frequently seen here.

At Manuel Antonio Beach, face the sea and look at the far right end near the rocks for a prehistoric turtle-trap built by Quepo Indians. The trap is a semicircular rock barrier that forms a pool at the beach's edge. Since low and high tides vary about 11 feet (3.4 m) here, some of the female turtles that came in over the rock wall at high tide to nest would be caught when the tide went out and water level dropped below the barrier. Both green and olive ridley turtles lay eggs here, though not in mass nestings. At low tide this is also a great place to see tiny tropical fish.

In addition to primary and secondary forest and beaches, there are marshes, a mangrove swamp, lagoons, and woodland. Warning signs point out the manzanillo trees along the beach; their leaves, bark, and apple-like fruit secrete a toxic white latex that stings the skin.

Even though Manuel Antonio is one of the most-visited parks, in rainy season it is sometimes possible in midweek to have the beach practically to yourself. To protect both vegetation and animals in this small park, camping is no longer allowed. Please do not feed the monkeys; some are becoming aggressive because of this practice.

New bathrooms and a visitor center with modest exhibits are in place now. If you wish a guided walk, inquire at the park entrance about certified local guides, trained by park personnel.

Dry season is December to March, but rains are possible even then; in wetter months mornings are usually clear, permitting hours of quiet enjoyment on the beach. Annual rainfall is 150 inches (3,800 mm); rainiest months are August, September, and October. Average temperature is 81°F (27°C).

A major concern for this small, beautiful park is that owners of almost half of the park have never been paid. Without payment, the government legally cannot expropriate land. Land prices have skyrocketed since 1972 when the park was created, and owners' patience is wearing thin. Donations designated to help purchase the land can be directed to the National Parks Foundation in Costa Rica or through The Nature Conservancy in the United States.

Getting There
By bus: Daily express buses between San José and Manuel Antonio, local Quepos–Manuel Antonio bus makes frequent runs.
By car: From Quepos, continue on paved road to the park.
By air: Daily scheduled flights from San José to nearby Quepos.

Where to Stay in Quepos
Two-story **Hotel Sirena,** telephone/fax (506) 777-0165, has 14 double rooms, air conditioning, private bath. Pleasant rooms are simply furnished and open onto a courtyard with a pool and bar/restaurant. Single $45, double $50, breakfast and taxes included. Conservation-minded local owners have put together interesting tours. On the $55 Savegre River horseback venture, travelers see crocodiles, white-face monkeys, and among 150 species of birds, as well as habitats that include mangrove, primary forest, beach, and river. A look at local agriculture—cattle, rice, and African palm—is included. Two-night, three-day packages include horseback riding, park tour, bilingual guide, lodging, and breakfasts, $158; or horseback riding and a tour in a yacht equipped for fishing and diving, $224.

Kamuk Hotel, (506) 777-0379, fax (506) 777-0258, on the main street in front of the Pacific has 28 rooms; single or double $45 without balcony, $56 with balcony. Each tastefully furnished room is air conditioned and has TV and telephone. A third-floor restaurant/bar offers sunset views, a ground-floor coffee shop allows people-watching. New swimming pool.

Where to Stay between Quepos and Manuel Antonio
(Listed according to rates—see map for locations)
Tulemar Bungalows, telephone (506) 777-0580, fax (506) 777-1579; e-mail tulemar@sol.racsa.co.cr, from the top of the hill, its octagonal roofs seem to hover among trees like visiting spacecraft. Each of the 14 spacious bungalows is spaced for maximum privacy and dynamite views of the blue Pacific. Half of the walls in each are full-length glass, with sliding screened windows. High wooden ceiling beams radiate out from a bubble skylight. Peach and blue are the colors in sofas in the large living area, comforters on the two double beds, and upholstered wooden chairs at the low breakfast bar. Each has air conditioning and ceiling fans, TV and VCR, and telephone. The kitchen has microwave, cooktop stove, and refrigerator. Double $185, breakfast included, $10 per person extra.

Nature trails lead past small waterfalls on 33 acres (13 ha) of lush forest and gardens. Through the forest below is an intimate, secluded beach, where I watched squirrel monkeys jump from tree to tree. Birds were everywhere. Daily afternoon guided nature tours in this beautiful private reserve are open to guests and nonguests, $25; on Mondays, when the park is closed, morning tours are added. An infinity-type pool has a forest setting.

Kayaks are free to guests. Tours include horseback riding, sportfishing, snorkeling, rafting, and a visit to Manuel Antonio Park.

Hotel & Villas Si Como No, (506) 777-0777, (506) 777-1250, fax (506) 777-1093; e-mail sicomono@sol.racsa.co.cr; Web site www.sicomono.com, is an experience. From the swimming pool with its waterslide and waterfall-fed Jacuzzi to a laser theater/conference center and nature trails through forested property, Si Como No reveals thoughtful planning by owner Jim Damalas. Energy-efficient air conditioners (remote-controlled), a water management system that processes gray waters for landscaping and turns hotel sewage into fertilizer, and insulated roofs and windows that conserve energy are noteworthy features.

Each suite has unobstructed views of forest, sea, and sunsets. Deluxe suites have king-size beds, a sitting room or extra bed, and a kitchen or wet bar, $190. Suites, some split-level, have minibars, king or queen beds, and balconies, $170. Junior suites with kitchens or minibars are $150. All have ceiling fans and air conditioning. Built-in sofas have brightly colored cushions—purples, reds, and oranges. Accents of cane adorn cabinets and furniture. Rates are double occupancy and include breakfast; children under 12 free.

The large atrium lobby incorporates tall trees which took root long before Si Como No was even a dream. A poolside snack bar is the place for breakfast and light lunches; there is a more formal dining room.

At **Hotel La Mariposa,** (506) 777-0355, fax (506) 777-0050; e-mail htlmariposa@msm.com; U.S. number (800) 416-2747, time seems suspended. Maybe it's the view of forest, sea, and white-sand beach curving out to Cathedral Point. Villas, refined in their simplicity and tasteful decor, are woven into the greenery of the hillside: Spanish red-tile roofs, white walls, bright colors in art and fabrics, bathrooms that incorporate tropical gardens, big windows, ceiling fans and air conditioning. The split-level villas have comfortable living rooms, large bedrooms, telephones, and two terraces, $180. One-level deluxe rooms, some with Jacuzzi tub, have private balconies, $140. Standard rooms are on the second floor of the main building, some with ocean view, $120. Rates are single or double occupancy and include breakfast and shuttles to airport and park. No children under 12.

The restaurant serves international cuisine (open to public, reservations December to April). A full meal plan for guests is $35 per night.

Makanda by the Sea, (506) 777-0442, fax (506) 777-1032; e-mail makanda@sol.racsa.co.cr; Web site www.makanda.com, is as elegant as its

Manuel Antonio Park from Hotel La Mariposa

name. Located about halfway between Quepos and Manuel Antonio, it is surrounded by tall forest. Squirrel monkeys like it here, and sloths come to call. The secluded beach is down a short trail through the trees. Each of seven studios and villas has an ocean view. Colorful purples and greens contrast with slate-gray tile. Louvered doors open up rooms to the natural world. Cushiony sofas, king- or queen-size beds gracefully draped with mosquito netting, kitchenettes or full kitchens, ceiling fans (one with air conditioning), reading lamps, split-level rooms, balconies or terraces, hammocks and lounge chairs, individual Japanese gardens—these are some of the features. The large "infinity" pool and Jacuzzi are set in the forest. Peace is palpable. Studios $125, villas $170. No credit cards; no children under 16. Turn right on the dirt road after Barba Roja Restaurant.

At **Hotel Casitas Eclipse,** telephone/fax (506) 777-0408, (506) 777-1738, dazzling white walls of Mediterranean-style villas stand out against the forest's green. Light and white furnishings inside contrast with dark-tile floors and rugs in the 25 suites and rooms. White columns and drapes separate living area from bedroom in first-floor suites, each with a kitchenette. Second-floor rooms with wood ceilings are large and comfortably furnished, private balcony. Each has telephone, refrigerator, ceiling fan, air conditioning and private entrance. Rooms $91, suites $119, double occupancy, breakfast included. *Casitas* for up to five, with kitchenette, are $200.

Three pretty blue pools are surrounded by clay tile lounge areas. A chef from St. Tropez presides over the restaurant. Tropical gardens include fruit trees that attract wildlife—the property is backed by Manuel Antonio park.

Hotel Arboleda, (506) 777-1056, telephone/fax (506) 777-0092, has 32 rooms plus two family units with kitchenettes, living area, and two bedrooms, built on a hillside sloping to the beach; plus two restaurants, a pool, and gift shop. Kayak rental is $10 per hour, a guided tour to Manuel Antonio is $40, and the hotel offers a half-day Damas Island tour. Beds are large and long for king-size guests. Some rooms are in a two-story building, others in bungalows. Single or double air-conditioned rooms $95; rooms with fans, $85. Airport pickup available.

The Barahonas, owners of Arboleda, have rustic cabins at the mouth of the Naranjo River for researchers or those interested in helping protect nesting turtles. Cabins have no electricity or hot water.

Costa Verde, (506) 777-0584, fax (506) 777-0560; e-mail costaver@sol. racsa.co.cr; Web site www.costaverde.co.cr; U.S. number (888) 412-3800, has a special feeling about it: wide tiled balconies with classy leather rocking chairs; terraces; gardens; big, sliding wood-framed glass doors; tití monkeys moving through the trees; and a panoramic view of forest, sea, and Cathedral Point. The openness of the 46 rooms built on hillsides above Manuel Antonio connects them with the forest just outside the door. All have kitchenettes and ceiling fans; 16 have a Jacuzzi and air conditioning. Superior rooms have a king and double bed, $90 single or double; standard rooms have double and twin beds, $65.

One restaurant serves lighter fare, while the original restaurant has a full menu—good food attractively presented. At 4 p.m., come for Monkey Hour. Relax with camera and a drink while you wait for squirrel monkeys to drop by. Bring camera and binoculars to breakfast, for that matter—a sloth rested in an eye-level treetop not 10 feet (3 m) from the open-air dining room the last time I was there.

Two pools with ample sun decks are surrounded by lush vegetation. Costa Verde's own 30 acres (19 ha) of forest reserve form part of a corridor for wildlife, with a 2-mile (3 km) nature trail open to guests—guided tours available. Other tours include a guided park walk, horseback tour, rafting, and an estuary boat trip. Costa Verde rents kayaks by the hour and offers guided kayak tours and a mangrove tour. This Costa Verde is affiliated with Costa Verde Inn in Escazú, outside San José.

At **Hotel Verdemar,** (506) 777-1805, fax (506) 777-1311; e-mail verdemar @sol.racsa.co.cr, on Playa Espadilla in Manuel Antonio, rooms and pool have a forest setting with ocean views from the pool deck. Deep-yellow walls are accented at the ceiling with coral borders that feature turquoise iguana motifs—turquoise-colored doors and drapes unite it all beautifully. Rooms feature one or two queen beds, most have kitchenettes: $65 to $80. A raised walkway to the beach minimizes disturbance to plants and animals. At least once a day, squirrel monkeys play in trees above the walkway. Verdemar has no restaurant, but at least 10 are a short walk away.

Karahé Hotel, (506) 777-0170, fax (506) 777-1075; e-mail karahe@ns
.goldnet.co.cr; Web site www.goldnet.co.cr/karahe/, has 16 air conditioned
junior suites in a two-story building near the beach. Rooms, with large windows and pretty quilted bedspreads, open onto balconies or terraces that
overlook an attractive pool and whirlpool with the sea beyond, $80. Nine
riverstone villas involve steps up through pretty gardens. Each has a private
porch, kitchenette with refrigerator (no stove), louvered screened windows in
a large, nicely furnished room, $50. Eight rooms tucked away in gardens up
a hillside are $70. Breakfast is included.

Plinio Hotel, (506) 777-0055, fax (506) 777-0558; e-mail plinio@sol.racsa
.co.cr, attracts people from all over the world. It's the kind of friendly place
where you hear, "If you're ever in Sweden, look me up." The restaurant is a
favorite with locals and visitors alike, cooking with a European flair. Accommodations vary. Jungle House has a king-size bed, living area, kitchen facilities, a loft with queen-size bed and a deck, $75. Three-story family suites
feature a rooftop sun deck, big living room, balcony, beds, and sofa beds,
$120 for four. There are two-story ocean-view studio suites for $75 and
rooms from $60 to $65, double occupancy. Rates include breakfast and
taxes. All units have ceiling fans or air conditioning.

Rooms overlook a swimming pool and small poolside restaurant. Plinio
also has 9 miles (15 km) of nature trails through its forested mountain slope,
one that leads to a 60-foot (18-m) wooden outlook tower with canopy-level
views; on clear days see the Talamancas, Dominical, and Nicoya Peninsula.
Isolde and Roger are wonderful hosts who invite you to experience the
canopy tower whether you stay here or not. Afterwards, drop by the restaurant and order a natural *piña* (pineapple) drink or a banana daiquiri. Plinio
Hotel is a mile (1.5 km) south of Quepos.

Hotel Villa Bosque, (506) 777-0463, (506) 777-1152, fax (506) 777-0401,
has 16 rooms with terraces, air conditioning and ceiling fans, and carved
wooden doors with palm motifs. Single $60, double $70, taxes included.
Guests enjoy the attractive open-air restaurant and swimming pool. A bilingual local guide leads four-hour tours to the park, $30.

Hotel Playa Espadilla, telephone/fax (506) 777-0903; e-mail spadilla@sol
.racsa.co.cr, has its own 22-acre (9-ha) private wildlife refuge where guests
can enjoy flora and fauna of the central Pacific region. The 18 pleasant, air-
conditioned rooms are near the park entrance. There's a tropical bar and
swimming pool. Single $65, double $70.

Hotel El Lirio, telephone/fax (506) 777-0403, has nine rooms, some with a
Southwestern United States flavor: rough-plastered white walls, tile floors,
and a splash of color from the bedspreads. Rooms are large, with queen-size
beds and ceiling fans. Four are in the two-story house next to the road; five

are across a pretty garden where orchids bloom; double $55, light breakfast and taxes included. A garden breakfast gazebo restaurant is next to the swimming pool.

Hotel Villa Nina, (506) 777-1628, fax (506) 777-1497; e-mail villanina@sol .racsa.co.cr, has eight rooms tucked away in a charming pink multistory building, each with its own decorator touches. Three are air conditioned with queen beds, a refrigerator, and private balcony, $65. Three have ceiling fans, standard beds, and views of the sea from balconies; the two nearest the road have ceiling fans, standard beds, and semiprivate balconies, $53. All have coffeemakers; breakfast included. A rooftop sun deck is next to a thatched, open-air bar; tropical foliage surrounds the pool. There's even an icemaking machine. Owned and operated by a Costa Rican family, the hotel is friendly and comfortable.

Cabinas Espadilla, telephone/fax (506) 777-0416; e-mail spadilla@sol .racsa.co.cr, has 18 rooms, some air conditioned. Those with ceiling fans also have equipped kitchenettes. Double $40, taxes included.

El Mono Azul de Manuel Antonio, (506) 777-1548, telephone/fax (506) 777-1954; e-mail monoazul@sol.racsa.co.cr, is an eight-room hotel with a natural-foods restaurant open to the public. Some rooms have air conditioning. There is a sparkling pool (candlelight dinners beside it), and nightly movies—the first to arrive gets to choose the film. The restaurant features salads, pizza, hamburgers, fish, pastas, and pastries—all baking done on the premises. Doubles $35 to $45, breakfast included. (VISA only accepted.)

Hotel Vela Bar, (506) 777-0413, fax (506) 777-1071; e-mail velabar@ maqbeach.com; Web site www.maqbeach.com, adjoins Manuel Antonio. Ten rooms with fans have balconies or terraces, furnished with hammocks, open onto a pretty tropical garden: singles $20 to $57, doubles $25 to $48, taxes included. A one-bedroom *casita* for up to three is $63; a one-bedroom apartment for two is $45, with fan, refrigerator, and stove. A local bilingual guide leads a morning park tour, $30 including park fee.

Cabinas Pedro Miguel, telephone/fax (506) 777-0035; Web site www .asstcard.co.cr, is a family affair, where hosts say people enter as strangers and leave as friends. Each of the 14 rustic, forest-surrounded rooms is different, some with hot water, all clean and simply furnished. There is a small pool, and the open-air restaurant has an unusual twist at dinnertime: salads and meats are set out, and guests cook their own meat over a long grill. The restaurant is open to the public, so drop by about 6 p.m. to join in the fun. Doubles $26 to $45; a cabin with kitchen is $70 for up to five.

Hotel Piscis, (506) 777-0046, has 18 modest rooms. Older ones are a bit dark, opening onto a long shaded porch, but immaculate, with fresh flowers on the table; newer rooms are brighter. All have fans. Double with private bath $30, shared bath $20, private bath and refrigerator $40, taxes included. No credit cards. Small restaurant.

Where to Eat from Quepos to Manuel Antonio

Barba Roja has been the place to eat for years—shrimp, lobster, steak. Quiet atmosphere with a nice view and good service. Open Tuesday to Sunday 7 a.m. to 10 p.m., Monday 4 to 10 p.m.

Look for **Café Milagro** as you enter Quepos; open daily 6 a.m. to 10 p.m. in high season, fewer hours in low season. Coffee is roasted on-site daily. Get pastries along with iced coffee, espresso, or cappuccino—brownies to die for. A small gift area has pottery made in Costa Rica.

El Gran Escape faces the beach in downtown Quepos; open 7 a.m. to 10 p.m., closed Tuesday. Menu includes Mexican food (fajitas, tacos), seafood, sandwiches (burgers, club sandwiches), black bean soup, and lots more.

Plinio Hotel's restaurant between Quepos and Manuel Antonio is a favorite: nice atmosphere and consistently excellent food from appetizers to desserts, specializing in Italian/German cuisine.

Karolas, open 7 a.m. to 10 p.m. daily, has full breakfasts (including banana pancakes or *huevos rancheros*), light lunches, and dinner that includes dishes from enchiladas and chicken cacciatore to fish. Try the chocolate macadamia nut pie.

Restaurante Isabel, on the main street coming into Quepos, has pastas as well as typical dishes and seafood. Closed Wednesday.

DOMINICAL AREA

Beaches; forest; waterfalls; small, secluded lodges; private wildlife refuges; Ballena marine park; and people who seem pleased to be where they are, doing what they're doing are all attractions in this southern Pacific zone. Tiny **Dominical** is where roads from Quepos and San Isidro de El General meet; from here travelers can continue on the Costanera Sur road to Ciudad Cortés to join up with the Inter-American at Palmar Norte.

Dominical is 28 slow miles (45 km) south of Quepos, via unpaved road with lots of one-lane bridges: allow about 90 minutes and take time to enjoy the birds along the road. San Isidro and the Inter-American are 22 miles (35 km) to the northeast via paved road, a pretty climb into the mountains; on this route, San José is about three hours away.

The town itself has the air of a frontier town, a casual place where everybody knows everybody else. A growing number of lodging options, from rustic to resort, and restaurants with an international flavor are sprinkled from

Dominical along approximately 30 miles (50 km) of sandy beaches with names like Matapalo, Barú, Playa Hermosa, and Uvita. Ballena National Marine Park and Caño Island Biological Reserve are easily reached from here. A number of the hotels are on forested property and cater to natural history travelers. Dry season for the area is November through April; average temperature, 83°F (28°C).

There is a filling station and even a small shopping center now, Plaza Pacífica. Restaurants offer Italian, Mexican, typical Costa Rican food, deli menus, and more. Try San Clemente Bar and Grill in town, the Roca Verde Bar & Restaurant less than a mile (1.5 km) south of the Barú River bridge, or drive 10 minutes south of town to Punta Dominical and enjoy a superb seaside setting and good food at the Cabinas Punta Dominical restaurant. Phones have not reached all the way down the costal road (*costanera*), so radio communication—the order of the day for most not so long ago—is still a lifeline for some.

Selva Mar tour agency, (506) 771-4582, fax (506) 771-1903; e-mail selvamar@sol.racsa.co.cr, based in San Isidro, makes reservations for hotels and lodges all through here (relaying reservations by radio) as well as lodges in the Cerro de la Muerte area.

Where to Stay in Dominical

Albergue Willdale, (506) 787-0023, fax (506) 787-0024; Selva Mar (506) 771-4582, fax (506) 771-1903, is set among the trees alongside the Barú River in Dominical. It has seven clean, simply furnished rooms: colorful painted cement floors, lovely purple heartwood, bright sheets, and fans. Single $25, $5 each additional person. There are bikes, an inflatable paddle boat, and kayaks. A stem of bananas is always out for guests. Owners, the Dales, also have a two-bedroom mountain villa, **Cabeza de Mono,** for those who seek solitude in beautiful surroundings. A spectacular view stretches from Cathedral Point in Manuel Antonio to Caño Island and Corcovado. The two-bedroom villa has a swimming pool and comes furnished with food for two meals per day; $125 a day or $900 per week, taxes included.

Hotel Villas Río Mar, Río Mar (506) 787-0052, fax (506) 787-0054; San José (506) 257-1138, fax (506) 257-1345; e-mail riomar@sol.racsa.co.cr, a short walk east of town along the Barú River, is an attractive resort of 40 thatched bungalows, restaurant, poolside bar, Jacuzzi, tennis court, and minigym set in lush tropical gardens against a backdrop of 16 forested acres (6.5 ha). Bungalows are a delight, with bedrooms opening via double louvered doors onto an outdoor living area with a wet bar, small refrigerator, breakfast bar, bamboo coffee table and comfy armchairs. Sheer tied-back drapes and the thatched overhang of the roof lend an intimate privacy to the open-air living space. Bedrooms have king or twin beds. Ceiling fans cool bedroom and terrace. Single $70, double $80. Multiday packages available. Breakfast $5, lunch or dinner $10, taxes included. The restaurant is open to the public.

Water Safety

Beaches in Costa Rica are no more dangerous than those in southern California, according to Donald Melton of Quepos, who has pushed lifesaving efforts in coastal areas for many years.

Basic rules apply whenever you swim in coastal waters: Do not swim alone, on a full stomach, or while intoxicated. Do not swim at the mouth of a river, where currents can be treacherous. For the same reason, be careful around rocky points. Look before you leap. How deep is the water—are people standing? Is the slope gradual or is there a steep drop-off? Ask local people how safe the water is.

According to Donald, about 80 percent of the 200 people who drown each year in Costa Rica are victims of riptides. Some rips are called "permanent"—always in the same place. In other areas, rips can come and go. Telltale signs are discoloration of the water—brown spots where turbulence is kicking up sand—and areas where breakers don't return directly to the surf but run parallel to the beach. Take a few minutes to watch the action of the sea before you go in.

If caught in a rip, remember that it will only take you out, not drag you under. Panic is a factor in drownings. Don't fight the current. See if you can use the energy of a big wave to push you toward the beach. Motion to shore for help, but while it is coming, swim parallel to the beach; then, as the rip weakens, swim at a 45-degree angle toward shore. Never try to swim directly toward the beach. If you can't swim, float; keep your legs and body close to the surface. If water is shallow enough that you can walk when you feel yourself being pulled out, also go parallel to the shore as fast as you can to try to get out of it.

Some dangerous beaches are Playa Bonita near Limón; near the entrance to Cahuita National Park; Doña Ana and Playa Barranca near Puntarenas; Jacó; and south Espadilla Beach at Manuel Antonio.

Villas Río Mar offers guided walks or horseback rides in the forest; nature trails lead to a viewpoint with spectacular vistas of the coastline. Off-site tours include snorkeling in Ballena park, tubing on the Barú River, mountain biking, river fishing, and visits to Caño Island, Corcovado, Manuel Antonio, and three-tiered Santo Cristo Falls.

HACIENDA BARU, PRIVATE NATIONAL WILDLIFE REFUGE

Location: On the Pacific coast a mile (2 km) N of Dominical, 29 miles (47 km) S of Quepos, 24 miles (38 km) SW of San Isidro de El General.
Rates: Lodging $50 double occupancy, breakfast included. Rates for tours and day visitors below.
Information/Reservations: (506) 787-0003, fax (506) 787-0004; e-mail baru@cool.co.cr; Web site www.cool.co.cr/usr/baru/baru.html.

Four young coatis had dashed across the trail and scampered up a tree, quickly disappearing in a leafy world hidden from our eyes. We had watched a blue-black grassquit doing rapid little song-jumps, seeming to somersault in the air as it fluttered up and down from the same low branch. What sounded like a giant crashing through the forest turned out to be monkeys feeding noisily, knocking down fruit and throwing branches to the ground in the process.

A hard act to follow? Doesn't seem to be at Hacienda Barú, an 800-acre (324-ha) private national wildlife refuge. On various visits I have ascended into the canopy, watched birds in mangroves on the way to the beach, hiked to a jungle tent camp, marveled at a giant ceiba, and traveled by horseback to see pre-Columbian petroglyphs—each time discovering more about the natural world from a master teacher who still calls himself a student: Jack Ewing. Jack and his wife, Diane, came to Costa Rica in the 1970s, expecting to stay four months. Come and discover what has kept them here.

Hacienda Barú has come a long way since the Ewings first managed it as a cattle operation, undergoing a metamorphosis that now brings two-legged beings to wander through regenerating pasture and along lowland forest trails. Steve Stroud and Mayra Bonilla joined the partnership in the nineties, equally committed to conservation and responsible tourism.

Some visitors arrive in the tropical forest expecting boas to be hanging from the trees and jaguars to appear on the trails. Boas are on Barú's reptile list, though you're not likely to see one. And no jaguars have been spotted here, though there are pumas, jaguarundis, and ocelots. But visitors still have plenty to see.

More than 310 species of birds have been counted, 57 species of mammals (including bats), and reptiles and amphibians that run the gamut from caimans to red-eyed tree frogs and tiny, colorful, poison-dart frogs. Humpbacked whales pass by offshore from December to April, and olive ridley and hawksbill sea turtles lay eggs on the beach from May through November. The hacienda helps with a nursery where about 2,500 baby turtles are hatched and released every year. Dolphins inhabit these warm waters.

About half of the hacienda is forested, both primary and secondary forest; the rest is mangrove, river, and beach habitats. Patches of lowland forest are being connected by a 100-acre (40-ha) biological corridor to protect biodiversity.

Day visitors are welcome at Hacienda Barú, choosing from a variety of hikes with naturalists or native guides: a three-hour Mangrove and Beach Walk includes a look at reforestation with native species ($15); the popular six-hour Rainforest Experience explores tropical wet forest ($30); and two- to three-hour horseback rides take in tropical waterfalls, beach, jungle trails, and pastures ($25). More than a mile (2 km) of self-guiding trails over level terrain are free to overnight guests, with a nominal fee for day visitors. Day and overnight guests can kayak through mangroves, no experience necessary; try whitewater kayaking; or experience a guided night estuary tour by kayak.

An incredible experience awaits those who ascend into the canopy by rope. Harnessed and helmeted, the visitor is gently lifted more than 100 feet (30 meters) to an observation platform—fantastic views of canopy vegetation and surrounding forest guaranteed. Possibilities of wildlife to be seen are countless ($35 for a minimum of 30 minutes on the platform). For more adventure, choose tree climbing, with a naturalist guide beside you all the way, $40.

Spend a night in the jungle, camping in tents next to a shelter with flush toilets and shower. Observe nocturnal animals; take a night hike. Morning bird-watching in the small clearing is excellent.

If your taste runs more to cabins, there are six two- and three-bedroom units with kitchenettes, fans, screened windows with shutters, bamboo sofas

Canopy climbing with Jack Ewing at Hacienda Barú

with flowered cushions, and double and single beds. A complimentary continental breakfast is served in an open-air dining room. Cabins are near both forest and beach. On a small hill nearby is a two-story observation tower, terrific for bird-watchers.

Be sure to see Diane's orchid collection: 250 species and growing. And do look in at the gift shop.

Getting There

By bus: Quepos–San Isidro de El General buses pass by the office.
By car: From Quepos (unpaved road), start watching for signs after passing El Ceibo gas station. From San Isidro, when the road dead-ends, turn right toward Quepos, continue about a mile (2 km); office on left.

Where to Stay from Dominical South to Ballena Area

(by location, going south from Dominical)
Bella Vista Lodge, (506) 771-4582, fax (506) 771-1903, via Selva Mar) above Punta Dominical lives up to its name—gorgeous views of forest and sea. Woody and Lenny Dyer have turned the old farmhouse (made of hand-cut hardwood) into a rustic place to get away from it all. A wide veranda surrounds the heart of the house. Four small bedrooms are off a central hallway that's open to catch the breeze. The two shared baths have solar hot water. Single $25, double $40. Two small cabins may be finished by your arrival.

No power lines here, so battery power kicks in at night. Meals are good: $4 for breakfast or lunch, $5 to $7 for dinner. Some gourmet dishes come with the candlelight dinner on the porch. Horseback tours are available for overnight guests and day visitors. An all-day rain forest–waterfall tour to double-tiered Nauyaca is $40; beach rides, $30; and a beach and Pozo Azul waterfall tour, $35. Explore walking trails in the forest. Transfers from Dominical arranged. If driving, watch for a sign on the left about 2 miles (3.5 km) south of Dominical.
Villas Escaleras, telephone/fax (506) 771-5247, is a complex of three villas set 1,200 feet (374 m) above the sea with a view of the coastline all the way to the Osa Peninsula. The main villa and a secluded guesthouse villa share a sky-high pool, while Villa II has its own pool. Each has a complete kitchen, orthopedic beds, and lots of privacy. The three-level main villa has three bedrooms, vaulted ceilings, beautiful purple-heart floors, brightly colored fabrics and art from Latin America, queen beds, and a wraparound balcony complete with hammocks and telescope: $300 for up to eight people, three-night minimum. The one-bedroom guesthouse, secluded among the trees, has a large bedroom, with king-size bed, living room, balcony, sun terrace, and rich colors from textiles and local hardwoods. Nearby creeks make this a great place for observation of birds and other forest animals: $125 for two.

Villa II has two bedrooms, king-size and twin beds, plus a futon in the living room. Fruit trees attract wildlife and sunset views are great: $200 for up to four people, three-night minimum.

Owners/managers Michael Holm and Denise Richards assist guests with visits to Bahía Ballena and Caño Island, boating, fishing, sea kayaking, river rafting, nature tours, and horseback riding. Watch for the Villas Escaleras sign about 2 miles (3.5 km) south of Dominical.

Cabinas Punta Dominical, telephone/fax (506) 787-0016; e-mail ehdpdsa @sol.racsa.co.cr, is 3 miles (5 km) south of Dominical. The spectacular setting, high on the point at Punta Dominical, puts the sea on both sides. Four spacious cabins of tropical hardwood, nestled discreetly among trees, have tremendous ocean views. Rooms have louvered, floor-length shutters on three sides, polished wood floors, two double beds and a bunk bed, ceiling fans, and screened windows. Each has a porch with a hammock. It's a peaceful, private place. Single or double $50, each additional person $12, taxes included. The thatched, open-air restaurant, open to the public, has excellent food; it's worth a trip just to sit here and drink in the panorama of sea and coastline, with Ballena National Marine Park at center stage.

Cabañas Escondidas, via Selva Mar (506) 771-4582, fax (506) 771-1903, is less than 6 miles (9 km) south of Dominical. In a forested hillside setting, each of nine very private cabañas is unique: Rancho Bamboo has Japanese-style sliding screen doors; Rancho Ambrosia is next to cacao trees; Panorama is a hexagon; Treehouse appears to be in the branches of the trees and remains without electric lights—nothing to dim the starlight. Electricity, however, has arrived for other cabins. These six are $25 to $45. Three beach cabins, El Sueño, Amapola, and Tesoro (with river rock decorating showers) are $75. Food is Thai, Chinese, and vegetarian gourmet, served in a large, thatched restaurant with a spectacular view of forest and ocean. Scrumptious desserts may include pineapple upside-down cake or specialties made with organic chocolate. Breakfast $3.50, lunch $5, dinner $10 (by reservation only).

Owners Gailon and Patricia have created beautiful gardens of native plants and trees, but 80 acres (32 ha) remain in natural forest. A horseback tour to waterfalls is $35, private nature reserve walks are $15, kayaking and snorkeling trips are arranged, mountain bikes available. A path leads to a secluded beach with tide pools for safe swimming.

Escondidas is a gentle, laid-back place, where you can take a tai chi chuan class, meditate, choose an energy awareness session, or have a therapeutic massage. Work-study programs are available from December to April, where people help out and learn either tai chi chuan, chi kung, massage, or vegetarian cooking. Write to Cabañas Escondidas, in care of Selva Mar, AAA Express Mail, 1641 NW 79th Avenue, Miami, FL 33126.

Las Casitas de Puertocito, telephone/fax (506) 787-0048, via Selva Mar (506) 771-4582, fax (506) 771-1903, has seven thatched split-level bungalows in a tropical forest setting. Each has a single bed, living area with bamboo furniture, and bath on the first level; queen-size bed on upper level; and ceiling fans. Cooking equipment is provided for stays longer than one week. Double

Going Bananas

Costa Rica is the world's second-largest exporter of bananas, after Ecuador. Native to Asia, bananas got their start in Costa Rica in the 1880s. Each trunk in a banana plant produces one bunch, then dies; but a continuous supply of new trunks emerges from the plant's base. It takes nine months from start of a trunk to cutting of fruit, three months from flower to harvest. Blue plastic bags, impregnated with insecticide and fungicide, are placed over a bunch at about two weeks; they concentrate heat, quickening growth.

At harvest time, the still-green stalk of bananas is cut from the trunk and pulled on a cable to the packing plant. The plastic is removed, and "hands" of bananas cut from the bunch soak in water to allow latex to drain from the cut stem. Fruit that survives a selection process is washed, labeled, sprayed with fungicide, loaded into a box, and put aboard a container ship. Costa Rica's bananas go mainly to the United States, Germany, Belgium, Italy, and the Netherlands.

The banana industry has come under attack for the cutting of forests for plantations, and for the eco-impact of pesticides and the plastic bags, which often end up in rivers and oceans. Banana companies are making changes under the ECO-O.K. program tied to environmental improvement by industry (See Chapter 2).

$49, breakfast included. Restaurant specializes in Italian food. Jungle hikes around the *finca*, swimming on three unspoiled beaches, and horseback rides (some multiday) are options. The property has three rivers with waterfalls.

Oro Verde Private Biological Reserve, (506) 771-4582, fax (506) 771-1903, via Selva Mar, above Uvita, managed by the Duarte family, offers day visits as well as overnight stays in rustic cabins. A visit involves a horseback ride and a hike in. This cultural/ecological tour lets you experience something of life on the Duarte farm. You may see an anteater, howler monkey, or *tepezcuintle*. You will see birds, butterflies, and waterfalls. A five-hour day tour into the forest is $20, including guide and lunch. Cabins are $10 per person, another $10 per day for meals.

Rancho La Merced, via Selva Mar (506) 771-4582, fax (506) 771-1903, is near Punta Uvita, adjacent to Ballena park. The working cattle ranch has 988 acres (400 ha) protected as a private wildlife refuge: primary and secondary forest, mangroves, and habitat on both the Morete River and along the beach. The rustic farmhouse has two bedrooms, no hot water (but owner Walter Odio explains that it isn't cold, either), living room, and equipped kitchen. A generator gives electricity for three hours at night. Double $45, $10 each additional person. Meals can be provided.

Play cowboy for a day; take a five-hour hike and horseback tour including river, mangrove, beach, and forest; or take a horseback trip to Punta Uvita—each $30. Two hiking tours in the refuge include either river and beach habitats or hiking in the forested mountains for a great view of the Morete River canyon and good birding, $25 for either.

The **Profelis Foundation**, which works on reintroduction of cat species into protected areas, is open to visitors; admission $10, free to Rancho La Merced guests. The visit includes a talk by one of the biologists carrying out the research-and-release program and observing some of the felines.

BALLENA NATIONAL MARINE PARK
Location: S of Punta Uvita on the Pacific.
Size: 13,282 acres (5,375 ha) of ocean and 272 acres (110 ha) of land.
Cost: $6.
Information: Telephone hotline 192 (see Appendix A: Parks and Reserve Information), (506) 786-7161 (in Palmar).

Created in 1990, Ballena park was established to protect marine resources. The 6-mile-(10-km)-long coast between Punta Uvita and Punta Piñuela is rich in well-preserved mangroves. Ballena Island and smaller rocky protrusions called Las Tres Hermanas are nesting sites for frigate birds, pelicans, and boobies. The park is named for the humpbacked whales that visit from December to March. Dolphins are common here.

This is the first marine park in Costa Rica to involve a fishing community, which has formed an association to assist in park development. There are no facilities for tourists yet, though visitors can snorkel around the coral reefs, dive, or visit by boat. Visits can be arranged from Dominical and Uvita.

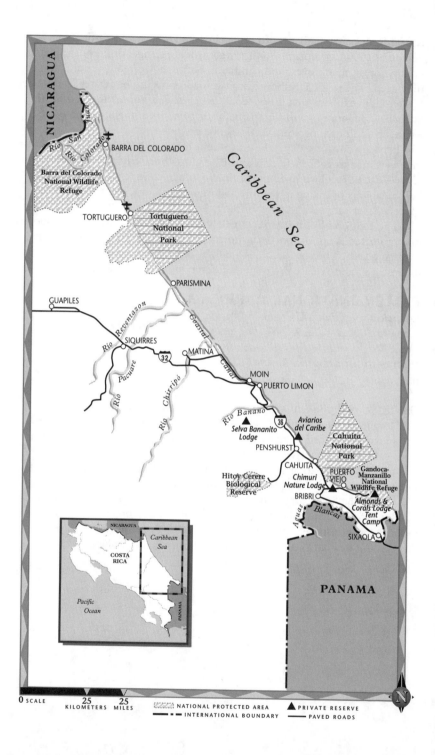

NICARAGUA

Río San Juan

Río Colorado

BARRA DEL COLORADO

Barra del Colorado
National Wildlife
Refuge

TORTUGUERO

Tortuguero
National
Park

Caribbean Sea

PARISMINA

GUAPILES

Río Reventazon

SIQUIRRES

Río Pacuare

Río Chiripó

MATINA

Canal Canal

MOIN
PUERTO LIMON

Río Banano

Selva Bananito
Lodge

Aviarios
del Caribe

Cahuita
National
Park

PENSHURST

Hitoy Cerere
Biological
Reserve

CAHUITA

Chimuri
Nature Lodge

PUERTO
VIEJO

Gandoca-
Manzanillo
National
Wildlife Refuge

BRIBRI

Agua

Blancas

Almonds &
Corals Lodge
Tent Camp

SIXAOLA

PANAMA

NICARAGUA

Caribbean
Sea

COSTA
RICA

Pacific
Ocean

PANAMA

0 SCALE   25   25
      KILOMETERS   MILES

NATIONAL PROTECTED AREA   ▲ PRIVATE RESERVE
INTERNATIONAL BOUNDARY   PAVED ROADS

N

10

COSTA RICA'S CARIBBEAN COAST

The Atlantic Coast, shorter than the Pacific, offers long, uncluttered beaches, high forested mountains, coconut palms, plantations of cacao and bananas, national parks and wildlife refuges, sleepy villages, and a commercial port. Mountains, coastal plains, and marine areas contain a rich mixture of species and habitats to explore.

The cultural landscape is unique—nowhere else in Costa Rica do Black and Indian influences leave such an imprint. While African Americans countrywide make up about 3 percent of the population, the percentage in Limón province is about one-third. This culture adds to the flavor of the Caribbean zone and, because many speak English, broadens communications for monolingual English-speaking tourists. It is, however, a Creole English whose expressions can surprise and delight.

Indian influence in the Caribbean is more heavily felt as you go farther south to the Talamanca coast—land of the Bribrí and Cabecar Indians. There are three main Indian reserves: KéköLdi, Talamanca-Bribrí, and Talamanca-Cabecar.

Two land routes bring travelers to this area: the highway through Braulio Carrillo National Park (see Chapter 7 for destinations before the turnoff to Las Horquetas) and the older road from San José through Cartago and Turrialba (described in Chapter 6). The two highways join at Siquirres for the final lap into Limón. Air and boat travel bring visitors to the Barra del Colorado and Tortuguero areas.

ROUTE TO LIMON

The newer highway through Guapiles and Braulio Carrillo National Park cuts travel time to 2½ hours by road from San José to Limón. Even after leaving the park, though, keep your eyes peeled for sloths in the trees. If driving, be careful of heavy fog and landslides, especially through the park, and also of speeding drivers.

If a landslide stops travel through Braulio Carrillo National Park to San José, officials can usually can tell you how long it may be before the road is clear. You can wait or consider two alternate routes: one is through Puerto Viejo de Sarapiquí, at least 3½ hours; another is back to Siquirres to return through Turrialba, at least 2½ hours. Both routes involve narrow, mountain-

EARTH

The Agricultural School of the Humid Tropical Region (EARTH) near Guácimo has a four-year, college-level program for students from Latin America, focused on balancing agricultural production and resource conservation in the humid tropics through teaching, research, and hands-on extension work. It was begun in 1986 to educate young Latin American leaders about sustainable agricultural systems and improved natural resource management.

Research at the school's banana plantations, whose earnings help provide scholarships, is aimed at developing an environmentally safer fruit. Visitors can see the plant where banana waste is recycled into paper; in the campus gift shop, they can buy products made from the recycled paper. Other tours encompass a banana plantation or packing plant and nontraditional plant crops such as pejibaye, yuca, pepper, plantain, *and* ñampi *(a tuber). Visitors may also visit the 865-acre (350-ha) forest reserve, mostly regenerating secondary forest, habitat for great green macaws, monkeys, toucans, poisonous frogs, fer-de-lance snakes, and morpho butterflies, plus 95 species of trees. Telephone (506) 255-2000, extension 4602, to arrange tours, or fax (506) 255-2540. Ask about the Adopt an Acre at EARTH program or the Plant a Tree scholarship initiative.*

ous potholed roads. If it's late in the day, consider lodging at one of the places mentioned below and waiting until morning.

Many travelers from earlier years made the journey from San José to Limón via the famous Jungle Train, discontinued in 1991. Even though the national railway system gave up the ghost in 1995, ending its freight and passenger service, the imprint of steel rails on this area is deep. It took from 1871 to 1890 to build the main line, with Chinese and West Indians brought in as workers. To help finance the project (and to feed the workers) bananas were grown for export, and that brought more African Americans from British colonies, many from Jamaica. That's how the United Fruit Company got its start in Costa Rica.

The highway crosses two mighty rivers famous for white-water rafting: the Reventazón just before Siquirres, and the Pacuare after. Siquirres is where the highland road through Turrialba comes in.

If you're driving, fill up at one of the several large gas stations along the highway; they are harder to find south of Limón.

Where to Stay on the Road to Limón

Casa Río Blanco, telephone/fax (506) 382-0957, fax (506) 710-6161; e-mail info@casarioblanco.com; Web site www.casarioblanco.com, has four stand-alone cabins with polished light-wood floors and rustic walls. Each has a double bed and day bed, screened windows on all sides, and a porch facing the forest above the river. Single $42, double $58, including breakfast; no credit cards. The river provides night music; during the day its pools are great for swimming, while the rushing white water is a natural Jacuzzi.

Guests can bird-watch, hike forest trails, walk along a river, climb into the canopy, discover small waterfalls, or stroll a self-guided walk through a small botanical garden, learning from a printed guide. Where the garden stops, a steep forested drop to the river begins. Rate includes a complimentary rain-forest tour on Casa Río Blanco's 12 acres (about 5 ha) and a canopy climb. Meals generally vegetarian: lunch $5, dinner $6.

Owner Dee Bocock, who taught school for 20 years, offers a day hike to a 275-foot (84-meter) waterfall—requires good physical condition and advance notice, $25 each for up to three. Discounts for Tortuguero and white-water rafting tours. For $150 a week, be a volunteer: help with bird, animal, or plant censuses; trail-blazing and -mapping; developing educational materials; or working in the organic garden; one-month minimum. The lodge is 36 miles (58 km) from San José; turn off 1,000 feet (300 m) after the Ponderosa Restaurant, just before Río Blanco—less than a mile (1.5 km) from the highway.

Happy Rana Lodge, (506) 710-6794 Spanish only, fax (506) 710-2301, U.S. number (520) 743-8254, has four cabins built 10 feet (3 m) off the ground in the middle of glorious rain forest. Each ample cabin is simply furnished and has a porch with hammock and chairs for watching birds and butterflies in surrounding trees. Paths connect cabins with the main lodge, where owners Alvaro and Heidi Monge serve tasty meals on a large covered terrace. Single $35, double $45, including breakfast. Cabins accommodate up to four.

Guests hike trails through 35 acres (14 ha) of forested property on both sides of the rushing Río Blanco. A long hanging bridge opens up access to the other side. See the poison-dart frogs (*rana*) here, inspiration for the lodge's name. Swim in river pools; hike to an impressive waterfall. Alvaro and Heidi arrange white-water rafting and Tortuguero canal trips. The lodge is 7 miles (11 km) past the Aerial Tram; turn right after La Ponderosa Restaurant on the road along the river and continue 2 miles (3 km). Signs point the way. Bus travelers can be picked up at the restaurant. Reserve at least one day in advance.

Hotel Río Palmas, (506) 760-0305, fax (506) 760-0296, before the town of Pocora, is a place I like. A delightful nature trail winds through riparian habitat, mostly between the Palmas and Dos Novillas Rivers. Walk it early in the morning when the light just begins to play on the waters. Kingfishers, herons, toucans, and poison-dart frogs (red with blue limbs) reward you. Just before the first long cement walkway along the water's edge, notice the woody vine that tied itself in a knot.

You're likely to see an armadillo on the hotel grounds, along with colorful basilisks. Owner Erick Berlin, also in the tropical plant business, has more than 500 varieties of tropical flowers on the property. A *palmito* plantation provides fresh heart of palm for the restaurant. Many species in the garden are labeled: loads of heliconias. High-ceilinged rooms with fans and private baths open to a landscaped courtyard with a small swimming pool and thatched rancho at one end. Superior rooms (local TV), are single $39, double $44; standard rooms, single $32, double $37. At the popular open-air restaurant, try your hand at cracking macadamia nuts found in the typical cart at the rear of the restaurant.

Hotel Río Palmas arranges tours to EARTH and offers a two-hour tour of its own trail plus a visit to Erick's ornamental plant farm, which exports 30 varieties. Other tour options are a macadamia farm, medicinal plant farm, three-hour horseback ride, or, for the truly fit, a six-hour trek to the Pocora waterfalls. Tortuguero tours are easily arranged from here. Public buses to Limón and points south pass in front of the hotel.

Where to Eat on the Road to Limón

La Ponderosa restaurant is a steak house and *chicharronera* (Costa Rica's *chicharrones* have no resemblance to the pork skins sold in the United States). Open 6:30 a.m. to 11 p.m. daily. Yes, it's named for the TV program: a photo of Ben Cartwright and his boys hangs above the bar, along with a map of the Old West spread.

Río Palmas Restaurant at Pocora, with pleasant surroundings and good

Hotel Río Palmas between Braulio Carrillo and Limón

food, is open daily 6 a.m. to 10:30 p.m. It's a good place to try natural fruit drinks such as cas, mango, or guanábana, and if you haven't yet tried fried yuca, do it here. Tired of *gallo pinto*? Breakfast can be pancakes or an omelette.

LIMON

Limón, or more correctly Puerto Limón, is capital of the province of Limón and the principal port on the Caribbean. Limón is 81 miles (131 km) east of San José, on the Caribbean coast. Christopher Columbus dropped anchor offshore near La Uvita Island, in front of Limón, on September 18, 1502. Though he stayed about 20 days, he apparently never set foot on the mainland. At that time, present-day Limón was called Cariay by the Indians who inhabited the area.

Around October 12, the day traditionally commemorating Columbus and his discovery and which *ticos* celebrate as Día de las Culturas (to recognize contributions of all cultures), Limón throws a party that draws about 200,000 people; population of the town itself is 58,324. It may not be Río, but this carnival is five days of music, parades, and dancing. During the rest of the year, Limón is a center of commerce (with deep-water docking facilities at nearby Moín) for fishing, shipping, agriculture, and tourism.

In Limón and south, you still see a few signs of the April 22, 1991, earthquake that walloped the region, though reconstruction of damaged buildings, roads, and bridges has whittled away at the physical evidence.

The quake, a 7.4 on the Richter scale, raised the Atlantic coast about 5 feet (1.5 m) at Limón and about a foot (30 cm) farther south at Gandoca, near Panama. One positive note is that scientists predict no major earthquake here for another 100 years.

Surfers are drawn to breaks at Playa Bonita and Playa Portete, north of downtown, and at Uvita Island, with December–January and June the best months. If sloths have so far eluded you, visit Vargas Park near the seawall, where several live. If you can't spot the well-camouflaged mammals, a passerby will usually help. At the Municipal Market, stop by one of the food stands to try rice and beans, a fried cake, or *agua de sapo*—literally, "toad water," but actually a kind of cold *agua dulce* with lemon. *Pan bon* is glazed bread with dried fruits.

Getting There

By bus: Frequent San José–Limón express buses.

By car: The San José–Braulio Carrillo route is the quickest; an alternate route is via Cartago and Turrialba to Siquirres, where the road joins the Braulio Carrillo route.

Where to Stay and Eat in Limón

Apartotel Corobicí, (506) 798-1670, telephone/fax (506) 758-2930, on Playa Bonita, has an open-air restaurant and patio area next to the ocean, along with a swimming pool. The 21 rooms are small, clean, and simply furnished, with ceiling fans, some with air conditioning. Single $21, double $27 to $32, taxes included. Six apartments, for up to five persons each, have cooking facilities and refrigerators, $54.

Hotel Maribú Caribe, San José (506) 253-1838, fax (506) 234-0193, hotel (506) 758-4543, has 52 air-conditioned rooms located in 14 upscale thatched bungalows, some with ocean views: single $68, double $78. The hotel has a restaurant featuring European and seafood specialties, a snack bar, and swimming pools. It offers seasonal turtle-nesting tours plus one-day tours to Tortuguero, $65; snorkeling in Cahuita National Park, $75; diving, $85; and a three-hour canal tour, $35. The hotel is situated on a hill, with grassy grounds going down to the sea. Transfer from San José, $40.

Hotel Matama, (506) 758-1123, (506) 758-1797, fax (506) 758-4499, near Playa Bonita is in a forest setting not far from the beach. The open-air restaurant/bar and rooms in scattered bungalows are nestled among the trees. Some bathrooms have small tropical gardens growing under their skylights. The 16 rooms are nicely furnished; cushioned wicker chairs add color. There's also a pool, air conditioning, car rental, and parking. Single $55, double $65.

Take the short botanical trail and a walk to an orchid garden on the 54 acre (22 ha) property. Day trips to Tortuguero are $65. Every Thursday, live music brings the sounds of salsa, reggae, and calypso. Restaurant open to the public 6:30 a.m. to 11 p.m. To get to the hotel without going downtown, turn north past the RECOPE refinery and follow the road 3 miles (5 km) to Matama.

NORTHERN CARIBBEAN

Roads have yet to link some of this area with the rest of the country. Canals, built in the 1970s, run parallel to the sea, connecting existing rivers and lagoons to provide an 80-mile (129-km) inland waterway from Moín, just north of Limón, to Tortuguero and Barra del Colorado on the northern Caribbean coast, top destinations for nature and adventure travelers and sportfishers. Famous for the wildlife in and along the waters, this lifeline of canals and rivers is a highway for canoes loaded with bananas and coconuts, logs that are floated south, and barges carrying supplies north. Families travel in tiny dugouts. Scheduled and charter flights offer a quicker option.

Most visitors to the protected areas arrive on package tours from San José that include transportation (bus/boat or air), food, naturalist guide, and, for multiday tours, lodging. Travel-related businesses from Limón south also arrange canal tours. An alternate river route is from Puerto Viejo de Sarapiquí in the north central region via the San Juan and San Carlos Rivers. To do the trip yourself, come by air or arrange for boat transfer at Moín outside Limón or at Puerto Viejo de Sarapiquí; once in Tortuguero or Barra del Colorado, hire a boat and local guide to explore waterways off the main canal.

TORTUGUERO AREA
Isolated for so long—the first public telephone was installed in 1972—Tortuguero still feels like an out-of-the-way place despite the thousands of tourists who arrive every year. The village of Tortuguero is small, with fewer than 500 residents who work mainly in farming (rice, coconuts, fruits, and vegetables) and tourism. Some visitors never get to the village, but I hope you do. Tortuguero is turtles and forest and rivers, but it's also a special kind of people who live on the edge of land and sea.

Things to See and Do
Caribbean Conservation Corporation's (CCC's) **H. Clay Frick Natural History Visitor Center**, a five-minute walk north of the village, is a must. Beautiful, colorful, informative exhibits focus on ecological relationships, highlighting turtles and the area's other diverse wildlife as well as the CCC's work. Founded in 1959 to support the work of the late Dr. Archie Carr, CCC is the oldest sea-turtle conservation organization in the world. It strives to preserve sea turtles and other marine and coastal life through research, training, education, and protection of natural areas. You can purchase some of Dr. Carr's books, T-shirts, and information packets on turtles and other

gift items. An 18-minute video (English or Spanish) describes Tortuguero's unique relationship with sea turtles. A biologist is on hand to answer questions. Open daily 10 a.m. to noon and 2 to 6 p.m. Admission $1 adults, children up to 12 free.

Volunteers are needed for both the CCC turtle-tagging program and a Neotropical bird study on resident and migratory species, one-week minimum stay. Contact the U.S. office for information: P.O. Box 2866, Gainesville, FL 32602, (800) 678-7853; Web site www.cccturtle.org. In Costa Rica, contact CCC at Apartado 246-2050, San Pedro; telephone/fax (506) 224-9215; telephone at center (506) 710-0547.

Stop by the **Joshua B. Powers Information Kiosk** to learn about the area's history: from settlement by peoples related to the Maya, to its fame in the 1700s among merchants and seamen for the thousands of turtles nesting here, to the impact of the Atlantic railroad and the canals. There is information on green turtles and the protected areas. Sign up here for nighttime turtle walks led by local guides July 1 through October 15: ticket office open 4 to 6 p.m., $5 per person plus 100 colones that go to the local development association. Wear dark clothes on the walk, stay quiet. Cameras are not permitted. Please respect your guide's instructions—rules have reason behind them.

Sodas and gift shops are tucked away on the few paths that meander through the village. A Travelair office is at **Paraíso Tropical**, a gift shop with artisan offerings and clothing as well as basics for travelers. Owner Jessie makes some of the things. The **Jungle Shop** and **Tienda de Artesanía** also offer gifts.

TORTUGUERO NATIONAL PARK
Location: Northern Caribbean coast, near Nicaragua.
Size: 46,816 acres (18,946 ha) of land; 129,147 acres (52,265 ha) marine habitat.
Hours: 8 a.m. to 4 p.m. daily.
Cost: $6, camping $2 per person per day.
Information/Reservations: Telephone hotline 192 (see Appendix A: Parks and Reserves Information), telephone/fax (506) 710-2929, (506) 710-2939.

Visions of Hepburn and Bogart on the *African Queen* come to mind as you wind through the rivers and canals of Tortuguero National Park. Flora, fauna, and the boat's condition may differ, but the feeling is here—you, the water, vegetation, and wildlife in an intimate and solitary encounter.

By boat, the dramatic contrast of the settled with the protected lands along the water vividly portrays the difference a park can make. From the air, Tortuguero is a mass of greens from the coastal plain to the Sierpe Hills, broken only by narrow ribbons of water.

However you get there, to explore Tortuguero is to discover a crocodile along the bank, a small turtle sunning on a trunk in the water, a monkey or sloth asleep in a tree, vultures peering down from a lofty perch. Perhaps a river otter will slip into the water as the boat approaches. Water and land birds keep binoculars busy: at least 405 species live here. Watch for green macaws, herons, egrets, parrots, kingfishers, oropendolas (notice their large, hanging nests), tanagers, toucans, and bananaquits.

Tortuguero is tall forest and palm groves, lianas trailing into the water, and floating gardens of water hyacinths. The endangered West Indian manatee feeds on these and other aquatic plants. This large sea cow can be 13 feet (4 m) long and weigh about 1,300 pounds (600 kg).

Tortuguero is also beaches, important nesting sites for the sea turtles (*tortugas*) that gave the place its name. Green, leatherback, hawksbill, and occasionally loggerhead turtles return to these beaches every year to lay eggs. Some come in massive *arribadas*, others singly. Though you could see a turtle any night, there are peaks. Best time to see hawksbills is July to October; leatherbacks, February to July with a peak in April and May; and green turtles, early July into October, peaking in August. Rangers from other parks help patrol the beaches during the busiest months to thwart egg-stealers. Researchers with the Caribbean Conservation Corporation have been tagging nesting turtles since 1955. Each female green turtle comes ashore to lay eggs an average of two or three times during her season here, staying not far offshore in between. It may be up to four years before she returns to Tortuguero.

There are many crustaceans (prawns feed under the water hyacinths), eels, 52 species of freshwater fish (including the gar, considered a living fossil because species of that genus lived 90 million years ago), and sharks.

Self-guided forest nature trails take off from ranger stations at either end of the park: one at the southern Jalova station, and four trails at the Cuatro Esquinas station near the village of Tortuguero. On foot in this wet tropical forest, you may spot small, brightly colored frogs that live here. Mammals include peccaries, raccoons, kinkajous, ocelots, pacas, cougars, and skunks. The park protects more than 15 endangered mammal species, including the tapir, jaguar, giant anteater, and three species of monkeys. All six species of kingfishers are here, along with three species of toucans—more than 300 species of birds in all.

Rain gear and rubber boots come in handy. Rainfall averages about 197 inches (5,000 mm), but can reach 236 inches (6,000 mm) in parts. It is hot and humid, with an average temperature of 79°F (26°C). Elevation is from sea level to 1,020 feet (311 m).

It is possible to visit Tortuguero in a day trip, but being there overnight allows for an after-dark boat ride to see nighttime animal life on the river, a chance to see the turtles, or simply more time to savor the flavor. Camping allowed near the stations.

Getting There
By boat: From Limón or from Puerto Viejo de Sarapiquí (see Chapter 7).
By air: Daily air service from San José.

Where to Stay and Eat near Tortuguero Park

Tortuga Lodge, (506) 222-0333, fax (506) 257-1665; e-mail costaric @expeditions.co.cr; Web site www.expeditions.co.cr, operated by Costa Rica Expeditions, has new facilities: 25 rooms in two-story modules set in a botanical garden that features palms, orchids, and heliconias, with the forest as a backdrop. Polished floors gleam in large rooms, which have almost as much window as wall; bright colors in furnishings are in tune with tropical colors outside. Each has ceiling fan, ample closet, and water-conserving features. Shady verandas invite relaxation while you watch river life in front or birdlife in the garden. The restaurant has views of the main canal—good food and lots of it. Guests enjoy another outdoor setting on the covered terrace by the dock.

Be generous with repellent and venture into the forest behind the lodge on a short loop trail (boots available, $1). Optional activities include a dawn boat trip, $15; turtle walks, $20; and transportation to Tortuguero Village, $8 one-way for up to three. Whether you take the turtle walk or not, attend the excellent natural history slide presentation about Tortuguero, turtles and other wildlife, and the park—it's free. Canal/river trips with a local guide are included in some packages. The one I took with Wallace as guide was magical—a flock of collared aracaris, my first look at the beautiful chestnut-colored woodpecker, a days-old howler clinging to his mother, bare-throated tiger herons, crocodiles, three-toed sloths, kingfishers, crocodiles, and Jesus Christ lizards. Wallace also knows about trees and plants.

Guests can fly both ways or do one way by boat. Two-day one-night trips start at $379 per person, double occupancy, including transportation (one-way by air), lodging, meals, and taxes. The three-day two-night trip is from $459. For lodging alone, single $96, double $116 per person, taxes included. Breakfast $13, lunch $19, dinner $21, taxes included. Meal plans available.

Jungle Lodge, (506) 233-0133, (506) 233-0155, fax (506) 233-0778; e-mail cotour@sol.racsa.co.cr; Web site www.expreso.co.cr/cotur/, operated by Cotur, has 50 comfortable rooms in buildings between the forest and Tortuguero River, many connected by covered walkways. Peach-colored quilted bedspreads and peach and turquoise drapes contrast with polished dark hardwood floors. A full-length mirror adds a nice touch. Cooling is by ceiling fan. Happy Hour is in a thatched bar, and tasty buffet-style meals are served in the separate dining room. A short loop trail in back of the hotel goes to Penitencia Lagoon and into a forest corridor. Remember repellent.

An early morning tour through canals is a delight. The naturalist guide told us about mating habits of the northern jacana—the male cares for the nest and the young—and about the buttress roots of the *gavilán* and other large trees. Seeing the ringed kingfisher in early morning light is a thrill. Packages include transportation (by boat, plane, or a combination), food, lodging, specified tours, and taxes. A one-day tour is $75: two-day, one-night tours, double occupancy, are $185 per person (round trip by boat) to $356

Jungle Lodge on the Tortuguero River

(round trip by air), including a stop at a banana-processing plant, visit to Tortuguero village and the CCC museum, and the morning canal tour. Tours run daily.

Hotel Ilan-Ilan, (506) 255-2031, (506) 255-2262, fax (506) 255-1946; e-mail mitour@sol.racsa.co.cr; Web site www.mitour.com, operated by Agencia Mitur, offers 24 rooms in two buildings. Large rooms are set in what the company calls a 20-acre (8-ha) botanical garden. Staff tell about the Italian biologist who would not believe that the "walking palm" really walks, so he took measurements and returned to see for himself—it did. The record for an individual bird count while staying at Ilan-Ilan is 300 birds in 72 hours. Every guest has the opportunity to plant a tree. The boat for the canal trip carries 44 persons and leaves from a dock in Hamburgo.

Three miles (5 km) of trails offer a half-day excursion. One kilometer is cement, fully wheelchair accessible, and the hotel has one room suitable for the handicapped. Tours depart daily. The two-day, one-night tour is one way by air, while a three-day, two-night tour is in and out by boat: $215 per person for either, including transportation, meals, lodging, and taxes. Ask about an optional Puerto Viejo de Sarapiquí–Tortuguero route.

Mawamba Lodge, (506) 223-2421, (506) 223-7490, fax (506) 222-5463; e-mail mawamba@sol.racsa.co.cr; Web site www.crica.com/mawamba/, is walking distance from Tortuguero village and the CCC natural history center. Find 36 comfortable rooms in pretty landscaped gardens (ceiling fans), pool, Jacuzzi, ranchos with hammocks, and a conference room for daily natural history programs. Walk on trails in the 7-acre (3-ha) private reserve. Food is served family-style, and there is an honor bar.

Night tours are $17 per person, and the turtle walk (July through September) is $10. A one-day tour to Mawamba is $72, including breakfast, lunch, bilingual guide, and transport between San José and the lodge. A two-day, one-night tour from San José is $201 per person, double occupancy, including ground transport from San José, meals, lodging, taxes, guide, and regular tours. A three-day, two-night tour is $252 per person, double occupancy. Options include air transport one or both ways or coming through Puerto Viejo de Sarapiquí.

Laguna Lodge, (506) 225-3740, fax (506) 283-8031, located on the ocean side of the river, has 26 ample rooms with ceiling fans and reading lamps. Buildings are set among 12 acres (5 ha) of gardens aflower with tropical plants, shaded by forest trees. The heliconia collection is spectacular. Meals are served family-style. The rancho-style bar on the lagoon is popular with guests as well as visitors from other lodges.

Standard two-day, one-night tour is $187 and three-day, two-night tour is $234; with one-way air, $329 each for two people. Packages include visits to the CCC museum, the village, and a lookout point above Tortuguero. Sarapiquí option available.

BARRA DEL COLORADO NATIONAL WILDLIFE REFUGE

Location: Northern Caribbean coast, across the San Juan River from Nicaragua.
Size: 242,158 acres (98,000 ha).
Cost: $1.
Information/Reservations: Telephone hotline 192 (see Appendix A: Parks and Reserves Information), telephone/fax (506) 710-2929, (506) 710-2939.

Access within the Barra del Colorado refuge is largely by its waterways. Virtually no land trails exist, and part of the western region has yet to be explored. But there's plenty to see from the network of rivers, channels, and lakes. Among endangered species are the West Indian manatee, tapir, cougar, jaguar, ocelot, and jaguarundi. Species most often seen are caimans and crocodiles, white-faced and howler monkeys, red brocket deer, and sloths. Birds include the great green macaw, great curassow, herons of various species, red-lored Amazon parrot, great tinamou, cormorant, and keel-billed toucan.

A very wet rain forest, the area averages from 158 inches (4,000 mm) of rain on the western edge to 221 inches (5,600 mm) at the town of Barra del Colorado. My two-day visit in one of the rainiest months, however, was sunny and beautiful. Go prepared for rain, but take your sunscreen.

See swamp forests, swamp palm forests, and mixed forests growing above the swamps. *Caña brava*, a wild cane, grows mainly along the rivers. Its stiff, solid stems are used to make decorative ceilings and prop up banana plants. Another forest species with commercial value is cativo, used in plywood. If you come via canals, you may see lumber being floated down to Moín; supposedly all being cut outside park lands.

Resident fish in the lakes, rivers, and estuaries include snook, tarpon, mackerel, snapper, gar, and guapote (a tropical rainbow bass). The area draws many sportfishers. You can easily combine a trip to Tortuguero and Barra del Colorado, either with a tour or by hiring a boat to take you from one to the other.

Getting There
By boat: Canal trip from Moín, six hours; from Puerto Viejo de Sarapiquí, via the San Juan River.
By air: Scheduled flights from San José to Barra del Colorado, 30 minutes.
Other: Tour companies offer one-day or multiday trips.

Where to Stay and Eat near Barra del Colorado
Río Colorado Lodge, (506) 232-4063, (506) 232-8610, fax (506) 231-5987; Web site www.sportsmanweb.com/Riocolorado/jungle; U.S. and Canada number (800) 243-9777, fax 813-933-3280, pioneered the boat tour to the Caribbean: from Puerto Viejo de Sarapiquí, follow the Sarapiquí River to the San Juan, then onto the Colorado River. Passengers are bused to Puerto Viejo, where they board the *Colorado Queen* for Barra del Colorado. Return trip is through Tortuguero, with a stop at the park, and on through the canals; then bus through Braulio Carrillo National Park to San José.

Set on the banks of the Colorado River, the lodge has 18 rooms, some air-conditioned. The complex is built on stilts, with covered walkways and dock. There is an aviary, recreation room, and bar, where rum drinks are on the house during happy hour. A two-day, one-night package is $196 from San José, going via Sarapiquí and returning through Tortuguero. From July through September, a night tour is offered to nesting sites at Tortuguero. Lodging and meals only is $90 per person. Fishing packages available.

Samay Lagoon Lodge, (506) 284-7047, fax (506) 383-6370; e-mail samaycr@sol.racsa.co.cr; Web site www.samay.com, on the Caribbean, has 22 comfortable rooms cooled by ceiling fans. Meals are served family style, with locally grown, natural ingredients. A three-day, two-night Samay Jungle Safari begins with a road trip to Puerto Viejo to travel the Sarapiquí River to the San Juan and Río Colorado. Day Two includes a canoe trip and jungle hike in the refuge and on Tortuguero canals, plus a night tour. Return on the third day through Puerto Viejo to San José, $278 per person. Options include flying in and out with more time for area tours, $375 per person. A budget package starts and ends at Puerto Viejo de Sarapiquí, $199. Sportfishing packages (catch-and-release) available.

Silver King Lodge (lodge (506) 381-0849, fax (506) 381-1403; U.S. number 800-847-3474, fax 813-943-8783; e-mail slvrkng@sol.racsa.co.cr, Web site www.silverkinglodge.com) has spacious, attractive rooms with tongue-and-groove floors and walls, bamboo ceilings, queen-size beds with orthopedic mattresses, and coffeemakers in each room. Gourmet meals are served buffet-style with complimentary wine; no charge for laundry service. Enjoy the enclosed ten-person Jacuzzi and explore backwater lagoons and rivers in aluminum canoes at no charge. Fiberglass kayaks are available for estuary trips into the rain forest at Barra del Colorado. Private paths also lead into the jungle. Take guided tours to the wildlife refuge, to Tortuguero, and to see turtle-nesting (July through September) or crocodiles at night.

A two-day, three-night option is $528 each, double occupancy, including round-trip airfare from San José, lodging, food, and two boat tours of Barra del Colorado and Tortuguero canals. Another package includes a guided canoe trip, lodging, meals, and drinks, $175 per person, double occupancy. Sportfishing packages available.

SOUTHERN CARIBBEAN

The road south from Limón goes all the way to Panama. Direct bus from San José to Sixaola at the border goes by Cahuita National Park and to the Indian village of Bribrí. It does not go all the way to Puerto Viejo de Limón; however, there is a direct San José–Puerto Viejo bus and buses go from Limón to Cahuita and Puerto Viejo de Limón. Several tour companies offer nature-oriented tours to the southern Caribbean region, and the area's lodges and hotels arrange visits to parks and reserves.

FROM LIMON TO CAHUITA

At Penhurst, a road west goes through miles of cacao plantations. Platforms are covered with seeds spread out to dry. You may see guanábana fruit covered with the same blue plastic, insecticide-impregnated bags that cover banana bunches. Follow this dirt road through big banana plantations to the Hitoy-Cerere Biological Reserve. Little visited, it holds treasures for those who reach its forests. Top private reserves are here.

HITOY-CERERE BIOLOGICAL RESERVE
Location: 37 miles (60 km) SW of Limón, 90 minutes from Cahuita.
Size: 22,622 forested acres (9,155 ha).
Hours: Daily 8 a.m. to 4 p.m.
Cost: $6.
Information/Reservations: Telephone hotline 192 (see Appendix A: Parks and Reserves Information), (506) 798-3170, telephone/fax (506) 758-3996.

Off the beaten path, Hitoy-Cerere is not a stopping-off point on the way to somewhere else but a destination in itself. Your map may not even show a road in, but it's there and passable even in wettest months.

Parts of this rugged portion of the Talamanca Mountains have yet to be explored. We do know some of the animals that live in its forested habitat: tapirs, jaguars, peccaries, pacas, porcupines, weasels, white-faced and howler monkeys, agoutis, anteaters, armadillos, kinkajous, sloths, squirrels, otters, and deer. Among the 276 bird species identified are the blue-headed parrot, keel-billed toucan, squirrel cuckoo, spectacled owl, green kingfisher, and slaty-tailed trogon. Frogs, toads, insects, and snakes have not been counted.

The forest canopy hovers at about 100 feet (30 m), but some species protrude through the top, reaching more than 160 feet (50 m). Buttresses from these giants' trunks widen their base of support, some with a horizontal reach of almost 50 feet (15 m). There are black palms with spiny stilt roots, tree ferns, orchids, and bromeliads. Mosses and lichens cushion trunks and branches.

Trails in this perpendicular place are difficult and not well marked. One researcher found it easier to stick to the rivers, though moss-covered rocks make streambeds slippery. *Hitoy* in Bribrí refers to moss- and algae-covered rocks in the river of that name; *Cerere* to another river's clear waters. Pools surrounded by exuberant vegetation invite a solitary dip, while waterfalls almost 100 feet (30 m) high inspire awe. Bring rain gear—no defined dry season. Yearly amounts average 138 inches (3,500 mm). Humidity is high year-round; temperatures average 77°F (25°C). Elevation ranges from 328 to 3,363 feet (100 to 1,025 m).

The reserve is surrounded by legally protected Indian lands: the Tayni, Telire, and Talamanca Cabecar.

A small biological station constructed with funds from Holland may be completed by your arrival. Check with the Amistad Caribe Conservation area about the possibility of bunking overnight at reserve headquarters.

Getting There

By car: Turn west at Penhurst and follow the road through plantations and settlements: Pandora, various *fincas*, and Concepción.
Other: Day tours are offered by agencies and lodges from Limón south to Cahuita and Puerto Viejo.

Where to Stay from Limón to Cahuita

SELVA BANANITO LODGE, PRIVATE RESERVE

Location: In the Talamanca Mountains, 12 miles (20 km) S of Limón and 9 miles (15 km) inland.
Rates: Single $100, double $95 per person, including lodging, meals, and taxes. One free tour with a two-night stay, two with three nights.
Information/Reservations: Telephone/fax (506) 253-8118, U.S. telephone/ fax (515) 236-3894; e-mail costari@netins.net; Web site www.netins.net /showcase/costarica/.

A Jesus Christ Lizard?

The remarkable Jesus Christ lizards are so named because they seem to "walk" on water: actually, they run. The secret to this phenomenon is quick movement and large hind feet with flaps of skin along each toe that allow them to skip over the surface of streams and ponds. Found on both Atlantic and Pacific slopes, species vary by size, form, and color.

Seven individual cabins built off the ground in the Caribbean style have forest out the back door—out the front, too, for that matter: 2,100 acres (850 ha) of the private Selva Bananito Reserve is a 10-minute walk away. A neighbor to La Amistad, the largest park in the country, Selva Bananito protects primary forest, waterfalls, wildlife, rivers and streams, and the chance to experience incredible rain-forest diversity.

The lodge and reserve are on the Stein family farm, which also has land in sustainable agriculture and cattle management. Conservation was paramount in lodge design and construction; those gleaming floors are of salvaged hardwoods. Hot water is supplied by solar energy, and wastewater is treated via a series of marshes and lily ponds. No electricity: nighttime reading is by lantern light, dinners by candlelight. Each spacious bungalow has a queen and double bed and wraparound balcony with a hammock waiting. It's rustic, but charming rustic. Meals are served in an open-air main lodge.

Guides accompany guests on a range of optional tours. A three-hour Jungle at Dawn tour for bird-watchers and photographers is $30. More than 300 species of birds have been counted on the preserve and environs. A forest tour is $15. On the waterfalls tour up the Bananito River, swim at one and eat lunch beside another, returning to the lodge through primary forest, $25.

Climb into a giant ceiba tree using ropes, harnesses, and ascenders: instruction in climbing techniques and safety, $20; jungle canopy climb, $50, including horseback ride to the ceiba. Overnight forest camping is another option, and guests can horseback ride and mountain bike. Bike down to the beach in the morning and be picked up in the late afternoon. Selva Bananito's tour company has several multiday packages that combine a visit to the lodge with other sites, such as Caribbean beaches, Tortuguero, Arenal, Poás Volcano, and Caño Negro.

Ten percent of the income from Selva Bananito activities goes to the Limón Watershed Foundation, established by the Steins; foundation goals include protection of rain-forest vegetation along watersheds of rivers such as the Bananito, which is the primary water source for Limón. Strategies encompass conservation programs, education targeted to sustainable agriculture techniques, patrols against illegal logging, and expansion of protected areas.

Getting There

By bus: From Limón, take bus south and get off at Bananito, where staff will pick you up. From San José, take a Cahuita or Puerto Viejo bus.
By car: Four-wheel-drive necessary for drive inland to the lodge.

AVIARIOS DEL CARIBE, PRIVATE WILDLIFE REFUGE

Location: 19 miles (30 km) S of Limón, 4 miles (7 km) N of Cahuita.
Rates: Single $50; double $60, including full breakfast.
Information/Reservations: Telephone/fax (506) 382-1335 (cellular phone).

At night, a flashlight revealed yellow caiman eyes along the bank of the Estrella River. At midmorning, from the same spot, I saw a river otter playing in the water, a purple gallinule strutting his stuff, and a little blue heron foraging at the river's edge—all of this from the upstairs veranda of the lodge.

Aviarios del Caribe is a labor of love for owners Luis and Judy Arroyo. Gracious hosts, they warmly share with guests their lives and their vision of humanity as caretaker of habitat and creatures. They have succeeded in having the island at the mouth of the Estrella River and the river delta declared a private wildlife refuge. Here are freshwater canals and lagoons, humid tropical forest, sandy beaches, and marshland, along with the forest and waterways. Its creatures are monkeys, sloths, river turtles, sea turtles, frogs, lizards, butterflies, and aquatic, arboreal, migratory, and marine birds, plus birds of prey—299 bird species so far. According to Luis, all six species of kingfishers found in Costa Rica are here, as well as white-collared manakins, migrating orioles and warblers, collared aracaris, toucans, and even the black-crowned night-heron, which nests here but is uncommon in the Caribbean lowlands.

On a quiet canoe trip with Cali, a local guide who takes guests through the canals to the river's mouth and the Caribbean, we watched a boat-billed heron 15 feet (4.5 m) away as he watched us. I was almost within touching distance of a northern jacana, a pretty black-and-chestnut-colored bird with a striking yellow patch above its bill, before it took flight, revealing the yellow underside of its wing. When we left the canoe for a walk on the island, Cali deftly whacked off the top of a coconut with his machete. The liquid tasted marvelous in the morning heat. The three-hour trip is $30 per person.

On short, self-guided trails through forest next to the lodge, you'll probably see a sloth. You're sure to see one upstairs in the lodge—Buttercup has a private tree there, though she seems to prefer a corner of the soft couch. Judy nursed the injured baby three-toed sloth back to health after its mother was killed on the highway; the sloth is now 6 years old. Judy has an album she refers to as "Friends of Buttercup"—filled with photos taken by former guests who have sent pictures. Buttercup is now the star of a master's thesis

Aviarios del Caribe near Cahuita

on vocalizations of female sloths and the responses of the males in and adjacent to her "territory." People continue to bring injured animals to Aviarios, so there's no telling what you'll find when you arrive.

The lodge has six bedrooms, all downstairs. Rooms are large with queen- or king-size beds and floor fans; fresh flowers say welcome. A small gym is available. Upstairs are both indoor and outdoor dining areas and an inviting living area with a library and TV/VCR. Mystical sea horses live in a salt-water aquarium, along with anemones, shrimp, and other fantastic sea creatures. A few steps away on the outdoor deck, see colorful poison-dart frogs in glass tanks; the Arroyos are successfully breeding them. Benches at the deck's rail are ideal for bird-watching; if you forget binoculars, a pair is there for you to use. Recently 51 species of birds, not including river birds, were sighted from this vantage point in a two-hour period, just in the yard and forest edge.

Next to the river is another covered deck and benches. The first time I met the Arroyos, Judy was cooking in a makeshift kitchen on that deck after the 1991 Limón earthquake. It hit just as they were finishing the lodge, so they started over. Now they are philosophical about the loss of new cabins at the mouth of the Estrella River, destroyed by a tropical storm.

Take a night frog walk, headlamps provided, $10. For off-site tours, talk to Brandon, who knows the Caribbean coast. He has a four-passenger vehicle or can accompany you in your car for trips to Hitoy-Cerere ($40 per person), Punta Uva, or Bribrí and the iguana farm ($35). Transport to Cahuita and back for dinner is $10.

Getting There

By bus: From San José, a Sixaola or Puerto Viejo de Limón bus passes the entrance; buses south from Limón pass by.

By car: Signs mark the entrance east off the main road between Limón and Cahuita, near the Estrella River.

CAHUITA

Still a small town (population 3,941) with unpaved streets, Cahuita draws thousands of visitors every year to the beauty of its natural surroundings, a combination of forest and beach showcased in Cahuita National Park. The laid-back lifestyle and the rich mix of cultures that form the Caribbean character of this place are also attractions. Visitors note the influence in food, dress, and music. And music is all over downtown Cahuita. Stroll the streets until you find the beat you like. Lodges and hotels tend to be small, each with a distinctive style. Cahuita is 27 miles (44 km) south of Limón by paved road.

Some of the best restaurants are at lodges and hotels, and you will find others along the main street.

Tour Companies

Cahuita Tours and Rentals (506) 755-0232, telephone/fax (506) 755-0082) is a full-service operation where you can send a fax; exchange money; buy newspapers, handcrafts, or postage stamps; make reservations; and find a public telephone. Owners Antonio Mora and Rudolfo Henriquez offer general information about the area. Snorkeling equipment is available, as well as bikes and scuba gear. For $20, enjoy a four-hour glass-bottomed-boat tour, viewing the marvels of the offshore coral reefs. Other tours include a morning guided nature walk ($18), visit to the Bribrí Indian reserve ($25), and trips to Manzanillo and the Gandoca-Manzanillo Wildlife Refuge or to Tortuguero National Park. A tour to Hitoy-Cerere Biological Reserve with a bilingual local guide is $35 per person, minimum three. Open 7 a.m. to noon and 1:30 to 7 p.m. daily.

CAHUITA NATIONAL PARK

Location: 27 miles (44 km) SE of Limón.
Size: 2,639 acres (1,068 ha) of land; 55,350 acres (22,400 ha) of sea.
Hours: Open daily: Puerto Vargas entrance 8 a.m. to 4 p.m., town entrance 8 a.m. to 5 p.m.
Cost: $6, camping $2.
Information/Reservations: Telephone hotline 192 (see Appendix A: Parks and Reserves Information), at park (506) 755-0302, conservation area telephone/fax (506) 755-0060.

Take white sands, coconut palms, a coral reef, the wreck of an 18th-century slave ship just offshore, and clear Caribbean waters; add at least 123 species of fish, abundant birdlife, and an assortment of other animals from monkeys to caimans. This winning combination is known as Cahuita National Park. Park offices are at Puerto Vargas, just north of Cahuita, and another entrance is from the town of Cahuita itself.

The 1,483-acre (600-ha) reef encircles Cahuita Point, forming a rich undersea garden of 35 species of varicolored coral some 1,640 feet (500 m) from shore. Brightly colored fish such as rock beauty, blue parrot fish, and angelfish swim among the formations, with sea urchins, barracudas, moray eels, sharks, lobsters, sea cucumbers, and green turtles, which feed on the expanse of turtle grass. Snorkeling and scuba diving are allowed, and glass-bottomed boats give visitors a glimpse of the Caribbean's best-developed coral reef.

There is, however, trouble in paradise. Increased erosion from deforestation in the Talamanca Mountains is affecting the reef, a vivid reminder of the distance damage can travel from a mismanaged forest.

Trails lead from both ends of the park. Take the 4-mile (7 km) nature trail that links the two entrances; allow at least 90 minutes to enjoy this experience in the exuberance of tropical moist forest vegetation. Abundance of land and sea birds makes it a bird-watcher's delight. Troops of up to 25 howler monkeys roam the area; look for coatis and raccoons. You may encounter a three-toed anteater, an otter, a four-toed armadillo, or a three-toed sloth.

Sea colors on a sunny day run from almost transparent near the white sand to bright green, turquoise, and aquamarine. At some points, water is knee-deep at quite a distance from shore. Some areas, however, have strong currents where swimming is not safe; two are in the first 1,312 feet (400 m) past the park entrance in Cahuita, and another is at Puerto Vargas. Heed the warning signs and ask if in doubt.

The park receives a little less than 118 inches (3,000 mm) of rain a year; distinction between wet and dry seasons is not as clear as in the Central Valley. Visibility around the reef, however, is better from December to April.

Stop by the information center at the town entrance, administered by a community group which also helps maintain trails and organize beach cleanups. New park headquarters at Puerto Vargas should be finished by your arrival. Camping is allowed at Puerto Vargas, and there are beachside picnic sites, rest rooms, and showers. The park is administered as part of the Amistad Caribe Conservation Area.

Getting There

See directions for the town of Cahuita. To reach the Puerto Vargas entrance by car, go south from Cahuita; watch for the sign on the east side of the road. Tour companies, lodges, and hotels offer day trips. Hire a local guide trained by the nonprofit Talamanca Association for Ecotourism and Conservation (ATEC).

Where to Stay and Eat in the Cahuita Area

Atlántida Lodge, (506) 755-0115, telephone/fax (506) 755-0213; e-mail atlantis@sol.racsa.co.cr; Web site www.atlantida.co.cr, has 30 rooms, each with its own porch separated from adjoining porches by a cane divider and fringed with a thatched-roof overhang. Rooms have fans, reading lamps, cane furniture, and wooden shutters over screened windows. Single $45, double $55, full breakfast and taxes included. There is an open-air restaurant, pool, Jacuzzi, gym, parking, gift shop, and a tour desk; at check-in, don't miss the antique crank cash register. The gardens are ablaze with color. A small bridge over a fish pond connects pool and snack bar. Playa Negra is in front. Atlántida offers 15 tours, including a four-hour jungle walk, snorkeling tour, and visit to Bribrí ($20 per person), bird-watching at Aviarios del Caribe ($30), tropical farm tour or visit to an orchid farm ($10), and an iguana farm tour ($15). Horseback riding to a waterfall is $35. Therapeutic massage available.

Bungalow Malú, (506) 755-0006, has four rooms in charming bungalows of river stone and wood, nestled among colorful tropical vegetation in expansive gardens across the road from the beach. Decorator touches abound. Wood washed ashore after storms has been polished and used as door handles and light fixtures—natural sculptures. Bathrooms have riverstone floors. Rooms have built-in desks, reading lamps, and small refrigerators, some have queen-size beds. Closets and headboards are wood and bamboo. Stone paths lead to a rancho-style restaurant where owner Alessandra Bucci features Italian dishes and fresh fish along with typical Caribbean dishes. Perhaps you can taste breadfruit here. Double $30, $3 more per extra person.

Chalet y Cabinas Hibiscus, (506) 755-0021, fax (506) 755-0015, is by the sea. Three bungalows; two two-story, two-bedroom houses; and a one-bedroom house are situated on palm-studded grounds. Private baths with hot water feature showers lined with smooth river stones. Lace curtains cover windows, and mosquito nets drape beds, though the owners, the Grafs, say they're more for show than necessity. Houses have balconies, sitting rooms, and completely furnished kitchens. Two-bedroom houses are $100 each; the one-bedroom, $50; bungalows $40 to $50. No restaurant here, but good ones are nearby.

El Encanto, telephone/fax (506) 755-0113, about three blocks from downtown on the road to Playa Negra, has three roomy bungalows, each furnished with queen-size bed and trundle bed, ceiling fan, reading lamps, walk-in closet, table, and chairs. Single $40 with breakfast, $37 without; double $45 with breakfast, $40 without. Owners Michael and Karen Russell offer a full breakfast. Dining room/lounge area opens to the large garden. Tours with local guides, certified by Talamanca Association for Ecotourism and Conservation, take guests for forest walks, horseback riding, and reef tours.

Hotel Jaguar, San José (506) 226-3775, fax (506) 226-4775, hotel (506) 755-0238; e-mail jaguar@sol.racsa.co.cr, has 45 rooms across the road from the beach at the north end of town. Building design incorporates cross-ventilation and thermo-siphoning, resulting in passively cooled rooms that have queen-size beds with orthopedic mattresses and louvered shutters over screened windows. Just outside the front door are lounge chairs on long porches facing the beach. Varied fruit trees draw birds to the hotel grounds. Watch for the flash of the scarlet-rumped tanager, and listen to parrots. Superior rooms: single $40, double $70; standard rooms: single, $30, double $55. Breakfast and taxes included.

Paul and Melba Vigneault, hotel owners, have created a menu fit for a gourmet, true elegance by the sea, with such delicacies as avocado omelets for breakfast and French Caribbean cooking that uses fresh herbs and spices in ten sauces served with fish, beef, or chicken. Sea bass with heart of palm sauce is memorable, or try chicken with cashew fruit sauce. The restaurant is open to the public. Lunches are light—salads and sandwiches, served only by prior reservation. The restaurant is in the garden, near the swimming pool.

Nature trails on the 18 acres (7 ha) offer hotel guests the possibility of seeing crocodiles, armadillos, sloths, kinkajous, agoutis, or colorful frogs. Trips arranged to Tortuguero, Bribrí reserve, and Panama. A rental shop has boogie boards, beach mats, fins, and snorkeling equipment, as well as books and souvenirs. Transfer from Cahuita bus stop available.

Magellan Inn, telephone/fax (506) 755-0035; Web site www.webspan.com/tropinet/magellani1, tucked away on a street back from the beach, has six delightful rooms. Original oil paintings adorn the white walls. There are big closets, a long desk, king-size beds, and beautiful woods in carpeted rooms. Each room has French doors that open onto a terrace facing the pool and a tropical garden colored by bright bougainvillea and hibiscus flowers as well as avocado, guava, orange, and lime trees. Ceiling fans are not only in the rooms but also on the individual terraces, which have cushioned bamboo furniture. Single or double $59, including continental breakfast.

Toucans, parrots, parakeets, and hummingbirds like the place, and sloths are not uncommon here. A garden path by the pool leads down to a coral hole that was once undersea. Guests may choose an exclusive morning canoe trip with an Indian guide on a river where manatees have been spotted—no promises. See monkeys, birds, orchids, and crocodiles, $26. Guided horseback rides and beach and Tortuguero tours arranged.

The terrace bar also opens to the garden. Classical music sets the tone for breakfast here. Owner Elizabeth Newton is an attentive hostess. Daughter Terry and son-in-law Etervé operate La Casa Creole restaurant for dinner, which offers seafood, French Creole, Polynesian, and other cuisines in an elegant, candlelit ambiance. Dessert of the day may be puffed pastry with vanilla ice cream and chocolate sauce or banana flambé. Lunches feature salads and sandwiches on baguettes; try milkshakes with a zing—for example, After Eight, with chocolate and creme de menthe. La Casa Creole has a separate entrance and is open to the public from 6 to 9 p.m. Watch for Magellan Inn signs at the first entrance to Cahuita.

PUERTO VIEJO DE LIMON

The village of Puerto Viejo de Limón is to the Caribbean what Montezuma is to the Pacific side. Laid back, it has its own slow and sultry beat. The village is a mecca for surfers; it is also home to ATEC, the Talamanca Association for Ecotourism and Conservation, an orgzanization that works from Cahuita south to Gandoca. Puerto Viejo is about five hours from San José, 40 miles (65 km) southeast of Limón.

Things to See and Do

The **Iguana Farm** in the KéköLdi Reserve is open daily 8 a.m. to 4 p.m., admission $1. KéköLdi people are raising green iguanas, an endangered species. Iguanas are traditionally important to this group for their meat and skins; even the fat is used for medicinal purposes. At a small shop, select from a variety of carefully carved gourds, baskets, drums, and other items made by local children and adults. Hikes into the reserve can also be arranged, led by certified local guides. A tour of the green iguana project and/or walks in the Indian reserve can also be arranged via the ATEC office (see sidebar). A word of caution: finding the farm can be challenging. Not long after taking the turnoff to Puerto Viejo and where pavement turns to gravel, watch on the right for an Iguana Farm sign and a road. The entrance is about 700 feet (200 m) down that road. Watch closely on the left for the entrance sign and parking area. If no one is in the small thatched artisan building, continue to the right up the hill. The iguanas are behind the private house here and someone will show you around. Juana was my charming guide.

The **Tropical Botanical Garden,** (506) 750-0046; e-mail jardbot@sol.racsa .co.cr, showcases bromeliads, heliconias, palms, orchids, gingers, and a variety of other native and exotic plants in 10 acres (4 ha) of garden areas that combine natural settings with landscaped grounds. The bromeliads, grown commercially as well, are fascinating not only in themselves but also as habitat for three varieties of poison-dart frogs. Cultivated crops here include pepper, cinnamon, vanilla, and ginger; 60 varieties of tropical fruits bring birds and butterflies. Visit the medicinal plant section. A loop trail opens access to 20 acres (8 ha) of the garden's private forest reserve, which borders Indian reserves. The trail is up-and-down and sometimes slippery, but owner Peter Kring offers this opportunity to those who want to walk in tropical forest without being concerned about getting lost or trespassing. Open Friday through Monday, 10 a.m. to 4 p.m., entrance fee $2.50, $8 with 2½-hour guided tour, or $2.50 for the loop trail in the forest.

Getting There

By bus: Direct bus from San José to Puerto Viejo, as well as buses from Limón. By car: Turn east off the main road to Bribrí and Sixaola near Hone Creek (Home Creek on some maps and signs); continue 3 miles (5 km) to the village of Puerto Viejo de Limón.

Where to Stay in and near Puerto Viejo de Limón

Beach Cottages, telephone/fax (506) 750-0119, is owned and managed by Mauricio Salazar, a Bribrí Indian, and his Austrian-born wife, Colocha. A two-person rustic bungalow is $25 per day, $150 a week; a three-person bungalow is $30 per day, $180 per week; each faces Black Sand Beach across the road and has an equipped kitchen (small refrigerator and hot plate), and upstairs bedroom. Furnishings are simple.

Cabinas Casa Verde, (506) 750-0015, fax (506) 750-0047, in downtown Puerto Viejo is surrounded by pretty gardens in a residential neighborhood. The friendly hotel encompasses 14 rooms in several small buildings, including a separate bathhouse for rooms with shared baths: single $16, double $22. Each room has a fan, mosquito net, garden view, and hammock. Six have balconies and private baths, double $30. A small bungalow with kitchenette (shared bath) is $25 for up to three.

On nature trails at **El Pizote Lodge,** San José telephone/fax (506) 229-1428, lodge telephone/fax (506) 750-0088, you're almost guaranteed to see small, colorful frogs. Eight rooms in a U-shaped wooden building have shared baths, single $34, double $50. The six bungalows have private baths: single $63, double $75. There are bright bedspreads, screened windows, cane ceilings, reading lamps, and ceiling fans. A two-bedroom *casita* has a king-size bed and two doubles, $113 for three persons. Meals in the restaurant are $2 to $5 for breakfast, lunch or dinner $9.

Kayaks, snorkeling equipment, and bicycles are available for rent; options include jungle hikes, bird-watching, and tours to orchid and banana plantations, Tortuguero and Cahuita, and nearby Indian reserves. A pool should be in place by your arrival. The lodge is on the main road into Puerto Viejo.

La Costa de Papito, telephone/fax (506) 750-0080, is small and charming. Four tropical-wood cabins, spaced for secluded privacy, have wraparound verandas with bamboo rails. Each is large, with wood and bamboo tables, ceiling fans, pitched ceilings, shuttered windows, and two double beds: double $50 for two, $5 each additional person. Breakfast is served at the bungalow upon request, while tropical drinks and *bocas* can be served among the tall palms or in a thatched rancho. Pretty gardens contain heliconias, palms, bananas, papayas, *guanábana*, plantains, and passion fruit; the ocean is beyond.

Owner Eddie Ryan is pleased to help guests arrange area tours such

ATEC and Responsible Tourism

The Talamanca Association for Ecotourism and Conservation (ATEC) promotes ecologically sound tourism along with cultural interchange and ethnic pride among indigenous and African Caribbean people of Talamanca. It was founded in 1990 by local residents when a new road brought development to previously isolated areas. ATEC now has a program called Talamanca Discovery, which aims to connect tourists with nature and with the peoples of this ethnically diverse area in healthy, responsible ways. Encouragement of small, locally owned business and tourist services is another of its ambitious goals.

Here is a sample of what travelers can experience. All tours are led by trained local guides. Guided walks are $12.50 half-day, $25 full day. The personalized naturalist/cultural trips go to Gandoca-Manzanillo for hiking and/or snorkeling, to Gandoca beach from March to July to watch leatherback turtles and gather data on turtle populations, to a family farm in Punta Uva for hiking and snorkeling, to the KéköLdi Indigenous Reserve for a tour and visit to a green iguana project, and to an Afro-Caribbean farm to learn about traditional farming methods within the forest.

A one-day trip from Limón to Tortuguero is $50 per person. Hiking and boat trips through Indian reserves in the Talamancas are an option with at least two weeks' advance notice. ATEC guides are available for birding trips to Cahuita, Puerto Viejo, Punta Uva, and Gandoca-Manzanillo.

The ATEC office, on the first main north–south street off the main road, is open daily from early to late, hours vary; (506) 750-0191, telephone/fax (506) 750-0188; e-mail atecmail@sol.racsa.co.cr; Web site greenarrow.com/x /atec.htm. Here you can purchase a copy of the booklet Coastal Talamanca *to learn more about area culture and ecology.*

as nature walks in an Indian reserve, visits to the green iguana farm, boat excursions, kayaking, horseback riding, or jungle treks in the Gandoca-Manzanillo Wildlife Refuge. The lodge rents bicycles and has a beautician and massage therapist. It's about a mile (2 km) south of Puerto Viejo on the beach road.

La Perla Negra Hotel, (506) 750-0111, fax (506) 750-0114, is indeed a gem. Set against a forest backdrop, the two-story hotel facing the beach is made of beautiful tropical woods. The 24 tasteful rooms have a view of either the open sea or the forest; double $65 including taxes, no credit cards. Some rooms have sleeping lofts; each has a ceiling fan, screened windows, and reading lights. Owners Marlena and architect Julian Grae designed and supervised the building, and nice touches abound. Double doors open onto terraces. The restaurant has an international menu. A swimming pool is in landscaped grounds with an ocean view. Perla Negra offers bird-watching, boating, kayaking, and jungle nature walks with local guides. Watch for a sign on the left as you enter Puerto Viejo.

Where to Eat in Puerto Viejo Area

The area's several restaurants offer a variety of foods. **Stanfords** is a landmark in the old two-story building by the ocean at the southern edge of town. Try delicious *patacones* here. The **Garden Restaurant** has good food; and for pizza or Italian dishes, try **El Coral**. The **Juice Joint** serves sandwiches (BLT, if you've missed it), Mexican food, waffles and pancakes, hot and cold espresso drinks, and slushies and smoothies. Desserts are scrumptious.

CHIMURI NATURE LODGE, PRIVATE RESERVE

Location: Outskirts of Puerto Viejo de Limón.
Rates: Double $24, four-person family cabin $36, bunk bed in dormitory $9.50, including taxes. One-day tour to KéköLdi $25, three-hour bird-watching/hiking tour $12.50 per person.
Information/Reservations: Telephone/fax (506) 750-0119; e-mail atecmail@sol.racsa.co.cr; Web site www.greenarrow.com/x/chimuri.htm.

For travelers seeking adventure in a rustic jungle setting, a stay at Chimuri Nature Lodge may fit the bill. This 49-acre (20-ha) natural reserve offers an out-of-the-ordinary experience.

Traditional Bribrí structures house guests. Built on stilts, the buildings are of tropical wood and bamboo, with cane-thatched roofs. There are three doubles and one unit for four persons; shared baths and flush toilets are steps away. A new dorm used principally for student groups is also open for low-budget travelers, bedding furnished. The complex, in a clearing surrounded by forest, is reached by a five-minute foot trail from the road below, and the Caribbean is 600 yards (500 m) away.

Managers Bruce and Ann Louise can prepare meals—chicken satay and other Thai dishes are Ann Louise's specialty—or guests can bring their own food and use the common kitchen. *Chimuri* means "ripe bananas" in Bribrí, and a stalk is always hanging at the main house, where any hungry hand may reach out and take one.

Owned by Mauricio Salazar, a Bribrí Indian, and his Austrian wife, Colocha, the lodge offers its guests good birding—a wide variety of species feed on the fruits and seeds of the surrounding jungle. Animals seen on the property include sloths, porcupines, agoutis, armadillos, tayras, coatis, anteaters, kinkajous, bats, poison-dart frogs, boa constrictors, opossums, and iguanas. There are birds of prey, parrots, hummingbirds, trogons, motmots, jacamars, toucans, manakins, orioles, and tanagers. On my latest visit, walking from the parking area to

Chimuri Nature Lodge on the outskirts of Puerto Viejo de Limón

the lodge, I saw oropendolas, keel-billed toucans, a black and green frog, and hummingbirds. For butterfly enthusiasts, multitudes live in the forest.

Hike trails alone or with trained local guides. Rubber boots are available. Bring repellent. An afternoon in the river's inviting pools is great after a morning of trekking trails. Explore farther than the Chimuri reserve or the nearby Caribbean coast on optional tours. A one-day walking tour goes through abandoned cacao plantations to traditional Bribrí stomping grounds in the KéköLdi reserve: learn about plants used for medicinal, construction, and other purposes. Along trails, see sloths, raccoons, toucans, iguanas, and perhaps a snake. The group, limited to five, stops by a private home to eat a picnic lunch and glimpse life on the Indian reserve. Return by a different trail. This tour is for people in good physical condition. Visit the green iguana farm and have a typical dinner with a local Black family.

Getting There
By bus: Ask to be let off at the Chimuri's sign on the way into Puerto Viejo—buses from either San José or Limón.
By car: Turn right at Chimuri's sign on road into Puerto Viejo, leave car in parking area; short trail leads up to cabins.

Where to Stay from Cocles Beach to Gandoca-Manzanillo
(in order of location south from Puerto Viejo area)
Villas del Caribe, San José (506) 233-2200, fax (506) 221-2801, hotel

(506) 381-3358, is an attractive red-tile-roofed complex on Cocles Beach. Twelve two-story villas sleep up to six each. The sitting room and equipped kitchenette open onto a private terrace. Upstairs balconies have hammocks. Large bedrooms have hardwood floors, ceiling fans, desk, and sitting areas: doubles $69, $10 each additional person. Vistas are through coconut palms and garden to the Caribbean. Enjoy the fragrance of a heliotrope hedge.

Go horseback riding on roads through a 125 acre (50 ha) private reserve, $5 an hour. Other options include coastal tours by motorboat with English-speaking guide, bicycle rental at $5 per day, and a visit to an old-fashioned *trapiche*—oxen-powered. Rent surfboards, boogie boards, snorkeling equipment.

Hotel Punta Cocles, San José (506) 234-8055, fax (506) 234-8033, hotel (506) 750-0117, U.S. number (800) 325-6927, is 3 miles (5 km) south of Puerto Viejo. The restaurants, 60 rooms, and pool are nestled by a tall forest housing toucans and parrots. Well-maintained nature trails lead through a 35-acre (14-ha) forest reserve. Watch for small, brightly colored frogs here, but do not touch them—the bright colors usually warn of strong toxins. Guests can make one- to two-hour self-guided forays into the lush forest. A checklist of area birds list 326 species in 55 families.

Trails lead across the road to golden-sand beaches and the hotel's seaside Blue Crab Bar. Other hotel amenities include a Jacuzzi and ice machines. Rooms are in bungalows connected to the restaurant and pool area by covered walkways. Each has its own terrace, and both fans and air conditioning: $70 for up to four. Five bungalows have furnished kitchens, $90 for up to six.

A tour desk is in the lobby. The hotel is an inviting base from which to explore nearby parks and reserves; it rents binoculars, bicycles, rain ponchos, boogie boards, and snorkeling equipment. Pick-up is available from the Puerto Viejo bus. The Limón–Manzanillo bus passes in front.

Miraflores Lodge, telephone/fax (506) 750-0038; e-mail mirapam@sol .racsa.co.cr; on Playa Chiquita is a bed-and-breakfast amid an exuberant tropical garden. Owner Pamela Carpenter Navarro not only attends to her guests but raises flowers for export. Guests live among 200 varieties of heliconia, ginger varieties (including the flamboyant torch ginger), calatheas, costus plants, and Musas (of the banana family), most of which are planted under pruned cacao trees. She also has bromeliads, orchids, and a medicinal plant garden. The plantings produce flowers, fruit, nectar, and seeds for animals and birds.

Each of the house's 10 rooms is different: decor reflecting Pamela's life and travels in Central America and her commitment to simplicity. Two upstairs rooms share a living area and bath, $45 per room. Downstairs suites, accented in bamboo and cane, have private baths, $50; rooms downstairs, $40; dorm-room bunk beds, $10 each. Breakfast is included. Total capacity is 45 people. A rancho restaurant, constructed by Bribrís, has the typical split chonta-palm floor—stop by to see it and have a cooling fruit drink.

Tours include an early morning bird walk to see toucans, trips to the iguana farm or Indian reserve, visit with a basketmaker, and dugout ride to Panama, along with bird walks, jungle hikes, sea kayaking, and a dolphin and snorkeling diving tour. Pamela also coordinates with ATEC for tours, and takes people to Bocas del Toro in Panama.

Shawandha Lodge, (506) 750-0018, fax (506) 750-0037, is as exotic as its name. Created by artist/designer Maho Diaz, each of 12 bungalows is unique, with its own theme and featuring furniture Maho designed. Exterior murals honor the area's multicultural diversity, with scenes from American and African native cultures. Spacious rooms open onto private terraces, each with a small sofa, table, and hammock. Bathrooms are enchanting: sinks with designs in small mosaic tiles, showers down spiral steps—no two alike. There are three double-bed rooms, five rooms with queen-size beds, and four with extra long king-size beds. Double $80 for two, including breakfast buffet; $15 per person extra.

Partner Nicolas Buffile brought to the project his creative experience with restaurants. The open-air restaurant and bar, with carved stone motifs reminiscent of Mexico, is striking with its towering rancho-style roof. Sofa, chairs, and tables offer places to relax with a drink and enjoy tropical garden colors before dinner. The menu has a French touch, with Caribbean, African, and Brazilian cuisine adding other flavors: open to the public only for dinner.

Guests may enjoy the 14 acres (8.7 ha) of the property, with trails into the forest on hills behind the lodge. A five-minute walk on a private trail leads to beautiful Playa Chiquita and the Caribbean. Shawandha Lodge is 3 miles (5 km) south of Puerto Viejo.

MANZANILLO AREA

The road goes past Punta Uva, which many claim is the prettiest beach on the Caribbean; here you're already in the Gandoca-Manzanillo National Wildlife Refuge, which has mixed private and government ownership. Though the road peters out after Manzanillo, walking trails continue through forest and along beach. Stand on a rocky point near Punta Manzanillo and see all the way north along the coast to Puerto Vargas and Cahuita National Park. Spectacular scenery. Hiking tours and boat trips to Gandoca Lagoon are available through local hotels and agencies. Stop by Maxi's Restaurant and Bar in Manzanillo.

GANDOCA-MANZANILLO NATIONAL WILDLIFE REFUGE

Location: *Along the Caribbean coast N of Panama, S of Puerto Viejo de Limón.*
Size: *23,348 acres (9,449 ha).*
Cost: *$1.*

That's Chocolate?

The cacao tree, whose seeds are used for cocoa, chocolate, and cocoa butter, is native to tropical America. Cacao is a short tree, about 26 feet (8 m) high with interesting biological peculiarities. Leaves are both green (mature) and red (young). They go from a horizontal to a vertical position depending on the amount of sunlight—the more intense the sun, the more they droop. The fruits, or pods (called mazorcas*), grow directly from trunk or branches, hanging like ornaments. As pods ripen, they change from green to yellow or red. As many as 60 seeds—the commercial cocoa beans—can be in one oval-shaped fruit. One opened for me had 43, all covered in a slippery, soft, tasty pulp. Watch for seeds drying on platforms in the Caribbean countryside.*

Information/Reservations: *Telephone hotline 192 (see Appendix A: Parks and Reserves Information), (506) 798-3170, telephone/fax (506) 758-3996.*

Gandoca-Manzanillo is a mixed-management reserve. That means its goal is not only to conserve the rich biological resources but also to work with the community in sustainable use of resources to promote economic development: tourism is one component. Several hotels and lodges exist on private land within the refuge.

Nature has spread a visual feast. Beaches here are often pictured on postcards: white sand, graceful palms with jungle-looking vegetation beneath, just the right amount of logs and coconuts washed up on the shore. Coral reefs about 650 feet (200 m) out create a snorkeler's paradise: blue parrot fish, green angelfish, white shrimp, red sea urchins and long-spined black ones, anemones, sea cucumbers, lobsters, sponges. Turtle grass sometimes attracts Pacific green turtles.

Explore the refuge's land portion by foot from Manzanillo, or take a boat to a more southern shore to begin a hike. Gandoca Lagoon is about a four-hour hike, but even a short walk on a trail that meanders from forest to beach to forest rewards with unexpected beauty. From the *mirador*, watch tropical fish through dazzlingly clear water or view coastline north to Puerto Vargas.

Terrain in the refuge ranges from flat to rolling country with small, forest-covered hills. You might discover a freshwater marsh, the only natural banks of mangrove oysters in the country, or the place where tarpon fish larvae grow to adulthood. Endangered species protected here include the manatee, crocodile, and tapir. There are also tepezcuintles, caimans, opossums, five species of parrots, sloths, ocelots, margays, otters, bats, falcons, hawks, frigate birds, pelicans, chestnut-mandibled toucans, and collared aracaris.

As for weather, forget the Costa Rican rule of thumb for wet and dry seasons. Rain falls year-round, though driest months are March through May and September through November. Expect cooler temperatures with wind and rain in December and January. Temperatures average 82°F (28°C).

An information center at Manzanillo may be open by the time you arrive; an office is already here. Check with the conservation area about camping. Consider lodging from Cahuita to Manzanillo.

Getting There
By bus: Bus as far as Puerto Viejo.
By car: From Puerto Viejo, follow the beach road south to Manzanillo.

ALMONDS AND CORALS LODGE TENT CAMP, PRIVATE RESERVE
Location: *South Caribbean coast, just N of Manzanillo.*
Rates: *Single $50, double $70. Breakfast $6, lunch $9, dinner $10, plus taxes. A three-day package includes guided walk in Gandoca-Manzanillo refuge, snorkeling at reef, and round-trip transfer from San José: $276 per person double occupancy with private shuttle, $192 with public bus.*
Information/Reservations: *Call Geo Expediciones, (506) 272-2024, (506) 272-4175, fax (506) 272-2220; e-mail almonds@sol.racsa.co.cr.*

Distant lightning played across the night sky. Forest giants loomed in the foreground, fireflies signaled among dense foliage. The sea and the cicadas harmonized in constant melody. And I? I savored lying in a hammock in the middle of the jungle in the darkness. My eyelids began to droop all too soon, and I resented missing a single magic moment of this unusual opportunity.

Almonds and Corals Lodge Tent Camp helps make such fantasies come true. My hammock was suspended inside a platform enclosure that held a tent, bathroom, and corner sitting area. Walls of netting make the experience one of being with the forest, not separated from it.

Twenty covered platforms on stilts are tucked among forest flora. In the cozy tent are a double or two single beds with pretty quilted spreads, floor fan, nightstand, and lamps. Drawers in the base of the beds provide storage space. Tent flaps can be closed at night for privacy. The bathroom, at one corner of the platform, is set off by a partition: flush toilet, built-in sink, and a rounded metal shower, where water at its natural temperature flows out of a pipe. There's even an electric plug. No smoking in tents.

Some visitors may be disappointed that they can glimpse other tents through the foliage; others, no doubt, will be grateful for near neighbors as darkness enfolds the jungle in sounds and shadows.

Raised wooden walkways connect the clusters of cabins with the dining room/bar and, on through the forest, with the beach. Nighttime lighting of walkways is unique; see for yourself. Meals in the open-air dining room are tasty, with a set menu each day. Staff is friendly and helpful, including delightful owners Aurora and Marcos.

Guests are treated to good birding even from their lodging, but I recommend an early morning walk to the beach. You may see toucans, parrots, or a slaty-tailed trogon. Howler monkeys seem to delight in leaving traces of their presence on walkways, so watch your step.

The Almonds and Corals reserve, itself within the Gandoca-Manzanillo National Wildlife Refuge, is small but beautiful. Tours to other parts of the refuge are led by excellent local guides, and sometimes by Marcos himself, who happens to be a physician. A hike starting at Manzanillo is a delight, $45. Eat sea grapes when they're ripe, walk on secluded beaches, and explore a blowhole. Climb to a *mirador* to look down through crystalline water at coral and look up at miles and miles of tropical coastline. Finally, check tide pools for sea urchins and tiny tropical fish, and learn something about medicinal plants and area history.

An array of other tours includes a dugout wooden canoe trip to Punta Mona with a look at Gandoca estuary, $65; bike to Punta Uva to snorkel at the coral reef, $45; kayak at Estero Negro, $65; and visit Volio Indian Ranch near Bribrí to meet an Indian woman and her clan, with the chance to buy handcrafts, $45. A few minutes from Volio is Chase, at the Panamanian border—the driver can take you there.

Aurora owns Geo Expediciones, a travel agency that specializes in the Caribbean area. Tours to the Hitoy-Cerere Reserve, Tortuguero, and Cahuita are arranged. One of the available packages combines Almonds and Corals with charming La Quinta de Sarapiquí Lodge, owned by Aurora's sister and brother-in-law.

Getting There

By bus: From San José and Limón to Puerto Viejo de Limón, San José–Sixaola bus passes the Bribrí intersection. Transfers arranged from either for a fee.

By car: From Puerto Viejo de Limón, go south; watch for sign about a mile (2 km) before Manzanillo.

Other: Some packages offer public or private transportation. A Geo Expediciones shuttle goes from San José to intermediate Caribbean stops and Almonds and Corals.

APPENDIX A
TRAVEL BASICS

ENTRY/EXIT REQUIREMENTS

Requirements for Entry
• Passport or tourist card
• Ticket out of the country (air or bus ticket)
• Length of stay permitted: 90 days with passport, 30 with tourist card
For U.S. and Canadian citizens, no visas are necessary. If you don't have a passport, purchase a tourist card at the airline ticket counter when you fly to Costa Rica; you will need a birth certificate or voter registration document along with photo identification, such as a driver's license. Citizens of other countries can check with the nearest Costa Rican consulate or the Costa Rican Tourism Institute for entry requirements.

The law requires travelers to carry a passport or tourist card at all times while in the country. A photocopy of the passport will do, so leave the original in the hotel safe-deposit box. Be sure to copy pages that show your name, photo, passport number, and date of entry into Costa Rica. (Copy machines abound—signs advertise "Copias.")

Exit Requirements
• Airport departure tax (exit visa): $17
When leaving the country by air, tourists must pay a departure tax, which may be paid in U.S. dollars or colones (*not* traveler's checks, *not* credit cards). The exit visa can be purchased at a window inside the airport or from authorized agents who meet arriving taxis and cars—look for the agents' badges.

If you leave Costa Rica within the time allotted—30 days for entry with tourist card, 90 days with U.S. or Canadian passport—you are not affected by government regulations that tighten up on those who overstay. At one time travelers who entered with a passport could apply for an exit visa at the end of the 90 days and receive a *de facto* extension of another month. No more. Travelers have only five days in which to leave after the exit visa is issued or they risk deportation and limitation on re-entry. For anyone who stays beyond the legal limit, the airport tax jumps to what Costa Ricans pay, about $43.

LANGUAGE

Spanish is the official language of Costa Rica. English is taught in some public schools, so you will encounter *ticos* who want to speak English with you or will try to help out if you don't speak Spanish. Do not expect to find English-speakers wherever you go. Major hotels have some bilingual staff, as do tour agencies and private reserves. However, the waiter, park attendant, or taxi driver may not speak English, and no one at the bus station may understand a word you say. But Costa Ricans will try hard to help as long as you are polite.

Ticos are delighted when you try out whatever Spanish you know, so learn a few words and phrases—at least *por favor* (pronounced por fah-VOR) and *gracias* (GRAH-see-ahs), "please" and "thank you." You will soon be saying *buenos días* (boo-EN-nos DEE-ahs), "good morning," with the best of them.

HEALTH AND SAFETY

Immunizations and Disease

No immunizations are required for entry. But even when staying at home, it is wise to have inoculations up-to-date. Is your tetanus booster current?

Incidence of malaria increased a few years ago in some parts of Costa Rica with the influx of refugees from neighboring countries, but is now on the decrease. Mosquito eradication programs are used to control its spread. Dengue, carried by the *Aedes aegypti* mosquito, has reappeared. An ongoing public education campaign stresses elimination of standing water, and a spraying program is in place. Check with your physician or local health office for advisory information. Contact the U.S. Centers for Disease Control for vaccine recommendations, (800) CDC-SHOT.

Insects

I am well acquainted with two insects in particular: chiggers (*coloradillas*—co-lo-rah-DEE-lyahs) and ticks (*garrapatas*—gahr-rah-PAH-tahs). Chiggers are actually mite larvae and live in grassy, bushy areas waiting to climb up the legs of passersby. Their bites itch like crazy, and the red bumps get worse if you scratch them. To discourage chiggers, dust sulfur powder on socks, feet, ankles, and lower calves before you walk in the grass. Put some on your pant legs. Mosquito repellents are not effective. For bites, Caladryl or Eurax cream helps; some people take an antihistamine for severe itching. The effect of the bites can last for weeks.

Ticks hang out especially where horses and cattle are found. You may notice some itching, but you also may feel nothing and then discover their reddish-black bodies under your skin when you undress. Be careful not to leave the biting end embedded because it can fester and cause infection. Apply alcohol, gasoline, or kerosene to the bite or hold a lighted match close to the tick to encourage it to come out. Squeeze gently to help it along. Ticks can carry disease, so if you get a fever after being bitten, see a doctor.

In an area where mosquitoes are bothersome, use repellent and wear protective clothing. (A tip: don't forget to apply repellent on your hands and, when wearing sandals, on the arches of your feet.) Some places provide mosquito netting for beds; if not, inexpensive mosquito coils help. Find them in grocery stores.

Ants in a wonderful assortment of sizes and colors can bite or sting. Try not to stand still without first checking out the area. Sounds easy, but the advice is hard to remember when you freeze in place to observe a great green macaw or a coati. Be alert in innocent-looking grass. A group of us waiting for a plane on a grassy airfield were bitten by ferocious fire ants, and when we landed back in San José, we had to do battle again with the swarms that had infiltrated the luggage. For hikes and trail rides, hats and long-sleeved shirts give some protection against ants that live in trees you might brush against.

If you are bitten by no-see-ums, the gnats known as *purrujas* in Costa Rica, use an antibiotic salve. You will not only be in more agony if you scratch the bites but also risk infection. No-see-ums live near the coast, preferring areas near salt marshes. Repellents are not too effective; protective clothing works best.

African (killer) bees arrived in Costa Rica in 1982, and you would do well to assume that all bee colonies are now Africanized. Keep your distance from hives or swarms. The stings of Africanized bees are no more venomous than those of your garden-variety bee, but these insects are aggressive and attack with less provocation. The cumulative effect of many bee stings is dangerous. If you're attacked, move in a zigzag motion; you can probably outrun them. Head for water if any is nearby, and cover your head. If someone with you is attacked and cannot move, cover both of you with something light in color and get the person to safety. Remove stingers with a knife or fingernails, being careful not to squeeze more of the stinger's venom into the bite. Apply ice or cold water, and, if badly bitten, see a doctor.

I routinely shake out boots or shoes before I put them on, and shake and inspect my clothes. Having once been stung by a scorpion when I did not, I rarely forget. None of the scorpion species in Costa Rica has fatal poison, but the sting can cause intense pain, itching, numbness of tongue and mouth, vomiting, and fever. Wash the bite with soap and water and disinfect it with alcohol. Anyone with allergies should seek medical help if the bite provokes breathing problems.

Snakes

Running on a path to catch a bus, I once came face-to-face with a snake racing to catch a gigantic frog. I had turned my head to glance at the frog as it leaped by and looked forward again to see a spectacular black snake with a luminous bright green stripe along the length of its long body about 4 feet in front of me. The top half of that body was reared in the air, the head at about the level of my knees. Startled, we stopped in our tracks and stared at each other for a timeless moment. Then in one graceful move, it melted to the ground and slid off into the leaves at the side of the trail. The lesson: if a giant frog passes you with incredible leaps and bounds, consider the possibility that something is in hot pursuit, headed your way.

Although seeing a snake in the tropical forest can be thrilling, be respectful and keep your distance. Minimize unpleasant surprises. First, running is not a good idea. Never sit on or step over a log or rock without checking out the other side. Some snakes live in trees, with protective coloration, so watch where you put your hands and your head. Most bites, however, occur below the knees, so consider high boots. Two pairs of eyes are better than one, so walk with a friend. At night, carry a strong light.

Costa Rica has 135 species of snakes. Only 18 species are poisonous. Fewer than 500 snakebites—most affecting farmworkers—are reported each year, with fewer than 15 fatalities. The fer-de-lance, or *terciopelo*, accounts for almost half the bites.

Bite marks of venomous and nonvenomous snakes differ. That of a nonpoisonous snake shows two rows of teeth marks but no fang marks. If the bite was from a poisonous snake, keep the victim still (especially the affected part), and squeeze out as much venom as possible with your mouth or hands within the first 10 minutes after the bite. Tourniquets and incisions are not recommended for amateurs. Get medical attention as quickly as possible. There is a polyvalent serum for use against all venomous Central American snakes except the coral, which has its own serum.

Food and Water Safety

Precautions make travel anywhere healthier. Give your body a break: keep to a diet it can recognize at first, adding a few new things each day. Get plenty of rest. If you would not eat in a "greasy spoon" or buy food from a street vendor at home, why risk it elsewhere in the world?

As for drinking water, reports of tap water contamination pop up from time to time, though larger towns have regulated water systems. I tend to exercise more caution in coastal areas and try to follow the saying, "When in doubt, don't." When you stay at a hotel or reserve in a rural area, you have every right to ask about the source of water. Many travelers take the precaution of drinking bottled water, available almost everywhere, or bottled carbonated drinks, beer, and packaged fruit juices. Contaminated ice continues to be a problem, mainly from the poor hygiene of those who handle it. And remember, if you don't trust the water as safe to drink, don't brush your teeth with it either.

A good substitute for water on a hot day on the coast is the liquid from a *pipa*, a green coconut. You can get *té de manzanilla* (chamomile tea) practically anywhere, with water that most likely has been boiled. Several companies offer a variety of delicious, packaged herbal teas. You can always get fine coffee.

The two largest dairy product companies are Dos Pinos and Borden; both are reliable and offer pasteurized products. Laser-treated milk that does not have to be refrigerated until opened is also available.

Raw fruits and vegetables that can be peeled are safer. (That's one reason you carry a pocketknife.) Be sure to try the *mamón chino* (an exotic-looking red, spiny fruit with a succulent white flesh inside that you suck off a large seed), several varieties of mangoes, pineapples, bananas with the taste of the sun still in them, and cas (wonderful in juice or ice cream). Be careful with the colorful cashew fruit (*marañón*)—it causes an allergic reaction in some people.

Crime

Theft is a worldwide phenomenon. Use common sense: don't wear expensive-looking jewelry or flash lots of cash when making simple purchases. Do watch your belongings. Don't leave cameras or binoculars lying unattended on the beach. Watch your pockets and bags on crowded buses and streets. Use a bag that closes securely and hold it tightly between arm and body. Carry your wallet in an inside coat or trouser pocket, not in a back pocket. Travel stores now carry all kinds of hidden pockets and pouches to wear on practically any part of the body; investigate which one serves your purposes. Keep your passport separate from your money. Better yet, carry a photocopy of your passport (the photo and entry date pages) and leave the original in the hotel safe-deposit box, along with your airline ticket. Carry only the credit cards you need.

Be alert on the street if approached by an overly friendly person who claims to have met you somewhere. There are expert pickpockets around. I lost a watch while trying to explain to a man that I did not believe I knew him. I would know him now.

The Costa Rican Tourism Institute (ICT) has published a "Passport for Your Safety" brochure, distributed at airports, hotels, and other tourism businesses, with tips for travelers on how to have a safer vacation. In case of emergency, call 911.

Traffic Hazards

For a tourist in San José, there are easier ways to get around than by rental car: parking space is limited, car theft is a problem, and traffic is fierce. I would suggest you walk or take a taxi or bus.

In the countryside, roads are for cars, buses, trucks, cows, dogs, chickens, people, and landslides. Be careful out there. Some specific driving habits to look out for are passing on curves, use of climbing lanes by cars going downhill, and driving on whichever side of the road has the best pavement or fewer rocks or ruts. Tailgating is a national pastime.

Watch out for two-lane roads that feed suddenly into one-lane bridges and for lethal *huecos* (WAY-kos), holes in the pavement, which can knock passenger and vehicle for a loop. Tree branches laid across the road warn of trouble ahead, and when an oncoming car flashes its headlights, it usually means "police ahead," an accident, or some other danger. Slow down.

Geography and climate team up to create landslides big and small. Fog is a permanent possibility on the highest section of the Inter-American Highway south of San José toward San Isidro de El General—the range known as Cerro de la Muerte. The earlier you get through that section, the better (and the scenery is magnificent). The same advice goes for the highway to Limón through Braulio Carrillo National Park.

On the San José–Puntarenas highway, you may find yourself in a string of cars, buses, and diesel-fume-belching trucks on a narrow, winding road. Adrenaline flows as vehicles jockey for position without a clue as to what may be approaching just around the curve. Avoid that road on weekends and after dark. In fact, avoid driving at night in general.

Even with road map in hand, you'll need to ask directions when traveling off main roads. Additional signs are going up along main tourism routes, but choices outnumber signs, especially on dirt roads. In the rainy season, always ask about the condition of the roads you plan to take before setting out each day.

Traffic police equipped with radar are on major roads. Watch the posted speed limit and buckle up. If you are stopped by transit police and cited, fines must be paid to a bank or the rental agency will handle it for you. You should not pay the officer.

GETTING TO COSTA RICA

Time, distance, and political considerations lead most tourists from the United States and Canada to opt for air travel to Costa Rica, which means landing at Juan Santamaría International Airport, 20 minutes from San José, or Daniel Oduber Quirós airport, 15 minutes west of Liberia in Costa Rica's northwest sector.

Some airlines have direct flights from the United States, while others have intermediate stops in Mexico or Central American countries. Check the Worldwide Web; most airline websites have information on schedules, along with luggage restrictions.

Commercial carriers include American, Continental, Delta and United (U.S. carriers); Aero Costa Rica and LACSA (Costa Rica); Mexicana (Mexico); and TACA (El Salvador). Find San José addresses and phone numbers for these airlines in Appendix B.

Several charter companies land at both the San José and Liberia airports.

TRAVEL WITHIN COSTA RICA

Taxis, buses, rental cars, charter and scheduled airplanes, horses, ferries, bicycles, helicopters, balloons, motorcycles, horses, foot-power—many options exist for moving a traveler around the country. Most of you will experience the country's highways and byways. Potholes are a serious hazard on paved roads, and unpaved roads definitely add an element of adventure, especially in rainy months. The kilometers of paved roads grow yearly, always with greatest increases (Costa Ricans say) in election years. Remember that highway construction and maintenance are expensive in this mountainous, rainy nation, to say nothing of the havoc wreaked by hurricanes and earthquakes. I traveled over the newly paved road between San Isidro de El General and Dominical in southern Costa Rica in 1987, just after it was finished, marveling at what an easy, quick trip it was through a spectacular landscape. Six months and Hurricane Joan later the landscape was still spectacular, but some of it had shifted onto the roadbed and potholes required full driver attention. Quality control in construction has also been lacking. As you travel, you'll encounter superb highways, potholes, unpaved gutbusters, and charming country roads.

Taxis

Licensed taxis are red except for the orange airport vehicles. Take an unlicensed taxi at your own risk. Meters, called *marías*, are required for distances of up to 7.5 miles (12 km). Before you get in, don't be embarrassed to ask the driver if his *maría* works or to look below the front dash to see if it's on. The meter will start with a minimum charge (at printing, 165 colones for the first kilometer); it goes up 75 colones for each additional kilometer in metropolitan areas. From 10 p.m. to 5 a.m., 20 percent is added. If you phone for a taxi, the driver can start the meter where he got the call. A driver who does not use the *maría* can be fined. To file a complaint at the Ministry of Public Works and Transport, be sure to get the taxi number and driver registration number and note the time.

Drivers are generally courteous, though some will refuse to take you if they consider the distance too short or the traffic too fierce. Don't be surprised if this happens to you at the taxi stand on Avenida 2 in front of Gran Hotel Costa Rica. It gets my vote for the greatest percentage of surly drivers.

You can hire a taxi to go practically anywhere there is some kind of road. In outlying areas, taxis are often four-wheel-drive Jeep types. The fare for hired trips is based on distance and time, more if the trip is over bad roads. If you don't want to arrange it yourself, ask your hotel to call, ascertain the fare, and reserve the taxi. The advantage is that the driver will stop wherever you want to take a picture or have an extra moment to soak up the scenery; the disadvantage is that he may not speak English. (Airport drivers usually speak some English, but their rates are higher.) See Appendix B: Travel & Environmental Contacts for San José taxi telephone numbers.

Buses

Bus service in Costa Rica is reliable and inexpensive. It offers a good opportunity to mix with the people, perhaps in closer quarters than we of automobile-minded societies are accustomed to. You may actually have to rub shoulders with someone, but you will sense the nature of those people by the time the trip is over. And they might have a glimpse of yours.

My bus travels have revealed a genuinely courteous people—helpful, friendly, good-humored, dignified. No pigs and chickens in these buses. The vehicles are usually clean (unfortunately, a few still carry a sign advising passengers to throw trash out the window rather than litter the bus!) and so are the Costa Ricans who use them. I have encountered some foreign tourists in Costa Rica who must have thought that "back to nature" in the tropics meant going without a bath. Not so for Costa Ricans: for them, personal cleanliness truly is next to godliness.

Intercity fares from San José usually do not exceed $12 one-way; once in the provinces, local bus services can usually move travelers to other destinations without a return to the capital. (See Appendix B: Travel & Environmental Contacts for departure points.)

Sometimes seats can be reserved with advance ticket purchase. If not, go to the bus stop at least an hour early. If the bus line has an office there, buy the ticket and get in line. If there is no office, you buy a ticket from the driver or his assistant. Ask if you are in line for the bus you want. Verify that it's the right bus when you get on. Most buses carry only seated passengers but not always so in outlying areas. Check your ticket to see if it is for an assigned seat; some routes assign seats, others don't.

As for luggage, some buses have compartments underneath; some have overhead luggage racks adequate only for a small pack or bag, and others allow luggage to be stored next to the driver. Newer long-distance buses have adequate legroom, while some of the old ones bring back memories of riding on a school bus: the seats are the same, but you are bigger.

Watch your belongings! If you end up standing in a crowded bus, watch your pockets. Even with those courteous, helpful, friendly, dignified people around you, a bad apple may be on board. Be especially careful with checked luggage. Get off the bus quickly to claim it at your destination. If you put a bag on an overhead rack, keep your eye on it, especially before the bus leaves and at intermediate stops.

On longer trips, carry bottled water, maybe a snack. Don't expect a rest room on board. If your destination is not the town itself, ask the driver to let you off as close as possible. In towns, taxis usually meet incoming buses.

I look forward to bus trips off the major highways. The driver may stop to chat a minute with another driver if you meet another bus on your route, or he may be flagged down by a housewife asking him to pick up something in town and drop it off on the return trip. These buses are a lifeline in rural areas.

Speaking some Spanish makes bus travel easier, but with politeness, persistence, and imagination, a non-Spanish-speaker can manage. Carry a map and point to destinations, or write the destination down and show it when asking for guidance. Bus is spelled the same in Spanish but is pronounced "boos."

Planes

Two domestic airlines offer scheduled service: SANSA and Travelair. SANSA rates are generally lower, while Travelair prides itself on the level of service it offers. SANSA flights leave from Juan Santamaría airport near Alajuela; Travelair flights leave from the Tobías Bolaños airport, 15 minutes from downtown San José in the suburb of Pavas.

Destinations, rates, and telephone/fax numbers for both of these airlines are in Appendix B. Baggage is limited to 26 pounds (12 kilos) on each. Store extra luggage at your hotel. Flights are generally less than one hour. Because planes are small, it's advisable to reserve as far in advance as possible, especially in high season.

Don't schedule yourself too tightly, and do be aware that flights can be canceled because of bad weather, more of a threat in the rainy season. Once, on a charter flight from Marenco, our pilot would only take two passengers at a time because of weather conditions; standing on the short, grass runway at Marenco with ocean on one side and rainforest-covered mountains on the other, not one of us questioned his decision.

Several charter companies provide air service. Look in the phone book under "Aviación" for other possibilities.

Aero Costa Sol, (506) 441-1444, fax (506) 441-2671; U.S. and
   Canada number (800) 245-8420
Aerobell, (506) 290-0000, fax (506) 296-0460
Aerolineas Turisticas de América, (506) 232-125, fax (506)
   232-5802
Aviones Taxi Aereo, (506) 441-1626, fax (506) 441-2713
Taxi Aereo Centroamericano, (506) 232-1438, fax (506) 232-1469
Travelair, (506) 220-3054, fax (506) 220-0413
Viajes Especiales Aéreos, (506) 232-1010, fax (506) 232-7934
Pitts Aviation, telephone/fax (506) 228-9912; e-mail skytours@sol
   .racsa.co.cr
Alas Anfibias, telephone/fax (506) 232-9567, a seaplane operation, opens
   up new possibilities for getting around in Costa Rica, especially to
   more remote places. Regular service goes to Drake Bay, Flamingo
   Bay, and Lake Arenal. Charters are available to Barra del Colorado,
   Coco Island, beaches on the Nicoya Peninsula and Gulf of Papagayo,
   and Tortuguero.

Helicopters

Helisa, Helicópteros Internacionales, (506) 231-6867, telephone/fax
   (506) 231-5885, does sightseeing tours as well as transfers.
Helicópteros del Norte, (506) 232-7534.

Trains

Trains are not an option. The famous Jungle Train from San José to Limón came to an end in 1991, when passenger service between the Central Valley and the Caribbean shut down. The Puntarenas route was also discontinued that year.

Ferries

On the Pacific side, three companies operate car/passenger ferries across the Gulf of Nicoya from the mainland to the Nicoya Peninsula. Each makes several round trips per day. The ferry between Puntarenas and Playa Naranjo takes about an hour; service between Puntarenas and Paquera takes about 90 minutes. There's no advance purchase of tickets, so if you are driving, get to Puntarenas at least 30 minutes early to get your ticket and get in line; even earlier on weekends.

A passenger launch also makes three trips a day from Puntarenas to Paquera.

The ferry across the Tempisque River at the upper end of the Gulf of Nicoya offers an alternate route to the central and northern regions of the Nicoya Peninsula and popular beach destinations, rather than going through Liberia. The continuous turnaround trips connect Puerto Níspero and Puerto Moreno. The crossing takes about 30 minutes.

A passenger launch also operates between Golfito and Puerto Jiménez, crossing the Golfo Dulce for a sea link between the mainland and the Osa Peninsula. It runs the 90-minute voyage once a day, each way.

See Appendix B: Travel & Environmental Contacts for departure times, rates, and telephone numbers.

Car Rental

To rent a car, you need a valid driver's license, passport, and credit card. The minimum age is usually 21 to 25. All major car-rental agencies have offices in Costa Rica, and there are several local companies as well. Offices are now not only in San José but in major towns, as well as some resorts. Few automatic transmissions are available.

Shop around. Deductibles can be high. Weekly rates are discounted, and travelers in the low season, May to November, may pay as much as 20 percent less. You may get better rates by reserving your car before you come, through international reservations. Ballpark figures for something like a Sentra or Tercel, based on current quoted rates, are $54 for one day and $330 for one week, including insurance and free mileage. Four-wheel-drives start at about $75 per day (Suzuki Sidekick), $475 for the week. There is usually a damage deposit, up to $1,000. Ask for a map and a handout sheet on basic Costa Rican traffic regulations.

As anywhere else, be sure to check the car over for dents, scratches, or other damage before you accept it and have those noted in writing by the agent. Also be sure to check the spare and jack and such details as brake fluid, oil, water, and lights.

Gas is sold by the liter. All petroleum is imported and refined in Costa Rica by RECOPE, the national refinery. Prices per gallon at printing range from $1 to $1.50, depending on whether it is regular, super, or diesel. In rural areas, watch the gas gauge. You will not find a service station at every intersection. In some small towns the attendant fills your tank not by pump but by *pichinga*, a plastic jug.

Speed limits are posted and the numbers are in kilometers, not miles. Before you rent a car, please read the Traffic Hazards section, above. Don't leave belongings visible even in a locked car, and don't leave luggage in the trunk at night or even unattended during the day. In fact, don't leave anything of value in an unattended car anytime. Use the seat belts.

Because of road conditions, driving times are usually longer than expected. See Intercity Buses in Appendix B for some idea of driving times.

Bicycles

Bicycle tourism is here. If you're going to do it on your own, remember that bike lanes do not exist. If this is your first trip to Costa Rica, you might consult one of the tour companies before you set off (see Chapter 4).

Hitchhiking

Hitchhiking on major roads is not common: bus fare is so cheap. However, in rural areas where bus service is nonexistent or infrequent, local people wait by the road for a ride. Tourists do not generally hitchhike in Costa Rica except in an emergency. For example, when my return flight from Golfito fell through and I had to be in San José the next day for an appointment—and all the buses were sold out—I hitchhiked for the first time in my life. At the end of the seven-hour trip, the kind young man who had rescued me said, "Ree, you should not do this any more. Not everyone is good." He delivered me right to my door.

WHAT TO BRING

Costa Ricans tend to dress on the conservative side, but they are becoming accustomed to the flavors of dress introduced by international visitors. In San José, it's common now to see local women wearing pants or jeans. Shorts worn by men or women are beginning to be seen, though much more on tourists than local folks. In coastal areas or for sports, shorts are common.

In the evening at a nice restaurant in San José environs, local men may wear a coat and tie or at least a dress shirt; women, a dress or nice pants outfit. In most other places, dress for dining out is casual.

For hikes in the forest, long pants give more protection from insects and plants than shorts. Throw in some cotton pants, especially in rainy season, since it takes forever and a day for jeans to dry. A long-sleeved shirt or two is wise for protection from the sun—remember, its rays are direct at 10 degrees from the equator—and from insects and scratches on narrow trails. Bring your bathing suit; nudity on public beaches is not acceptable in this culture.

Tuck in a sweater or light jacket for chilly evenings or wet, windy weather. Light clothes that can be layered will serve you well.

If you will be staying at hotels or nature reserves that have shared baths, consider a lightweight sweatsuit for trips to the shower. It can double as sleeping attire if the night is chillier than expected or as something comfortable to change into after a day of sightseeing or travel.

A comfortable pair of walking shoes is paramount. Some prefer tennis shoes to hiking boots for forays into the tropical world. Whichever, they probably will get wet at some point, even in the dry season if a trail leads through small streams, so have a backup. In rainy times, locally available rubber boots are handy. You can buy them in markets and shoe stores, especially in rural towns; they are standard footwear for campesinos. Some lodging places have rubber boots available to guests. (You probably won't find any for extra-large feet.)

Rain poncho or umbrella? I pack both, but make sure the poncho is lightweight and hooded. The poncho gives better protection to backpacks, fanny packs, binoculars, and cameras, and can be useful for boat rides or trips on horseback. The umbrella is great for town time and for when you're not carrying 20 other things on the trail. In warmer areas, I suggest you try simply getting wet one time, especially on a forest walk. Experience the elements. Just protect your camera or binoculars (plastic bags) and go for it.

Leave expensive jewelry at home. Much to Costa Ricans' dismay, thievery is on the upswing, especially in San José. I had a chain snatched from my neck on a downtown street at midday.

Though the electric current is 110 volts, same as in the United States and Canada, some outlets do not accommodate the larger grounding plugs on new appliances. So if you're bringing your computer on vacation (heaven forbid), bring an adapter without the larger prong. When packing electric razors, hair dryers, and such, be aware that travel in the boonies may put you in a room without an electric outlet.

Pack light. Travel to a remote spot by small plane, boat, or jeep may limit what you can take. Some domestic airlines limit luggage to 26 pounds per person. Bring a smaller bag, with enough room to carry a change, and store your larger bag at the hotel until you return.

A day pack also comes in handy, even for city sightseeing. You can stick in a jacket, camera, umbrella, and guidebook. Be sure it closes securely. To further foil the light-fingered in heavy street traffic or on crowded buses, wear your fanny pack to the front or move your day pack to your shoulder where you can control access to it. A water-resistant pack helps.

As for film, you can get Fuji, Kodak, Agfa, and other brands in San José and some outlying towns, but it's best to bring a few extra rolls just in case.

Slide film is generally hard to find outside San José. You will not find the variety of ASA ratings and types of film you may be accustomed to. Don't forget spare camera batteries.

Imported goods are expensive, so if you run out of toilet items, consider local brands. Keep any medicines you require with you, not packed in luggage to be checked.

One item you should not bring along is impatience. Leave it at home. Who knows? After a time in Costa Rica without it, you may find you don't need to lug it around anywhere anymore.

Checklist of other items:

Wide-brimmed hat for rain or sun.

Flashlight for nighttime hikes, to get from your cabin to the dining room in the middle of the forest, and in case the power goes off in town or the generator is shut off before you're ready for bed at one of the remote reserves.

Sunscreen

Insect repellent

Pocket calculator—simplifies currency calculations.

Moist towelettes

Pocketknife

Small mirror—some rustic facilities lack a bedroom mirror.

Anti-itch ointment—an antihistamine cream for insect bites or even an antihistamine to take orally to reduce discomfort. If you do find yourself with bites and no ointment, juice from the stem of the impatiens (china) plant, abundant in many parts of Costa Rica, is an excellent natural remedy.

Antidiarrheal medicine—better to have the kind you are comfortable with, just in case.

Washcloth—many Costa Rican hotels don't supply them.

Reclosable plastic bags—small ones are ideal for keeping a passport or other important papers dry; a larger one is handy for packing a wet bathing suit, or even for your camera or extra lens.

Plastic water bottle—or buy bottled water for hikes, bus rides, etc.

Binoculars, to see the expression on the face of the sloth high in the tree. You'll be sorry if you don't bring a pair.

Antifogging agent for eyeglasses, especially during the rainy season, when putting binoculars or a camera to your glasses can result in one big blur. (If you're in the forest with Amos Bien of Rara Avis, he can show you a plant leaf that will do the trick, but otherwise bring your own stuff.)

Old tennies or sandals, for climbing over rocks at the beach to explore tide pools.

Tissues—public rest rooms in Costa Rica may not have toilet paper.

Coin purse, to accommodate an ever-growing supply of change. (Unfortunately, only the small denominations seem to self-generate.)

RESERVATIONS

Reservations for hotels and for lodges at private nature reserves are highly recommended for visits from December to April and are increasingly advisable in the low season, now marketed as the Green Season. They are essential for Christmastime and Easter week—some hotels have higher rates at these times as well. Some hotels and reserves offer substantial discounts during off-season months, especially in beach areas.

You will note that I've emphasized smaller hotels, many of them owner-operated. I believe they give the traveler a better opportunity to taste the flavor of the country. Phone numbers, faxes, and, where available, e-mail and Web site addresses for hotels, private reserves, and tour companies are included in regional chapters. The 506 prefix is the country code for calling to Costa Rica. Once inside the country, do not dial 506. Mailing addresses are not listed because service is slow and unreliable.

Once you're in the country, call to reconfirm reservations you made from home; and bring copies of your confirmation. Prices listed, high-season rates, are valid at the time of printing, however, rates do change. Use these as guidelines. I have not included taxes in these rates unless specified.

Tourist attractions also feel the impact of Costa Rican vacationers during school vacation from December through February and during a two-week midyear break in July. Beaches and parks are prime destinations.

AT THE AIRPORT

When you arrive in Costa Rica at the San José airport, look for the Costa Rican Tourism Institute (ICT) airport information office after you make your way past *migración* (Immigration) and *aduana* (Customs). From 9 a.m. to 5 p.m. Monday to Friday, except holidays, ICT staff (aided by student interns studying tourism) can answer your questions, help you make hotel reservations, and give you a road map of Costa Rica. You can pick up brochures published by ICT as well as by hotels and tour companies and get free copies of the English-language newspapers published in Costa Rica.

The bank at the airport is open for dollar transactions from 5:30 a.m. to 8 p.m. Monday through Friday, except holidays. It's across from the ticket counters on the ground floor near the airport information desk.

A taxi ride for the 11 miles (18 km) into San José is $10 U.S. If there are four or more people in your group, you may be directed to a van, which costs $17. If you are put in one of these vans with other travelers, ask the person assigning taxis what your share will be. Fare on the frequent public buses from the airport to San José or Alajuela is about 50 cents but there are no luggage racks, so if you have big bags, forget that option.

Outside the front door of the airport terminal are offices of half a dozen rental-car agencies; near the passenger exit is a private tourist information and reservation agency called Travel Center. Open daily from 9 a.m. to 9 p.m., the center has maps, books, and lots of travel folders—bilingual staff.

When you leave the country, you will be told to be at the airport two hours early. It's good advice; check-in lines can be long, and you need time to pay the departure tax and change your remaining colones into dollars. It's best to reconfirm your return flight at least 24 hours before departure. Baggage handlers will carry your luggage from curbside and leave it as close as possible to the check-in counter. Many an unsuspecting tourist has followed his or her luggage, only to receive disapproving looks from fellow passengers for not going to the end of the line. Leave the bags at the front—you go to the back.

Travelers who land at the Daniel Oduber Quirós International Airport, 11 miles (17 km) west of Liberia in northwestern Costa Rica, will also find car rental agencies and taxis. At this printing, only charters and LACSA land at this airport.

MONEY MATTERS

Currency

The monetary unit is the *colón* (co-LONE). Its symbol is ¢. Take time to look at the coins—some are *colones* (co-LONE-ess) and some are *céntimos* (SEN-tea-mos). Each is clearly marked, but it pays to recognize that the coin marked "20" is 20 colones, not 20 céntimos. Bills come in denominations of 50, 100, 500, 1,000, and 5,000. (The 50- and 100-colon bills are being replaced with coins). Pretty 5- and 10-colón notes are rarely used now, though you can buy them as souvenirs. Coins are 1, 2, 5, 10, 20, 25, 50, and 100 colones: 10, 25, and 50 céntimos are still around but are an endangered species. Newer coins have a golden finish.

The colón floats in relation to the U.S. dollar; as of July 1998, the exchange rate was 257 to the dollar. Continuing mini-devaluations will change this rate.

From my experience, you sometimes pay a premium for colones in a departure airport, so change a minimum or wait until you get to Costa Rica. You may change money legally at banks or at your hotel. It is certainly more convenient at the hotel, but sometimes the cash drawer is low, so don't wait until the last minute to ask. Do not change dollars on the street: it's both illegal and risky. The difference in the legal and black-market rate is only a few colones, and you risk receiving counterfeit money or being otherwise short-changed or robbed.

Western Union has offices at Calle 9, Avenidas 2/4, and in San Pedro if you need to transfer cash. Telephone is (506) 283-6336, toll-free inside Costa Rica (800) 777-7777.

Hotels and banks usually charge a small amount for changing traveler's checks or give a lower exchange rate. Ask. Some have a minimum service charge whether you change $50 or $500 worth of checks. Do not assume that all hotels will accept credit cards, especially outside San José; be sure to inquire when you make your reservation. In listings, I indicate if a lodge or hotel does not accept credit cards. Also, some establishments add a surcharge for use of credit cards even though it is illegal.

Always have some smaller bills with you. Taxis or rural restaurants or shops may not have change for a 5,000-colón note.

Banks

Hours vary but banks are open at least from 9 a.m. to 3 p.m., closed on holidays and weekends. A few have longer hours and are open Saturday morning. In San José the most efficient bank I have found for changing money is Banco Metropolitano (Avenida 2 between Calle Central and Calle 1), open weekdays from 8:15 a.m. to 4 p.m. But at any bank, just tell the guard at the door that you want to change U.S. dollars (that much English everybody understands), and he will point you in the right direction.

Before you take a place in any bank line, ask to be sure you are in the right one. You sometimes must hand over your identification documents (passport, tourist card) at one window and complete the transaction at another. It can be a happy five-minute experience, or it can take 30 minutes or more. Non-U.S. currency is difficult to change.

Banks generally assess a small percentage for changing traveler's checks. Bank holidays are listed at the end of this appendix.

Credit Cards

More and more establishments accept credit cards, but ask before you spend if you're depending on plastic. Some establishments—hotels especially—add a surcharge for use of a credit card, even though it's illegal. You may want to check when you make your hotel reservation.

In downtown San José, an American Express office is on the third floor of the Banco de San José across from the Hotel Europa on Calle Central, Avenidas 3/5, open 8:15 a.m. to 4:15 p.m. weekdays. Call (506) 257-1792 for information.

For VISA and MasterCard, automatic teller machines with 24-hour service (some for Plus and some for Cirrus) are increasingly available in the Central Valley, with at least one in places like Liberia, Limón, Ciudad Quesada, and Puntarenas. A Credomatic office on Calle Central, Avenidas 3/5, deals with both of these cards. It's open 8 a.m. to 7 p.m. weekdays, Saturdays from 9 a.m. to 1 p.m.; for information call (506) 257-0155.

For VISA, I have also used the Banco Crédito Agrícola de Cartago, Avenida 4, Calle 2, near the Metropolitan Cathedral.

You will need to show your passport or tourist card for any credit-card transactions at banks.

TOURIST INFORMATION

The toll-free 24-hour information line within Costa Rica is (800) 012-3456. In any kind of emergency, call 911.

In addition to the Costa Rican Tourism Institute office at the airport, ICT has two downtown information offices: at Plaza de la Cultura on Calle 5, Avenidas Central/2, and in the tall ICT building at Avenida 4, Calles 5/7 (go down steps to the entrance and take an elevator to the 11th floor). You'll find brochures, books of hotel photos to flip through, and staff to answer your questions. You can get a free ICT road map and lists of hotels, restaurants, museums, galleries, and such. If you will be traveling by bus, ask for an up-to-date list of public transportation. Hours at downtown offices are 8 a.m. to 4 p.m. Monday through Friday, closed holidays.

For information on Costa Rica before your trip, see Appendix B.

COMMUNICATIONS

Mail
Some hotels sell postage stamps and will mail cards and letters for guests. However, it's fairly painless to do it yourself at the local post office, and Spanish usually is not necessary. Just hand the card to the person at the window, who will sell you beautifully colored stamps. Move away from the window to affix the stamps and put them in the appropriate slot: interior or exterior. Don't expect your cards or letters to get to recipients before you get home.

The line moves quickly at the Central Post Office in San José, Calle 2, Avenidas 1/3. Hours of window service are 7 a.m. to 9 p.m. weekdays, 8 a.m. to noon on Saturday. Elsewhere, look for a CORTEL sign to find the post office.

Telephones
International calls are easy, once you have access to a phone. From a private phone you can dial direct, using the appropriate country code (001 for the United States and Canada), followed by the area code and the number. Call person-to-person collect, or charge a call to your credit card by dialing 09, the country code (1 for the United States and Canada), area code, and phone number. An operator will come on the line for billing and person-to-person specifics. You can also dial 116 for the international operator, but service is quicker and cheaper using the 09 service. At most hotels, you must go through the switchboard, and there may be a fee. Ask.

Prepaid telephone cards have arrived in Costa Rica. Buy a Viajera Internacional 199 card for calls to anywhere in the world. Another is the Colibrí card. With these, users dial numbers indicated on the cards for service. You can also buy cards for card-operated public phones, good for local and international cards; insert the card and make your call. Buy cards from vending machines at the airport, from ICE telephone agencies, or from banks and other entities that display emblems for them.

Two communications centers in San José allow travelers to make international calls or send a fax or e-mail and pay on the spot (or call collect or use a telephone credit card). Radiográfica Costarricense in downtown San José, Avenida 5, Calle 3, is open from 8 a.m. to 10 p.m. weekdays and 8 a.m. to 8 p.m. weekends. Comunicaciones Internacionales on Avenida 2 just west of the Gran Hotel Costa Rica and Plaza de la Cultura is open daily from 7 a.m. to 8:30 p.m. Comunicaciones Internacionales also has an office in Puntarenas and some tour offices around the country offer international services.

From any phone in the country, you can contact an operator in Canada or the United States to place collect or credit card calls.

	United States	Canada
AT&T	0-800-0114-114	0-800-015-1161
MCI	0-800-0122-222	
Sprint	0-800-0130-123	

New in Costa Rica are public phones that use prepaid phone cards for local calls. Coin phones require a supply of 5-, 10-, or 20-colón coins (look on the phone to see which it accepts). Place the coin in the slot; if the phone is working properly, it will drop only when your call goes through. If the phone starts beeping after you have talked awhile, feed it another coin or you'll be cut off. When calling a friend, give the person the number you are calling from (posted near the phone) so s/he can call you back.

There are no area codes for different parts of the country, so just dial the seven-digit number; omit the 506 country code. Even local calls on private phones cost: amount of time is added to a basic charge, which is one reason most businesses do not let the public use their private phones.

Calls from your hotel can be expensive; ask.

Notice the many public telephone signs as you travel around the country. Often they are in the local grocery or sometimes even in a private home. To call from one of these, give the person in charge of the phone the number to be dialed. Time is metered, and you pay when you finish.

NOTE: Numbers change regularly. If repeated calls to a hotel or lodge get no answer, assume the number has changed; call information.

Telex, Fax, E-mail

If your hotel does not offer these services, go to Radiográfica or Comunicaciones Internacionales in San José, where you can both send and receive. Most post offices have telegraph services. Western Union has an office at Calle 9, Avenidas 2/4. A very few hotels have Internet access for guests.

TAXES AND TIPPING

The sales tax is 13 percent. Currently there is a lodging tax of about 3 percent, so hotel bills will reflect 16.39 percent tax. (The 13 percent tax is also levied on the 3 percent). Efforts to eliminate the lodging tax have not yet succeeded. I do not include taxes in hotel rates—except where specified—because the tax rate seems to change more often than the editions of my book. At restaurants, you pay the 13 percent sales tax and a 10 percent service charge that is usually automatically added to your bill. Tipping beyond that service charge is at your discretion.

Tipping for services is a personal matter, of course, but here are some suggestions to guide you.

Taxi drivers: Tip not expected, but if they load luggage or provide extra-special service, you may want to tip.

Bellboys, porters, etc.: At least 50 cents per bag.

Housekeeping staff or cooks at private reserves: 50 cents to $1 per person per day.

Naturalist and river guides: $3 to $5 per day, a little less for local guides without naturalist training.

Bus or van driver on a tour: $2 or $3 per person per day

Riverboat captains: $2 or $3.

COSTA RICAN CUISINE

Gallo pinto is the staple of the Costa Rican diet: black beans and rice. Try to eat it somewhere other than a first-class hotel. A *gallo* is something with a tortilla wrapped around it—beef, cheese, beans, chicken, or pork. When faced with an unfamiliar menu in the countryside, you usually can't go wrong ordering one of the rice dishes such as *arroz con pollo* (chicken and rice) or a *casado*, which often comes with beef, chicken, or pork and vegetables such as yuca (cassava, a tuber similar to a potato), plantain, or squash with the ever-present rice and black beans. A vegetarian *casado* may also be available.

Olla de carne is a soup of beef and vegetables—chunks of yuca, squash, potato, corn on the cob, plantain, or whatever is in the house recipe.

Tico tamales, traditional at Christmas, are wrapped in banana leaves rather than cornhusks; a filling of pork is most common, though it can be chicken. Try a *tortilla de queso*, a substantial tortilla with cheese mixed in the cornmeal. *Pupusas*, of Salvadoran origin, have found their way into typical restaurant menus in Costa Rica. Basically they are two tortillas fried with cheese inside—tasty and greasy.

Sea bass (*corvina*), prawns (*langostinos*), and lobster (*langosto*) are among the fresh seafood available. An appetizer of ceviche, certain types of raw seafood "cooked" in lime or lemon juice and mixed with onion and coriander (*cilantro*) leaves, can serve as a good light lunch.

The big bunches of bright red or orange fruit you see for sale along roadsides are *pejibayes*, a palm fruit that has been harvested for food since Indian times. When boiled, it is often served as an hors d'oeuvre with a dollop of mayonnaise on top. Try it. You may not like it—the flesh is quite dense and on the dry side—but most *ticos* love it. Another product of the *pejibaye* palm is *palmito*, or heart of palm, served cooked or fresh. Some palm species do not resprout when cut for the "heart." The *pejibaye* does, and commercial plantations now supply the market, so you don't have to worry that your heart of palm salad cost a forest tree its life. Natives also make a fermented drink from the sap when a tree is cut. Have a guide point out the tree, a stately palm with hairy spines on the trunk.

Naturales, or natural fruit drinks, may come mixed with milk, in which case they will be listed as *en leche*, or with water (*en agua*). Popular fruits for the *naturales* include *mora* (a berry), *piña* (pineapple), papaya, mango, and cas. Let your surroundings guide you as to which is safest, or stick to bottled drinks. In the *campo* (country) I sometimes order *agua dulce*, a hot drink made of boiling water and brown sugar. You can also have it mixed with milk (*con leche*). It's especially good in the mountains when there is a chill in the air. Cane-based *guaro* is the national liquor.

For sweets, try a dessert (*postre*, pronounced POS-tray) of flan, a sweet custard, or *tres leches*, a moist cake. *Cajeta* is similar to fudge.

BUSINESS HOURS

Banking hours, which are at least 9 a.m. to 3 p.m., are covered above. Government and professional offices are usually open from 8 a.m. to 5 p.m., though some government offices close at 4 p.m. Shops are generally open from 9 a.m. to 7 p.m., though some still observe the long lunch hour—closing from noon to 1 or 2 p.m. Downtown San José used to close up at midday Saturday and reopen on Monday. These days, more stores observe weekday hours on Saturday, and a few are open on Sunday. Some restaurants close on Sunday, some on Monday; check before you charge off in a cab.

A note on daylight hours. Since Costa Rica is near the equator, it does not have the seasonal variations in daylight hours that lands to the north have. If you get up with the sun, you will be getting up between 5 and 5:30 a.m. Darkness falls between 5:30 and 6:30 p.m. year-round.

CURRENT HAPPENINGS

The *Tico Times* is an English-language newspaper published every Friday. It's an excellent source of information on what's going on in Costa Rica and is widely available in downtown San José.

Costa Rica Today comes out every Thursday, distributed free at many hotels and other tourist-related businesses throughout the country. It has a restaurant section and articles on health, language, hotels, and tours, plus a calendar of events and delightful natural history pieces.

Radio 2 at 99.5 FM has English-language programming with music from the 1960s to the '90s (including a request line), news, weather, and a Friday-morning segment devoted to tourist information.

HOLIDAYS

On official national holidays, most businesses, including banks, close.
January 1—New Year's Day.

Holy Week—Maundy Thursday and Good Friday rival Easter in importance. Banks and businesses close, some of them all week.

April 11—Day of Juan Santamariá, national boy-hero in the 1856 battle against William Walker and his filibusterers.

May 1—Labor Day.

July 25—Annexation of the Province of Guanacaste, formerly part of Nicaragua.

August 2—Day of the Virgin de Los Angeles (Our Lady of the Angels), patron saint of Costa Rica.

August 15—Mother's Day.

September 15—Independence Day (independence from Spain).

October 12—Day of the Cultures (Discovery of America).

December 25—Christmas (many businesses close from Christmas to New Year's Day).

APPENDIX B
TRAVEL & ENVIRONMENTAL CONTACTS

> Note: The international country code for Costa Rica is "506"
> Add it to seven-digit numbers when calling from outside Costa Rica.
> In Costa Rica, use only the seven digits.

INTERNATIONAL AIRLINE INFORMATION

AIRLINE	ADDRESS	RESERVATIONS	AIRPORT
American	Across from Hotel Corobicí, Avenida 5b, Calle 42	257-1266 441-0841	442-8800
Continental	From U.S. Embassy, 700 feet (200 m) south, 1,000 feet (300 m) east, 200 feet (50 m) north	296-4911	442-1904
Delta	Calle 34, Paseo Colón/Avenida 2	257-4646	440-4802
LACSA	Calle 1, Avenida 5	296-0909	443-3555
Mexicana	Calle 5, Avenidas 7/9	257-6334	441-9377
TACA	Avenida 3, Calle 40	222-1790	442-3606
United	La Sabana, Edificio Oficentro	220-4844	441-8025

DOMESTIC AIRLINE SCHEDULED SERVICE

SANSA

San José office, Calle 24, Paseo Colón/Avenida 1,
(506) 221-9414, fax (506) 255-2176.

Following are flights and fares as of January 1998. All are to and from San José except where noted differently, and all are scheduled at least once a day. No reduction for round trip. Reduced rates for children. There are SANSA ticket agents at most of these destinations.

DESTINATION	ONE-WAY FARE ($)
Barra del Colorado	45
Carrillo (Sámara)	55
Coto 47	55
Golfito	55
La Fortuna (planned)	45
Liberia	55
Nosara	55
Palmar Sur	55
Puerto Jiménez	55
Quepos	35
San Vito (planned)	55
Tamarindo	55
Tambor	45
Tortuguero	45
Quepos–Tamarindo	50
Tamarindo–Quepos	50
La Fortuna–Tamarindo (planned)	50
Tamarindo–La Fortuna (planned)	50
Quepos–Palmar Sur	50
Palmar Sur–Quepos	50

TRAVELAIR

San José office, Tobias Bolaños Airport, Pavas, (506) 220-3054, (506) 232-7883; fax (506) 220-0413; e-mail airplane@sol.racsa.co.cr; Web site www.centralamerica .com/cr/tran/travlair.htm.

Following are flights and fares as of January 1998. All are to and from San José except where noted differently, and all are scheduled daily. There are reduced fares for most round trips. Travelair ticket agents are located at most of these destinations. In addition to these scheduled flights, Travelair offers charter service. It is the only domestic airline in Costa Rica supervised both by Costa Rica Civil Aviation as well As the U.S. FAA.

DESTINATION	ONE-WAY FARE ($)
Carrillo (Sámara)	80
Golfito	81
Jacó	37
Liberia	88
Palmar Sur	78
Puerto Jiménez	87
Punta Islita	80
Quepos	48
Tamarindo (Flamingo)	88
Tambor	66
Tortuguero	45

Interdestination flights are available without changing planes or returning to San José. Here are some:

Golfito: to Carillo, Liberia, Palmar Sur, Puerto Jiménez, Punta Islita, Quepos, Tamarindo, Tambor.

Quepos: to Carillo, Golfito, Liberia, Palmar Sur, Puerto Jiménez, Punta Islita, Tamarindo, Tambor.

Tortuguero: to Carillo, Golfito, Palmar Sur, Puerto Jiménez, Punta Islita, Quepos, Tamarindo, Tambor.

FERRIES

Puntarenas–Playa Naranjo Ferry: between Puntarenas and the Nicoya Peninsula, at Playa Naranjo.
661-1069, 661-3834, fax 661-2197.
Cost: car fee plus driver is $10.50, passengers $1.50 each.
Leaves Puntarenas 3:15 a.m., 7 a.m., 10:50 a.m., 2:50 p.m., 7 p.m.
Leaves Playa Naranjo 5:10 a.m., 8:50 a.m., 12:50 p.m., 5 p.m., 9 p.m.

Ferry Tambor: between Puntarenas and the Nicoya Peninsula at Paquera.
661-2084, 661-2160
Cost: car and driver $9, passengers $1.50 each or $3.50 first class.
Leaves Puntarenas 5 a.m., 12:30 p.m., 5 p.m., 7:30 p.m.
Leaves Paquera 8 a.m., 2:30 p.m., 8:30 p.m.

Ferry Peninsular: between Puntarenas and the Nicoya Peninsula at Paquera.
Telephone/fax 661-3674
Cost: car and driver $9, passengers $1.50 each.
Leaves Puntarenas 8:45 a.m., 2 p.m., 8:15 p.m.
Leaves Paquera 6 a.m., 11:45 a.m., 6 p.m.

Puntarenas–Paquera Launch: between Puntarenas and the Nicoya at Paquera, passengers only
661-2830, fax 641-0241, passengers only, less than $1.50 each.
Leaves Puntarenas from behind market 6:15 a.m., 11 a.m., and 3:15 p.m.
Leaves Paquera 8 a.m., 12:30 p.m., 5 p.m.

Tempisque Ferry: across the mouth of the Tempisque River, connecting the mainland with the Nicoya Peninsula.
685-5295.
Cost: car and driver about $2, passengers less than 25 cents each.
Leaves Puerto Níspero (mainland side) at 5 a.m. and Puerto Moreno (on the peninsula) at 5:30 a.m., continuous service until 7 p.m.

Golfito Launch: across the Golfo Dulce between Golfito and Puerto Jiménez, passengers only.
Cost: less than $1
Leaves Golfito at 11:30 a.m. and Puerto Jiménez at 6 a.m.

TAXIS

If you have access to a phone directory, check the yellow pages for taxis, or your hotel can call one for you. Here are a few in San José.

CGT Taxi	254-6667
Coopetico R.L.	224-7979
Multiservicos Alfaro	221-8466
	223-3373
Taxis San Jorge	222-0025
	221-3434
	221-3535
Taxis Unidos	221-6865
(airport)	233-6637

INTERCITY BUSES

Regular intercity bus service provided by different companies covers practically the entire country, with varying frequency and levels of service. Departure locations are listed below alphabetically by town or destination, along with phone numbers and length of trip. Buses start from San José unless otherwise indicated. Sometimes there is a terminal, but sometimes there's only a sign alongside the street indicating the bus stop. Bus stops sometimes move; check with the ICT information office if you have trouble.

Airport (Juan Santamaría): Calles 10/12, Avenida 2, 24-hour service, leaving every 10 minutes from 5 a.m. to 10 p.m., then less frequently, 222-5325, 30 minutes

Alajuela: Calles 10/12, Avenida 2 (same as above), 222-5325

Arenal from Ciudad Quesada: See Tilarán from Ciudad Quesada

Barva Volcano/Braulio Carrillo: From central market in Heredia (bus to Paso Llano), three times daily except twice on Sunday, then walk to park

Boca Tapada: see Pital

Braulio Carrillo (via highway to Limón): Calle Central, Avenidas 9/11, every 30 minutes from 5 a.m. to 9:45 p.m., 257-8129 (this is the Guapiles bus; get off at the ranger station), 40 minutes

Cahuita: Calle Central, Avenidas 9/11, three times daily, 257-8129, 4½ hours

Cahuita from Limón: 75 meters north of Radio Casino, four times a day, 758-1572

Cañas: Calle 16, Avenidas 3/5, buy ticket in advance, five times daily, 222-3006, 3 hours

Cartago: Calle 5, Avenidas 18/20, every 10 minutes from 5 a.m. to 7 p.m., then less frequently, 233-5350, 35 minutes

Chirripó: See San Isidro de El General

Ciudad Quesada (San Carlos): Calle 12, Avenidas 7/9, every hour from 5 a.m. to 7:30 p.m., 255-4318, 3 hours

Ciudad Quesada/La Fortuna: Municipal bus station in Ciudad Quesada (take bus for El Tanque), eight times daily, 460-0326, 1 hour

Ciudad Quesada/Arenal/Tilarán: Municipal bus station in Ciudad Quesada (goes through Fortuna and around Lake Arenal and volcano), twice daily, 4 hours

Conchal: Calle 20, Avenida 3, once a day, 221-7202

David, Panama: Calle 14, Avenida 5, twice daily, 221-4214

Dominical: Calle 16, Avenida 3, once a day, 777-0318

Dominical from San Isidro: four times daily, 771-1348

Flamingo Beach: Calle 20, Avenida 3, twice a day, 222-7202

Flamingo from Santa Cruz: twice daily

Fortuna: Calle 12, Avenidas 7/9, three times daily, 255-4318, 4½ hours

Fortuna from Ciudad Quesada: see Tilarán from Ciudad Quesada

Guapiles: Calle Central, Avenidas 9/11, every 30 minutes from 5 a.m. to 9:45 p.m., 257-8129.

Golfito: Calle 12, Avenidas 7/9, express bus, buy ticket in advance, twice a day, 221-4214, 8 hours

Guayabo National Monument from Turrialba: twice daily

Heredia: Calle 1, Avenidas 7/9, every 10 minutes from 5 a.m. to 10 p.m., 233-8392, 25 minutes; Calles 10/12, Avenida 2, every 15 minutes from 6 a.m. to 10 p.m.; Calle 4, Avenida 5/7, every 15 minutes from 6 a.m. to 11 p.m.

Irazú Volcano: Calles 1/3, Avenida 2, 8 a.m. Saturday and Sunday only

Jacó: Calle 16, Avenidas 1/3, three buses daily, 233-1109, 3 hours

Jacó from Puntarenas: three times daily, 90 minutes

Junquillal: Calle 20, Avenida 3, one express bus daily, 221-7202, 5 hours

La Cruz or Peñas Blancas: Calle

16, Avenidas 3/5, five buses daily, 222-3006, 5 hours

Lankester Garden from Cartago: south side of Central Park, every 30 minutes from 4:30 a.m. to 10:30 p.m., 574-6127, 15 minutes

Liberia: Calle 14, Avenidas 1/3, several express buses daily, buy ticket in advance, 222-1650, 4 hours

Limón: Calle Central, Avenidas 9/11, hourly from 5 a.m. to 7 p.m., through Braulio Carrillo, 223-7811, 2½ hours

Los Chiles: Calle 12, Avenidas 7/9, twice daily, 255-4318, 5 hours

Manuel Antonio: see Quepos

Monteverde: Calle 14, Avenidas 9/11, twice daily, buy ticket in advance, 222-3854, 4 hours

Monteverde from Tilarán: once daily from Santa Elena 3 km from Monteverde, 3 hours

Monteverde from Puntarenas: once daily, 222-3854

Montezuma from Paquera: from Paquera dock when ferry arrives, 642-0219

Nicoya: Calle 14, Avenidas 5, buy ticket in advance, 222-2750, 6 hours

Nicoya from Liberia: every hour from 5 a.m. to 7 p.m.

Nosara Garza and Guiones: Calle 14, Avenida 5, 222-2666, 6 hours

Nosara from Nicoya: Main terminal, once a day, 685-5352, 90 minutes

Orosi Valley from Cartago: daily between 6 a.m. and 10 p.m., bus stop is 1 block east and 3 blocks south of Cartago Ruins

Orotina: Calle 16, Avenidas 1/3, seven times daily

Palmar/Ciudad Cortés: Calle 14, Avenida 5, twice daily, 221-4214

Palmar to Sierpe: six times daily

Peñas Blancas: Calle 16, Avenidas 3/5, six times daily, 5 hours

Pital: Calle 12, Avenida 9, twice daily, connection to Boca Tapada

Playa del Coco: Calle 14, Avenidas 1/3, twice a day, 222-1650, 5 hours

Playa del Coco from Liberia: four times daily

Playa Hermosa from Liberia: five times daily

Poás Volcano: Calles 12/14, Avenida 2, 8:30 a.m. daily

Puerto Jiménez: Calle 12, Avenidas, 7/9, twice daily, 257-4121, 8 hours

Puerto Viejo de Limón: Calle Central, Avenidas 9/11, once daily, 255-1025, 5 hours

Puerto Viejo de Sarapiquí: Calle 12, Avenidas 7/9, five times daily through Braulio Carrillo 2½ hours

Puerto Viejo de Sarapiquí from Ciudad Quesada: Municipal Terminal, six times daily, 460-0638, 3 hours

Puntarenas: Calle 16, Avenidas 10/12 every 30 minutes from 6:30 a.m. to 9 p.m., 233-2610, 2 hours

Quepos and Manuel Antonio: Calle 16, Avenidas 1/3, express from lot beside Hotel Musoc advance tickets in adjacent market, 223-5567, 3½ hours

Quepos from Puntarenas: Next to Puntarenas Terminal, three times daily, 643-3135

Quepos from San Isidro: Municipal market in Quepos, twice daily, 771-1384, 3½ hours

Sámara and Carrillo: Calle 14, Avenidas 3/5, daily express, 222-2666, 6 hours

San Isidro de El General: Calle 16, Avenidas 1/3, every hour from 5:30 a.m. to 5 p.m., buy ticket in advance, 771-0414, 3 hours; in San Isidro three buses a day for San Gerardo de Rivas 506-233-4160 and Chirripó

San Isidro to San Gerardo: twice daily

San Vito: Calle 14, Avenida 5, buy ticket in advance, 222-2750, 6 hours

Santa Cruz: Calle 20, Avenidas 3/5, 221-7202, 5 hours

Santa Cruz to Nicoya: every hour from 6:30 a.m. to 9:30 p.m.

Santa Cruz from Liberia: every

hour from 5:30 a.m. to 7:30 p.m.
Santa Rosa/Peñas Blancas: Calle
14, Avenidas 3/5, 6 times daily
Sarchí from Alajuela: in Alajuela
from same block as Alajuela–San José
TUASA bus, every 30 minutes
5 a.m. to 10 p.m., 441-3781
Sixaola: Calle Central, Avenidas 9/11,
257-8129
Tamarindo: Calle 14, Avenidas 3/5,
once daily, 222-2750, 223-8229, 5½
hours
Tilarán: Calle 14, Avenidas 9/11, five
times daily, 222-3854, 4 hours
Tilarán from Ciudad Quesada:
Parada Municipal Municipal
Terminal, twice a day, 4 hours passes
by Fortuna and Arenal
Turrialba: Calle 13, Avenidas 6/8,
hourly express from 6 a.m. to 9 p.m.,
556-0073, 90 minutes
Zarcero: Calle 16, Avenidas 1/3, hourly bus from 5 a.m. to 7:30 p.m., Ciudad
Quesada bus, 255-4318, 90 minutes

INFORMATION SOURCES

COSTA RICAN TOURISM INSTITUTE (ICT)
San José Information Offices
Weekdays 8 a.m. to 4 p.m.
Avenida 4, Calles 5/7
Telephone (506) 223-1733
Fax (506) 223-5452
Plaza de la Cultura
Calle 5, Avenidas Central/2
Telephone (506) 222-1090
In Costa Rica, free hot line
(800) 012-3456
In U.S., (800) 343-6332
(8 a.m. to 5 p.m. Central Time),
(305) 858-7277, fax (305) 857-0071
E-mail: info@tourism-costarica.com
Website: www.tourism-costarica.com

NATIONAL CHAMBER OF TOURISM (CANATUR)
E-mail info@tourism.cr
Website: www.tourism.co.cr/

PARKS AND RESERVES INFORMATION
Telephone Hotline: 192 (within Costa
Rica) Operates Monday to Friday, 7:30
a.m. to 5 p.m. English- and Spanish-
speaking staff give information on how
to get there, weather, entrance fees, and
hours and days each area is open—some
protected areas are closed one or two
days a week. You cannot make reservations at this number, but staff can give
you the appropriate number to call.
Information can also be sent by fax.

CONSERVATION AREA NUMBERS
Contact appropriate conservation area
for overnight reservations or for
answers to more detailed questions
about individual parks, reserves, and
wildlife refuges.

Amistad Pacific Conservation Area:
La Amistad National Park (Pacific
    Region), (506) 771-3297, tele-
    phone/fax (506) 771-3155
Chirripó National Park, (506)
    771-3297, telephone/fax
    (506) 771-3155
Tapantí National Park, (506)
    771-3297, telephone/fax
    (506) 771-3155

Amistad Caribe Conservation Area:
Cahuita National Park, telephone/fax
    (506) 755-0060
Gandoca-Manzanillo Wildlife Refuge,
    (506) 798-3170, telephone/fax
    (506) 758-3996
Hitoy-Cerere Biological Reserve, (506)
    798-3170, telephone/fax (506)
    758-3996

Arenal-Huetar Norte Conservation Area:
Arenal Volcano National Park, (506)
    460-1412, fax (506) 460-0644
Caño Negro National Wildlife Refuge,
    (506) 460-1412, fax (506) 460-
    0644

Arenal Conservation Area:
Tenorio Volcano National Park, (506) 695-5908, fax (506) 695-5982

Central Volcanic Range Conservation Area:
Braulio Carrillo National Park, (506) 290-1927, (506) 290-8202, fax (506) 232-5324
Guayabo National Monument, (506) 290-1927, (506) 290-8202, fax (506) 232-5324
Irazú Volcano National Park, (506) 290-1927, (506) 290-8202, fax (506) 232-5324
Poás Volcano National Park, (506) 290-1927, (506) 290-8202, fax (506) 232-5324

Guanacaste Conservation Area:
Guanacaste National Park, telephone/fax (506) 695-5598, (506) 695-5577
Junquillal National Wildlife Refuge, telephone/fax (506) 695-5598, (506) 695-5577
Rincón de la Vieja National Park, telephone/fax (506) 695-5598, (506) 695-5577
Santa Rosa National Park, telephone/fax (506) 695-5598, (506) 695-5577

Coco Island Conservation Area:
Coco Island National Park, (506) 233-4533, telephone/fax (506) 256-0365

Osa Conservation Area:
Ballena National Marine Park, (506) 735-5282, telephone/fax (506) 735-5036
Caño Island Biological Reserve, (506) 735-5282, telephone/fax (506) 735-5036
Corcovado National Park, (506) 735-5282, telephone/fax (506) 735-5036

Golfito National Wildlife Refuge, (506) 735-5282, telephone/fax (506) 735-5036

Central Pacific Conservation Area:
Carara, (506) 416-6576, fax (506) 416-7402
Manuel Antonio, (506) 777-0644, fax (506) 777-0654

Tempisque Conservation Area:
Barra Honda National Park, telephone/fax (506) 659-9039, (506) 659-9194
Cabo Blanco Absolute Natural Reserve, telephone/fax (506) 642-0093
Las Baulas National Marine Park, (506) 653-0470, telephone/fax (506) 680-0779
Ostional National Wildlife Refuge, telephone/fax (506) 659-9039, (506) 659-9194
Palo Verde National Park, telephone/fax (506) 671-1290, (506) 671-1062

Tortuguero Conservation Area:
Barra del Colorado National Wildlife Refuge, telephone/fax (506) 710-2929, (506) 710-2939
Tortuguero National Park, telephone/fax (506) 710-2929, (506) 710-2939

EMBASSIES IN SAN JOSE

ARGENTINA
Avenida 6, Calles 2½5, (506) 221-3438, fax (506) 283-9983

CANADA
Oficentro Ejecutivo La Sabana, Sabana Sur (Building 5, 3rd floor), (506) 296-4149, fax (506) 296-4270

FRANCE

Road to Curridabat, 200 m south, 25 m east of Indoor Club, (506) 225-0733, (506) 225-0933

GERMANY

Rohrmoser, (506) 232-5533, (506) 222-6671

GREAT BRITAIN

Edificio Centro Colón, 11th floor, Avenida Colón, Calle 38, (506) 221-5566, (506) 221-5816, fax (506) 233-9938

HOLLAND

Oficentro Ejecutivo, La Sabana, Sabana Sur (Building 3, 3rd floor), (506) 296-1490

ITALY

Los Yoses, Avenida 10, Calles 33/35, (506) 234-2326

JAPAN

Residencial Rohrmoser, 400 m west, 100 m north of La Nunciatura, (506) 232-1255

MEXICO

Los Yoses, (506) 234-2466, fax (506) 234-9613

SPAIN

Calle 32, Paseo Colon/Avenida 2, (506) 222-1933, (506) 222-5745, fax (506) 222-4180

SWITZERLAND

Centro Colon, 10th floor, Paseo Colón, Calle 38, (506) 233-0052

UNITED STATES

Rohrmoser, road to Pavas in front of Centro Comercial (any taxi driver can take you), (506) 220-3939, fax (506) 220-2305; Consulate, (506) 220-3050, fax, (506) 231-4783

FAUNA: ENGLISH AND SPANISH NAMES

English . . . . .Spanish
agouti . . . .*guatusa*
anteater, silky . . . .*serafín*
anteater, tamandua . .*oso hormiguero*
armadillo . . . .*cusuco*
bat . . . .*murciélago*
bird . . . .*pájaro, ave*
butterfly . . . .*mariposa*
caiman . . . .*caimán, lagarto*
coati . . . .*pizote*
cougar, mountain lion . .*puma, león*
crocodile . . . .*cocodrilo*
deer, brocket . . . . . .*cabra de monte*
deer, white-tailed *venado cola blanca*
frog . . . .*rana*
gopher . . . .*taltusa*
hummingbird . . . .*colibrí*
jaguar . . . .*jaguar, tigre*
jaguarundi . . . .*león breñero*
kinkajou . . . .*martilla*
macaw . . . .*lapa*
margay . . . .*caucel, tigrillo*
monkey, howler . . . .*mono congo*
monkey, squirrel . . . .*mono tití,*
. . . .*mono ardilla*
monkey, white-faced capuchin
. . . .*mono cara blanca*
ocelot . . . .*manigordo*
opossum . . . .*zorro*
otter, river . . . .*nutria, perro de agua*
paca . . . .*tepezcuintle*
parrot . . . .*loro*
peccary, collared . . . .*saíno*
peccary, white-lipped . . . .*cariblanco*
raccoon . . . .*mapache*
skunk . . . .*zorro hediondo*
sloth . . . .*perezoso, perico*
snake . . . .*serpiente, culebra*
spider monkey . . . . .*mono colorado,*
. . . .*mono araña*
squirrel . . . .*ardilla, chisa*
tapir . . . .*danta*
tayra . . . .*tolomuco*
toad . . . .*sapo*
turtle . . . .*tortuga*

METRIC CONVERSION TABLES

To Change	to	Multiply by
Hectares	Acres	2.471
Meters	Feet	3.2808
Meters	Yards	1.094
Kilometers	Miles	.6214
Millimeters	Inches	.0394
Centimeters	Inches	.3937
Square kilometers	Square Miles	.3861
Liters	Gallons (U.S.)	.2642
Liters	Pints	2.113
Kilograms	Pounds	2.205
Grams	Ounces	.0353

TEMPERATURE CONVERSION

Celsius to Fahrenheit: multiply by 9/5 (or 1.8) and add 32.
Fahrenheit to Celsius: subtract 32 and multiply by 5/9 (or .56).
Here are some reference points to save some of the math:

Celsius	Fahrenheit
0°	32°
10°	50°
20°	68°
30°	86°
35°	95°
40°	104°

RECOMMENDED READING

The Biodiversity of Costa Rica, Zaldett Barrientos and Julián Monge-Nájera (eds.). Instituto Nacional de Biodiversidad, 1995.

The Butterflies of Costa Rica and Their Natural History, Philip J. DeVries. Princeton, N.J.: Princeton University Press, 1987.

Costa Rica National Parks, Mario A. Boza. Madrid: Incafo (for Fundación Neotrópica de Costa Rica), 1996.

Costa Rica: Politics, Economics, and Democracy, Bruce M. Wilson. Boulder: Lynne Rienner Publishers, Inc., 1998.
Costa Rican Natural History, edited by Daniel H. Janzen. Chicago: University of Chicago Press, 1983.

The Costa Ricans, Richard Biesanz, Karen Zubris Biesanz, and Mavis Hiltunen Biesanz. Englewood Cliffs, N.J.: Prentice-Hall, 1982.

A Guide to the Birds of Costa Rica, F. Gary Stiles and Alexander F. Skutch. Ithaca, N.Y.: Cornell University Press, 1989.

An Introduction to Cloud Forest Trees: Monteverde, Costa Rica, William A. Haber, Willow Zuchowski, and Erick Bello. 2nd edition. Monteverde, Costa Rica, self-published, 1998.

Journey through a Tropical Jungle, Adrian Forsyth. Toronto: Greey de Pencier Books, 1988.

A Naturalist in Costa Rica, Alexander F. Skutch. Gainesville, Fla.: University of Florida Press, 1971.

The New Key to Costa Rica, Beatrice Blake. San José: Publications in English, 1998.

The Quetzal and the Macaw: The Story of Costa Rica's National Parks, David Rains Wallace. San Francisco: Sierra Book Club, 1992.

The Rivers of Costa Rica: A Canoeing, Kayaking, and Rafting Guide, Michael W. Mayfield and Rafael E. Gallo. Birmingham, Ala.: Menasha Ridge Press, 1988.

A Travel and Site Guide to the Birds of Costa Rica, Aaron Sekerak and Elissa Conger. Edmonton: Long Pine Publishing, 1996.

INDEX